In the Shadow of the Steamboat

NUMBER 137 • 2022

In the Shadow of the Steamboat

A Natural and Cultural History of North Warner Valley, Oregon

Geoffrey M. Smith

With contributions by Pat Barker, Erica J. Bradley, Anna J. Camp, Judson B. Finley,
Denay Grund, Eugene M. Hattori, Bryan S. Hockett, Christopher S. Jazwa, Jaime L. Kennedy,
Donald D. Pattee, Evan J. Pellegrini, Richard L. Rosencrance, Daniel O. Stueber,
Madeline Ware Van der Voort, and Teresa A. Wriston

THE UNIVERSITY OF UTAH ANTHROPOLOGICAL PAPERS
THE UNIVERSITY OF UTAH PRESS
Salt Lake City

The Defiance House Man colophon is a registered trademark
of The University of Utah Press. It is based on a four-foot-tall
Ancient Puebloan pictograph (late PIII) near Glen Canyon, Utah.

ISBN 978-1-64769-074-8 (paper)
ISBN 978-1-64769-076-2 (ebook)

Cataloging-in-Publication data for this title
is available online at the Library of Congress.

Errata and further information on this and other titles available online at UofUpress.com
Printed and bound in the United States of America.

DEDICATION

*For the students and staff of the 2011–2013 UNR Field Schools
in Great Basin Prehistory and Paleoecology,
who made teaching and learning in the Big Empty an amazing experience,
and for Bill Cannon for convincing me to kick the tires and give Warner Valley a chance.*

Contents

Part III. North Warner Valley Settlement-Subsistence Patterns

Part IV: Synthesis and Conclusions

Figures

Tables

Supplemental Tables (Available Online)

Acknowledgments

North Warner Valley lies in the traditional homelands of both the Northern Paiute and Klamath Tribes. I appreciate the opportunity to work in their territories. Teresa Wriston codirected the 2011–2013 UNR Field Schools in Great Basin Prehistory and Paleoecology and was instrumental in planning and executing the survey and backhoe trenching programs. Field school students conducted the bulk of the fieldwork on which this volume is based. They were supervised by UNR graduate students Chrissina Burke, Anna Camp, Peter Carey, Danielle Felling, Stephen LaValley, and Anthony Taylor. Bill Cannon, Lucille Housley, Anan Raymond, Dave Rhode, and Mike Rondeau provided supplemental instruction on various topics. Bill Cannon and Kathryn Stewardson (Lakeview Resource Area, Bureau of Land Management) provided critical logistical support. Much of the research was funded through the Great Basin Paleoindian Research Unit, which was established with a generous gift from the late Joe and Ruth Cramer.

The work reported here builds upon master's theses by Donald Pattee, Evan Pellegrini, Madeline Ware Van der Voort, and Emily Whorton, and PhD dissertations by Anna Camp and Jaime Kennedy. Bill Cannon, Catherine Fowler, John Fagan, Gene Hattori, Dennis Jenkins, Julien Pellegrini, and Dave Schmitt provided feedback on some of the ideas presented here as I developed them. Pat Barker and Richie Rosencrance read and commented on the full manuscript draft. Richie assisted with many of the figures. Don and Kay Fowler generously shared their knowledge and memories of UNR's previous work in Warner Valley.

Foreword

UNR Archaeology in the Warner Valley Region, 1987–1998

DON D. FOWLER AND CATHERINE S. FOWLER

At the 1986 Great Basin Anthropological Conference, Bill Cannon, Archaeologist for the Bureau of Land Management (BLM) Lakeview Resource Area, approached us with an offer of a joint University of Nevada, Reno (UNR)-BLM archaeological field school to be held in Warner Valley, Oregon. He had initiated similar programs in his district with Washington State University, the University of Oregon, and, for paleontological work, the South Dakota School of Mines (Cannon 2019). Bill said he could provide vehicles, some funding and equipment, and a location for the field school headquarters at the site of a Civilian Conservation Corps (CCC) camp located at the base of Hart Mountain toward the north end of the valley. We agreed, and a contract was signed between the BLM, the U.S. Fish and Wildlife Service, and UNR.

The CCC camp, occupied 1933 to 1941, had concrete pads for wall tents, a vehicle repair garage, and a mess hall. The garage had been torn down when the camp closed, but the pads were left in place. The gable-roofed wooden mess hall also remained intact. It had small offices at either end and a central room large enough to seat 30 people at long tables with built-in benches and ample space for a kitchen. Water for the camp had been piped down from a spring on the bajada of Hart Mountain, but the system had fallen into disrepair by the 1980s. When the CCC left, the mess hall was taken over by the U.S. Fish and Wildlife Service, which operates the nearby Hart Mountain National Antelope Refuge. The BLM also provided two trailer houses for visitors and equipped the mess hall kitchen with a propane stove and oven plus a refrigerator. Students brought their own tents. A full-time cook was hired for each field season; students handled KP duties, as assigned.

The main CCC project in the 1930s had been to build a road up the west side of Hart Mountain and a Refuge headquarters complex (shops, garages, offices, and staff living quarters) on the top. The CCC had also drilled the now-defunct well. When the UNR field school took over the CCC building, we hauled culinary water from the Refuge headquarters in 5-gallon cans down to our camp. Periodically, we towed a 300-gallon water buffalo up the mountain to get dishwashing water and water for solar shower bags.

Eugene Hattori was the Field School Director from 1987 to 1994. Gene is a native Nevadan who attended UNR as an undergraduate student before obtaining a master's degree there and, ultimately, a PhD from Washington State University. He had worked with Don Fowler intermittently from 1966 until 1980 in eastern and southern Nevada. After 1980, he went on to do CRM work in California, taking summer leave to direct the UNR field schools. D. Craig Young, who came to UNR with a master's degree in hand, attended the field school in 1988 and continued as Hattori's assistant from 1989 to 1994. Craig later served as Field School Director in 1995 and 1996 and was assisted by Julie Tipps and Elizabeth (Molly) Moore. In 1997 and 1998, the field school was codirected by Alanah Woody, Julie Tipps, and B. Sunday Eiselt. Moore (1995), Tipps (1997), and Eiselt (1997a) all wrote master's theses, and Craig Young (1998) a doctoral dissertation, on Warner Valley archaeology. Summary reports of the field school research were prepared annually (e.g., Cannon et al. 1990; Fowler et al. 1989). The field school initially concentrated on sites in dunes around Flagstaff and Crump Lakes, but the focus later shifted to pit house sites on the edges of marsh areas in the southern and central parts of Warner Valley (see Eiselt 1997a).

In 1993, the Susanville and Cedarville, California, BLM offices contracted with UNR to conduct archaeological survey and testing programs in their districts. The Lakeview BLM office, through Bill Cannon, provided similar contracts for work northwest and east of Warner Valley. These projects were implemented by UNR graduate students each summer, in the weeks following the end of the field schools, through 1998. Contract work in the three districts continued through 2001 (e.g., Kolvet 1995). Work in the Cedarville District centered on rock art (Woody 1996). Annual reports of the various projects remain on file in the three BLM district offices and the UNR Anthropology Department. The data these projects collected supplemented those generated by the UNR field schools.

ETHNOGRAPHIC CONSULTING AND TEACHING

From 1988 until the end of our field schools in 1998, we were privileged to have Northern Paiute elders Clarence and Julia DeGarmo, from the Fort Bidwell Indian Tribe in northern Surprise Valley, as consultants, monitors, and lecturers each summer. Clarence had been in the U.S. Navy in World War II, steering Marine landing barges onto the shores of Pacific islands—although he was not old enough to serve. He had returned to Fort Bidwell, married Julia, had a family, and worked for the U.S. Forest Service until he retired.

Clarence was a close student of traditional Paiute culture, history, and oral tradition but also of Great Basin and North American Indigenous culture histories written by academic archaeologists and anthropologists. He had an artist friend make him a set of flip charts portraying both Northern Paiute and academic views of culture history. Using the charts, he gave talks in public schools in northern California. He also volunteered his time as an athletic coach for local girls' and boys' teams and was much admired. Clarence and Julia's field school lectures were on Northern Paiute and New World culture history and featured his flip charts. He made atlatls and darts, which he taught the students to use in a contest he created and called the Warner Valley Olympics. He also taught them how to play Northern Paiute games such as hoop and pole, ring and pin, and others. Another of his creations was his "deadly" milk of magnesia blue glass projectile points—beautifully flaked objects he sometimes bestowed on friends or left on sites about to be surveyed to see whether the students were paying attention!

Clarence and Julia were very knowledgeable about the plants and animals of their homeland, often pointing out edible taxa, those with medicinal uses, and good places to hunt or collect. In 1997, they helped the students build an experimental pit roast of root vegetables, including Valerian root, camas bulbs, wild onions, and bitterroot—a simulation of long-ago practices that Clarence remembered from his boyhood. Both he and Julia enjoyed interacting with the students, as well as the more serious work of monitoring the archaeological excavations and providing valuable information as to what was being recovered. Their warmth as well as their knowledge and willingness to share enriched the students' experiences immensely. Julia's beautiful beadwork followed many students, faculty, and visitors home as keepsakes.

UNR's Paleoindian Research Program in the Northwestern Great Basin

In 1994, Joseph and Ruth Cramer provided a $1 million endowment, the Sundance Archaeological Research Fund, to UNR to survey and excavate early sites in the northern Great Basin. As part of that effort, the UNR field school was moved for two seasons to the BLM facility at Poor Jug, Oregon. Surveys and test excavations were conducted to the north, primarily around Alkali Lake and in the Dietz Basin, where Clovis and Early Archaic sites had been investigated by the University of Oregon (Willig et al. 1988). The field school was discontinued after 1998, with full field seasons thereafter being devoted to the work of the Sundance Program in south-central Oregon and northwestern Nevada.

The work presented in this volume picks up where UNR left off in the late 1990s. Under the auspices of the Great Basin Paleoindian Research Unit (born from the Sundance Archaeological Research Fund), UNR continues to pursue the goals laid out by Joe and Ruth Cramer, namely, searching for and excavating terminal Pleistocene and early Holocene archaeological sites in the northwestern Great Basin. The results presented here add to our collective understanding of the natural and cultural history of Warner Valley, Oregon, with a focus on the earliest chapters of human history in the region.

PART I

Project Setting

Research Perspectives

Geoffrey M. Smith

Warner Valley is located near the intersection of Oregon, Nevada, and California (Figure 1.1). It measures ~135 km north–south by ~50 km east–west and contains four sub-basins: North Warner Valley, Rabbit Basin, South Warner Valley, and Coleman Valley (Figure 1.2). Together, the sub-basins cover ~4,900 km² and are in the traditional territories of the Penutian-speaking Klamath and Numic-speaking Northern Paiute Tribes (C. Fowler and Liljeblad 1986; Stern 1998).

Over a century of paleoenvironmental research has been conducted in Warner Valley (Hansen 1947; Russell 1884; Van Winkle 1914); archaeological work began in the late 1930s (Cressman 1937, 1942; Cressman et al. 1940). But efforts in both realms have been sporadic, and our understanding of past conditions and how they influenced human use of the area remain incomplete—particularly for North Warner Valley. Bill Cannon (Archaeologist for the Bureau of Land Management [BLM] Lakeview Resource Area) has long recognized Warner Valley's research potential and supported fieldwork by crews from the University of Nevada, Reno (UNR) throughout the late 1980s and 1990s. Much of this work focused on the Warner Lakes and produced a good understanding of middle and late Holocene environmental conditions and human adaptation (Cannon et al. 1990; Eiselt 1997b, 1998; D. Fowler 1993; D. Fowler et al. 1989; Tipps 1998; Young 1998, 2000). However, most sites lacked fluted and Western Stemmed Tradition (WST) artifacts, thus the terminal Pleistocene and early Holocene chapters of Warner Valley's history remained largely unwritten.

To address this shortcoming, Bill reached out to me in 2010 to establish a long-term research program

in North Warner Valley, where a series of pluvial beach ridges above the basin floor suggested that the area may contain Paleoindian sites. In fact, preliminary reconnaissance of the ridges below Steamboat Point, a prominent rimrock feature that rises above North Warner Valley, demonstrated that the area contains a rich record of WST sites. That summer, Bill also directed us to 37Ha3735, a series of small rockshelters along the base of Little Steamboat Point. In August, we excavated a 1 m² test pit in Little Steamboat Point-1 (LSP-1), the largest of the shelters. That work established that LSP-1 contained stratified and cultural deposits spanning the Holocene.

The co-occurrence of a stratified rockshelter and surface record dating to the early Holocene and, perhaps, the terminal Pleistocene led us to work for five years in an area that we designated the North Warner Valley Study Area (NWVSA). The NWVSA is a 221 km² area that encompasses the LSP-1 rockshelter and various physiographic features including volcanic rimrock and incised tablelands, relict beach ridges, and the basin floor. Our research goals in the NWVSA were: (1) develop a history of pluvial Lake Warner through backhoe trenching, mapping, and paleoenvironmental reconstruction; (2) study Native American settlement patterns through survey, site recording, and artifact analysis; and (3) excavate part of the LSP-1 rockshelter to provide chronological and subsistence data to help us interpret the surface archaeology of the NWVSA. Between 2011 and 2015, we achieved our first two goals. Unfortunately, LSP-1 was badly looted sometime in spring of 2012, at which point we had only excavated 4 m². That event destroyed much of the shelter's remaining late and middle Holocene deposits. However, the terminal early

FIGURE 1.1. Overview of the Great Basin showing the distribution of Pleistocene lakes and location of the North Warner Valley Study Area (NWVSA; adapted from Wriston and Smith 2017).

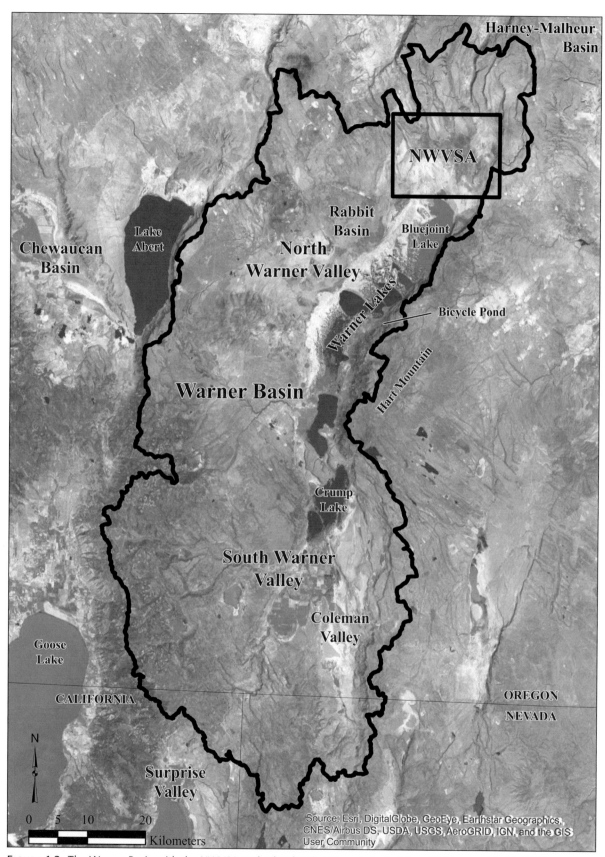

FIGURE 1.2. The Warner Basin with the NWVSA and other key locations (adapted from Wriston and Smith 2017).

Holocene deposits generally escaped damage. Realizing that the BLM could not effectively guard against future damage given the site's remote location, and recognizing the shelter's research potential, Bill encouraged us to return to the site to excavate some of the remaining deposits. This allowed us to recover a more substantial record of human occupation from ~26 m³ of excavated deposits. This record offers a clear picture of technological and dietary change throughout the Holocene. These changes occurred in concert with major environmental shifts that took place in North Warner Valley across almost 10 millennia.

NATURAL SETTING

The Warner Basin was created by faults through volcanic rocks in a complex horst-and-graben system (Personius and Sawyer 2002). The basin floor (graben) dropped, and the surrounding north-to-south ridges (horst) rose, moving along the faults. Although no known fault scarps cut through Quaternary deposits, deformation of Pleistocene lake shorelines, along with numerous lineaments across its floor, suggests some vertical deformation (Craven 1991; Personius and Sawyer 2002; Pezzopane 1993; Pezzopane and Weldon 1993; D. Weide 1975; Weldon et al. 2002).

The Warner Lakes, a chain of small lakes and ponds joined by sloughs and separated by dunes, straddle the divide between South Warner Valley and North Warner Valley. Water draining from the mountains first collects in Crump Lake, which usually maintains a level of ~1,364 m above sea level (ASL), before emptying northward. Moving north, the lakes' levels gradually decrease to a low of ~1,360 m asl at Bluejoint Lake. At the end of the chain and perpetually starved for water, Bluejoint Lake has often been a dry playa during the historic period. In fact, most of the Warner Lakes have dried and refilled at least once during the past 50 years (Cannon 1993).

Water in the Warner Basin usually originates high in the mountains as winter snow, which when it melts slowly moves into the ground or flows toward the valley floor. Some of it is lost to evaporation across the large flat pans on the valley bottom. However, if there is a lot and it is relatively cool then pools and/or lakes form. Of course, higher amounts of precipitation foster higher lake levels (Enzel et al. 1989; Mohammed and Tarboton 2012; Oviatt et al. 2015; Reheis et al. 2014). Mountain spines control the direction of runoff and so mark the edges of each drainage basin.

Today, North Warner Valley is vegetated by grasses and shrubs, with abundant Indian ricegrass (*Achnatherum hymenoides*) in sandy areas and big sagebrush (*Artemisia tridentata*) and rabbitbrush (*Ericameria* sp.)

covering its slopes. The vegetation transitions to saltgrass (*Distichlis spicata*), greasewood (*Sarcobatus* sp.), and shadscale (*Atriplex confertifolia*) on the valley floor where the sediment is salty and groundwater levels are high. Black-tailed jackrabbits (*Lepus californicus*) and cottontail rabbits (*Sylvilagus nuttallii*) are by far the most abundant game animals, although pronghorn (*Antilocapra americana*), mountain sheep (*Ovis canadensis*), mule deer (*Odocoileus hemionus*), and elk (*Cervus elaphus*) also occur in the area. Warner Valley lies along the Pacific Flyway, and more than 30 species of migratory birds visit it each year (Fowler et al. 1989). Four species of fish—tui chub (*Gila bicolor*), dace (*Rhinichthys osulus*), redband trout (*Oncorhynchus mykiss*), and the Warner sucker (*Catostomus warnerensis*)—are native to the valley (Cannon 1993). Freshwater mussels (*Anodonta oregonensis*) occur in some of the lakes today and were sufficiently abundant in the past to serve as a food source for both Native Americans and early Euro-American settlers (Cannon 1993; Eiselt 1998).

RESEARCH QUESTIONS AND FIELD METHODS

Our work was aimed at addressing six basic questions about the natural and cultural history of North Warner Valley: (1) when did pluvial Lake Warner's highstand occur; (2) did Lake Warner rise during the Younger Dryas (12,900–11,600 calendar years before present [cal BP]);[1] (3) when did North Warner Valley become free of surface water; (4) when did humans first visit the area; (5) when did they occupy LSP-1; and (6) how did people's use of the area change across time? Our efforts to answer these questions form the basis of this volume. Here, I summarize our major field methods. Subsequent chapters provide additional details about our field and lab methods.

We primarily focused our geomorphological field investigations, which included 37 backhoe trenches (BTs), near shoreline features associated with archaeological sites but also offsite areas that might provide data related to lake transgressions and recessions. Each BT provides clues about local conditions. Their profiles record stratigraphic and sedimentary information about the presence, absence, and nature of surface water, as well as the deposition and erosion of lacustrine, paludal, and aeolian sediment. Some of the BT profiles also produced tephras or shells that provided some chronological controls, and ostracods, gastropods, and bivalves that, in addition to providing radiocarbon dates, offer a sense of local conditions. Not every BT produced datable materials or information key to our interpretations, thus in Chapter 3 we focus mostly on those that did. With this information and the elevations of productive BTs,

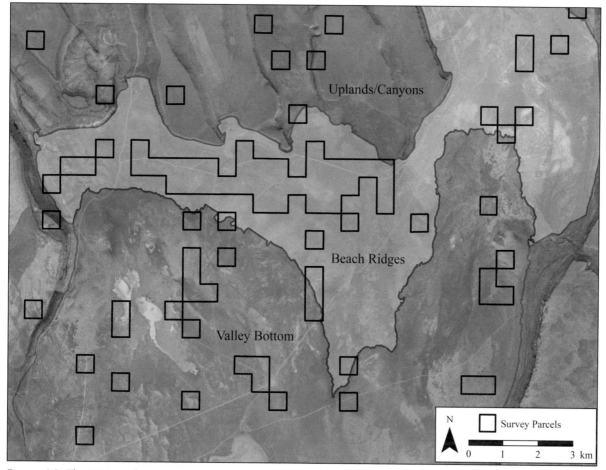

FIGURE 1.3. The NWVSA showing the locations of different landforms and survey parcels.

we produce a lake-level curve based on multiple data points. Each data point consists of an elevation, age, and picture of local conditions. Together, they tell the story of pluvial Lake Warner's rise and fall. In some cases, we use the vertical distribution of diagnostic artifacts such as stemmed and fluted points to help tell that story.

For our pedestrian survey, we divided the NWVSA into four general landforms: (1) uplands (tablelands surrounding North Warner Valley); (2) canyons (drainages cut into tablelands); (3) beach ridges (locations characterized by relict lakeshore features sometimes capped with sand sheets); and (4) the valley bottom. As the project progressed, we grouped canyons and uplands into a single landform type (upland/canyon) because we did not sample canyons sufficiently. In 2011, our first summer of survey, we used a stratified random sampling strategy, selecting 500 m × 500 m quadrats aligned with the NAD83 UTM grid and surveying them at 20–30 m intervals. In 2012 and 2013, we switched to a nonrandom survey strategy focused on beach ridge and valley bottom quadrats that held the best potential to contain Paleoindian sites. We surveyed 21.0 km², or ~10 percent of the NWVSA (Table 1.1 and Figure 1.3). We mapped

TABLE 1.1. Sample Fractions of landform types in the NWVSA

Landform Type	Area (km²)	No. of Quadrats	Area Surveyed (km²)	Sample Fraction (%)
valley bottom	82.0	29.5	7.4	9.0
beach ridge	61.0	48.0	12.0	19.7
upland/canyon	78.0	10.5	2.6	3.3
Total	221.0	88.0	22.0	10.0

all sites (10 or more associated artifacts) and isolated resources (fewer than 10 associated artifacts) and recorded basic information about both (Smith and Wriston 2018).

Our work in the LSP-1 shelter unfolded in two stages: testing and data recovery. In 2010, we excavated a 1 m² test pit (TP-1, later designated N105E99) according to the natural stratigraphy using 10 cm arbitrary levels within each stratum. We recorded all depths below a temporary datum initially set at the southwestern corner of the unit. In 2011, we established a permanent datum at an arbitrary point (N100E100) near the mouth of the shelter and excavated three additional 1 m² units along the E99 gridline south of our initial test pit. At the end of that summer, we made the decision to stop excavating LSP-1.

The following spring, we discovered that looters had destroyed a substantial portion of the shelter's middle and late Holocene deposits. Given the ongoing threat from looting, we spent an additional three years excavating behind the dripline. Our early efforts focused on relocating the site datum, reestablishing our grid system, and squaring off the edges and bottoms of the looters' pit. Later efforts focused on carefully excavating intact early, middle, and late Holocene deposits. All totaled, we excavated ~26 m³ at LSP-1. Except for our initial test pit and the tops of units disturbed by looting, we excavated using 5 cm arbitrary levels within natural strata and passed all sediment through ⅛ in hardware cloth. We recorded the X, Y, and Z coordinates of all in situ tools and other notable artifacts, ecofacts, and features. We bagged artifacts and ecofacts recovered from the screen by level.

ORGANIZATION

This volume is organized into four sections. Part I, Project Setting, reviews the history of the northern Great Basin, with a focus on southeastern Oregon and northwestern Nevada. It also summarizes the ethnographic lifeways of the Northern Paiute and Klamath peoples who call the area home. Finally, it presents the results of our lake-level reconstructions with a focus on the terminal Pleistocene/early Holocene (TP/EH).

Part II, the Little Steamboat Point-1 Rockshelter, presents the results of five years of excavations in the largest of the 35Ha3735 rockshelters. The shelter contained a well-preserved record of human use beginning ~9,775 years ago, featuring robust flaked and groundstone tool assemblages; various other artifact types that include stone, shell, and bone ornaments and tools; basketry; and a sizeable faunal assemblage. This record offers a clear picture of human subsistence during the early Holocene and later periods. The spatial distribution of

these materials across the shelter floor provided an opportunity to address questions related to site structure.

Part III, North Warner Valley Settlement Patterns, uses data from three years of pedestrian survey to place LSP-1 into a broader context. We recorded 114 sites and 355 isolated archaeological resources. Of these, 69 sites and 55 isolated resources contained time-sensitive artifacts ranging from Clovis to Desert Series projectile points. The character of these sites and the raw materials that people used changed across time, suggesting that North Warner Valley's place in northern Great Basin prehistory also varied across time.

Part IV, A Natural and Cultural History of North Warner Valley, integrates the major results of our lake-level reconstruction, rockshelter excavation, and pedestrian survey. These programs generated data that provide a cohesive picture of a changing natural and cultural landscape. Of course, they have also raised new questions that will drive future research in North Warner Valley and beyond.

SUMMARY

Paleoenvironmental reconstructions, large-scale surveys, and cave/rockshelter excavations have historically formed the foundation of archaeological research in the Great Basin. Ideally, these efforts will occur as part of a long-term, multidisciplinary research program (e.g., Aikens and Jenkins 1994; Aikens et al. 1982; Jenkins et al. 2004a; Thomas 1970, 1983, 1988). With its prominent but understudied pluvial lake and surface archaeological records, as well as a nearby stratified rockshelter, North Warner Valley offered an opportunity to pursue such an undertaking. We sought to understand the nature of environmental and cultural change in a remote part of the Oregon desert and how those processes were related. In the following pages, we present the salient results of our efforts and outline how they inform our understanding of traditional lifeways and hunter-gatherer adaptation in the northern Great Basin.

NOTES

1. I will present all dates as calibrated years before present (cal BP). I calibrated radiocarbon dates to 95.4 percent ranges (traditionally referred to as 2σ though that is technically not appropriate because it implies a normal distribution) using OxCal 4.2 (Bronk Ramsey 2009) and the IntCal13 Curve (Reimer et al. 2013). I used Reimer et al.'s (2013) Marine13 Curve, Moss and Erlandson's (1995) marine reservoir correction rate of 240 ± 50 developed for the Oregon Coast, and Long and Rippeteau's (1974) method of averaging multiple radiocarbon dates for the *Olivella* shell

beads (see G. Smith et al. 2016a). I followed Stuiver and Polach's (1977) guidelines for presenting uncalibrated and calibrated dates, which in some cases produced age ranges that differ slightly from those I have presented in previous publications about Warner Valley. In cases where I refer to the ages of sites or events published before authors routinely calibrated radiocarbon dates, I used Appendix 1 in Grayson (2011) to convert them to roughly equivalent cal BP ages.

2 Archaeological and Ethnographic Context

Geoffrey M. Smith and Pat Barker

Our work in North Warner Valley builds on a century of anthropological research in the northern Great Basin. This chapter outlines the cultural history of northwestern Nevada and southeastern Oregon, focusing initially on the archaeological record and later the ethnographic record. We divide the archaeological record into three major environmental periods (the terminal Pleistocene/ early Holocene, middle Holocene, and late Holocene) within which we delineate five cultural periods (Paleoindian, Early Archaic, Middle Archaic, Late Archaic, and Terminal Prehistoric; Figure 2.1). Our discussion of the ethnographic record is not meant to serve as a comprehensive review of Klamath and Northern Paiute lifeways. We present it to guide our interpretations of archaeological data in later chapters. Thus, we focus on aspects that may be visible in the archaeological record, namely, technology, settlement, and subsistence. In Chapter 14, we use these records to place the major results of the NWVSA research program into our broader understanding of northern Great Basin prehistory.

ARCHAEOLOGICAL OVERVIEW

The Terminal Pleistocene and Early Holocene (~15,000–9000 cal BP)

During the terminal Pleistocene and early Holocene (TP/EH), the landscape of the northern Great Basin was dramatically different than it is today. Lakes filled many valleys, including the Lahontan, Fort Rock, Abert-Chewaucan, Alkali, Guano, and Warner basins (Grayson 2011; see Figure 1.1). Lake histories for individual basins range from detailed to nonexistent. Much work remains to be done, but lakes generally reached

highstands 16,000–14,000 cal BP (Adams et al. 2008; Friedel 1994; Licciardi 2001; Negrini 2002). During the relatively warm and dry Bølling Allerød (14,700–12,900 cal BP), many lakes receded or disappeared completely, only to rise again during the cooler and wetter Younger Dryas (12,900–11,600 cal BP). The rise and fall of lakes dictated the number and size of wetlands in the region, and as deep lakes gave way to shallow lakes and wetlands, biotic productivity likely increased for a time in some places (Young 1998). As the early Holocene (11,500–9000 cal BP) unfolded, some lakes and wetlands disappeared forever, while others shrank but persisted (Grayson 2011).

The distributions of plants and animals during the TP/EH were also different from today, although changes in vegetation were primarily altitudinal rather than latitudinal (Wigand and Rhode 2002). Prior to the Younger Dryas, trees grew at lower elevations in many places (Minckley et al. 2004; Wigand and Rhode 2002). High and occasional mid-elevation zones featured forests of whitebark pine (*Pinus albicaulis*) and white fir (*Abies concolor*), or sagebrush steppe (Mehringer 1985; Minckley et al. 2007). Later, during the early Holocene, trees began to retreat upslope in places. On valley floors, greasewood communities moved into territories vacated by disappearing wetlands (Hansen 1947; Wigand and Mehringer 1985). Numerous genera of megafauna went extinct in the Great Basin during the terminal Pleistocene. Horses (*Equus*), camelids (*Camelops* and *Hemiauchenia*), and mammoths (*Mammuthus*) were probably the most common but likely never abundant (Grayson 2016). Bison (*Bison bison*), elk, pronghorn,

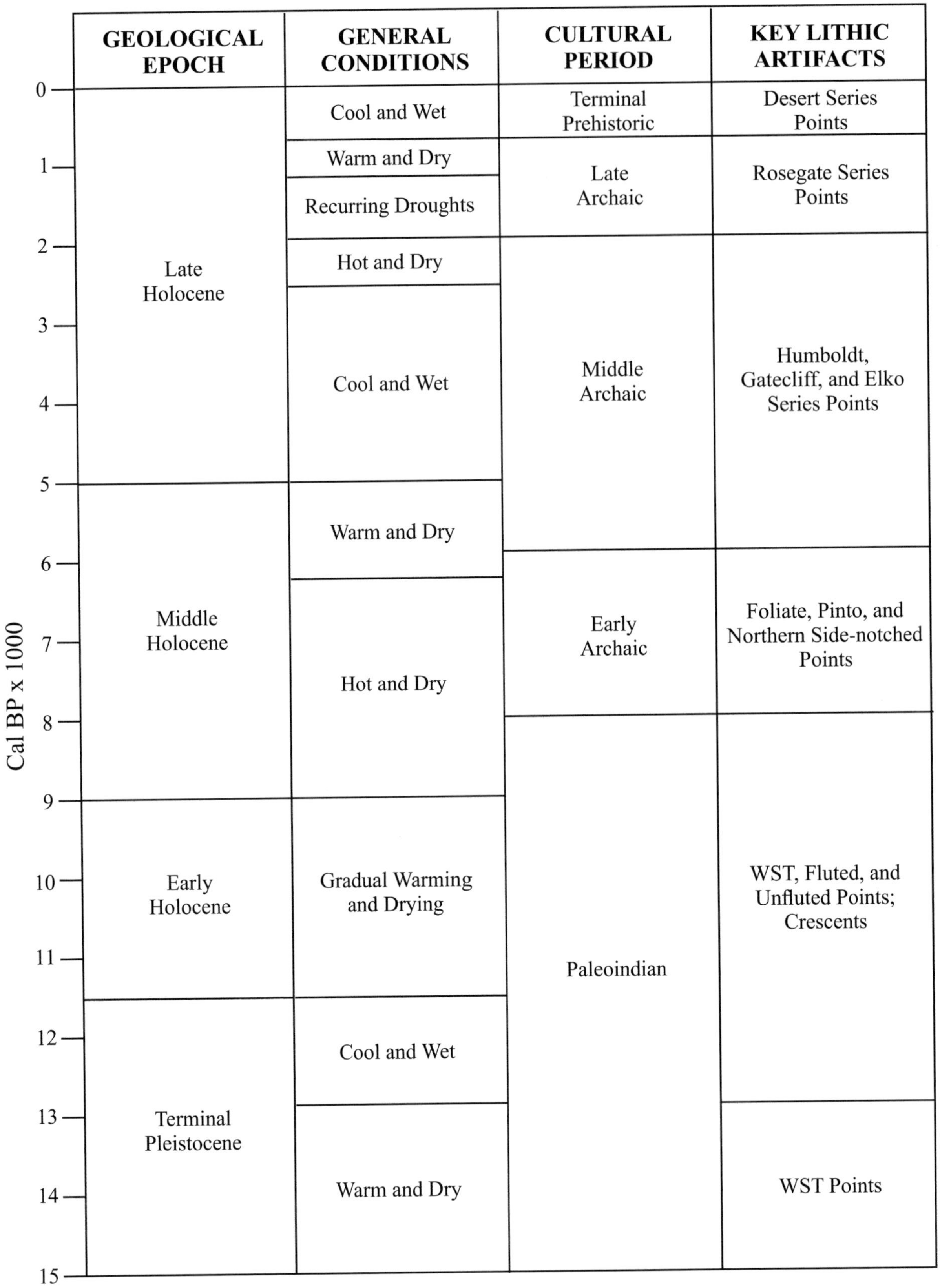

GEOLOGICAL EPOCH	GENERAL CONDITIONS	CULTURAL PERIOD	KEY LITHIC ARTIFACTS
Late Holocene	Cool and Wet	Terminal Prehistoric	Desert Series Points
	Warm and Dry	Late Archaic	Rosegate Series Points
	Recurring Droughts		
	Hot and Dry	Middle Archaic	Humboldt, Gatecliff, and Elko Series Points
	Cool and Wet		
Middle Holocene	Warm and Dry	Early Archaic	Foliate, Pinto, and Northern Side-notched Points
	Hot and Dry		
Early Holocene	Gradual Warming and Drying	Paleoindian	WST, Fluted, and Unfluted Points; Crescents
Terminal Pleistocene	Cool and Wet		
	Warm and Dry		WST Points

Cal BP x 1000

FIGURE 2.1. Cultural and environmental sequences for the northwestern Great Basin.

mountain sheep, and mule deer persisted, but their numbers may have been relatively low during the early and middle Holocene (Broughton et al. 2008; but see Grayson 2011). Bison populations waxed and waned in the northern Great Basin throughout the Holocene, at times seeming to disappear only to reemerge centuries or millennia later (Grayson 2006). The distributions of smaller fauna were also somewhat different, with pikas (*Ochotona princeps*) and pygmy rabbits (*Brachylagus idahoensis*) being more widespread and found at lower elevations than today (Grayson 2005).

Currently, the earliest evidence for human occupation in the northern Great Basin occurs at the Paisley Five Mile Point Caves in Oregon's Summer Lake Basin. There, Dennis Jenkins and colleagues uncovered WST projectile points and other obsidian tools, debitage, modified mammal bones, coprolites containing human DNA, and hearth features in terminal Pleistocene deposits (Hockett and Jenkins 2013; Jenkins et al. 2012, 2013; Shillito et al. 2020). Coprolites returned both Clovis (13,400–12,700 cal BP [D. Miller et al. 2013]) and pre-Clovis ages, and Jenkins's team recovered three WST points from Clovis-aged deposits. Importantly, they found no fluted points. Jenkins concluded that the Paisley Caves show that Paleoindians used WST technology in the northern Great Basin coincident with Paleoindian use of fluted points elsewhere in North America and that people first visited the site 1,000 years or so before the Clovis Era (Jenkins et al. 2012, 2013).

Cooper's Ferry in western Idaho has also produced WST points associated with pre-Clovis radiocarbon dates. The earliest occupation probably occurred 16,500–15,300 cal BP, a millennium or so before the Paisley Caves, but there are no diagnostic projectile points from the site's deepest cultural deposits. Cooper's Ferry likely served as a residential base where groups butchered game (including horse) and, later, excavated storage pits (L. G. Davis et al. 2019). Davis and colleagues argue that the site supports the hypothesis that the first groups to reach temperate North America did so via a Pacific coastal route (Davis et al. 2012, 2014, 2019).

These interpretations of the Paisley Caves and Cooper's Ferry records have both been questioned (Fiedel 2014; Fiedel et al. 2020; Goebel and Keene 2014; Manning 2020; Sistiaga et al. 2014). Because reporting is ongoing, it will be some time before we learn how the sites ultimately fit into the broader discourse about the peopling of the Americas. However, the consensus seems to be that both sites represent early occupations where WST and not fluted points have been found. The fact that they both contain WST points suggests that fluted points do not mark the earliest occupations in the Inter-

mountain West. In turn, this calls into question both the Clovis First model and the role of the Ice-Free Corridor in the initial dispersal of people into the New World.

Despite Stephen Bedwell's (1970, 1973) claim that Oregon's Fort Rock Cave contained a ~15,000-year-old occupation—which Connolly and colleagues (2017) failed to corroborate upon returning to the site—the Paisley Caves remain the only well-dated site in the northern Great Basin with a pre-Younger Dryas occupation. Well-dated Younger Dryas occupations are also rare (Smith et al. 2020), but among these, Connley Cave 4 (Jenkins et al. 2017), the Paisley Caves (Jenkins et al. 2016), and Cougar Mountain Cave (Rosencrance et al. 2019) have yielded the best information. The number of dated sites—mostly caves and rockshelters but a few open-air sites as well—rises sharply during the early Holocene, which presumably marks increasing populations (Louderback et al. 2010) or changing land-use patterns (Smith and Barker 2017).

Both these dated and numerous other undated TP/EH sites are marked by WST, fluted, and unfluted concave-base points that are probably younger than Clovis points from other regions (Beck and Jones 2010, 2013). Crescents and other flaked stone tools are also found at these sites. While a handful of sites have produced multiple fluted points (e.g., Sheep Mountain, Sage Hen Gap, Trout Creek Paleo Camp, and the Dietz Site; Smith and Barker 2017 and references therein), they generally occur as isolates (Grayson 2011). Pinson (2011) suggested that the Dietz Site was used as a stopover by Clovis groups moving between pluvial basins; other fluted point concentrations could represent similar stops in a mobile settlement system.

Concentrations of WST points are also known from the Dietz Basin (Pinson 1999; Willig 1989), Guano Valley (Reaux et al. 2018), Hawksy Walksy Valley (Bradley et al. 2020; Christian 1997), Five Mile Flat (Smith 2007), and many other valleys. Stemmed points have also been found in several Fort Rock Basin caves (Fort Rock Cave, Cougar Mountain Cave, and the Connley Caves), as well as Last Supper Cave and Hanging Rock Shelter in northwestern Nevada (Felling 2015; Layton 1970; Smith et al. 2011; Smith et al. 2015a).

The relationship between fluted and WST technology in the region is a topic of debate. Some researchers have argued that they mark sequential Pleistocene technologies (Fagan 1988; Jennings 1986; Willig 1988). Others see them as contemporary terminal Pleistocene technologies marking either separate ethnolinguistic populations descended from different founding populations (Beck and Jones 2010, 2013) or components of the same toolkit (Tuohy 1974). Unfortunately, no sites contain both technologies in a stratified context. There are also no well-dated fluted point sites in the Great Basin or California. As we outlined above, however, the Paisley Caves and Cooper's Ferry indicate that stemmed points are at least as old as Clovis points from the Great Plains and U.S. Southwest.

Some early sites have produced bags, mats, sandals, and nets that reflect a complex Paleoindian textile industry (Connolly et al. 2016). Shell beads from the Pacific Coast also occur in some early Holocene assemblages (Jenkins et al. 2004b; Smith et al. 2016a). Residential structures are rare but not unknown (Connolly 1999; Hildebrandt et al. 2016). Early groups produced Great Basin Carved Abstract petroglyphs in mid-elevation settings likely associated with productive root grounds (Benson et al. 2013a; Cannon and Ricks 1986, 1999; Middleton et al. 2014; Ricks and Cannon 1993).

Food residues are primarily restricted to dry caves and rockshelters. They are dominated by jackrabbits and other small game, with fish, shellfish, waterfowl, and other birds also represented (Grayson 1979, 1988; Greenspan 1994; Hockett et al. 2017; Napton 1997; Oetting 1994a). In the Fort Rock Basin, and, as we discuss later, North Warner Valley, groups probably held communal rabbit drives during the early Holocene (Oetting 1994a). Artiodactyls are uncommon relative to small game in many assemblages, which may reflect a risk-minimization strategy (Pinson 1999, 2007) or low population densities of big game (Broughton et al. 2008). Although people and some taxa of megafauna coexisted in the northern Great Basin for a time, there are no unequivocal kill sites in the region. Grayson (2011, 2016) suggests that this could be a function of preservation bias: hunters would have killed, processed, and consumed large prey in open-air settings where those animals lived, not in caves and rockshelters where preservation is good. The role of plants in Paleoindian diets is not well understood, although, based on the paucity of groundstone in most TP/EH assemblages, intensive seed processing was probably uncommon.

Edible root and grass pollen and starch were recovered from one of the Paisley Caves coprolites, suggesting that early groups consumed some plants (Jenkins et al. 2013; also see Kennedy 2018, and Blong et al. 2020). This possibility is supported by the distribution of Great Basin Carved Abstract rock art sites, many of which contain completely repatinated bedrock milling surfaces suggestive of plant processing (Middleton et al. 2014). Paleoindians also consumed berries (Connolly 1999) and, likely, marsh plants (Bradley et al. 2020; McGuire and Stevens 2017).

Our understanding of Paleoindian mobility and land use is based largely on source provenance studies, technological analyses of lithic artifacts, and regional studies of site location. There is some evidence that early groups were residentially mobile and far ranging. With few exceptions, residential and storage features are absent (Elston and Zeanah 2002; Elston et al. 2014). The Paleoindian toolkit, comprised of a few generalized implements, appears to have been well suited for mobile groups (Graf 2001; Pratt et al. 2020; Smith 2007). Finally, groups conveyed obsidian substantial distances (Jones et al. 2003; Reaux et al. 2018; Smith 2010). Jones and colleagues (2003, 2012; also see Smith 2010) have argued that toolstone conveyance patterns reflect TP/EH foraging ranges. However, such patterns can be influenced by myriad factors (Smith and Harvey 2018). Wetlands figured prominently in early land-use strategies, but whether they served as longer-term residential hubs from which logistical hunting or foraging parties came and went or places that residential groups revisited periodically is unknown (Bedwell 1973; Elston et al. 2014; Jones et al. 2003; Madsen 2007; Smith et al. 2013a). During the early Holocene, groups probably started to use other parts of the landscape due to the diminution of lakes and wetlands (Felling 2015; Grayson 2011).

The Middle Holocene (9000–5000 cal BP)

Although not as uniformly hot and dry as Antevs (1948) once proposed, the middle Holocene was generally warmer and drier than both the preceding TP/EH and subsequent late Holocene. The period from 9000 to 6300 cal BP was especially dry (Rhode 2016; Wigand and Rhode 2002). Mount Mazama erupted ~7700 cal BP and blanketed the region in ash. Many remaining lakes and wetlands dried completely for a time and produced downwind dune systems (Dugas 1998; Mehringer and Wigand 1986; Young 2000). In western Nevada, Lake Tahoe fell below its sill (Lindström 1990) and the lower Humboldt River ceased flowing (House et al. 2001).

Vegetation shifted in response to elevated temperature and reduced precipitation. On Steens Mountain, sagebrush moved upslope (Mehringer 1985), while in the Harney Basin greasewood and shadscale covered much of the valley floor (Wigand 1987). This was also the case in the Lahontan Basin (Mensing et al. 2004). Wetter conditions returned after 6300 cal BP, fostering increases in sagebrush in lower elevation areas along with grasslands and pine-fir forests in higher elevation areas (Minckley et al. 2007; Rhode 2016; Wigand and Rhode 2002). Lake Tahoe resumed feeding the Truckee River and, in turn, Pyramid Lake (Lindström 1990; Mensing et al. 2004), and the Humboldt River's flow increased (House et al. 2001).

Prolonged aridity affected small and large game in the region. As may have been the case during the early Holocene, increased seasonality probably reduced artiodactyl herds when the winter-wet, summer-dry precipitation pattern likely produced insufficient forage for young animals (Broughton et al. 2008). This could explain the low numbers of artiodactyls in middle Holocene assemblages in the northern Great Basin, although there are other possible explanations (Pinson 1999, 2007). The distribution of small game also changed. Pygmy rabbits became restricted to more northern latitudes due to a loss of sagebrush habitat, and pikas moved upslope in response to rising temperatures (Grayson 2005). While the middle Holocene is often viewed as unfavorable, expanding greasewood communities—a favored jackrabbit habitat—in many valley bottoms may have benefitted people (Schmitt et al. 2004).

The Early Archaic period (8000–5750 cal BP) roughly corresponds to the most arid part of the middle Holocene (Rhode 2016). Stemmed points disappeared ~9000 cal BP (Rosencrance 2019), and Early Archaic sites are marked initially by foliate (i.e., Cascade) points and, later, Northern Side-notched points (Aikens et al. 2011; King 2016a; Oetting 1994b). Other artifacts include groundstone, which occurs in greater numbers than during the TP/EH, shell and stone beads, and wood and bone tools (Jenkins et al. 2004b; McGuire and Hildebrandt 2016; O'Connell 1975). Multiple Warp and Spiral Weft type sandals replaced Fort Rock type sandals (Connolly et al. 2016). Except for sandals, this constellation of artifacts generally occurs north of the Humboldt River, suggesting the presence of particular ethnolinguistic groups—perhaps Penutian speakers (Delacorte and Basgall 2012).

Although food remains from middle Holocene sites are rare, because occupations from that period are rare (see below), Early Archaic groups seem to have targeted a wider range of resources. Large pit houses in California's Surprise Valley dated to 7400–5200 cal BP produced bison and elk remains (James 1983; O'Connell 1975), while fish, marsh plants, rabbits and hares, waterfowl eggshell, and seeds have been recovered from Fort Rock Basin sites (Jenkins et al. 2004a). Most researchers think that the increased number of milling stones at middle Holocene sites marks an increase in diet breadth, as groups added seeds to their diets (Jenkins et al. 2004a; Ruby 2016). However, we will discuss later the probable use of such tools to process roots, small game, and pigment as well.

For decades, researchers assumed that harsh conditions during the middle Holocene led to reduced human populations (Baumhoff and Heizer 1965; Grayson 2011;

Layton 1985). There is some evidence for this possibility; for example, many cave and rockshelters show prolonged hiatuses during that time (Ollivier 2016). Middle Holocene radiocarbon dates are also relatively rare (Louderback et al. 2010), although, at least in northwestern Nevada, the number of sites increases during the Early Archaic period when adjusted for time (Ruby 2016).

These trends may imply decreased human populations, but they may also reflect a reorganization of settlement-subsistence strategies that brought people away from caves and rockshelters and closer to water sources. In the Fort Rock Basin, people repeatedly stopped at the Locality III site between 8600 and 6300 cal BP—a generally arid period—during wet intervals when nearby ponds and sloughs would have held water (Aikens et al. 2011). Other middle Holocene sites in the Fort Rock Basin, such as Bowling Dune, DJ Ranch, Big M, and Bergen, were occupied slightly later than Locality III when wetter conditions returned. Those sites contained houses, storage features, and other evidence of longer-term occupations (Aikens et al. 2011). In that regard, they are like the Surprise Valley pit houses, which are clustered around thermal springs (O'Connell 1975). Finally, many middle Holocene sites are clustered around upland springs, which may reflect a narrowed settlement system focused on dependable water sources (Fagan 1974).

Obsidian sourcing data suggest relatively long stays at some middle Holocene sites. Smith (2010, 2011) noted that in the northwestern Great Basin, middle and initial late Holocene projectile points were conveyed shorter distances than early Holocene and terminal late Holocene types. In addition, middle Holocene points were made of fewer obsidian types, suggesting an increased reliance on local sources. McGuire (2002) and King (2016b) observed the same pattern in northeastern California and northwestern Nevada, which they attribute to increased residential stability, especially during the Middle Archaic period (5750–2000 cal BP). Alternatively, given the ephemeral nature of many middle Holocene residential sites, groups may have operated within smaller territories but relocated their camps more often. Finally, trade networks may simply have changed in ways that emphasized local toolstone.

The Late Holocene (5000–150 cal BP)

The late Holocene saw increased precipitation and lower temperatures than the middle Holocene (Minckley et al. 2007; Rhode 2016). A summer-wet pattern likely produced more favorable conditions for artiodactyls (Broughton et al. 2008). Lakes and marshes deepened, woodlands expanded, and sagebrush communities replaced some greasewood communities. There were some interruptions in these general trends though. For example, from 2500 to 2000 cal BP, conditions grew nearly as hot and dry as those that characterized the middle Holocene. Recurrent droughts have also occurred during the past 2,000 years, including during the Medieval Climatic Anomaly, 1100–700 cal BP (Stine 1994). Those droughts are evident in the Pyramid Lake (Benson et al. 2002; Mensing et al. 2004) and Carson Sink (Adams 2003) records, but so too are wetter intervals. The frequency, perhaps more than the amplitude, of these shifts may have negatively affected people in the region. After 700 cal BP, the Little Ice Age brought about colder and wetter conditions.

The late Holocene encompasses most of the Middle Archaic (5750–2000 cal BP), Late Archaic (2000–600 cal BP), and Terminal Prehistoric (600–150 cal BP) periods. Middle Archaic projectile point types include Humboldt, Gatecliff, and Elko series points (King 2016a; Oetting 1994b), all of which tipped atlatl darts. After 2000 cal BP, these were replaced by Late Archaic Rosegate points that mark the arrival of the bow and arrow. After 600 cal BP, Terminal Prehistoric groups adopted smaller Desert Series arrow points. Groundstone is common at sites from all late Holocene periods (Hildebrandt et al. 2016).

Residential stability continued to increase in the northern Great Basin during the late Holocene, although it varied in some places. The Fort Rock Basin contains several Middle Archaic sites with houses, storage features, and diverse artifact and faunal assemblages, which Jenkins and colleagues (2004a) suggest marks a regional population increase. A sharp rise in the number of radiocarbon dates during the late Holocene supports this idea (Louderback et al. 2010). Many residential sites are in marsh-grassland ecotones, which would have enabled residents to exploit several environments close to home.

Many caves and rockshelters were reoccupied after lengthy hiatuses (Ollivier 2016). McDonough (2019) suggests that some caves in the Fort Rock Basin served as summer–fall logistical camps. Residential stability decreased after 3000 cal BP in the Fort Rock Basin—which roughly corresponds to a reduction in marshlands (Jenkins et al. 2004a)—but increased again after 2000 cal BP. Carlon Village, a cluster of eight large domestic structures, was constructed after 2350 cal BP (Wingard 2001), while in the Abert-Chewaucan Basin, pit house villages along the Chewaucan River and near Lake Abert appeared around the same time (Oetting 1989, 1990). Parts of South Warner Valley saw increased use after

3500 cal BP (Weide 1968), and habitation sites near the Warner Lakes were occupied primarily after 3000 cal BP (Tipps 1998; Young 1998) These sites suggest a heavy Middle Archaic presence. In northwestern Nevada, residential stability was high until 1300 cal BP, after which time people appear to have employed more of a residentially mobile strategy that produced a scattered Terminal Prehistoric record that can be difficult to recognize (Hildebrandt et al. 2016).

Increased large game availability is reflected in Middle Archaic faunal assemblages across the region (McGuire et al. 2016; Pinson 2007). In addition to artiodactyls, Middle Archaic assemblages from the Fort Rock Basin contain rabbits and hares, waterfowl, canids, and fish (O'Grady 2004; Singer 2004). Milling equipment is also common, and the taxonomic diversity of archaeological-botanical assemblages peaks. Root procurement appears to have been important (McGuire and Stevens 2017). Together, these trends suggest that subsistence pursuits were varied and that people consumed a wide range of foods.

Hildebrandt and McGuire (2002; see also McGuire and Hildebrandt 2005; McGuire et al. 2016) have argued that within this generalized subsistence strategy men targeted large game to reap both the caloric and social benefits that successful hunts provided. During the Late Archaic period, large game hunting may have initially continued to be important, but artiodactyl use had declined by the onset of the Terminal Prehistoric period—at least in northeastern California (Carpenter 2002). McGuire and colleagues (2016) link this decline to the arrival of the Numa and their ethnographically documented family-band level of socioeconomic organization (Steward 1938). As expected, based on Steward's observations, milling equipment and archaeological-botanical assemblage diversity are high at Terminal Prehistoric sites (McGuire et al. 2016).

THE NUMIC SPREAD

When and from where Native Americans came to occupy the linguistic territories present at the time of Euro-American arrival remains a controversial topic (Madsen and Rhode 1994). Today, southeastern Oregon is home to both the Klamath and Northern Paiute. Those groups speak different languages: the Klamath language (and the languages of several other nearby California groups) is part of the broader Penutian language family, while Northern Paiute is part of the Numic branch of the Uto-Aztecan language family. Many archaeologists and linguists believe that the Numa moved from eastern California north and east across the Great Basin within the past 2,000 years (Bettinger and Baumhoff 1982;

Camp 2017, 2018; Delacorte 2008; Hill 2006; Lamb 1958; W. Miller 1983, 1986). Others argue that Numic speakers have been in the region much longer (Aikens and Witherspoon 1986; Goss 1977; Thomas 2019).

Linguists have proposed three models to account for the geographic distribution of Numic languages. The first postulates a recent expansion out of the southwestern Great Basin. Sydney Lamb (1958) initially suggested that this event took place within the past 1,000 years, although he has since acknowledged that it may have occurred a few millennia earlier (Thomas 1994). Jane Hill (2001, 2002) refined and expanded this model with the argument that the Numic spread marked the final part of a larger process in which Uto-Aztecan languages moved north and west from northeastern Mesoamerica. In her interpretation, that process began 6500–5000 cal BP and involved the migration of maize farmers rather than simply the spread of language across in situ populations.

A second model proposed by Catherine Fowler (1983) holds that the Uto-Aztecan language family emerged around the Arizona-Mexico border ~7000 cal BP and then spread to surrounding areas sometime after 5000 cal BP. This model is compatible with Lamb's model but not Hill's because Fowler does not see Numic languages being spread by maize horticulturalists migrating north from northeastern Mesoamerica.

A third model holds that Uto-Aztecan speakers were emplaced in central Nevada for a considerable amount of time and began to radiate outward during the middle Holocene (Goss 1968, 1977; Merrill 2012; Merrill et al. 2009). While it remains unclear which of these models, if any, best captures what took place, it is important to note that all suggest Uto-Aztecan languages did not diverge from their proto–Uto-Aztecan ancestor until 7000–6500 cal BP. Further, all suggest that any movement of Numic speakers within the Great Basin likely did not occur until after 3000 cal BP (Madsen and Rhode 1994). Finally, they all describe the same boundary between Numic and Penutian speakers in the northern Great Basin.

Assigning ethnolinguistic membership to archaeological assemblages is a challenging endeavor, but basketry may provide one of the best means of matching evidence (Camp 2017). For example, based on differences in trays, baskets, hats, and other items, Hattori (1982) argues that Penutian speakers ancestral to today's Klamath and Modoc groups occupied the northern Great Basin until 600 cal BP. Camp's (2017) comparison of Catlow Twine basketry from archaeological contexts and Klamath and Modoc basketry supports this possibility. Other researchers have argued that Desert Series projectile points may serve as a Numic marker (Bettinger and Baumhoff 1982; Delacorte 2008; Delacorte and Basgall 2012). Barker (2018) recently suggested that V-twined sandals may also be a Numic marker in northwestern Nevada. Finally, some researchers have suggested that shifts in house form, toolstone conveyance, or more broadly, settlement-subsistence patterns across the Late Archaic–Terminal Prehistoric boundary may signal the Northern Paiute displacement of the Klamath from part of their ancestral homeland (Aikens 1994; Connolly and Jenkins 1997; Eiselt 1998; Hildebrandt et al. 2016; Oetting 1989, 1990).

THE ETHNOGRAPHIC PERIOD

At the time of initial direct Euro-American contact in the 1820s, Warner Valley lay within Northern Paiute territory (specifically, the *Kidütökadö*, or Marmot Eaters) and adjacent to Klamath territory (C. Fowler and Liljeblad 1986; Stern 1998; Stewart 1939). However, ethnographic accounts suggest that it was previously in Klamath hands. The Northern Paiute claim that they won a war with the Klamath and forced them to retreat from northern Nevada and beyond the territorial boundaries observed at the time of Euro-American contact (Camp 2017; Sutton 1986, 1993). To the south, Loud and Harrington (1929) were told of an earlier, presumably non-Numic, group that occupied the Humboldt Sink, Winnemucca Lake, and Pyramid Lake areas. Those earlier inhabitants were identified as being related to the Hokan-speaking Pit River Tribe or Penutian-speaking Klamath Tribe. Closer to North Warner Valley, the Surprise Valley Paiute told Isabel Kelly (1932) of a similar group that they believed was related to the Pit River or Shasta/Hat Creek Tribes.

Because Warner Valley may have seen shared use by the Klamath and Northern Paiute, ethnographic and ethnohistoric studies of both groups form the basis for this section (Barrett 1910, Coville 1897; I. Kelly 1932; Spier 1930). Unfortunately, ethnographers did not begin recording traditional lifeways until long after both groups had been affected by Euro-American contact. Exposure to epidemic diseases, trade for arms and other European goods, slave trading, and the introduction of the horse altered Native cultures (Malouf and Findlay 1986; Shimkin 1986; Spier 1930; Walker and Sprague 1998). By 1870, substantial Native populations had relocated to reservations or communities adjacent to Euro-American settlements. Ethnographers largely relied on people's memories, and as time passed people were increasingly only able to recount their parents' or grandparents' memories, not firsthand observations (I. Kelly 1932; Spier 1930). This issue was compounded by the increasing integration of Western and Indigenous culture, which accelerated the loss of traditional knowledge and practices. Yet, it is important to note that while some information about Native American culture was lost, activities such as plant gathering (Couture 1978; Couture et al. 1986; Gleason 2001), jackrabbit drives (Peden 1995), and fishing (Foster 1996) continue today in ways like those practiced in the past.

The Klamath

Among the Klamath, work was typically divided along gender lines. Economic efficiency and diet breadth were facilitated by men and women working on different tasks, depending on seasonal resource availability (Barker 2016, 2019; Elston and Zeanah 2002; Zeanah 2002, 2004; Zeanah and Simms 1999). Men were generally responsible for fishing, but men and women worked together during major runs (Spier 1930; Stern 1998). Women gathered wokas (yellow pond lily [*Nuphar lutea*]) and other plants, while men hunted upland game. Men who were too old to hunt and fish helped women with plant gathering and processing. Men and women both built pit houses—semisubterranean dwellings excavated up to 1 m deep and 4–10 m across, with roofs comprised of dirt or vegetation supported by mats, wooden planks, and central posts (Spier 1930). Klamath houses were like the pit houses that O'Connell (1975) reported in Surprise Valley but different from Northern Paiute houses. The Klamath also had semisubterranean sweat lodges and temporary summer shelters, the latter being like those of the Northern Paiute except that they lacked rock ring foundations.

Men made weapons, fishing nets, and wooden tools. Stone-tipped arrows were only used in warfare (Barrett 1910; Spier 1930). Barrett (1910) noted that the Klamath used obsidian and chert knives and other tools but did not use stone arrowheads or spear points for hunting. Spier (1930) noted that they used stone arrowheads for both war and hunting but did not elaborate. Both Kelly (1932) and Barrett (1910) described Klamath war arrows as tipped with relatively large obsidian or chert points. Game, fish, and birds were taken using fletched and unfletched arrows with reed shafts and sharpened greasewood foreshafts. Bows were sinew-backed juniper staves pointed on the ends. Men built large dugout canoes but were assisted by women.

Women made clothing and cordage and wove textiles. All Klamath textiles were twined rather than coiled and included both soft and ridged forms (Barrett 1910). Soft textiles included decorated hats, bags, mats, trays, and bowls related to Catlow Twine textiles from archaeological contexts (Camp 2017). Soft parching and sifting trays were used in food processing. Hard conical burden baskets, flat-sided storage baskets, trays, and spoon-shaped baskets were used for food gathering and processing. The Klamath wore woven sandals that differed from those made by the Northern Paiute (Ollivier 2016; Smith et al. 2016b). They used a wide array of groundstone implements including mortars and pestles, shaft straighteners, mauls, plain manos and metates, and two-handed horned metates.

Subsistence activities were centered on rivers, streams, and marshes (Spier 1930). Winter was the most stressful season, with starvation often a threat (Spier 1930). Although travel was limited in winter, men fished year round in streams and rivers. The Klamath avoided winter extremes by living in pit house clusters and subsisting on stored foods (e.g., dried fish and plants) supplemented by fresh fish or game. Winter houses were often situated adjacent to running water. Resources were shared as needed and many communities maintained large communal storage pits to supplement private food storage in individual houses (Spier 1930). Unguarded storage pits were sometimes raided during hard times. As winter gave way to spring, food supplies often ran short while people waited for fishing and plant collecting locales to become productive. Most years, marsh plants began sprouting in April or early May, and salmon and suckers started their spawning runs in March.

In the spring, people moved out of their winter houses, which were dismantled for the summer, and into temporary houses built at food collecting sites. Canoes, stored over winter in shallow water to prevent cracking, moved people and gear to fishing or gathering spots (Stern 1998). Rushing streams and rivers were quieted with rock dams to create pools suitable for net fishing, often undertaken with large triangular dip or long gill nets (Stern 1998). Other fishing tools included two-prong harpoons, multipronged spears, and barbed spears. Sometimes fish were taken with baited hooks on poles.

Anadromous fish available to the Klamath included coho salmon (*Oncorhynchus kisutch*), chinook salmon (*Oncorhynchus tshawytscha*), steelhead trout (*Oncorhynchus mykiss irideus*), Lost River sucker (*Deltistes luxatus*), shortnose sucker (*Chasmistes brevirostris*), cutthroat trout (*Oncorhynchus clarkii*), chum salmon (*Oncorhynchus keta*), and Pacific lamprey (*Entosphenus tridentatus*). Major resident fish included bull trout (*Salvelinus confluentus*), rainbow trout (*Oncorhynchus mykiss*), and, locally, Warner suckers.

Fish that spawn in late winter and early spring (coho salmon, Lost River and shortnose suckers, and Pacific lamprey) were important because they provided fresh food as stored foods ran out. Anadromous fish with spawning runs in the summer or fall (chinook and chum salmon, steelhead trout) were gathered, processed, and stored as winter provisions. Bull trout and rainbow trout are available year round and were taken in all seasons. When early spring runs were especially abundant, people congregated at good fishing spots. In good years, people camped for two to three months and hunted and gathered other resources from there. These longer-term gatherings were major social events, and people developed and/or maintained economic, political, and familial ties (Spier 1930).

While men fished spawning runs, women gathered marsh and upland roots (Spier 1930). Important marsh resources included yellow pond-lily, sedge (*Carex* sp.), cattail (*Typha* sp.), Indian potato (*Sagittaria latifolia*), and bur-reed (*Sparganium eurycarpum*). Upland root crops included wild onion (*Allium anceps*), balsam root (*Balsamhoriza saggitata*), camas (*Camassia quamash*), bitterroot (*Lewisia redivva*), biscuitroot (*Lomatium cous*), yampa or epos (*Perideridia* sp.), sego lily (*Calhortus nutalli*), and mariposa lily (*Calochortus macrocarpus*).

Women's spring gathering focused on desert parsley (*Lomatium canbyi*), epos, and camas. Summer and early fall were devoted to gathering, processing, and storing *wokas*, which served as the primary winter plant food. While *wokas* was readily available, gathering and processing it was laborious. In addition to gathering and drying, it had to be fermented in a pit for up to five weeks. Spier (1930) reported that a woman could gather 4–6 bushels of *wokas* per day and endeavored to have 7–10 50–lb sacks of dried *wokas* by summer's end.

The Surprise Valley Northern Paiute

The Northern Paiute in Surprise Valley lived in fairly permanent villages composed of five or six families occupying separate houses (I. Kelly 1932). Most families had at least two winter settlements and moved when food was exhausted at one of them. Their northernmost winter camp was in the vicinity of Plush, Oregon, ~40 km south of North Warner Valley. The Surprise Valley Paiute built aboveground winter houses in sheltered locations with ready access to water. They were generally large, single-family conical buildings constructed with willow (*Salix* sp.) poles and covered with sewn or twined tule (*Schoenoplectus acutus*) or grass mats. They were large enough to accommodate eight or nine people and tall enough for someone to stand upright. The Surprise Valley Paiute also made summer shade roofs (ramadas)

associated with a brush sleeping enclosure. People used the shades for cooking and general work and houses for storage and sleeping.

In contrast to the Klamath, the Surprise Valley Paiute made and used small triangular obsidian and chert arrowheads (I. Kelly 1932). In archaeological contexts, Northern Paiute arrowheads classify as Desert Series points (Thomas 1981). They were hafted onto an arrow shaft up to 4 ft long. Except for fishing arrows, all arrows were fletched with three feathers and decorated to identify the owner (I. Kelly 1932). Bipointed, sinewbacked bows were made from juniper staves 3–4 ft long. Groundstone tools included manos and metates, mortars and pestles, and shaft straighteners. Men made weapons, flaked stone tools, and large hunting, fishing, and birding nets. Women usually made cordage for those nets. They also made predominantly twined baskets and, occasionally, coiled baskets. In contrast, Klamath baskets were exclusively twined. Woven Northern Paiute tools included open and closed conical burden baskets, parching and winnowing trays, mats, seed beaters, cooking baskets, bowls, fish traps and baskets, and pitched water bottles. In Surprise Valley, people did not use woven sandals or woven hats.

In contrast to groups with access to pinyon pine nuts, which could be stored, subsistence pursuits among the Northern Paiute groups in northwestern Nevada, northeastern California, and southeastern Oregon—north of the pinyon zone—were more continuous and less seasonal (I. Kelly 1932; Riddell 1978). Food accumulation and storage sufficient to avoid late winter shortages was more problematic in the north. As a result, there was a greater emphasis on root gathering and animal procurement, especially pronghorn and jackrabbits.

The *Kidütökadö* provide a good example of a nonpinyon Northern Paiute adaptation. Beginning in spring when snow was still on the ground, people fished along creeks and streams on the valley bottom. As the snow melted, winter settlements were abandoned, and people moved into the eastern hills for early shoot and root gathering, supplementing their diet with food from strategically located caches. Throughout the spring and well into summer, people stayed in relatively fixed camps whose location allowed food gathering from both the valley bottom and adjacent hills. People generally did not make logistical trips to known resource patches but instead foraged opportunistically in an expanding radius from camp. They gathered plants and small game for daily consumption and harvested dense root patches for winter storage. Depending on local conditions, gathering could be wide ranging, from collecting camas in swamps to gathering epos and other roots in higher and drier country. Women's access to plant resources, especially roots, determined camp locations, and men hunted from the base camp but more often went on longer hunting trips (I. Kelly 1932).

As fall approached, plant gathering declined and people turned to hunting for winter storage. From late summer into fall, they gathered for communal jackrabbit drives and waterfowl hunts. Participants usually divided the fruits of these labors equally. People returned to relatively permanent settlements in Surprise Valley to subsist on seeds, dried roots, and dried meat from caches (I. Kelly 1932). People also traveled in winter among several camp areas to participate in communal antelope and jackrabbit drives.

Geophytes were an especially important dietary staple in the northern Great Basin (Couture 1978; Couture et al. 1986; I. Kelly 1932; Riddell 1978; Scholze 2011; Trammell et al. 2008). Important root crops occur in valley bottom wetland habitats, on sandy or rocky sagebrush-covered slopes, and in upland meadows and flats. They are available in spring when their stems and flowers become visible, and people harvested them with simple tools, mainly digging sticks. Lowland plants were harvested first in the early spring and consumed to stave off starvation as winter stores became exhausted. As conditions ameliorated through spring and into summer, other geophytes became available at higher elevations. The most important of these were dryland taxa like epos, biscuitroot, and bitterroot. People gathered them for daily consumption and, more importantly, to dry them for winter storage. Other important upland root plants included desert parsley, wild onion, balsam root, sego lily, and mariposa lily (I. Kelly 1932).

Winter hunting was critical (I. Kelly 1932; Riddell 1978). In addition to daily individual and small group hunts for deer, rabbits, and other small game, people organized communal jackrabbit drives using nets and pronghorn drives using corrals and wing traps. Pronghorn drives were usually held in mid- or late winter, using the wet ground to tire the animals. Riddell's (1978) consultants described how families gathered for the drive and meat was shared equally among them. These communal hunts provided much-needed winter food, but, equally as important, they were social gatherings at which individuals found mates, developed trade relationships, and nurtured alliances to gain access to neighboring resource areas (I. Kelly 1932). While an antelope boss managed the drive itself, the social gathering was managed by a group of household heads.

From late September through January, the Surprise Valley Paiute participated in communal jackrabbit hunts using individually owned large nets (1 m × 30 m or longer; I. Kelly 1932). One or more net owners (bosses) organized the hunt, which involved members of four or five camps. Men and women drove jackrabbits into nets strung across a valley and clubbed them. Once an area's jackrabbit population was exhausted, people moved elsewhere to continue the hunt. The boss divided the catch among all families, and most of the meat was dried. Both men and women cut rabbit skins into long strips, which they used to make blankets and robes (I. Kelly 1932).

PREDICTIONS FOR THE ARCHAEOLOGICAL RECORD OF NORTH WARNER VALLEY

Based on what we know about the archaeological record of the northern Great Basin, Klamath and Northern Paiute lifeways, and the history of pluvial Lake Warner (see Chapter 3), we anticipated that the archaeological record of North Warner Valley would be characterized by the following trends:

1. The Younger Dryas (12,900–11,600 cal BP) should mark the period of highest site density, when lakes and/or wetlands were extensive and productive.
2. Stemmed- and fluted-point sites should be found on the same landforms, reflecting the use of both projectile technologies during the terminal Pleistocene.
3. Early Holocene (11,500–9000 cal BP) sites should be largely located below 1,390 m asl., if groups followed Lake Warner as it regressed.
4. The middle Holocene (9000–5000 cal BP) should mark a period of low site density, when surface water was scarce and overall biotic productivity was probably low.
5. If present, Early Archaic (8000–5750 cal BP) sites should be concentrated around areas that might have remained periodically productive during the middle Holocene (e.g., close to Bluejoint Lake).
6. The late Holocene (post-5000 cal BP) should mark a period when people returned to North Warner Valley.
7. Middle and Late Archaic (5750–2000 cal BP and 2000–600 cal BP) site density should be moderately high.
8. Middle and Late Archaic sites should occur in all parts of North Warner Valley.
9. The Terminal Prehistoric period (600–150 cal BP) should be characterized either by a new suite of diagnostic artifact types (e.g., Desert Series points instead of Rosegate points), if the Northern Paiute displaced the Klamath, or by a very low site density

if North Warner Valley was largely abandoned after the Klamath-Northern Paiute territorial boundary shifted to the west.

10. Terminal Prehistoric sites should generally be small and located in all parts of North Warner Valley.

11. At stratified and/or radiocarbon-dated sites, artifact types attributed to the Klamath should be older than artifact types attributed to the Northern Paiute.

Summary

Warner Valley lies between two areas of the northern Great Basin that have received considerable attention from archaeologists and ethnographers alike. To the west and north, work in the Abert-Chewaucan, Alkali, and Fort Rock Basins has revealed an extensive record of human occupation ranging from WST and Clovis times to the Terminal Prehistoric period. To the south, Nevada's High Rock Country and California's Surprise Valley contain an equally impressive record of human use spanning the Holocene and, in places, the terminal Pleistocene. Prior to our work, North Warner Valley was largely terra incognita to professional archaeologists. Fortunately, the archaeological work done in the adjacent areas and the information collected by ethnographers in the early twentieth century provide a framework within which to situate the archaeological data we present here.

3 The History of Lake Warner

Teresa A. Wriston and Geoffrey M. Smith

When people first laid eyes on North Warner Valley during the terminal Pleistocene, a large lake covered the basin. From the tops of Steamboat Point and nearby Little Steamboat Point, they could have watched waves crash into the steep slopes and bedrock outcrops of the basin's eastern and western margins. Immediately below them, the water would have reached midway up a more gradual slope. There, the lake would have been ringed by stands of marsh vegetation in sheltered coves and bays. The lake, marshes, and the mammals and birds drawn there would also have made it a good place for people.

A few thousand years earlier, the lake had been much higher. It lapped at the bases of Steamboat Point and Little Steamboat Point, carving alcoves that later sheltered people. Roughly 200 generations after the first groups arrived, the view from the same vantage point would have looked quite different. There would have been no surface water, and the valley floor would have been dominated by brilliant white playas interspersed with tan silts and sands. People would have had to walk a considerable distance south to find cattail, waterfowl, and fish near a chain of lakes—remnants of pluvial Lake Warner. When Mount Mazama erupted ~7,700 years ago, ash fell into those lakes and marshes. After that time, the lakes continued to evolve, with those farther away from springs and mountain drainages probably drying during the middle Holocene before rising again in the late Holocene, albeit in smaller basins reshaped by wind and surrounded by dunes. Today, these small basins hold the Warner Lakes.

Water has always played an important role in the natural and cultural history of North Warner Valley. In this chapter, we outline the history of pluvial Lake Warner, drawing upon geomorphological and chronometric data collected using a variety of methods including extensive backhoe trenching. In places, we also draw upon archaeological data presented later (see chapters 4 and 13). Together, these data tell a story of a changing landscape and people's response to those changes.

PREVIOUS RESEARCH

Israel C. Russell was one of the first researchers to recognize that the gravel ridges and bedrock cuts ringing many Great Basin valleys were traces of ancient lakes. In 1884, Russell visited Warner Valley and concluded that despite coming close, the lake never topped its drainage divide. Three decades later, Van Winkle (1914) and Stewart (Grover et al. 1917) reached a different conclusion, arguing that at one time Lake Warner overflowed into Harney Basin to the north. Stewart discovered what he thought was a water-worn basaltic dike to support this claim. As part of his dissertation work, David Weide (1975) reexamined the dike and conclusively argued that Lake Warner in fact never overtopped its spill point. This is important because it means that Lake Warner's levels, albeit with some consideration of tectonic activity and rebound, are good indicators of the balance of moisture and evaporation in the region through time. The lake rose when the climate was cold and wet and fell when it was warm and dry. Of course, there are other factors that influence this simple equation. For example, sometimes lakes rose when it was cold and dry due to decreased evaporation. As a rule, however, more moisture produces greater lake level.

Weide (1975) used what was known at the time about the distant and much larger Lake Bonneville and Lake Lahontan systems for temporal control. He deduced that Lake Warner's last highstand occurred during the Last Glacial Maximum (LGM), 24,000–17,000 cal BP. Young (1998, 2000) later worked in Warner Valley to assess the effect of changing lake levels on human adaptive strategies. He recognized two major late Holocene lake stands using the distribution of diagnostic artifacts: (1) a pre-2000 cal BP level of 1,365.5 m asl, when the Warner Lakes coalesced and expanded northward to cover much of the valley floor; and (2) a post-2000 cal BP level of 1,361 m asl, which approximates the level of many of the Warner Lakes today. In both cases, Young (1998) recognized that while marshes offer a range of foods, they require quiet water that is neither too shallow nor too deep (C. Fowler 1990a, 1992; R. Kelly 2001; Madsen and Kelly 2008; Raymond and Parks 1990; Wheat 1967). He studied the Warner Basin's topography and found that protected embayments where gradual slopes produced water depths of ~1.5 m likely fostered the most productive marshes. It is in those places that we expected to find substantial evidence of human occupation.

These earlier studies—in particular, Weide's (1975) and Young's (1998, 2000)—were important because they provided a foundation for understanding Lake Warner's history; however, there remained ample opportunity to refine the lake's history by conducting geoarchaeological research to establish better chronometric control through radiocarbon ages and geochemical tephra identification.

METHODS

A major goal of our research program was to construct a lake-level curve to guide our interpretations of the archaeological record. Ancient shorelines offer many types of data useful for understanding when a lake occupied that elevation. For instance, people obviously do not live under water, and many artifacts, particularly those made of obsidian, quickly become waterworn if exposed to currents or wave action. It follows that if we find artifacts at an elevation that are not waterworn, then the lake was below that elevation when people discarded the artifacts and stayed below that elevation thereafter. Gravel-capped beach ridges or bars are useful because the gravel is resistant to erosion and protects finer-grained sediment found beneath it. Trenching into these gravel beach ridges often reveals buried tephras or materials that can be radiocarbon dated (e.g., shell, charcoal, organic-rich sediment). Fortunately, we discovered a rich record of WST and Clovis occupations along Lake Warner's shorelines. Their vertical distribu-

tion helped us to reconstruct the lake's history. Tephras, marsh sediment, and freshwater shells provided dates that suggested periods during which people most likely occupied Lake Warner's shores.

Over three seasons, we excavated 37 backhoe trenches (BTs) into shoreline features, usually targeting the backsides of gravel beach ridges. We photographed, profiled, and described most trenches, but here we report only those that contained dateable remains or materials important to our interpretations. We recorded precise locations for the trenches using Global Positioning System (GPS) units and established their elevations using a total station and USGS benchmarks, when possible.

We collected tephra, shell, and sediment samples from the trenches for various laboratory analyses including geochemical identification and Accelerator Mass Spectrometry (AMS) radiocarbon dating. Franklin Foit (Washington State University Geoanalytical Laboratory) identified the tephras. Beta Analytic Inc. and the University of Arizona Accelerator Mass Spectrometry Laboratory processed the radiocarbon samples. We classified shells, ostracods, and diatoms using a tabletop scanning electron microscope and comparative online databases (Forester et al. 2015; Spaulding et al. 2010) and other references (Burch 1972, 1982; Burch and Tottenham 1980; Delorme 2001; Herrington 1962; Schmid and Crawford 2001; D. Taylor 1981).

We derived contours and basin cross-section profiles using ESRI's ArcGIS contour and 3-D Analyst line/profile tools applied to the 10 m National Elevation Dataset (NED) data. We did not correct for rebound or tectonic movement, given that the contours trace shoreline features on aerial imagery within an acceptable range of error for the goals of our study. We used USGS and USDA hydrological data sets in drainage basin area calculations with modification to represent the Warner Basin's hydrology during the lake's maximum extent. We calculated changes in surface area and lake volume in ArcGIS using the 10 m NED dataset. We did not apply any corrections for sediment fill and dune-and-slough topographic development or sediment displacement from the floor of the basin via wind activity, although these factors may affect volume calculation accuracy (Currey 1990).

We coupled topographic maps and aerial imagery with cross-section profiles to analyze shoreline feature location and elevation. Given that constructional features (e.g., beach gravel ridges and bars) can form quickly (Adams and Wesnousky 1998; Oviatt et al. 2015), we used wave cuts or cross-section elevation drops to represent still stands. Although we recognize that some features may be relics of previous lake cycles, wave cuts

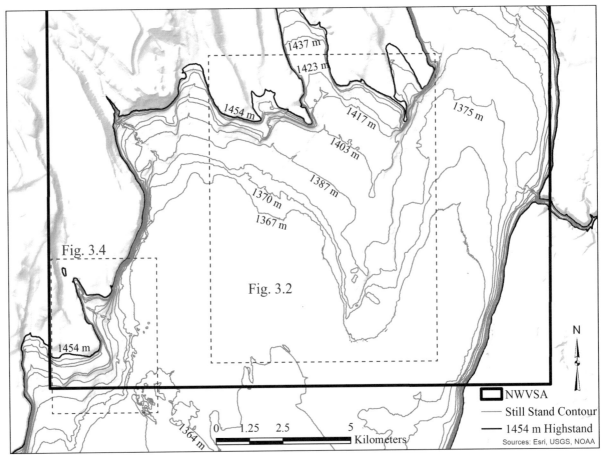

FIGURE 3.1. Lake Warner's maximum highstand (1,454 m asl) and still stand shore zones within the NWVSA. The location of figures 3.2 and 3.4 are shown by dashed lines (adapted from Wriston and Smith 2017).

take time to form and are presumably more representative of long-term lake levels than beach ridges created by storms, which reflect wave height (Taylor and Stone 1996). A sample of cross-section profiles around the lake helped us determine which nick-points were most common. Following Adams and Wesnousky (1998) and Reheis and colleagues (2014), we assume that variations in shoreline elevation can be expected to vary at least 1 m below and up to 3 m above these still stands due to differences in substrate, sediment supply, fetch (the distance over which wind has blown without obstruction), and topographic location. Therefore, these shore zones encompass 4 m around each still stand.

RESULTS

Field visits, aerial imagery, and topographic maps demonstrate that the sill separating the Warner Basin from the Harney-Malheur Basin sits at 1,464 m asl. The highest shoreline features—constructional gravel beach ridges—sit at 1,454 m asl (one exception is discussed below), with more regular occurrences at 1,452–1,453 m asl (Figure 3.1). The highest wave-cut shoreline

sits at 1,448 m asl, suggesting only brief transgression(s) to higher elevations. However, the 1,454 m asl constructional shoreline features occur on all shores. It follows that we found no evidence that Lake Warner topped its 1,464 m asl drainage basin divide. At its 1,454 m asl highstand, Lake Warner would have covered ~1,345 km² with a volume of ~95 km³ (Table 3.1).

A short, weathered beach ridge at 1,461 m on the northern side of Rabbit Basin is higher than all others, but the slope also has the distinct and relatively unweathered gravel beach ridge at 1,454 m asl that corresponds to the highest shoreline features found elsewhere in Warner Valley. This old beach ridge predates the highstand represented on the other shores and, given its limited extent, suggests that 7+ m of tectonic deformation has occurred in this area between the lake highstand that created this beach ridge and the latest one. Within Warner Valley's floor below Rabbit Basin, historic accounts testify to large earthquakes (Patton 1985; Pezzopane and Weldon 1993; Weldon et al. 2002) that did not cause much deformation but probably released tension along the same fault(s).

TABLE 3.1. Lake Warner surface area and volume changes at select elevations (adapted from Wriston and Smith 2017)

Shoreline Elevation (m asl)	Surface Area (km²)	Volume (km³)	Surface Area: Volume Ratio[4]
1,464[1]	1,398.38	108.52	13
1,454	1,345.18	94.81	14
1,448	1,314.34	86.83	15
1,442	1,284.43	79.03	16
1,437	1,260.51	72.66	17
1,425	1,185.78	55.52	21
1,417	1,145.12	48.51	24
1,403	1,052.43	33.1	32
1,387	905.41	17.35	52
1,375	787.15	7.26	108
1,370	714.54	3.48	205
1,366[2]	470.12	1.02	461
1,364[3]	273.02	0.27	1,011

[1] Sill level.
[2] Basin floor filled.
[3] Near modern level.
[4] The surface-area-to-volume ratio provides a simple illustration of how quickly the lake would have responded to changes in precipitation and/or evaporation at different elevations, with higher ratios having a quicker response.

We identified nine erosional wave-cut terraces that mark still stands of sufficient duration to erode bedrock steps in the tuff and basalt shorelines and construct beach ridges at corresponding elevations. These shore zones can be traced around the basin margin and are, from highest to lowest: 1,451–1,447 m asl; 1,445–1,441 m asl; 1,440–1,436 m asl; 1,426–1,422 m asl; 1,420–1,416 m asl; 1,406–1,402 m asl; 1,390–1,386 m asl; 1,378–1,374 m asl; and 1,373–1,369 m asl. More than 20 constructional shoreline features (e.g., gravel beach ridges) are discernable on gradual slopes with abundant sediment supply but, as noted above, wave cuts take longer to form and are better indicators of relatively stable lake levels useful for regional comparisons. Weide (1975) identified similar shorelines but believed that up to 12 m of south-to-north tectonic displacement had occurred since the last highstand. He cited the anomalously high 1,461 m asl shoreline at the north end of Rabbit Basin (discussed above) as support for that possibility, which accounts for 7 of the 12 m of displacement. With the modern advantage of aerial imagery and 1-m digital elevation models, we found good correspondence of shorelines throughout the basin suggesting that, contrary to Weide's (1975) assertion, no major tectonic deformation has occurred since the 1,454 m asl highstand.

Two of the shore zones represent major changes in surface area to volume, as rising water spread south into Coleman Valley just above 1,368 m asl and then above 1,384 m asl northwest into the Rabbit Basin. Increased surface area relative to depth/volume increases the amount of evaporation for the same amount of water. We use this simple surface-area-to-volume ratio to represent the lake's responsiveness to changes in precipitation, temperature, cloud cover, wind, and seasonality. The higher the ratio, the more responsive and erratic lake levels should be, unless there is a substantial ground-water contributor. This is especially true for broad areas with little vertical relief (Weide 1975), including North Warner Valley.

Backhoe Trenching

Eight of our 37 BTs (BT1, BT2, BT14, BT17, BT18, BT19b, BT21, and BT33) provided dateable remains or identifiable tephras relevant to lake-level reconstructions (Table 3.2). We describe these below according to their location within the NWVSA.

Northern Shore Trenches

We excavated BT1, BT2, BT18, BT19b, and BT33 on the gradually sloping northern shoreline below Steamboat Point (Figures 3.2 and 3.3). We excavated BT21 at a higher elevation and into a relatively steep rocky slope. The gradual slope has relatively wide spacing between gravel beach ridges created as Lake Warner receded. These ridges allowed greater spatial separation of any artifacts deposited along its shores than on steeper shorelines. Archaeological survey showed that the elevations of BT1 and BT2 midslope are closely associated with sites containing both WST and Clovis points, presumably left behind by the first groups to visit North Warner Valley.

We excavated BT1 into the backside of a gravel beach ridge (1,394 m asl at its top). It exposed fine lake bottom sediment at its base, topped by lakeward-dipping gravels from a past landward beach ridge. In the trough between this beach ridge and the one located upslope from it, loamy fine sands accumulated as overwash while the lake level hovered around 1,391.55 m asl. These fine sands continued to accumulate as lagunal conditions were created when ponded water was trapped upslope of the beach ridge that also protected it from wave action. The deposits are relatively dark and organic-rich with reduction features (i.e., greenish with manganese staining) that suggest emergent marsh conditions. The marsh was probably short lived and formed a ring around the northern shore while the lake remained high. However, even after the lake receded, water may have ponded there (e.g., a playette) with seasonal input from a nearby drainage. Ponding would have lasted at

TABLE 3.2. North Warner Valley geochronological data (adapted from Wriston and Smith 2017)

BT	Dated Material	Elevation (m asl)	Context	Lab Number	¹⁴C Date	Cal BP, 95.4% confidence (median)	Reference
1	humates	1,391.55	back bar lagoon/playette	AA95109-H	10,300±55	12,385–11,830 (12,110)	Wriston and Smith (2017)
1	bulk carbon	1,391.55	back bar lagoon/playette	AA95109	10,470±65	12,575–12,095 (12,335)	Wriston and Smith (2017)
14	Pisidium sp. shell	1,377.00	shoreline	Beta-414459	11,940±40	13,965–13,585 (13,775)	Wriston and Smith (2017)
33	Pisidium sp. shell	1,388.50	shoreline	Beta-414929	12,100±40	14,105–13,795 (13,950)	Wriston and Smith (2017)
2	Pisidium adamsi shell	1,390.91	shoreline	AA95087	12,355±65	14,760–14,100 (14,430)	Wriston and Smith (2017)
17	Mount St. Helens M tephra	1,364.63	lacustrine	n/a	between 19,160±250 & 20,350±350	between 23,660–22,490 (23,090) & 25,395–23,665 (24,530)	Mullineaux (1996)
19b	Vorticifex effuse shell	1,369.35	shoreline	Beta-414460	22,840±80	27,430–26,990 (27,220)	Wriston and Smith (2017)
18	Trego Hot Springs tephra	1,368.16	nearshore	n/a	23,200±300	27,900–26,810 (27,445)	Benson et al. (1997)
17	Trego Hot Springs tephra	1,364.23	lacustrine	n/a	23,200±300	27,900–26,810 (27,445)	Benson et al. (1997)

least until the drainage floodwaters were of sufficient strength to cut through the impounding beach ridge gravels and below the trough's elevation. We dated the bulk carbon from these lagunal sediments to 10,470±65 ¹⁴C BP (12,575–12,095 cal BP [12,335 cal BP median]) and the humate (a product of biological decay) fraction to 10,300±55 ¹⁴C BP (12,385–11,830 cal BP [12,110 cal BP median]). Because soil continues to accumulate new carbon until it is deeply buried, we expect this age to be younger than when the marsh existed. It dates to a time when the sediment was sufficiently buried to prevent the input of younger carbon. Based on this age and the character of the overlying deposits, the lake stayed below 1,391.55 m asl after 12,000 cal BP.

Lakeward, the cross section of beach ridge exposed in BT1 has overlapping gravel layers separated by sand lenses. We collected a few weathered freshwater clam shells (*Pisidium* sp., or peaclams) from these sands and gravels but have yet to date them. These pea clams generally prefer well-oxygenated waters in ponds and lakes up to 3 meters deep, with soft, vegetated substrates (Thorp and Rogers 2011; Wriston and Smith 2017, Table 3). The top of the trench exposed wind-deposited sands mixed by roots and burrowing animals. A weak soil separates these sands into lower and upper strata. This soil between deposits of wind-blown sand reflects a stable period when sand stopped accumulating on top of the beach ridge and the surface stabilized, allowing formation of the weak soil on top of the lower sands. Given that the source of sand is primarily the basin floor, this halt in deposition suggests that the lake may have risen to cover the basin floor below the trench. After the lake again receded, the wind again blew sand particles up to the top of the beach ridge, depositing the upper sands.

We excavated BT2 in the trough between the beach ridge profiled in BT1 and the one downslope (1,392 m asl at its apex). The base of the trough has dense, wave-deposited gravels covered by clean, coarse beach sands. In these sands, we discovered many shells, including those of Adam Peaclam (*Pisidium adamsi*), Pygmy Fossaria (*Fossaria parva*), and Artemesian Rams-horn (*Vorticifex effusa*). These clams and snails prefer shoreline habitats (Wriston and Smith 2017, Table 3). Closer to the beach ridge crest, loamy, fine sand interbedded with occasional lenses of pebbles or coarse sand is preserved but is abruptly truncated at an oblique angle toward the trough. The bulk of these fine sands was deposited horizontally and below storm-wave turbulence, suggesting a lake level exceeding 1,394 m asl. However, lenses of small gravels and pebbles with abundant *P. adamsi* shells suggest periodic lake recessions as the top of the stratum was laid down. A channel draining waters from the trough likely truncated these sands. This truncation marks an unconformity that extends across the short side of the trench where it is covered by overwash gravels carried over the top of the 1,392 m asl beach ridge by waves. Continued channel activity in the trough is suggested by alluvial reworking of gravels and sands into channel swales cutting parallel into the beach ridge and draining westward.

We sampled lenses of shell from within layered gravels near the beach ridge crest. Two shell concentrations contained *V. effusa*, *P. adamsi*, Great Basin Rams-horn (*Helisoma newberryi*), *F. parva*, Ridgedbeak Peaclam (*Pisidium compressum*), and *Promentus umbiliatellus*, all typical of lakeshore environments in the region. A *P. adamsi* shell from these beach gravels at 1,390.91 m asl returned a date of 12,355±65 ^{14}C BP (14,760–14,100 cal BP [14,430 cal BP median]). Waves continued to lay down gravels above this shell until reaching 1,391.4 m asl when the waters receded and wind-blown sands began to accumulate. This sand mixed with the underlying gravels as it was churned by plant roots, burrowing animals, and insects. But in the northern portion of the trench, two sand strata can be differentiated due to the presence of reworked tephra in the lower package. As in BT1, these wind-blown sands were deposited during periods of low lake levels when sands on the basin floor were available for transport.

Around the corner, on the leeward slope of a bedrock finger that extends toward the basin, we excavated BT33 at 1,389 m asl. At least 80 cm of tephra with secondary alteration is present at its base. The bottom part of the tephra layer is pinkened, presumably by biogenic activity, but it transitions to clean white tephra midprofile. In its top 30 cm, the lower tephra stratum has abundant 0.5–1.0 cm diameter silica-coated balls created by rolling in wind or water. Another 7 cm of clean white tephra was deposited on top of these balls. These tephras remain unidentified but are surprisingly thick, spanning 1,386.9–1,387.7 m asl. We used a tabletop SEM to verify that diatoms are not a contributing component of these strata. These tephras are likely aeolian accumulations of the Trego Hot Springs and/or Mount St. Helens M tephras identified elsewhere. A large, infilled root cast indicates that the tephra was at the surface for some time before a thin bed of poorly-sorted sand and gravels was deposited over them by a rising lake that then deposited clean, fine sand and then well-sorted coarse beach sand topped by layered beach gravels. A *Pisidium* sp. bivalve shell found at 1,388.5 m asl within the base of the layered beach gravels returned a date of 12,100±40 ^{14}C BP

(14,105–13,795 cal BP [13,950 cal BP median]). After that time, the lake again receded, and alluvium of poorly sorted loamy sands and gravels accumulated.

We excavated BT18 into the landward slope of the lowest gravel beach ridge (1,370 m asl) on the northern shore. The base of the trench has well-sorted nearshore lake deposits that alternate between fine and medium sand with manganese staining. Dense ostracod (e.g., seed shrimp) shell layers of *Limnocythere ceriotuberosa*, *Limnocythere friabilis*, and possible *Cypria* sp. or *Cypricercus* sp. are found amongst these sands along with bivalve and snail shells that include *P. compressum*, *P. adamsi*, *F. parva*, *V. effusa*, and a single diatom (microalgae with silica walls) type—*Ellerbeckia arenaria*. Taken together, the overlapping habitat preferences of these species corroborate deposition in shallow water near the lake margin (see Wriston and Smith 2017, Table 3), which would have been ~1,368.5 m asl. These fine and medium sands were then topped by a thin 5-cm layer of clean coarse sand, pebbles, and gravels when the lake receded slightly, and the trench was at the beach line.

The character of the overlying deposits then changes to silty clay loam that likely formed in a relatively large back-bar lagoon, with many vertical in-filled root casts, manganese stains, and abundant calcium carbonate. Occasional pebbles were also noted. Trego Hot Springs tephra fell into these waters ~27,445 cal BP (Benson et al. 1997; but see Benson et al. 2013b [we prefer the 1997 radiocarbon age constrained curve to the 2013 GISP2 comparison, given that we are comparing radiocarbon dates]), depositing a clean, white, 5–10 cm thick horizontal bed of tephra on the lagoon's floor. The water was sufficiently deep to protect the tephra layer while manganese-rich loose sands containing dense ostracod layers were deposited atop it. The ostracods are dominated by *L. ceriotuberosa* and wave ripples are evident in the sand. Together, this information suggests that the lagoon and the adjacent lake were at ~1,369 m asl. Over 50 cm of alternating fine and medium sand layers with lenses of ostracods accumulated before a layer of gravel was deposited by rising lake waters that broke over the gravel beach ridge protecting the lagoon. These gravels increase in size and abundance on the lakeward side of the trench. Calcium carbonate-rich, loamy, medium sand continued to accumulate for another 70 cm, but plant roots and burrowing animals have mixed this layer that is topped by very loose wind-blown sand.

We excavated BT19b into the lakeward slope of the lowest gravel beach ridge remnant at 1,370 m asl. The base of the trench is rock-like silcrete (surface sand and gravel cemented by silica), with abundant manganese

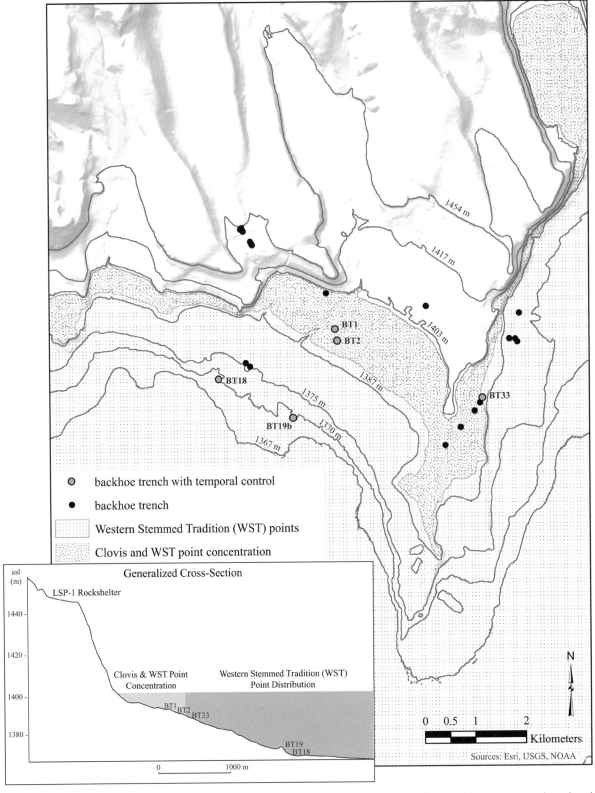

FIGURE 3.2. Northern shore of the NWVSA with excavated trench locations. Trenches discussed in text are numbered and included on a generalized cross section to show their relative shoreline elevation. The vertical distribution of Clovis and Western Stemmed Tradition (WST) point types shows that Clovis types are restricted to the moderately high shore zones, while WST types are there and continue lower into the basin (adapted from Wriston and Smith 2017).

staining on its fine-grained platy surfaces. The deposit's abundant ostracods include *L. ceriotuberosa, L. friablis,* and either *Cypria* sp. or *Cypricercus* sp. We noted three types of diatoms but only positively identified *Campylodiscus hibernicus.* These fine-grained deposits relate to an older lake cycle and are overlain unconformably at 1,368.9 m asl by medium sand with occasional gravel and shell. Above the unconformity, a nearly complete 5-cm-long freshwater mussel (*Anodonta* sp.) bivalve was noted within a burrowed trail. Ostracods from these sands were identified as *L. ceriotuberosa* and either *Cypria* sp. or *Cypricercus* sp. The only diatom type present is *C. hibernicus.* The top of this stratum is manganese-stained, loose, and has abundant shell and ostracod beds.

At 1,369.35 m asl, the horizontal sands transition to wave ripples formed in a shallow nearshore environment. A *V. effusa* shell extracted from these deposits returned a date of 22,840±80 ^{14}C BP (27,430–26,990 cal BP [27,220 cal BP median]). Other identified shells include *P. compressum* and *F. parva.* Ostracods include *L. ceriotuberosa* and *L. friabilis,* and the single diatom type *C. hibernicus.* The wave forms are covered by 5–10 cm of massive medium sand, suggesting a change in lake level before wave ripples again form in medium sand deposits interbedded with ostracod lenses to 1,369.65 m asl. These upper ripples include beds of *L. ceriotuberosa* and either *Cypria* sp. or *Cypricercus* sp. ostracods. Medium sands continue to accumulate to the trench's surface at 1,370 m asl, but the upper 40 cm is mixed by plant roots, burrowing animals, and insects. These sands contain many shells including examples of *F. parva* and *V. effusa,* ostracods *L. ceriotuberosa* and either *Cypria* sp. or *Cypricercus* sp., and *C. hibernicus* diatoms.

We excavated BT21 upslope of the highest beach ridge within our project area at 1,446.5 m asl, a pocket beach ridge formed in a saddle between two ridges. This shoreline was created shortly after Lake Warner's highest still stand. Clean, loose gravels occur at the base of the trench with increasing amounts of loam incorporated in the upper gravels due to dirty slopewash accumulating behind the bar during rainstorms. Unfortunately, we did not recover dateable remains in the high-energy gravel deposits. The beach ridge gravels are topped by reworked Mazama tephra incorporated into loamy alluvium. Another 40 cm of loamy sediment has accumulated since the reworked tephra's deposit. The presence of reworked Mazama tephra atop the beach gravels with no alluvial deposition outside of upward gravel void infilling suggests that these beach ridges and, in turn, the last lake highstand, are relatively young (i.e., post–LGM).

Western Shore Trenches

We excavated 12 trenches on the lake's northwestern shoreline (Figures 3.4 and 3.5) within a slight embayment formed by a bedrock ridge extending into the basin. This ridge divides Rabbit Basin and North Warner Valley and blocks winds from the south, helping to protect deposits on its northern slope from wave action and wind erosion. A series of trenches excavated into this embayment's northeast-facing slope revealed large cobbles and boulders in its upper shores, reworked sand and gravels topped by dunes midslope, and fine lake deposits near the basin floor. This shore is steeper than the northern shore, and water would have quickly deepened over a relatively short horizontal distance when the lake rose. Here, we only describe the two most important trenches: BT14 and BT17.

We excavated BT14 into a swale between dunes at 1,378 m asl and found coarse beach sand with occasional shells at its base. A fine, crusty sand separates it and the overlying alternating fine- and medium-grained sands with occasional bivalve shells. These lead up to clean, coarse, loose sand. On top of these sands, 12 cm of small beach gravels were deposited. We dated a *Pisidium* sp. bivalve shell retrieved from the base of these gravels to 11,940±40 ^{14}C BP (13,965–13,585 cal BP [13,775 cal BP median]). On top of the gravels are mixed poorly sorted sands with occasional gravels. These sands are reworked beach and nearshore sands but with inputs from wind and slopewash. We discovered some gravels that may have been worked up from below or deposited during a later lake transgression and then churned into the sand by plant roots or burrowing animals.

We excavated BT17 lakeward of the western shore dunes at 1,367 m asl, which exposed sandy clay loam laid down in deep, quiet waters at its base. Trego Hot Springs tephra fell into these waters ~27,445 cal BP (Benson et al. 1997), depositing a clean white 5 cm thick horizontal layer at 1,364.23 m asl. Reworked tephra and loamy fine sand continued to be deposited until lenses of sand and small pebbles became frequent, indicating that the lake had receded, introducing turbulent flow. The lake rose again later, depositing loamy fine sand before a 12-cm-thick horizontal layer of clean white tephra was deposited at 1,364.63 m asl. This tephra was identified as Mount St. Helens M, dated to between 19,160±250 (23,660–22,490 cal BP [23,090 cal BP median]) and 20,350±350 ^{14}C BP (25,395–23,665 cal BP [24,530 cal BP median]; Mullineaux 1996). Atop the tephra, reworked tephra and loamy sand transition to sandy clay loam, again suggesting that the lake deepened. These lake-bottom muds are interrupted by 15 cm of wave ripple deposits of coarse

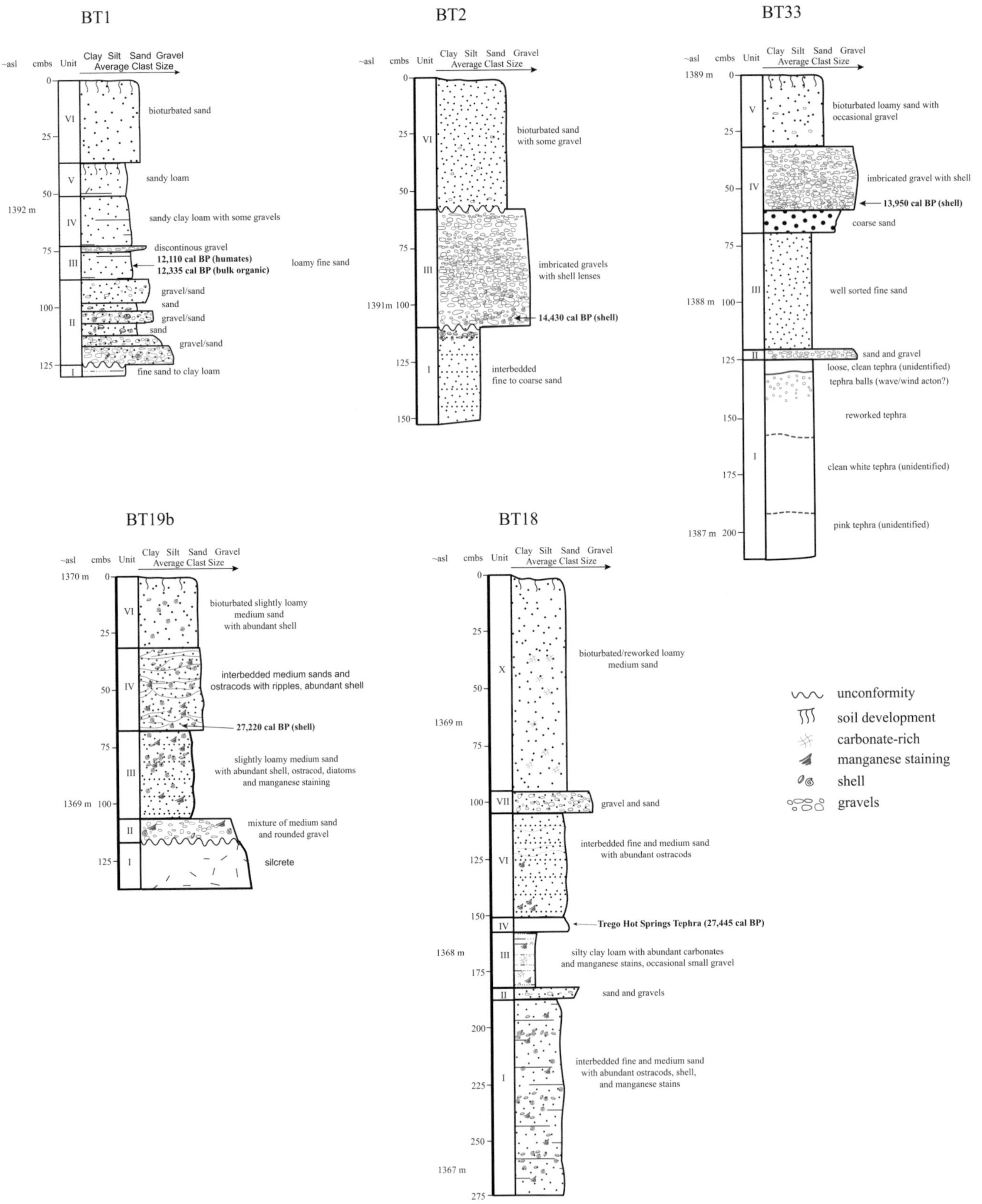

FIGURE 3.3. Northern shore backhoe trench logs. Elevations are shown in meters asl and in cm below surface (cmbs) (adapted from Wriston and Smith 2017).

sand and pebbles lain down at 1,365.3 m asl before sandy clay loam deposits were again deposited in deeper water. This deposition continued but is truncated by a weathered unconformity at 1,365.9 m asl.

These relict lake deposits weathered for some time, with weak, platy structure developing at its surface. Poorly sorted gray sand containing occasional manganese-coated subrounded gravel covered the weathered surface. These are probably beach sands deposited during a lake transgression, but they grade to calcium carbonate-rich, loamy sand topped by sandy clay-to-sandy-clay loam hardpan playette deposits. This playette has a single, coarse gravel layer on its surface at 1,366.5 m asl that was then overtaken by a wind-blown sand sheet later mixed by plant roots and animal burrows. Except for the identified tephras, we did not recover dateable material from BT17. However, these deep-water deposits suggest the lake stayed above 1,367 m asl (filling the valley floor) for a long time. We observed additional support for this scenario in BT16, which was located upslope and contained reworked tephra that is likely Trego Hot Springs and/or Mount St. Helens M in beach sands at 1,368.5 m asl.

Although imprecise, if we use the deposits between the dated tephras to calculate a general sediment accumulation rate, then 40 cm of deposits accounts for an average of 91 years per cm of deposition between 27,445 cal BP and 23,800 cal BP (the mean age of Mount St. Helens M tephra). If we then assume that this rate was relatively constant and subtract the width of the tephras, it suggests that the lake remained above 1,367 m asl for 11,375 years and above the highest tephra to deposit another 125 cm of lacustrine sediment before water levels permanently receded. This would mean that the lake remained above 1,367 m asl until at least 12,425 cal BP with two exceptions. Assuming the same sedimentation rate, the nearshore wave ripples and pebbles above the Mount St. Helens M tephra would approximate 18,340 cal BP, while those between the tephras would approximate 24,985 cal BP, signaling recessions to 1,365–1,366 m asl before rebounding.

THE ARCHAEOLOGICAL EVIDENCE

In addition to the geomorphological evidence from the backhoe trenches, we used the vertical distribution of time-sensitive projectile points to help reconstruct Lake Warner's history. As we outlined earlier, the locations of such artifacts provide a minimum age for the shoreline features upon which they rest.

The earliest demonstrated evidence of human occupation (~14,200 cal BP) in the northern Great Basin comes from the Paisley Caves in the nearby Abert-

Chewaucan Basin. On the Columbia Plateau, Cooper's Ferry in western Idaho has produced artifacts dating to a millennium or more before groups first occupied the Paisley Caves. As we outline in Chapter 13, archaeological survey and backhoe trenching revealed that except for the LSP-1 rockshelter (see Chapter 4), the NWVSA record is predominantly a surface one. Despite that fact, the dated shorelines described above provide some rough chronological controls for associated artifacts. For example, the densest concentrations of WST and fluted points correspond to shorelines dated to between 14,385 cal BP and 12,090 cal BP (Figure 3.6). Though broad, this range encompasses both the Clovis Era (13,400–12,700 cal BP) and earliest period of the WST in the Intermountain West (Davis et al. 2019; Jenkins et al. 2012, 2013; Smith et al. 2020). Those shorelines would have provided access to abundant food including waterfowl, fish, small mammals, and cattail or tule in a ring of emergent marshes situated in protected back-bar lagoons. A nearby drainage and lake waters would have also attracted large game such as pronghorn, mule deer, bison, and possibly camel and horse.

Fluted points are generally absent from shorelines below 1,390 m asl, which probably signals their disappearance in North Warner Valley by 12,090 cal BP, if not before. Shorelines below 1,390 m asl contain numerous WST points—mostly shorter-stemmed varieties. People likely followed the receding lakeshore onto the floor of North Warner Valley and, eventually, south to the Warner Lakes. Together, the vertical distributions of fluted and WST points suggest that Lake Warner receded from the gravel beach ridges on the northern shore down to current Warner Lake levels (1,360–1,364 m asl) between 12,700 cal BP and 9000 cal BP (the end of the WST in the northern Great Basin), a scenario that is in line with the geomorphic evidence outlined above.

Decades of archaeological investigation around the Warner Lakes—located at a lower elevation and south of the NWVSA—have revealed not only the presence of WST points but also younger and more abundant Cascade, Humboldt, Northern Side-notched, Gatecliff, and Elko dart points and younger-still Rosegate and Desert Series arrow points (Cannon et al. 1990; Eiselt 1997b; D. Fowler et al. 1989; Tipps 1998; Weide 1968; Young 1998, 2000). Except for fluted points, which are restricted to higher and older shorelines, virtually the entire Great Basin projectile point sequence is found at dune and slough sites around the Warner Lakes. This reflects the importance of this basin's relatively reliable water and marsh systems and supports M. Weide's (1968) and D. Weide's (1975) assertions that the dune-and-slough topography that required a dry basin floor

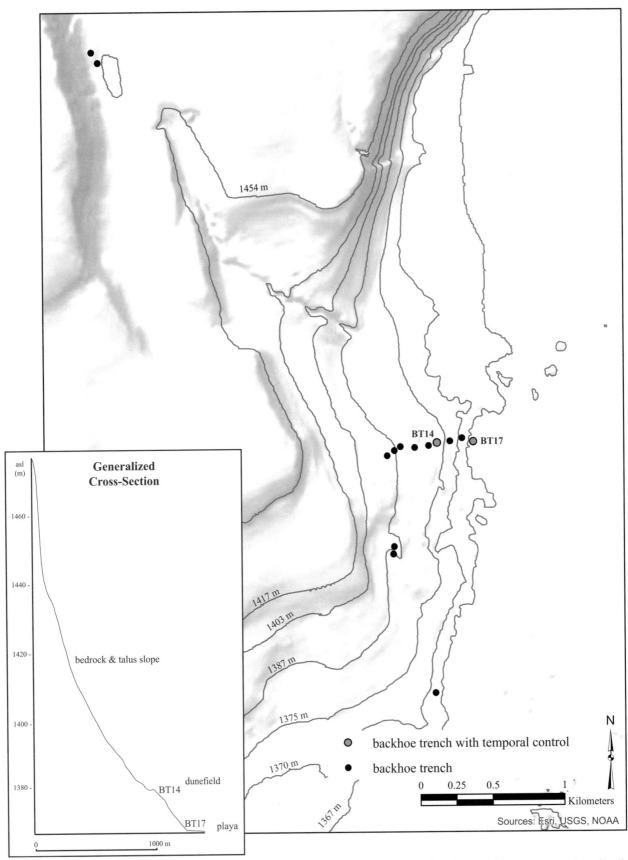

FIGURE 3.4. Western shore of the NWVSA with excavated trench locations. Trenches discussed in text are numbered and included on a generalized cross section to show their relative shoreline elevation (adapted from Wriston and Smith 2017).

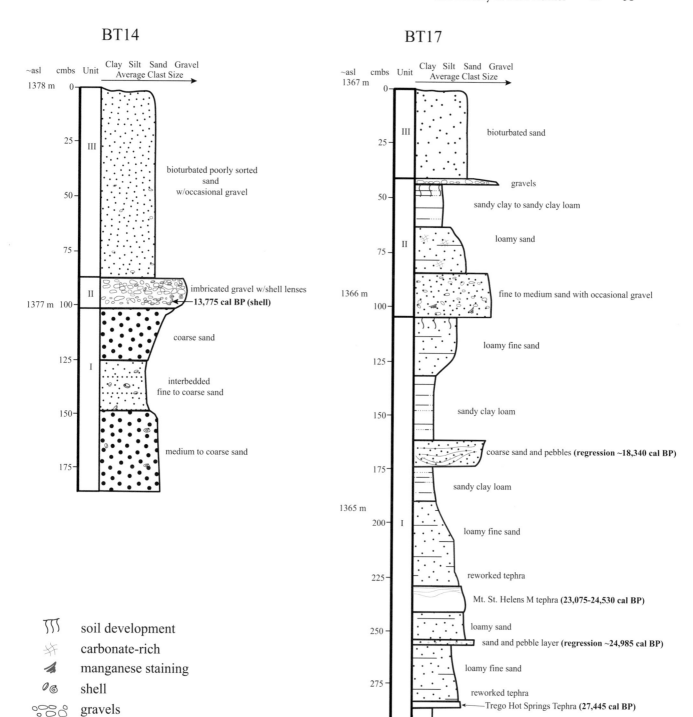

FIGURE 3.5. Western shore backhoe trench logs. Elevations shown in meters asl and in cm below surface (cmbs) (adapted from Wriston and Smith 2017).

to form was first established during the early Holocene. This fact further supports our contention that pluvial Lake Warner had dried by that time and was replaced by the much smaller Warner Lakes.

As we outline in the next chapter, the LSP-1 rock-

shelter offers additional information relevant to our interpretation of Lake Warner's history. The shelter was cut by the lake and has a basal elevation of 1,449 m asl. After the lake receded below the shelter, alternating layers of gravel and sand accumulated as the shelter

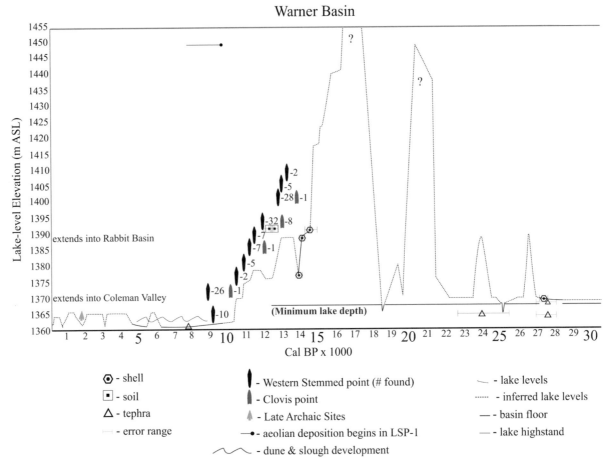

FIGURE 3.6. Late Pleistocene to Holocene lake-level reconstruction for Lake Warner (adapted from Wriston and Smith 2017).

walls unloaded. Radiocarbon dates of 11,685±45 ^{14}C BP (13,585–13,430 cal BP) and 12,280±45 ^{14}C BP (14,485–14,035 cal BP) on noncultural leporid bones from the lowest stratum indicate that this occurred during the terminal Pleistocene.

Minimal allogenic sediment accumulated in the shelter until shortly before people first visited it 9775 cal BP. Thereafter, fine-grained aeolian sediment accumulated rapidly for ~1,500 years and continued to contribute to alluvial deposits and roof fall throughout the middle Holocene. Wind, which in the Great Basin predominantly blows from the southwest to northeast (Wriston 2009), brought fine sands and silt from the newly exposed basin floor into LSP-1. As such, we know that Lake Warner had disappeared from North Warner Valley by the time people first occupied the shelter, if not a little earlier.

While there is no evidence that a major lake occupied the NWVSA during the middle or late Holocene, it is possible that during mesic conditions shorter-term marshes or wetlands returned. After all, Whistler and Lewis (1916) reported stands of tule north and west of Bluejoint Lake. The presence of periodic late Holocene marshes in North Warner Valley is further suggested by charred cattail and/or bulrush/tule seeds in hearths from LSP-1 dated to 1015±30 ^{14}C BP (975–805 cal BP), 2490±25 ^{14}C BP (2725–2475 cal BP), and 4010±20 ^{14}C BP (4520–4420 cal BP; see Chapter 5). We cannot rule out the possibility that groups brought marsh plants into the shelter from more distant locations (e.g., the Warner Lakes), but it seems equally likely that visitors to LSP-1 collected them from the valley floor closer to the shelter during wet intervals.

SUMMARY

Our lake-level curve for Lake Warner is based on the data presented here, information collected by other researchers working in the area, and data from nearby basins (see Wriston and Smith 2017 and references therein). While the curve marks a step forward in understanding the hydrographic history of North Warner Valley, we view it more as a starting point than a final product. We expect the curve to change as more data become available, and further paleoenvironmental work in North Warner Valley refines the ideas presented here.

Based on our reconstruction, Lake Warner was situated between 1,368.5 m and 1,370 m asl when Trego Hot Springs tephra fell ~27,445 cal BP (Benson et al. 1997). This is confirmed by a shell date of 27,220 cal BP in near-shore wave ripples at 1,369.35 m asl. Lake Warner maintained a minimum elevation of 1,367 m asl based on the lacustrine fine-grained deposition in the BT17 profile until 24,990 cal BP. Around that time, sedimentation rates and changes in clast size deposition show that the lake receded to 1,365 m asl and then quickly rebounded to a minimum elevation of 1,367 m asl.

Mount St. Helens M tephra fell into a moderately deep lake ~23,800 cal BP, and for approximately 5,000 years the lake maintained a minimum elevation of 1,367 m asl. By 18,340 cal BP, based on sedimentation rates and changes in clast size deposition, the lake had receded to around 1,365 m asl before quickly rebounding again to 1,367 m asl.

Yet, there is surprisingly little evidence indicating when pluvial lakes reached their last highstands in the northern Great Basin. We do know that Lake Warner continued to exceed 1,367 m asl and likely rose to its maximum highstand between 17,000 and 16,100 cal BP (Figure 3.7). This is based on lake-level correspondence to adjacent Surprise Valley (Egger et al. 2016; Ibarra et al. 2014) and better-studied lakes in northern Nevada including Lake Franklin (Munroe and Laabs 2013). In the nearby Abert-Chewaucan Basin, pluvial Lake Chewaucan receded from its highstand before 15,940 cal BP, based on duck bone dates in the Paisley Caves' basal stratum (Jenkins et al. 2012). Data from these nearby basins suggest that Lake Warner's last highstand may have preceded 16,100 cal BP but probably not by much.

Shell dates from within the beach ridges show that Lake Warner was moderately high (1,390 m asl) between 14,430 cal BP and 13,950 cal BP before dropping to 1,377 m asl ~13,770 cal BP. The lake rebounded to 1,390 m asl during the Younger Dryas before depositing lagoon sediment that then developed a soil dated to between 12,355 cal BP and 12,110 cal BP. During this interval, people likely first occupied North Warner Valley, leaving WST and fluted points and associated debris along its shorelines.

Lake Warner had receded and retreated southward from the NWVSA by 10,300 cal BP, based on peat ac-

cumulation rates in Hansen's (1947) core near Crump Lake (Weide 1975; Wriston and Smith 2017). By that time, Lake Warner's remnant had reached a near-modern lake elevation. People using WST points (but not fluted points) continued to visit North Warner Valley. As we discuss in Chapter 6, they responded to the loss of wetlands and marshes by shifting from a probable marsh-focused subsistence strategy to one that featured communal rabbit drives.

Marsh peats began accumulating below 1,364 m asl in Warner Valley and continued even as the rest of the basin dried out and old lake-bottom clays, silts, and fine sands began blowing into dunes. Some of this fine sediment escaped the valley floor by blowing upslope into nearby catchments, including LSP-1. Aeolian sediment began to accumulate in the shelter ~9775 cal BP and continued to do so throughout the middle Holocene.

Although conditions in Warner Valley were much drier during the middle Holocene than during the terminal Pleistocene and early Holocene, wetlands, lakes, and/or springs persisted to the south of the NWVSA even as dunes accumulated around them. Mazama tephra fell ~7700 cal BP atop dunes and into these small lakes and wetlands (e.g., Crump Lake [Hansen 1947]). People continued to visit those relatively lush places, leaving dart and arrow point types that collectively span the entire Holocene around small lakes and sloughs (Cannon et al. 1990; Eiselt 1997b; D. Fowler et al. 1989; Tipps 1998; Young 1998).

Bulrush/tule and cattail seeds from LSP-1 dated to 4520–4425 cal BP and 2725–2475 cal BP may signal wetter conditions and a possible lake rebound during the Neoglacial period (4200–2500 cal BP). Increasing artifact densities dated to 2000 cal BP in the dunes surrounding the Warner Lakes certainly suggest that conditions grew more favorable for people around that time (Tipps 1998; Young 1998). Bulrush/tule seeds from LSP-1 dated to 975–805 cal BP may also signal increased surface water in or near the NWVSA during the Medieval Climatic Anomaly. Lastly, increased surface water may have once again characterized North Warner Valley during the Little Ice Age (Wigand 1987). These possible late Holocene lake-level increases may have been slightly more substantial than the one that filled North Warner Valley with tule during the late 1860s. We hope that additional geomorphological and paleoecological studies in the vicinity of our project area will serve to test and refine these ideas.

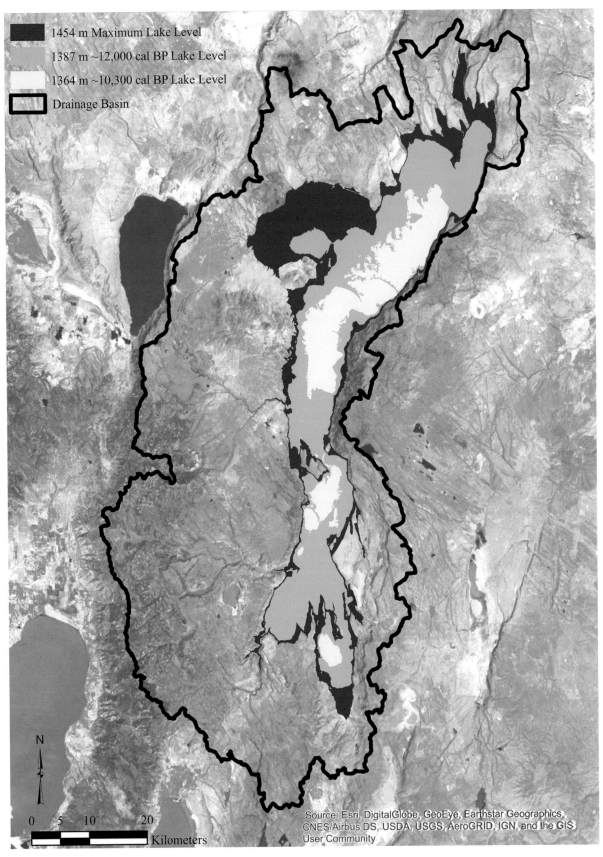

FIGURE 3.7. Select reconstructed lake levels of Lake Warner, including its maximum level at 1,454 m, approximate level when people first occupied its shores, and approximate early Holocene level (adapted from Wriston and Smith 2017).

PART II

The Little Steamboat Point-1 Rockshelter

History of Work, Stratigraphy, and Cultural Chronology

Geoffrey M. Smith, Judson B. Finley, and Bryan S. Hockett

Part I of this volume provides some context for our archaeological investigations in North Warner Valley. These investigations included excavations in the LSP-1 rockshelter, which we describe here in Part II, and extensive pedestrian survey of the area surrounding the shelter, which we describe later in Part III. The LSP-1 shelter was critical to our study because it contained a record of human occupation replete with hearths and other features, food residues, fiber artifacts, and stone, bone, and shell tools and ornaments. That record spans most of the Holocene and offers a detailed picture of human behavior and how it changed across time. It also allows us to better understand how people used the surrounding area.

The LSP-1 shelter sits at the base of Little Steamboat Point, which consists of welded tuff and andesite rimrock. Little Steamboat Point is part of the late Miocene-aged Rattlesnake Tuff Formation that covers parts of eastern Oregon (Walker 1979). LSP-1 is the largest of eight south-facing wave-cut shelters located along Little Steamboat Point (Figure 4.1). It overlooks the floor of North Warner Valley, ~90 m below, and measures ~8 m across at its mouth and ~6 m deep (Figure 4.2). Prior to our excavations, the shelter's deposits were within 1–2 m of the ceiling, but when people first visited it during the early Holocene there would have been ~4 m between the ceiling and floor. An alcove in the shelter's northwestern quadrant was created by counterclockwise wave action, and a crack in the ceiling has periodically brought water into the rear of the shelter. Our sense is that this process has contributed to poorer organic preservation toward the rear of the shelter.

HISTORY OF WORK

In 2009, Bill Cannon recorded the shelters, which span a ~1-km stretch of rimrock, as site 35Ha3735. In 2010, he asked UNR to test some of the shelters to determine whether they contained stratified archaeological deposits. Over the course of a week, we tested both the largest shelter (LSP-1) and a smaller shelter (LSP-2), the latter of which contained few artifacts. At LSP-1, we established a grid system along the cardinal directions with grid north offset 16° east of magnetic north. We excavated a 1-m² test pit (TP-1, later designated N105E99) according to natural strata, using 10 cm arbitrary levels within each stratum (Figure 4.3A). We recorded all depth measurements below a temporary datum initially set at the southwestern corner of TP-1. Excavations produced a modest lithic assemblage, including one foliate and one WST projectile point, as well as a well-preserved faunal assemblage. We recorded 11 major stratigraphic units (1–11, with some additional subunit designations; Table 4.1) and terminated TP-1 176 cm below datum (cmbd), or ~169 cm below the surface, without reaching bedrock. Radiocarbon dates of 8290±40 ^{14}C BP (9425–9135 cal BP), 8340±40 ^{14}C BP (9470–9260 cal BP), and 8400±50 ^{14}C BP (9520–9300 cal BP) on charcoal collected 103–131 cmbd indicated that LSP-1 contained a stratified record extending back to the terminal early Holocene (Table 4.2).

Given the site's potential to inform our understanding of trans-Holocene lifeways, we returned to LSP-1 in 2011 during the first of three archaeological field schools in North Warner Valley. From June to August, we excavated three 1-m² units in a north–south line extending south from TP-1. We established a permanent datum at

FIGURE 4.1. Overview of the LSP-1 rockshelter, the largest of eight wave-cut shelters recorded as 35Ha3735. (A) Crewmember at the shelter opening for scale. (B) The debris fan that is the source of much of the allogenic deposits. Photo taken in August 2010.

FIGURE 4.2. The interior of LSP-1 prior to excavation. Photo taken in August 2010.

TABLE 4.1. Correlation of 2010–2012 and 2013–2015 stratigraphic designations

2010–2012	2013–2015	Sediment Package	Periods of Use (cal BP)[1]
1	I dung		sterile (stratum postdates 150)
2	II upper fan facies	upper	1300–900
3a			
3b			
4			
4a			
4b			
5a	III upper loess		1300–900 1900–1600[2]
5b			
5c			
5d			
5e			
6	IV lower fan facies		1300–900 2700–2500 3400–3200 4500–4400 9775–8875[3]
6a			
6b			
7			
8a	V massive	middle	4500–4400[4] 8200–8000 9775–8875
8b			
9	VI lower loess		
10	VII upper gravel	lower	9775
11	VIII upper sand		sterile (stratum dates to 10,250–9775)
12[5]	IX lower gravel		sterile (stratum dates to 12,200–10,250)
13[5]	X lower sand		sterile (stratum dates to 14,250–12,200)

[1] Delineated based on peaks in the summed probability distribution presented in Figure 4.7.
[2] Most dates from this period come from textiles in F.14-10, a pit that also contained textiles dated to the 1300–900 cal BP period.
[3] Restricted to the very rear of the shelter.
[4] Several of these dates come from features that were likely excavated into Stratum V from the overlying Stratum IV.
[5] We did not encounter Strata 12 and 13 until 2012.

N100E100 near the mouth of the shelter, 44 cm below the elevation of our 2010 temporary datum set at the southwestern corner of TP-1 (N105E99). Subsequently, we recorded all elevations (and *x* and *y* coordinates) relative to the permanent datum with an adjusted elevation of +44 cm to maintain consistency between our 2010 and later elevations. We excavated the three units to 126 cmbd, at which point the artifact density dropped off considerably and a stratigraphic change occurred. This 1 × 4 m excavation block became known as the E99 Trench, and it has served as the main basis of our stratigraphic interpretations (see Figure 4.3b). We recovered

another foliate point and obtained a radiocarbon date of 8670±40 ^{14}C BP (9730–9540 cal BP) on a charcoal fragment 97 cmbd in N102E99. At the end of the 2011 field season, our understanding of the site had not changed considerably: it contained a stratified record dating back to the early Holocene but not earlier. Because UNR's Great Basin Paleoindian Research Unit focuses primarily on the terminal Pleistocene, we elected to stop excavating in LSP-1.

During a visit on Memorial Day weekend in 2012, we discovered that LSP-1 had been extensively looted, probably not long before we arrived. Roughly 12 m² of

TABLE 4.2. Radiocarbon dates from LSP-1

Stratum	Elevation (cmbd)	¹⁴C Date	Cal BP, 95.4% Confidence	Lab Number	Material	Unit	Notes
II	20–26	1250±30	1275–1080	Beta-536738	*Lepus* tibia DC[1]	N102E99	
II	21–26	1200±30	1235–1010	18B/0570	*Brachylagus* tibia DC[1]	N106E98	
II	21–26	3170±25	3450–3360	D-AMS 32563	*Sylvilagus* tibia DC[1]	N107E99	
II	26–31	1060±30	1055–925	18B/0571	*Sylvilagus* tibia DC[1]	N106E98	
II	26–31	1145±30	1175–975	D-AMS 32560	*Sylvilagus* tibia DC[1]	N107E98	
II	25–35	1290±30	1285–1180	Beta-536771	*Lepus* mandible	N103E99	
II	36–41	1100±30	1065–935	18B/0572	*Lepus* tibia DC[1]	N106E98	
II	50	1015±30	975–805	D-AMS 10587	F.11-14 (hearth) *Juniperus* seed	N104E99/100	dug into II
II/III	33	1850±25	1865–1715	UGA-16803	unidentified charcoal	N102E99	
II/III	52	1790±20	1815–1625	UGA-18235	F.14-10 (pit) Catlow Twine textile	N101.5E103	dug into IV from II/III
II/III	59	1340±20	1300–1190	UGA-18237	F.14-10 (pit) *Artemisia* bark bundle	N102E103	dug into IV from II/III
II/III	62	1760±20	1720–1610	UGA-18239	F.14-10 (pit) *Artemisia* sandal	N102E103	dug into IV from II/III
II/III	62	1860±20	1865–1730	UGA-18236	F.14-10 (pit) *Artemisia* sandal	N102E103	dug into IV from II/III
II/III	66	1300±20	1285–1185	UGA-18238	F.14-10 (pit) *Artemisia* sandal	N102E103	dug into IV from II/III
II/III	76	1880±20	1880–1735	UGA-18240	F.14-10 (pit) *Artemisia* sandal	N102E103	dug into IV from II/III
III	41–44	1255±25	1275–1090	D-AMS 10590	*Artemisia* charcoal	N105E99	column sample
III/IV	45	6550±20	7490–7425	UGA-15595	unidentified charcoal	N105E99	
IV	36–41	1350±25	1315–1185	D-AMS 32559	*Sylvilagus* tibia DC[1]	N107E98	
IV	46–51	1030±30	1050–835	18B/0573	*Sylvilagus* tibia DC[1]	N106E98	
IV	46–51	8595±35	9630–9500	D-AMS 32562	*Lepus* tibia DC[1]	N107E99	
IV	51–56	1115±35	1175–935	D-AMS 32564	large mammal bone	N107E99	
IV	51–56	4560±25	4620–4275	UGA-21830	*Olivella* bead	N107E99	
IV	57	2490±25	2725–2475	UGA-16800	F.11-05/15 (hearth) unidentified charcoal	N104E99	dug into IV
IV	56–61	8385±35	9485–9305	D-AMS 32558	*Lepus* femur DC[1]	N107E98	
IV	56–61	8440±40	9530–9405	18C/0574	*Sylvilagus* tibia DC[1]	N106E98	
IV	62	880±40	915–705	Beta-283901	unidentified charcoal	N105E99	
IV	61–66	3040±25	3345–3165	D-AMS 10591	*Artemisia* charcoal	N105E99	column sample
IV	61–66	8640±30	9670–9540	Beta-536771	*Lepus* femur DC[1]	N103E99	
IV	61–66	8360±40	9475–9285	18B/0575	*Sylvilagus* tibia DC[1]	N106E98	
IV	61–66	8500±45	9545–9450	D-AMS 32567	*Sylvilagus* tibia DC[1]	N102E101	
IV	66	3985±25	4520–4415	D-AMS 10588	F.14-02 (hearth) cordage	N102E100/101	
IV	66–71	3090±25	3370–3230	D-AMS 10592	*Artemisia* charcoal	N105E99	column sample
IV	72	2910±30	3160–2960	Beta-317155	F.11-19 (hearth) *Artemisia* charcoal	N104E99	
IV	72	3160±30	3450–3270	Beta-406150	F.14-06 (hearth) *Salix* charcoal	N102E102	

TABLE 4.2. (cont'd.) Radiocarbon dates from LSP-1

Stratum	Elevation (cmbd)	¹⁴C Date	Cal BP, 95.4% Confidence	Lab Number	Material	Unit	Notes
IV	74–75	3990±25	4520–4415	D-AMS 10589	F.11-06/14-04 (hearth) *Artemisia* charcoal	N102E99/100	
IV/V	51–56	8290±40	9425–9135	D-AMS 32561	*Sylvilagus* tibia DC[1]	N107E99	
IV/V	56–61	8670±30	9685–9545	Beta-536770	*Lepus* radius	N102E99	
IV/V	56–61	8375±50	9500–9265	D-AMS 32565	*Lepus* proximal radius	N102E99	
IV/V	67	3140±25	3445–3255	UGA-15593	*Rhus* charcoal	N105E99	
IV/V	71–76	8200±35	9270–9030	D-AMS 32557	large mammal bone	N107E98	
V	68	4010±20	4520–4425	UGA-16801	F.11-07 (hearth) unidentified charcoal	N102E99	
V	71–76	8740±50	9910–9550	D-AMS 27315	*Lepus* femur DC[1]	N107E99	
V	76–81	8500±40	9545–9460	D-AMS 32566	*Lepus* femur DC[1]	N102E101	
V	76–81	8570±40	9600–9485	18B/0576	*Sylvilagus* tibia DC[1]	N106E98	
V	81	1200±20	1180–1065	UGA-16859	F.14-01 (midden) Catlow Twine textile	N103E101	*Neotoma* midden
V	82	1160±20	1175–990	UGA-16860	F.14-01 (midden) Catlow Twine textile	N103E102	*Neotoma* midden
V	82	4010±25	4525–4420	UGA-15260	*Bison* femur	N104E101	
V	85	4030±20	4565–4425	UGA-16802	unidentified charcoal	N103E99	
V	86	8350±30	9460–9295	UGA-14916	*Artemisia* charcoal	N103E101	
V	81–86	3045±30	3350–3170	D-AMS 10593	*Artemisia* charcoal	N105E99	column sample
V	86–91	7890±30	8260–7970	UGA-21827	*Olivella* bead	N102E100	
V	86–91	8550±40	9555–9480	18B/0577	*Sylvilagus* tibia DC[1]	N106E98	
V	91–96	8360±35	9470–9295	D-AMS 27316	*Lepus* humerus DC[1]	N107E99	
V	96	4000±25	4520–4420	UGA-14917	*Artemisia* charcoal	N103E101	
V	97	8670±40	9730–9540	Beta-306419	unidentified charcoal	N102E99	
V	96–101	8140±40	9245–9000	18B/0578	*Lepus* tibia DC[1]	N106E98	
V	101–106	8265±40	9410–9125	D-AMS 10594	*Artemisia* charcoal	N105E99	column sample
V	102	30±15	Modern	PSU-AMS 5252	*Sarcobatus* charcoal	N105E101	
V	103	8340±40	9470–9260	Beta-287251	unidentified charcoal	N105E99	
V	107	7320±35	8190–8025	D-AMS 27318	large mammal bone	N107E99	
V	107	8930±15	9475–9230	UGA-21826	*Olivella* bead	N104E101	average of 4 dates
V	106–111	8270±35	9405–9130	D-AMS 27317	*Lepus* tibia DC[1]	N107E99	
V	111–116	8870±30	9435–9120	UGA-21825	*Olivella* bead	N105E100	
V	111–116	8520±40	9545–9470	18B/0579	*Lepus* tibia DC[1]	N106E98	
V/VI/VII	121–126	8545±35	9550–9480	D-AMS 27319	*Lepus* tibia DC[1]	N107E99	
V	121–126	8630±20	9140–8765	UGA-21829	*Olivella* bead	N102E102	average of 2 dates
V	121–126	9200±30	9815–9490	UGA-21828	*Olivella* bead	N102E102	
V	125	8700±30	9735–9550	UGA-15142	F.13-01 (hearth) *Artemisia* charcoal	N103E100	
V/VII	106	8300±20	9420–9250	UGA-15594	*Rhus* charcoal	N105E99	
VI	120	8290±40	9425–9135	Beta-282809	unidentified charcoal	N105E99	average of 2 dates
VI/VII	124	8340±25	9450–9290	PRI-14-069	*Artemisia* charcoal	N107E99	
VI/VII	131	8400±50	9520–9300	Beta-297186	unidentified charcoal	N105E99	
VII	111–116	5240±25	6175–5920	D-AMS 10595	*Artemisia* charcoal	N105E99	column sample
VII	123	2070±25	2120–1950	UGA-15596	*Artemisia* charcoal	N105E99	

TABLE 4.2. (cont'd.) Radiocarbon dates from LSP-1

Stratum	Elevation (cmbd)	¹⁴C Date	Cal BP, 95.4% Confidence	Lab Number	Material	Unit	Notes
VII	123–126	7340±30	8275–8030	Beta-495442	*Lepus* tibia DC[1]	N106E98	
VII	142	7310±40	8185–8020	Beta-306418	unidentified charcoal	N105E99	
VII/VIII	126–131	8080±30	9115–8800	Beta-495443	*Sylvilagus* tibia DC[1]	N106E98	
VIII	126–131	7920±30	8975–8610	Beta-493989	*Lepus* tibia DC[1]	N107E98	
VIII	128–131	1175±25	1180–1000	D-AMS 10596	*Artemisia* charcoal	N105E99	column sample
VIII	131	8290±25	9420–9145	UGA-18011	*Lepus* ulna	N107E99	
VIII	131–136	7945±35	8980–8645	D-AMS 10597	*Artemisia* charcoal	N105E99	column sample
VIII	141–146	8335±40	9470–9255	D-AMS 27320	*Lepus* tibia DC[1]	N107E99	
VIII	147	8120±30	9125–9000	Beta-493990	*Lepus* tibia DC[1]	N107E99	
VIII/IX	141	9100±30	10,295–10,200	UGA-15259	*Sylvilagus* humerus	N105E99	bioapatite date
IX	141–146	10,320±40	12,385–11,975	Beta-495444	*Sylvilagus* calcaneus	N106E98	
VIII/X	155	8625±40	9680–9530	D-AMS 27322	*Lepus* tibia DC[1]	N102E103	
X	151–156	11,685±45	13,585–13,430	D-AMS 27321	*Lepus* calcaneus	N107E99	
X	221–226	12,280±45	14,485–14,035	D-AMS 27323	*Sylvilagus* humerus	N104E100	
Unknown	Unknown	1230±35	1265–1065	AA-103861	diagonally twined textile fragment	Unknown	looters' backdirt

[1] Diaphysis cylinder

deposits were hastily excavated between the E99 Trench and the shelter's eastern wall (Figure 4.3c and Figure 4.4). In conjunction with the BLM, we made the decision to excavate most of the remaining deposits in the shelter's interior to collect as much data as possible before it was looted again. From late July to early August, we screened the looters' backdirt, reestablished our grid system, and began excavations in three additional units in which the upper deposits had been destroyed: N104E100, N105E100, and N106E100. In N104E100, we reached bedrock at 226 cmbd. We also resumed excavations in N104E99 and terminated it at 176 cmbd.

Between 2013 and 2015, we excavated a good portion of the remaining deposits in the shelter's interior, focusing mostly on the units east of the E99 Trench in which the upper deposits had been destroyed (Figure 4.3d), but later also on the northwestern quadrant of the shelter where intact deposits spanning the Holocene remained. When fieldwork ended in 2015, we had excavated ~26 m³ of deposits within the shelter's interior. Deposits in a small area at the back of the shelter and larger areas along the western and southern edges of our excavation block remain unexcavated and undisturbed.

As our work progressed, it became clear that substantial portions of the middle and late Holocene deposits had been destroyed by looters. Fortunately, the E99 Trench and, later, other undisturbed units provided stratigraphic and chronological data for those periods as well as modest artifact assemblages. Furthermore,

the terminal early Holocene and latest Pleistocene deposits remained essentially intact across the shelter's interior, including below the looters' pit. The materials contained within those deposits provide a record of hunter-gatherer behavior that has allowed us to examine myriad topics including diet, technology, toolstone procurement, and site structure. Finally, data collected during our extensive pedestrian survey of North Warner Valley (see Chapter 13) allow us to understand how LSP-1 fit into broader patterns of trans-Holocene settlement and subsistence in the area.

STRATIGRAPHY

Sediment Sources, Modes of Transportation and Deposition, and Postdepositional Processes

The LSP-1 sediment derives from a combination of allogenic, autogenic, and anthropogenic sources. Two sources of allogenic sediment have contributed the bulk of the deposits. First, physical weathering of Little Steamboat Point's welded tuff and andesite has produced a debris fan on the west side of the shelter that has brought coarse clastic sediment into its interior (see Figure 4.1). The andesite has weathered into cobble-sized blade- and plate-shaped clasts with angular edges that have been transported into the shelter across the fan via gravity and water. In some cases, this sediment forms an open framework, clast-supported matrix with no interstitial fine-grained component. In other cases,

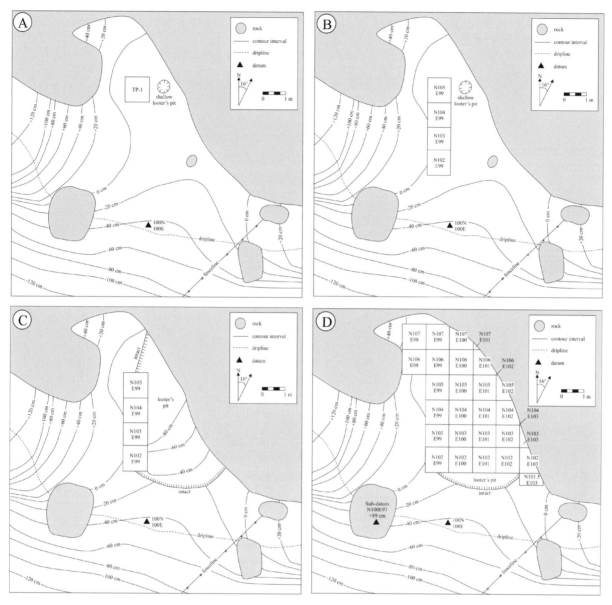

FIGURE 4.3. The progression of work at LSP-1: (A) 2010, test pit TP-1; (B) 2011, the E99 Trench; (C) 2012, the looters' pit; and (D) 2012–2015, excavation block.

while still clast-supported, fine-grained sediment fills interstitial spaces. Second, the floor of North Warner Valley has provided abundant fine-grained sediment that has blown into the shelter. This includes sediment blown directly into the shelter and windblown sediment that has mantled the surrounding hillslope and subsequently transported into the shelter as shallow, surface sheet flows.

Autogenic sediment also occurs in LSP-1 and is the product of physical and chemical weathering of the shelter's walls, most notably during its initial formation by wave action and subsequent freeze-thaw cycles. These processes have contributed autogenic sediment of two

distinct lithologies and grain sizes. Fine-grained, buff-colored subangular to subrounded pebbles originate from the coarse component of the surrounding welded tuff. The fine-grained matrix of the tuff contributes well-rounded, coarse black sand and granules composed of devitrified glass and other pyroclastic materials. Since the rimrock's face is the same lithology, those two sediment classes also occur as allogenic sediment transported into the shelter via the debris fan and deposited in massive beds. We primarily encountered those deposits in the western part of our excavation block, closest to the fan. The welded tuff also occasionally weathers as large clasts maintaining the coarse and fine components.

FIGURE 4.4. The interior of LSP-1 in May 2012: (A) the extent of the damage to the deposits from looting; (B) the remnants of N105E99; and (C) the location of the E99 Trench.

Those clasts occur as subangular to subrounded cobbles that are also transported into the shelter as fan debris.

Finally, anthropogenic processes contributed to the LSP-1 deposits. In the lower cultural deposits (mainly Strata V and VI, see below), people discarded tens of thousands of animal bones. These bones became "organic clasts" and, in some units, comprise a significant portion of the site matrix. In the upper cultural deposits (mainly Strata II and III), people brought substantial amounts of plant material into the shelter. Together, these materials affected the rates at which the strata accumulated and contributed to their overall character.

Three postdepositional processes of concern are: (1) pedogenesis; (2) bioturbation; and (3) anthropogenic processes. Calcium carbonate accumulations appear to be related to airfall associated with aeolian deposition rather than pedogenic processes. Otherwise, pedogenesis is not a major factor. Some evidence of animal burrowing occurs throughout the deposits, but it is not widespread in the lowest strata, probably due to the coarse-grained nature of those deposits. Some date re-

versals in the upper part of Stratum V suggest that those deposits are mixed in places, likely due in part to recurrent human activity at the end of the early Holocene. Pit excavation occurred at the site, mostly during hearth construction, but it was recognizable. The final and most substantial anthropogenic process is the looting event, which affected ~12 m² of the deposits inside the shelter. It removed up to 1 m of late and middle Holocene deposits, which limited the sample from which we can draw conclusions about site use during those periods. In some places, looting also disturbed the uppermost early Holocene deposits. We have kept those facts in mind when discussing artifact density and distribution in later chapters.

The LSP-1 Strata

We initially described the stratigraphic sequence at LSP-1 during the excavation of TP-1 in 2010 using 23 alphanumeric designations and retained that system during our 2011 excavations (see Table 4.1). Following the 2012 looting event and expansion of our excavation

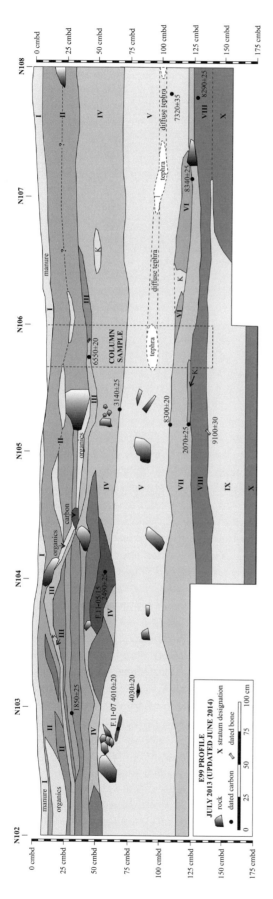

Figure 4.5. The E99 Trench profile looking west.

block, it became clear that the stratigraphy varied across the shelter's interior. Many of the upper strata became impossible to track horizontally because they were destroyed during the looting event. Furthermore, some of the distinctive strata noted in our 2010 and 2011 excavation units turned out to be localized lenses. As such, during the 2013 field season we consolidated our initial alphanumeric strata designations into broader units denoted by Roman numerals (see Table 4.1). Our understanding of the ages of those strata and when people used LSP-1 is based on 89 AMS radiocarbon dates obtained on artifacts, features, and ecofacts (see Table 4.2). The E99 Trench profile is the most representative depiction of the shelter's stratigraphy along a north–south axis (Figure 4.5), while the N102 profile best captures it along an east–west axis (Figure 4.6). Here, we outline the character and ages of the 10 major stratigraphic units at LSP-1 from youngest to oldest.

Stratum I (cattle dung) ranged from 5 to 10 cm in thickness and consisted of indurated cattle dung and <10 percent subangular gravel (roof fall). We did not obtain any radiocarbon dates for Stratum I, but, given that Euro-American ranching did not begin in the region until the mid-nineteenth century, it necessarily postdates that time.

Stratum II (upper fan facies) contained interfingering coarse and fine facies of autogenic material entering the shelter via the western debris fan. It measured up to 25 cm thick, and its color ranged from light yellowish brown to very pale brown (10YR 6/4 to 10 YR 7/4, dry). Texture consisted of sets of massive, gravelly medium to very fine sand and massive sandy gravel. Gravels ranged in size from granules to pebbles. Some gravel sets were clast supported. Organic debris was common closer to the shelter's mouth but uncommon closer to the back of the shelter. Deposits were strongly effervescent. Stratum II had an abrupt, smooth, lower boundary in the shelter's interior and a gradual wavy boundary near the shelter's mouth. Seven radiocarbon dates from Stratum II cluster between 1300 and 900 cal BP, while an eighth date of 3170±25 ^{14}C BP (3450–3360 cal BP) is an obvious outlier. The period between 1300 and 900 cal BP marks one of at least seven periods of occupation. Rosegate Series points (n=4) were the only projectile point type recovered from Stratum II (see Chapter 7).

Stratum III (upper loess) was a discontinuous deposit generally <15 cm thick. It was most clearly manifested near the mouth of the shelter and interdigitated with Stratum II. Stratum III was very pale brown (10YR 7/3, dry), slightly gravelly, and slightly silty medium- to very fine sand. It contained laminated beds 1–2 mm thick and was violently effervescent. It had an abrupt,

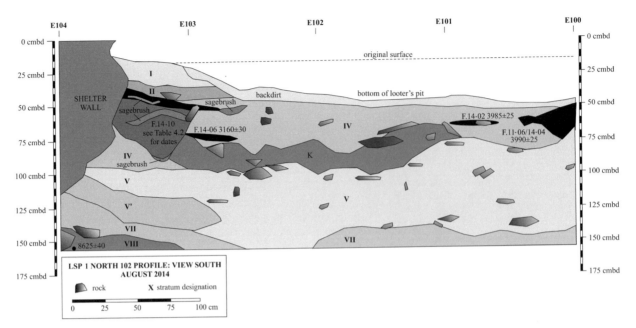

FIGURE 4.6. The N102 profile looking south.

smooth, lower boundary. The fine texture and laminated beds indicate secondary transport of aeolian sediment into the shelter interior as localized sheetwash. A radiocarbon date of 1255±25 ^{14}C BP (1275–1090 cal BP) suggests that Stratum III dates to the same general period as Stratum II. A second date of 6550±20 ^{14}C BP (7490–7425 cal BP) from the Strata III/IV contact is incongruent with both the date of 1275–1090 cal BP and those from the underlying Stratum IV. Finally, feature F.14-10, a storage pit filled with fiber artifacts (see chapters 5 and 11) dug into Stratum IV from either Stratum II or III, provided six additional radiocarbon dates that possess a bimodal age distribution: two items date to the 1300–900 cal BP period of occupation represented in Stratum II, and four date to an earlier period (1900–1600 cal BP). There is little additional evidence that people used LSP-1 ~1900–1600 cal BP. Therefore, the four dated textiles from F.14-10 likely do not accurately reflect the age of Stratum III. Instead, Stratum III is likely roughly the same age as the overlying Stratum II.

Stratum IV (lower fan facies) was recognizable throughout the shelter's interior and was 40 cm thick in places. It was similar in color and texture to Stratum II—especially in the southwestern portion of the excavation block—but contained substantially more charcoal fragments. Eighteen radiocarbon dates from Stratum IV range from 880±40 ^{14}C BP (915–705 cal BP) to 8640±30 ^{14}C BP (9670–9540 cal BP). We also obtained dates of 3140±25 ^{14}C BP (3445–3255 cal BP), 8200±35 ^{14}C BP (9270–9030 cal BP), 8290±40 ^{14}C BP (9425–9135 cal BP), 8375±50 ^{14}C BP (9500–9265 cal BP), and 8670±30 ^{14}C BP

(9685–9545 cal BP) along the Strata IV/V contact. The dates from Stratum IV vary widely but most correspond to five general periods of use: (1) 1300–900 cal BP; (2) 2700–2500 cal BP; (3) 3400–3200 cal BP; (4) 4500–4400 cal BP; and (5) 9775–8875 cal BP (restricted to the very rear of the shelter). In a few places, vertical mixing within Stratum IV hindered our ability to assign the contents of some excavated levels to cultural components. We recovered 10 Elko Series points and one Rosegate point from Stratum IV. We also recovered one Elko point, one Rosegate point, and one foliate point near the Strata IV/V contact, which supports our belief that Stratum IV generally recorded Middle Archaic occupations.

Stratum V (massive) was the primary artifact-bearing deposit at LSP-1. It measured up to ~60 cm thick and was light brownish grey (10YR 6/2, dry) in color. The deposit consisted of massive, poorly sorted gravelly, silty, very fine sand. Gravels ranged in size from granules to cobbles (<20 cm). Gravel shape was primarily angular to subangular. Stratum V was strongly effervescent and littered with leporid bones from top to bottom. It had an abrupt wavy boundary with Stratum IV and a clean wavy boundary with Stratum VII. A bed of laminated tephra was embedded within Stratum V in the center-rear of the shelter and filled voids in the lower portion of the stratum (see Figure 4.5). It was most clearly manifested in the deposits beneath the large crack in the shelter's ceiling. Franklin Foit (Washington State University School of the Environment) analyzed the bed, which contains at least four different tephras. Five shards strongly correlated to the Mount Mazama eruption

(~7700 cal BP), while others weakly correlated to Paulina Creek tephra (~55,000 cal BP [Kuehn and Foit 2006]) and two unknown tephras. The vertical position of the tephra bed and abundant older radiocarbon dates overlying it suggest that the tephra did not originate from the middle Holocene Mount Mazama eruption. Instead, due to its mixed composition and lack of a clear geochemical signature, the tephra bed is probably somehow derived from the volcanic formation into which LSP-1 is cut.

We obtained 24 radiocarbon dates on isolated charcoal fragments, bone, shell beads, and two features from Stratum V. These range from 3045±30 ^{14}C BP (3350–3170 cal BP) to 9200±30 ^{14}C BP (9815–9490 cal BP). The dates cluster within three general periods: (1) 4500–4400 cal BP; (2) 8200–8000 cal BP; and 9775–8875 cal BP. Two basketry fragments from a packrat midden (F.14-01, see Chapter 5) built into Strata IV and V returned younger dates of 1160±20 ^{14}C BP (1175–990 cal BP) and 1200±20 ^{14}C BP (1180–1065 cal BP). They do not accurately reflect the age of those deposits. We recovered side-removed points (*n*=2), foliate points (*n*=2), WST points (*n*=10), indeterminate foliate/WST point fragments (*n*=4), and a crescent from Stratum V.

Stratum V' was a localized lens of light brownish gray (10YR 6/2), gravelly sand in the southeastern quadrant of the excavation block. It is visible in the N102 profile (see Figure 4.6). It contained blocky to subangular clasts <2.5 cm in diameter. Stratum V' was strongly effervescent and possessed a smooth boundary with the underlying Stratum VII. We did not obtain radiocarbon dates from Stratum V', but it is likely the same age as Stratum V and younger than Stratum VII.

Stratum VI (lower loess) was an isolated 1.5 × 1.5 m lens of very pale brown (10YR 7/4, dry) massive, slightly gravelly, silty, very fine sand in the western excavation block. The lens was compact, violently effervescent, and had an abrupt lower boundary. It measured ~20 cm thick near its center. It sat at the base of Stratum V and above Stratum VII and probably represents a sand sheet that banked against the back of the shelter. One radiocarbon date from within Stratum VI (8290±40 ^{14}C BP [9425–9135 cal BP]) and three radiocarbon dates of 8340±25 ^{14}C BP (9450–9290 cal BP), 8400±50 ^{14}C BP (9520–9300 cal BP), and 8545±35 ^{14}C BP (9550–9480 cal BP) along its contact with the underlying Stratum VII indicate that Stratum VI dates to the same general period as the lowest portion of Stratum V (~9775 cal BP). We recovered one foliate point, two WST points, and one corner-notched point base that we tentatively typed as an Elko point from Stratum VI or mixed Strata V/VI sediment.

Stratum VII (upper gravel) occurred throughout the shelter's interior and was generally 25 cm thick. It consisted of very pale brown (10YR 7/3, dry), massive, sandy gravel and gravel. Gravels ranged from subangular and subrounded welded tuff pebbles to blade- and plate-shaped andesite cobbles. The materials that comprised Stratum VII are derived from the surrounding rimrock. Some cobbles formed an open framework clast-supported matrix. It was violently effervescent and possessed a clear, wavy lower boundary. We obtained four radiocarbon dates on isolated charcoal fragments and animal bone: 2070±25 ^{14}C BP (2120–1950 cal BP); 5240±25 ^{14}C BP (6175–5920 cal BP); 7310±40 ^{14}C BP (8185–8020 cal BP); and 7340±30 ^{14}C BP (8275–8030 cal BP). Clearly, none reflect the true age of Stratum VII. Based on the ages of the surrounding strata, we estimate that Stratum VII dates to ~9775 cal BP. We recovered two corner-notched point bases that we tentatively typed as Elko points from mixed Strata V/VII deposits. Their position suggests either that they were displaced from higher up in the shelter's deposits—Elko points are fairly old in the northern Great Basin—or that they are fragments of some older but unrecognizable point type. We return to this topic in Chapter 7. Artifact density was very low in Stratum VII.

Stratum VIII (upper sand) consisted of very pale brown (10YR 7/3, dry) gravelly sand. It was generally <25 cm thick and separated from Stratum X (lower sand) by Stratum IX (lower gravel) in places. Where Stratum IX was absent, Stratum VIII rested atop Stratum X. The two were difficult to distinguish given their similar lithology, color, and texture. Gravels included subangular to subrounded welded tuff pebbles. Much of the sand was black, owing to the fact that it consisted of well-rounded devitrified glass and other pyroclastic materials from the surrounding welded tuff. It was compact, mildly effervescent, and possessed a clear, wavy lower boundary. A piece of isolated and apparently intrusive charcoal also produced an aberrant date of 1175±25 ^{14}C BP (1180–1000 cal BP). Eight other dates obtained on isolated charcoal fragments or animal bones returned ages ranging from 7920±30 ^{14}C BP (8975–8610 cal BP) to 9100±30 ^{14}C BP (10,295–10,200 cal BP), suggesting either that the bottom of Stratum V and the top of Stratum VIII are somewhat mixed in places or that Stratum VIII dates to essentially the same period as the lower portion of Stratum V. Based on the ages of the overlying and underlying strata, our best age estimate for Stratum VIII is 10,250–9775 cal BP. We recovered few artifacts from Stratum VIII and suspect that those that we did find migrated down from the overlying stratum.

Stratum IX (lower gravel) was like Stratum VII (upper gravel) in lithology, color, and texture. It possessed a clear, wavy lower boundary. We encountered it in the western half of the excavation block, where it was thickest (~35 cm). It gradually tapered and disappeared to the east. As noted, where present, it served to separate Strata VIII and X (upper sand and lower sand). A lone date of 10,320±40 ^{14}C BP (12,385–11,795 cal BP) on noncultural animal bone and the ages of the overlying and underlying strata indicate that Stratum IX spans 12,200–10,250 cal BP. We recovered few artifacts from Stratum IX and suspect that all of them originated in the overlying strata.

Stratum X (lower sand) was consistent in lithology, color, and texture with Stratum VIII (upper sand). It was compact, fluvially reworked, autogenic welded tuff resting atop bedrock. It was ~60 cm thick in units N104E100 and N105E100, which we excavated to bedrock. The bedrock, which slopes downward toward the shelter's mouth, indicates that Stratum X was probably thinner near the shelter's rear and thicker near the shelter's mouth. We obtained three radiocarbon dates for Stratum X: 8625±25 ^{14}C BP (9680–9530 cal BP); 11,685 ^{14}C BP (13,585–13,430 cal BP); and 12,280±45 ^{14}C BP (14,485–14,035 cal BP). The 8625±25 ^{14}C BP date is clearly incongruent with the other two dates, which both suggest that Stratum X dates to 14,250–12,200 cal BP. Stratum X marks the initial sedimentation of LSP-1 after Lake Warner receded below the shelter's elevation. We recovered virtually no artifacts from Stratum X, and any that we did were likely translocated from the overlying cultural strata.

Cultural Chronology

Radiocarbon dates on features and fiber artifacts suggest seven major periods of use at LSP-1 (Figure 4.7) that we ultimately grouped into three cultural components. Except in cases where they were mixed or disturbed by the looting event, we assigned artifacts and ecofacts from each excavation level to one of these three components (Tables 4.3 and S1 [online]). The oldest and most substantial component consists of Late Paleoindian occupations marked by WST, foliate, and side-removed points as well as a crescent dated to ~9775–8875 cal BP. We encountered it mostly in the lower portion of Stratum V (generally below 76–86 cmbd). In places, it extended down into the upper part of Stratum VII and/or up into the lower part of Stratum IV (the latter appears to have largely been the case toward the rear of the shelter). A less intense period of use occurred ~8200–8000 cal BP.

The Middle Archaic component is marked by Elko Series points. Radiocarbon dates on features suggest three periods of use: (1) ~4500–4400 cal BP; (2) ~3400–3200 cal BP; and (3) ~2700–2500 cal BP. Middle Archaic artifacts were primarily restricted to Stratum IV

and, in a few cases, the uppermost levels of Stratum V. They occurred throughout the shelter's interior except in the very back, but they were most common toward the apron.

Finally, the Late Archaic component is marked by Rosegate points. Radiocarbon dates on features and fiber artifacts suggest two use periods: (1) ~1900–1600 cal BP; and (2) 1300–900 cal BP. We encountered Late Archaic artifacts mostly in Strata II and III, though in places they extended down into the upper portion of Stratum IV. At the rear of the shelter, the Late Archaic component rested atop the Late Paleoindian component.

Despite a rich surface record containing fluted and WST points associated with the 1,390 m asl Younger Dryas shoreline below the shelter (see Chapter 13), there is no evidence that people visited LSP-1 during the terminal Pleistocene. Instead, the first and heaviest period of use of the site postdates the disappearance of pluvial Lake Warner from North Warner Valley. As is the case with many rockshelters in the northern Great Basin (Ollivier et al. 2017), there was a substantial hiatus at LSP-1 during the middle Holocene. In addition to the ~3,500-year hiatus from ~8000 to 4500 cal BP exhibited in Figure 4.7, we did not find any Northern Side-notched points at the site. It is possible that the looting event destroyed evidence of Early Archaic shelter use, but our excavations in intact units along the E99 Trench and the front and rear of the shelter suggest otherwise. Finally, there is no evidence of Terminal Prehistoric use of the LSP-1. Following a ~400-year period of heavy use by Late Archaic groups, use of the shelter ceased.

Synthesis: Depositional History, Site Formation, and Use

The 10 LSP-1 strata may also be characterized as consisting of three major sediment packages (see Table 4.1). From bottom to top, these are differentiated black sands and gravel layers (lower package), poorly sorted aeolian sands and fan gravels (middle package), and debris fan gravels (upper package). These packages recorded periods of site formation and use. The lower package consisted of alternating sets of coarse gravel and black sand. It began to accumulate before 14,485–14,035 cal BP (the oldest radiocarbon date from Stratum X)—after pluvial Lake Warner had carved the shelter—and ceased accumulating at ~9775 cal BP, when aeolian deposition increased sharply. The upper and lower gravel layers (Strata VII and IX) included a mix of blade- and plate-shaped andesite cobbles and subangular and subrounded pebbles derived from the welded tuff. The clasts formed an open-framework, clast-supported matrix with varying degrees of fine-grained sediment

TABLE 4.3. Cultural components by excavation unit

| Excavation Unit | Component[1] | | | | | |
| | Late Archaic | | Middle Archaic | | Late Paleoindian | |
	Strata	Elevation (cmbd)	Strata	Elevation (cmbd)	Strata	Elevation (cmbd)
N106E98	I, II, III, IV	to 51	IV	51–56	IV, V, VI	56–126
N107E98	I, II, IV	to 56	absent[3]	—	IV, V, VI, VII	56–126
N102E99	I, II, III	to 31	IV	31–56	V	76–126
N103E99	I, II, III	to 36	III	36–61	IV, V	81–126
N104E99	I, II, III	to 51	IV, V	51–81	V, VI, VII	81–136
N105E99	I, II, III	to 56	IV, V	46–86	V, VI, VII	86–136
N106E99[2]	I, II, III, IV	to 51	IV, V	56–86	V, VI, VII	86–131
N107E99[2]	I, II, III, IV	to 46	absent[3]	—	V, VI, VII	66–131
N102E100[2]	looted	looted	IV	61–76	V, VII	76–141
N103E100[2]	looted	looted	looted	looted	V	81–126
N104E100[2]	looted	looted	looted	looted	V, VI, VII	86–131
N105E100[2]	looted	looted	looted	looted	V, VI, VII	91–131
N106E100[2]	looted	looted	looted	looted	V, VI, VII	96–126
N107E100[2]	looted	looted	looted	looted	V, VI	96–126
N102E101[2]	looted	looted	IV, V	56–76	V, VII	76–141
N103E101[2]	looted	looted	looted	looted	V, VII	76–141
N104E101[2]	looted	looted	looted	looted	V, VI, VII	91–136
N105E101[2]	looted	looted	looted	looted	V, VI, VII	91–136
N106E101[2]	looted	looted	looted	looted	V, VII	85–126
N107E101[2]	looted	looted	looted	looted	V, VII	91–126
N102E102[2]	looted	looted	IV, V	66–76	V	76–141
N103E102[2]	looted	looted	IV, V	66–76	V, VII	76–146
N104E102[2]	looted	looted	IV, V	71–76	V, VII	76–136
N105E102[2]	looted	looted	looted	looted	V, VII	71–136
N101.5E103	I, II, II, IV	to 61	unexcavated	—	unexcavated	—
N102E103*	I, II, III, IV	31–56	IV	76–91	V, V'	91–131
N103E103*	looted	looted	looted	looted	V, V'	111–131

[1] Gaps in elevation ranges of components reflect levels in which materials from different periods were mixed.
[2] The opening depths delineated for these units reflect the bottom of looters' pit and/or top of intact deposits. We do not know whether the units once contained Late or Middle Archaic components.
[3] We did not encounter evidence of a Middle Archaic component in these units.

filling interstitial spaces. Stratum VII contained more fine-grained sediment filling voids and cavities, while Stratum IX contained virtually no fine-grained component. The clasts showed no preferred orientation indicative of transport and deposition in high-energy fluvial events. Instead, Strata VII and IX were likely deposited as the initial unloading of gravelly sediment stored on the hillslope west of the shelter opening took place. The upper and lower sand units (Strata VIII and X) both contained abundant, black, coarse sand and granules with subangular to subrounded welded tuff clasts. While Stratum VIII may have had a small aeolian component, which made it mildly effervescent, Stratum X showed no reaction to hydrochloric acid and thus may have lacked an aeolian component. Stratum VIII originated as either autogenic sediment weathered from the shelter walls or allogenic sediment stored on the surrounding hillslope and transported in via the incipient debris fan. Stratum X marks the initial sedimentation of LSP-1 following the shelter's formation via wave action sometime before 14,485–14,035 cal BP. People first occupied LSP-1 near the end of Stratum VII's accumulation, ~9775 cal BP.

The middle package consisted of two distinct strata: (1) a massive unit of poorly sorted fan gravels mixed with a component of fine to very fine sand (Stratum V); and (2) a distinct layer of massive, silty, very fine aeolian sand (Stratum VI). It spans a narrow period from ~9775 cal BP to ~8025 cal BP. Due to the mixed grain-size component of Stratum V, the middle package likely reflects a period when aeolian sand from the valley floor was abundant and/or the availability and transport of coarse, clastic debris fan gravels was reduced. Based on

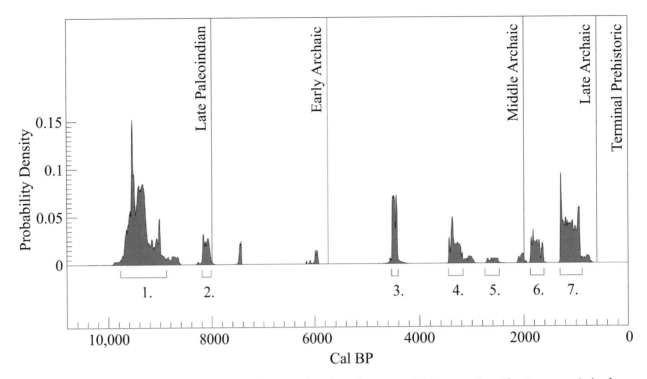

FIGURE 4.7. Summed probability distribution of radiocarbon dates from Strata II–VII suggesting at least seven periods of use.

our lake history presented in Chapter 3, the former scenario is especially relevant. The floor of North Warner Valley had dried by ~10,300 cal BP. Initially, the exposed lakebed would have offered a major supply of sediment to be transported into the shelter by prevailing southwesterly winds. Dates from Strata V and VI suggest that sediment accumulated very rapidly: ~60 cm over ~1,750 years. This rapid accumulation was aided by a buildup of anthropogenic debris including ~100,000 faunal elements (see Chapter 6) and flaked- and groundstone artifacts during an especially heavy period of use between 9775 and 8875 cal BP.

There is a gap in the ages of the middle and upper sediment packages. The top of Stratum V, dated to ~8000 cal BP, rested immediately beneath the bottom of Stratum IV, dated to ~4500 cal BP. Essentially, most of the middle Holocene record is missing. At least two scenarios could produce such a gap. First, Stratum V may span ~9775–4500 cal BP but became hopelessly bioturbated over the years. For this to be the case, we should see dispersed middle Holocene dates and diagnostic middle Holocene artifact types (e.g., Northern Side-notched points). We do not. Only nine of 89 dates from LSP-1 fall during the middle Holocene and, again, we did not recover any Northern Side-notched points. Second, there was a major unconformity in the LSP-1 deposits that either marked a period of erosion or nondeposition. Because caves and shelters are generally sediment traps (Wood-

ward and Goldberg 2001), and because erosion would only remove fine-grained sediment and leave a massive, clast-supported stone line, which is not present in the LSP-1 strata, we discount the possibility that erosion removed middle Holocene sediment. Instead, it appears that the period from ~8000 to 4500 cal BP was a time of little to no sediment accumulation or occupation. Paraconformities, or periods of nondeposition like that observed at LSP-1, are not uncommon in western North American rockshelters, where even the effects of physical and chemical weathering are reduced (Finley 2016).

Finally, the upper package (i.e., debris fan gravels) consisted of interfingering coarse- and fine-grained debris fan facies that we divided into two strata (Strata II and IV) separated by a thin stratum of aeolian sand (Stratum III). It accumulated over the past 4,500 years and marked a wholly different depositional regime than the middle sediment package. The upper fan materials of Stratum II formed distinct lenses of varying grain size typical of distributary channels on the surface of alluvial fans. Grain size reflects an energy regime where larger grain sizes indicate higher energy conditions and smaller grain sizes indicate lower energy conditions. While some lenses were present in Stratum IV, coarse- and fine-grained facies are horizontally continuous, indicating that distinct distributary channels may have not yet formed, and depositional conditions were stable across the surface of the debris fan. Stratum III marks a period of increased aeolian contribution in the upper sediment package that had two distinct facies to the north (i.e., interior) and south (i.e., exterior) of the shelter's west wall. Stratum III was thickest in the north section where it contained laminated beds 1–3 mm thick, indicating fluvial reworking of fine and very fine aeolian sand. The stratum became thin toward the center of the west wall where it rose over the crest of the debris fan. South of that, Stratum III became mixed with fan gravels but maintained its distinct color and texture. Strata II–IV contained evidence of episodic use of LSP-1 by people including three Middle Archaic occupations and two Late Archaic occupations dating to 1900–1600 cal BP and 1300–900 cal BP.

As is the case with many caves and rockshelters, understanding LSP-1's stratigraphy and chronology proved to be challenging. The loss of a substantial portion of the site's deposits to looting destroyed much of the site's late and middle Holocene record. A paucity of hearths or other features in the middle and lower sediment packages led us to turn to isolated charcoal fragments or animal bones for dating. In some cases, these produced dates that are discordant with numerous other dates from the same strata. Out-of-sequence dates, especially near stratigraphic contacts, suggest that some minor mixing occurred in the LSP-1 deposits. Nevertheless, the depositional history and site formation processes at LSP-1 are clear. The three major sediment packages record local environmental conditions that almost certainly influenced human use of LSP-1 and, more broadly, North Warner Valley. They record pluvial Lake Warner's TP/EH regression, the exposure, erosion, and transport of valley floor sediment during the early–middle Holocene and ameliorating conditions during the late Holocene. Further, they reflect periods of heavy use and hiatuses that correspond closely to changes in settlement patterns on the valley floor below. Most importantly, they contain clues about how, when, and why people visited North Warner Valley. We explore these topics in detail in the subsequent chapters.

Feature Distribution, Content, and Plant Use

Jaime L. Kennedy, Geoffrey M. Smith, and Bryan S. Hockett

In this chapter, we describe the morphology, distribution, and content of the LSP-1 features with a focus on what they can tell us about chronology, subsistence, and paleoenvironmental conditions in North Warner Valley. We also compare the macrobotanical contents of the features to those collected from a column sample in the west profile of Unit N105E99. Finally, we describe the animal bones recovered from the various features. In doing so, we build upon Kennedy's (2018) recent analysis of macrobotanical remains from LSP-1.

METHODS

Feature Recordation and Collection

We assigned 35 feature numbers during our excavations using a two-part numbering system. The first part denotes the year in which we first encountered the feature; the second part denotes the order in which we encountered it that year (e.g., F.11-02 was the second feature designation we made in 2011). In many cases, we designated something a feature in the field that ultimately proved to be less significant than we initially believed (e.g., a light charcoal or ash lens). We omitted those cases from our macrobotanical analysis. Occasionally, we assigned two numbers to the same feature (this happened a few times if it crosscut units excavated during different field seasons). In such cases, upon recognizing that the two numbers denoted the same feature, we combined them (e.g., F.11-06/14-04 represents a single feature first encountered in 2011 and again in 2014 an adjacent unit). Excluding those features that we ultimately deemed insignificant and combining those that we initially recorded separately left 14 features that war-

rant discussion (Table 5.1 and Figure 5.1). Because looting removed much of the site's Middle and Late Archaic deposits, the horizontal distribution of features from those periods primarily reflects the area we excavated before the looting event (the E99 Trench) or units that were not extensively damaged (N102E100, N102E101, N102E102, N102E103, and N101.5E103). The interior of the shelter probably contained more features dating to those periods than we encountered during our work.

Laboratory Methods

We analyzed 15 bulk sediment samples from 11 hearths and one *Neotoma* midden, and 25 bulk sediment samples from a single macrobotanical column (Table 5.2). The hearth and midden samples consisted of fill collected from the densest organic components of each feature. The column sample includes sediment from Strata I–VIII and spans the upper, middle, and lower sediment packages from the west profile of N105E99 collected in contiguous 5 cm intervals (see Figure 4.5).

Kennedy processed the samples following the wash-over flotation procedures outlined by Cummings (1989) in which light fraction remains such as seeds/fruits/nuts, charcoal, and other plant material were recovered. She added soil from each bulk sediment sample to ~3 gal of water in a clean 5-gal bucket and stirred the water until a strong vortex formed and botanical remains floated to the surface. She then poured the light fraction through a 250 µm mesh sieve. Kennedy added more water to the bucket and continued mixing, repeating this process as many times as necessary to ensure the entire light fraction was successfully transferred to the

TABLE 5.1. LSP-1 features

Feature ID	¹⁴C Date	Cal BP, 95.4% Confidence	Stratum	Unit(s)	Elevation (cmbd)[2]	Interpretation
11-05/15	2490±25	2725–2475	dug into IV	N103E99, N104E99	60	hearth
11-06/14-04	3990±25	4520–4415	IV	N102E99, N102E100	65	hearth
11-07	4010±20	4520–4425	V	N102E99, N102E100	69	hearth
11-14	1015±30	975–805	dug into II/III	N104E99, N104E100	60	hearth
11-19	2910±30	3160–2960	IV	N104E99, N104E100	70	hearth
13-01	8700±30	9735–9550	V	N103E100, N104E100, N103E101, N104E101	125	hearth
13-02	EH[1]	n/a	V	N103E102	121	hearth
14-01	LH[1]	n/a	dug into IV/V	N102E100, N103E100	85	*Neotoma* midden
14-02	3985±25	4520–4415	IV	N102E100	66	hearth
14-03	LH[1]	n/a	IV	N102E101	63	hearth
14-06	3160±30	3450–3270	IV	N102E102, N102E103	72	hearth
14-07	LH[1]	n/a	dug into IV	N102E103	52	hearth
14-08	LH[1]	n/a	dug into IV	N102E103	40	hearth
14-10	LH[1]	n/a	dug into IV	N102E103	65	storage pit

[1] Estimated age based on depth and proximity to other dated features (LH=late Holocene; EH=early Holocene).
[2] Approximate midpoints of features.

sieve. Flotation continued until no visible light fraction was floating on the surface and the water turned clear (i.e., clays and silts were washed through the screen). After the light fractions dried, Kennedy weighed and passed them through graduated dry sieves with openings of 4 mm, 2 mm, 1 mm, 500 μm, and 250 μm. She then removed the macrobotanical materials from the sample for analysis.

Kennedy weighed all charcoal >2 mm and selected a subset of 20 fragments per sample for identification. She examined the tangential, transverse, and radial surfaces of each charcoal fragment using a Nikon AZ 100 microscope with 200× zoom optics. She recovered and identified seeds and fruits with the help of a Nikon binocular stereo zoom microscope with 10×–70× zoom optics. Kennedy consulted various identification manuals (e.g., Adams and Murray 2004; Cappers et al. 2009; L. W. Davis 1993; Delorit 1970; Friedman 1978; Hoadley 1990; Martin and Barkley 1973; Minnis 1987; Schopmeyer 1974; Sharp 1990) and compared the rockshelter constituents to modern reference collections housed at the University of Oregon Museum of Natural and Cultural History to identify specimens to the lowest taxonomic level possible. She collected and weighed charred plant tissue fragments, leaves, buds, and stems but did not assign them to taxa. Kennedy consulted ecological data associated with plant taxa at LSP-1 (e.g., calflora.org; USDA 2014, 2019; Weber and Hanks 2008) to infer seasonality of occupation and environmental trends.

Our nomenclature generally follows Meyers et al. (2015) and Hitchcock and Cronquist (1973). The use of a specific epithet indicates a confident species-level attribution. The use of a genus name alone specifies certainty in genus-level attribution but not species-level attribution. Also, while other plant tissues can be sorted into descriptive categories, macrobotanical analysis cannot identify amorphous charred vegetative materials to taxon. Here, we define three categories of charred plant tissues: (1) fruity edible tissues likely representing berries or other sugar-laden vegetative materials; (2) starchy edible tissues representing unidentified geophytic materials; and (3) vitrified tissues (glassy, bubbly unidentifiable plant materials). We used both inferential statistics (ubiquity and density measures) and quantitative analyses (analysis of variance and chi-square tests for heteroscedasticity) to compare macrobotanical data. We used soil volume instead of weight to quantitatively compare the samples.

FEATURE DESCRIPTIONS
Late Paleoindian Features

F.13-01 marks the oldest feature we recorded in LSP-1. It represents the remains of a hearth built at the Strata V/VII contact. We encountered it at the intersection of the N103/104 and E100/101 grid lines. The hearth measured 60 cm across and 3 cm deep. It returned a radiocarbon date of 8700±30 ¹⁴C BP (9735–9550 cal BP) and contained limited plant remains. The charred macrobotanical assemblage included *Artemisia* charcoal, a small fragment of fruity edible tissue, and several *Chenopodium* (50 percent) seeds and cheno-am perisperms (50 percent) (Tables 5.3 and 5.4).[1] *Amsinckia*

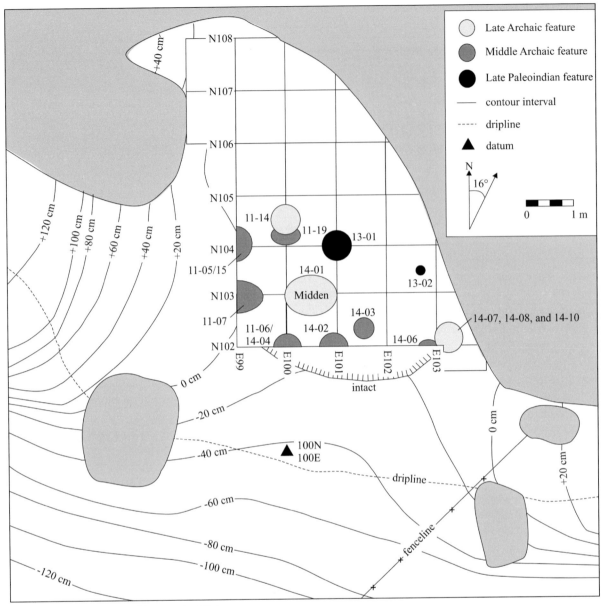

FIGURE 5.1. Distribution of features in LSP-1.

seeds dominated (99 percent) the uncharred plant assemblage, which also included *Chenopodium* seeds (1 percent). The hearth contained one *Sylvilagus* bone and 14 burned and unburned small mammal bones (Table 5.5).

F.13-02 represented the remains of a very small (15 × 15 × 3 cm) hearth or possible hearth clean-out surrounded by several burned rock fragments. We encountered it near the bottom of Stratum V in Unit N103E102. Although it remains undated, its stratigraphic position suggests that it is terminal early Holocene in age. Fuel wood was limited to small *Artemisia* charcoal fragments. Like F.13-01, it contained a modest charred plant assemblage featuring *Eriogonum* (33 percent), *Descurainia* (17 percent), Montiaceae (17 percent), *Agrostis* (17 percent),

and *Galium* (17 percent). The uncharred plant assemblage was identical to F.13-01, with only *Amsinckia* (99 percent) and *Chenopodium* (1 percent) seeds identified. Of note, F.13-02 produced the most animal bones of any hearth. These included one *Lepus* element, two leporid elements, roughly four dozen burned and unburned small mammal bones, and two burned large mammal bones.

Middle Archaic Features

We initially recorded F.11-05/15 as two separate features in units N103E99 and N104E99. It was a large hearth dug into Stratum IV. The feature extended into the west wall of the units and its cross section remains visible in the E99 profile (see Figure 4.5). The excavated portion

TABLE 5.2. Column and hearth sample proveniences

Sample No.	Sample Volume (L)	Sediment Package	Excavation Unit	Stratum	Feature	Elevation (cmbd)	Description
5b	0.9	upper	N105E99	I	—	28–31	column sample
6	1	upper	N105E99	II	—	31–36	column sample
7	1	upper	N105E99	II	—	36–41	column sample
8a	1	upper	N105E99	II	—	41–44	column sample
8b	1	upper	N105E99	II	—	44–46	column sample
9	1	upper	N105E99	III	—	46–51	column sample
10	1	upper	N105E99	III	—	51–56	column sample
11	1	upper	N105E99	III/IV	—	56–61	column sample
12	1	upper	N105E99	III/IV	—	61–66	column sample
13	1	upper	N105E99	IV/V	—	66–71	column sample
14	1	middle	N105E99	IV/V	—	71–76	column sample
15	1	middle	N105E99	V	—	76–81	column sample
16	1	middle	N105E99	V	—	81–86	column sample
17	1	middle	N105E99	V	—	86–91	column sample
18	1	middle	N105E99	Tephra	—	91–96	column sample
19	1	middle	N105E99	Tephra	—	96–101	column sample
20	1	middle	N105E99	V/VI	—	101–106	column sample
21	1	middle	N105E99	V/VI	—	106–111	column sample
22	1	middle	N105E99	V/VI	—	111–116	column sample
23	1	lower	N105E99	VI/VII	—	116–121	column sample
24	1	lower	N105E99	VI/VII	—	121–126	column sample
25a	0.2	lower	N105E99	VI/VII	—	126–128	column sample
25b	0.8	lower	N105E99	VI/VII	—	128–131	column sample
26	0.75	lower	N105E99	VI/VII	—	131–136	column sample
27	0.6	lower	N105E99	VIII	—	136–141	column sample
1653	0.9	upper	N104E99/100	II/III	11-14	50	hearth
1658	0.9	upper	N104E99	Dug into IV	11-05/15	64	hearth
—	0.45	upper	N104E99	Dug into IV	11-05/15	60	hearth
1654	0.65	upper	N104E99	Dug into IV	11-05/15	58	hearth
2438	0.5	upper	N102E103	Dug into IV	14-07	52	hearth
1292	1.0	upper	N102E103	Dug into IV	14-08	40	hearth
1649	0.6	upper	N104E99	IV	11-19	72	hearth
2432	0.25	upper	N102E100/101	IV	14-02	66	hearth
2429	0.25	upper	N102E99/100	IV	11-06/14-04	75	hearth
1665	0.35	upper	N102E99	IV	11-06/14-04	65	hearth
2437	0.5	upper	N102E101	IV	14-03	58	hearth
2430	0.5	middle	N102E100	Dug into IV/V	14-01	81–86	rat midden
1657	0.7	middle	N102E99	V	11-07	69	hearth
1270	0.4	lower	N103E102	V	13-02	122	hearth
1031	0.6	lower	N103E100	V	13-01	125	hearth

measured 100 × 50 × 20 cm. Charcoal returned a date of 2490±25 ^{14}C BP (2725–2475 cal BP). An Elko point (Artifact 303) and a foliate point (Artifact 304) lay immediately adjacent to the hearth. Fuel wood consisted of *Artemisia* charcoal. Both fruity and starchy edible tissues were recovered. The feature fill contained a small but diverse assemblage of charred seeds including *Chenopodium* (43 percent), *Agrostis* (23 percent), *Descurainia* (11 percent), *Eriogonum* (4 percent), *Leymus cinereus* (3 percent), *Amsinckia* (2 percent), Montiaceae (2 percent), *Typha latifolia* (2 percent), Poaceae (2 percent), *Plagiobothrys* (1 percent), *Ribes* (1 percent), Lamiaceae (1 percent), and *Galium* (1 percent). The uncharred seed assemblage was limited to *Atriplex confertifolia* (40 percent), *Amsinckia* (38 percent), *Chenopodium* (14 percent), Poaceae (2 percent), *Mentzelia* (2 percent), and cheno-am perisperms (1 percent). Animal bones included one unidentified, burned, large mammal bone

TABLE 5.3. Charcoal and charred tissues from hearth features

Component	Feature ID	Sample Volume (L)	Charcoal Taxa Weight (g)		Charred Plant Tissue Weight (g)	
			Artemisia	*Atriplex*	Fruity Tissue	Starchy Tissue
Late Archaic	11-14	0.9	0.35	0.01	<0.01	<0.01
	14-07[1]	0.5	0.34	—	0.02	<0.01
	14-08[1]	1.0	0.32	0.02	—	<0.01
Middle Archaic	11-05/15	2.1	0.91	—	<0.01	<0.01
	11-06/14-04	0.6	1.01	—	—	—
	11-07	0.7	0.41	—	<0.01	—
	11-19	0.6	0.19	—	—	—
	14-02	0.25	0.36	0.06	<0.01	<0.01
	14-03[1]	0.5	6.67	—	0.02	<0.01
Late Paleoindian	13-01	0.6	0.08	—	<0.01	—
	13-02[1]	0.4	0.04	—	—	—

[1] We did not obtain radiocarbon dates for these features but assigned them to components based on their stratigraphic positions.

and 30 unburned and burned small mammal bones, some of which represent leporids.

We recorded F.11-06/F.14-04 as two separate features in the field and later combined them. It was a hearth in Stratum IV that we encountered in units N102E99 and N102E100. The excavated portion measured 50 × 25 × 13 cm. Charcoal produced a radiocarbon date of 3990±25 ^{14}C BP (4520–4415 cal BP), which is essentially identical to the age of another hearth (F.14-02) located at the same elevation 15 cm to the east. *Artemisia* was the only identified charcoal type in the feature. Although we collected numerous charred seeds from the macro-botanical samples, most were identified as *Agrostis* (47 percent), *Descurainia* (34 percent), or *Chenopodium* (14 percent). The remaining 5 percent of the charred assemblage included *Atriplex* (3 percent), *Eriogonum* (<1 percent), *Phacelia* (<1 percent), and *Mentzelia* (<1 percent) seeds. The uncharred seed assemblage also contained several of these taxa but with different ratios. It included *Chenopodium* (53 percent), *Descurainia* (33 percent), *Atriplex confertifolia* (5 percent), *Amsinckia* (2 percent), *Agrostis* (1 percent), Poaceae (1 percent), Brassicaceae (1 percent), *Mentzelia* (1 percent), *Amaranthus* (<1 percent), and *Cryptantha* (<1 percent). We recovered a single animal bone—an unidentified, unburned, small mammal element—from F.11-06/F.14-04.

F.11-19 was a small hearth encountered near the top of Stratum V in Unit N104E99. It lay atop a 10 cm thick silt lens. Both the hearth and silt lens extended to the east into the adjacent Unit N104E100, but that portion was destroyed during the looting. The hearth measured 55 × 50 × 8 cm. Charcoal consisted exclusively of *Artemisia*, a piece of which returned a date of 2910±30 ^{14}C BP (3160–2960 cal BP). The feature fill also included charred and uncharred seeds. *Chenopodium* (83 per-

cent), Brassicaceae (3 percent), *Descurainia* (3 percent), Montiaceae (3 percent), *Leymus cinereus* (2 percent), *Agrostis* (2 percent), *Phacelia* (2 percent), and *Plagiobothrys* (2 percent) charred seeds were identified along with uncharred seed types identified as *Amsinckia* (67 percent), *Atriplex confertifolia* (17 percent), cheno-am perisperms (8 percent), Brassicaceae (4 percent), and *Descurainia* (4 percent). The F.11-19 fill did not contain animal bones larger than 4 mm.

We recorded F.14-02 in units N102E100 and N102E101, and a portion of it remains visible in the N102 profile (see Figure 4.6). It was a hearth that measured 80 cm across by 5 cm deep, situated near the bottom of Stratum IV. F.11-06/14-04, which dates to the same period, was located immediately west of F.14-02, but the two features appear to be separate entities. Several pieces of burned rock surrounded the charcoal and ash lens. F.14-02 produced a radiocarbon date of 3985±25 ^{14}C BP (4520–4415 cal BP). Identified fuel wood included *Artemisia* and *Atriplex*, and this feature contained the highest density of charcoal of the analyzed features. We also recovered fragments of fruity and starchy edible tissues. The charred seed assemblage included *Agrostis* (77 percent), *Chenopodium* (13 percent), *Leymus cinerus* (7 percent), and *Galium* (3 percent). The uncharred seed assemblage included *Atriplex* (79 percent), *Amsinckia* (20 percent), and *Chenopodium* (1 percent). We collected a fragment of cordage from the feature fill. The F.14-02 fill did not contain any animal bones larger than 4 mm.

F.14-03 represented a 50 × 50 × 5 cm hearth encountered in Unit N102E101. Although we did not date it, F.14-03 was in Stratum IV at roughly the same elevation and near three other Middle Archaic features (F.14-02, F.14-06, F.11-06/14-04). It likely dates to around the same time (either ~4500 cal BP or ~3300 cal BP). Several pieces of groundstone and two Elko points (artifacts 2196 and 2198) lay scattered around the hearth. *Artemisia* was the only charcoal taxon identified in F.14-03, but charcoal density was high. Like F.14-02, F.14-03 contained fragments of fruity and starchy edible tissues. We identified charred Poaceae (34 percent), *Chenopodium* (20 percent), *Descurainia* (20 percent), *Amsinckia* (14 percent), cheno-am perisperms (7 percent), and *Mentzelia* (2 percent) seeds, along with uncharred *Chenopodium* (22 percent), cheno-am perisperms (21 percent), Brassicaceae (13 percent), *Mentzelia* (7 percent), Poaceae (5 percent), *Atriplex confertifolia* (4 percent), *Descurainia* (3 percent), and *Scirpus/Schoenoplectus* (<1 percent) seeds. F.14-03 did not contain any animal bones larger than 4 mm.

F.14-06 was a small hearth exposed in Unit N102E102 during cleaning of the N102 profile (see Figure 4.6). It measured 40 cm across and 6 cm deep and was situated near the bottom of Stratum IV. It returned a radiocarbon date of 3160±30 ¹⁴C BP (3450–3270 cal BP). We did not collect a fill sample because we noted it during wall cleaning and do not discuss it further.

F.14-10 was a pit excavated into Stratum IV near the shelter's eastern wall. It occupied the southwestern corner of Unit N102E103 and is visible in cross section in the N102 profile (see Figure 4.6). The pit measured 60 cm across and 48 cm deep. It was capped with a dark lens of ash, charcoal, and sagebrush, but it is unclear whether that marked part of the pit or a separate feature. The pit sloped slightly down and to the west, as do most of the strata in that part of the shelter. Its cross section suggests that it was excavated in an east–west direction away from the shelter wall. Numerous bits of shredded sagebrush were found along the pit's edges, further suggesting that it may have been lined before it was filled. Fill was variable in color and texture but predominantly dark gray sandy gravel. The N102 profile shows a burrow extending west from F.14-10. Disturbances within the pit noted during excavation suggest that the burrow penetrated it following its construction.

We recovered five sandals/sandal fragments, a piece of twined basketry, and a bundle of shredded sagebrush bark from the pit. They are described in detail in Chapter 11 (also see Smith et al. 2016b). Radiocarbon dates on four of the sandals (1300±20 ¹⁴C BP [1285–1185 cal BP], 1760±20 ¹⁴C BP [1720–1610 cal BP], 1860±20 ¹⁴C BP [1865–1730 cal BP], and 1880±20 ¹⁴C BP [1880–1735 cal BP]), the twined basketry fragment (1790±20 ¹⁴C BP [1815–1625 cal BP]), and the sagebrush bark bundle (1340±20 ¹⁴C BP [1300–1190 cal BP]) reflect two periods separated by a few centuries. Elsewhere (Smith et al.

2016b), we suggested that the bimodal distribution of dates from the pit may indicate that people placed the items in the pit on two separate occasions. Alternatively, and perhaps more likely, the items were discarded in the shelter over the course of a few centuries, and someone later collected and buried them during a single event ~1300–1200 cal BP. Of note, the twined basket fragment recovered from F.14-10 is ~600 years older than the two twined basketry fragments recovered from F.14-01 (the *Neotoma* midden) located ~2 m to the west, indicating that the fragment in the pit is not part of the same vessel as the fragments from F.14-01. Kennedy did not analyze the storage pit fill.

F.11-07 was a hearth located in the western part of the shelter. A remnant of it is visible in the E99 Trench profile (see Figure 4.5). It measured 50 cm across by 3 cm deep and was built in the mid-to-upper portion of Stratum V. F.11-07 returned a radiocarbon date of 4010±20 ¹⁴C BP (4520–4425 cal BP). A second, smaller, charcoal lens located 15 cm north and 15 cm below F.11-07 (also visible in the E99 Trench profile) returned a nearly identical date of 4030±20 ¹⁴C BP (4565–4425 cal BP) and likely represents some of the F.11-07 hearth fill displaced downward by rodent burrowing. Charcoal abundance in F.11-07 was low, with a density similar to Middle Archaic features F.11-19 and F.11-05/15. *Artemisia* was the only identified fuel wood. The fill included small fragments of charred, edible, starchy tissues along with charred *Chenopodium* (61 percent), *Descurainia* (18 percent), *Leymus cinereus* (12 percent), Poaceae (6 percent), *Atriplex* (3 percent), and cheno-am perisperms (1 percent). *Atriplex confertifolia* (94 percent) dominated the uncharred seed assemblage, which also included *Amsinckia* (3 percent), cheno-am perisperms (1 percent), *Chenopodium* (1 percent), *Scirpus/Schoenoplectus* (<1 percent), *Mentzelia* (<1 percent), Poaceae (<1 percent), and *Achnatherum* (<1 percent). It also contained two *Lepus* elements and a dozen burned and unburned small mammal bones.

Late Archaic Features

F.11-14 was a hearth built at the bottom of a shallow pit excavated into Strata II/III. We uncovered it in Unit N104E99. It extended into Unit N104E100, but that portion was destroyed by looting. The pit measured up to 110 cm across and 25 cm deep, while the hearth measured 60 cm across and 8 cm deep. F.11-14 contained *Artemisia* and *Atriplex* charcoal, a piece of which returned a date of 1015±30 ¹⁴C BP (975–805 cal BP). Other charred remains included fruity and starchy plant tissues and *Chenopodium* (57 percent), *Descurainia* (31 percent), *Leymus cinereus* (3 percent), Poaceae (2 percent), Brassicaceae

TABLE 5.4. Charred seeds from hearth features

Plant Taxon	Late Archaic (53.6%)					Middle Archaic (44.0%)				Late Paleoindian (2.4%)		Ubiquity (%)
	11-14 (11.5%)	14-07 (12.9%)	14-08 (29.4%)	11-05/15 (2.8%)	11-19 (1.3%)	11-06/14-04 (23.0%)	14-02 (3.8%)	14-03 (4.2%)	11-07 (8.9%)	13-01 (1.1%)	13-02 (1.3%)	
Amsinckia	230	20	87	94	27	32	56	54	26	107	120	100
Cryptantha	—	—	—	—	—	2	—	—	—	—	—	9
Phacelia	1	—	1	—	2	2	—	—	—	—	—	36
Plagiobothrys	—	—	—	1	2	—	—	—	—	—	—	18
Brassicaceae	2	—	—	—	5	8	—	58	—	—	—	36
Descurania	81	390	496	6	5	813	—	28	27	—	3	82
Cheno-Am	172	30	48	3	3	—	—	74	0	7	—	73
Amaranthus	—	—	—	—	—	2	—	—	—	—	—	9
Atriplex	61	2	41	98	7	103	220	14	749	—	—	82
Chenopodium	532	810	2,216	57	80	833	20	90	99	5	—	91
Monolepis	—	—	1	—	—	—	—	—	—	—	—	9
Eriogonum	2	4	4	3	—	3	—	—	—	—	5	55
Fabaceae	—	—	1	—	—	—	—	—	—	—	—	9
Galium	—	—	2	1	—	—	4	—	—	—	3	36
Juniperus	4	34	125	—	—	—	—	—	—	—	—	27
Lamiaceae	—	—	—	1	—	—	—	—	—	—	—	9
Carex	—	2	4	—	—	—	—	—	—	—	—	18
Scirpus	6	2	19	—	—	—	—	6	1	—	—	45
Juncus	—	—	1	—	—	—	—	—	—	—	—	9
Typha	—	—	—	1	—	—	—	—	—	—	—	9
Mentzelia	30	6	8	5	—	8	—	26	1	—	—	64
Ribes	1	—	—	1	—	—	—	—	—	—	—	18
Montiaceae	1	—	—	1	3	—	—	—	—	—	3	36
Nicotiana	12	—	3	—	—	—	—	—	—	—	—	18
Poaceae	48	24	12	6	—	18	—	48	10	—	—	64
Achnatherum	1	4	1	1	—	—	—	—	—	—	—	36
Agrostis	—	2	7	12	2	567	96	—	1	—	3	73
Leymus	8	—	—	1	2	—	8	—	19	—	—	45
Prunus	1	—	—	—	—	—	—	—	—	—	—	9
Rosa	—	6	—	—	—	—	—	—	—	—	—	9
Unidentified	23	30	35	4	—	50	—	50	—	—	—	n/a
Total	1,216	1,366	3,112	296	138	2,441	404	448	943	117	137	n/a

TABLE 5.5. Fauna from features

Feature ID	Lepus	Sylvilagus	Leporid	Unburned Small Mammal	Burned Small Mammal	Unburned Large Mammal	Burned Large Mammal	Total
11-05/15	—	2	1	23	4	—	1	31
11-06/14-04	—	—	—	1	—	—	—	1
11-07	2	—	—	7	5	—	—	14
11-14	—	1	—	5	3	1	—	10
13-01	—	1	—	6	8	—	—	15
13-02	1	—	2	20	26	—	2	51
Total	3	4	3	62	46	1	3	122

Note: Fill from features 11-19, 14-02, and 14-03 did not contain any bones ≥4 mm. We did not collect a fill sample from 14-06.

(1 percent), *Scirpus/Schoenoplectus* (1 percent), *Eriogonum* (1 percent), *Phacelia* (<1 percent), Montiaceae (<1 percent), *Ribes* (<1 percent), and *Prunus* (<1 percent) seeds. The uncharred seed assemblage included *Chenopodium* (40 percent), *Amsinckia* (24 percent), cheno-am perisperms (18 percent), *Atriplex confertifolia* (6 percent), Poaceae (5 percent), *Mentzelia* (3 percent), *Nicotiana* (1 percent), and Brassicaceae (<1 percent). The fill contained one *Sylvilagus* bone, eight burned and unburned small mammal bones, and one unidentified and unburned large mammal bone.

F.14-07 was a basin-shaped hearth with some oxidized sediment observed in the eastern profile of Unit N102E102. We first noted it while excavating the southeastern corner of Unit N102E102 but did not assign it a feature number until later, at which time we also noted F.14-08 immediately above it in the eastern profile of Unit N102E102 (described below). F.14-07 measured 50 cm across and 8 cm deep and was excavated into Stratum IV. It was immediately underlain by a large burrow, which may have truncated the feature's bottom. F.14-07 remains undated but is likely Late Archaic in age. Identified charcoal in F.14-07 was limited to *Artemisia*. We also observed both fruity and starchy charred tissues. The charred seed assemblage contained *Chenopodium* (64 percent), *Descurainia* (28 percent), *Juniperus* (2 percent), cheno-ams (2 percent), Poaceae (1 percent), and *Eriogonum* (1 percent). We also recovered a charred rosehip (*Rosa*) fragment with an intact achene. Uncharred seeds included *Chenopodium* (51 percent), *Descurainia* (29 percent), *Amsinckia* (4 percent), *Juniperus* (3 percent), cheno-am perisperms (2 percent), Poaceae (2 percent), *Mentzelia* (1 percent), *Achnatherum* (1 percent), *Atriplex confertifolia* (<1 percent), and *Carex* (<1 percent). We did not recover any animal bones larger than 4 mm.

Like F.14-07, we first encountered F.14-08 while excavating the southeastern corner of Unit N102E102 but

did not assign it a number until we mapped the unit's eastern profile. It consisted of a concentration of unburned and burned vegetation located near the shelter's eastern wall. It was partially destroyed by looting. The remaining portion measured 55 cm across and 20 cm deep. It is unclear whether and how it was related to the underlying F.14-07 but may have simply represented the upper portion of that hearth. Charred macrobotanical constituents in F.14-08 included *Artemisia* and *Atriplex* charcoal, charred starchy edible tissues, and *Chenopodium* (76 percent), *Descurainia* (20 percent), *Juniperus* (2 percent), *Amsinckia* (<1 percent), *Agrostis* (<1 percent), Poaceae (<1 percent), *Eriogonum* (<1 percent), *Phacelia* (<1 percent), *Atriplex* (<1 percent), *Carex* (<1 percent), *Juncus* (<1 percent), *Mentzelia* (<1 percent), and *Galium* (<1 percent) seeds. A diverse, uncharred seed assemblage was dominated by *Chenopodium* (63 percent) but also included *Descurainia* (10 percent), *Juniperus* (8 percent), *Amsinckia* (6 percent), cheno-am perisperms (4 percent), *Atriplex* (3 percent), *Scirpus/Schoenoplectus* (2 percent), *Mentzelia* (1 percent), Poaceae (1 percent), *Monolepis* (<1 percent), Fabaceae (<1 percent), *Achnatherum* (<1 percent), and *Nicotiana* (<1 percent). We did not recover any animal bones larger 4 mm. F.14-08 remains undated but is likely Late Archaic in age.

F.14-01 was a concentration of mostly unburned organic debris that occupied portions of units N102E100, N102E101, N103E100, and N103E101. Its top was destroyed during the looting event. The remaining portion measured 110 × 80 × 25 cm and crosscut the Strata IV/V boundary. Two small textile fragments found in and immediately adjacent to it returned nearly identical dates of 1160±20 ^{14}C BP (1175–990 cal BP) and 1200±20 ^{14}C BP (1180–1065 cal BP), which indicates that the feature is intrusive into the surrounding older stratum. Charred plant remains were limited to *Artemisia* charcoal, but we identified numerous uncharred *Chenopodium*

TABLE 5.6. Ethnographic and environmental associations of plant taxa

Family	Genus/Species	Common Name	Traditional Uses[1]	Available for Harvest	Ecological Attributes[2]
Amaranthaceae	*Amaranthus*	pigweed	FO, ME	fall	DR
Anacardiaceae	*Rhus*	sumac	—	—	—
Asteraceae	*Artemsia*	sagebrush	FU, TE, TO, ME	—	DR
Boraginaceae	*Amsinckia*	fiddleneck	FO	summer/fall	—
	Cryptantha	cat's eye	—	summer/fall	—
	Plagiobothrys	popcorn flower	—	summer/fall	FW
Brassicaceae	*Descurainia*	tansymustard	FO	summer	—
Chenopodiaceae	Cheno-am	—	FO	fall	HA
	Atriplex	saltbush/shadscale	FO	fall/winter	HA, DR
	Chenopodium	goosefoot	FO	fall	HA, DR, FU
	Monolepis	povertyweed	—	fall	HA
Cupressaceae	*Juniperus*	juniper	FO, FU, ME, DY, TE	fall	DR
Cyperaceae	*Carex*	sedge	FO, TE	summer/fall	OW
	Scirpus/ Schoenoplectus	bulrush, tule	TE	summer/fall	OW
Fabaceae	Legume family	—	—	—	—
Grossulariaceae	*Ribes*	currant, gooseberry	FO, ME	summer/fall	DR
Hydrophyllaceae	*Phacelia*	phacelia	ME	summer/fall	—
Juncaceae	*Juncus*	rush	FO, TE	summer/fall	HA, FW
Lamiaceae	Mint family	—	—	—	—
Loasaceae	*Mentzelia*	blazing star	FO	fall	—
Montiaceae	Montia family	—	—	—	FU
Poaceae	*Achnatherum hymenoides*	Indian ricegrass	FO	summer/fall	DA, OU
	Agrostis	bentgrass	FO	summer/fall	DA, FW
	Leymus cinereus	Great Basin wildrye	FO, ME, FI	summer/fall	DA
Polygonaceae	*Eriogonum*	buckwheat	FO, ME	fall	DA
Rosaceae	*Prunus*	chokecherry, klamath plum	FO, ME	fall	DA
	Rosa	wild rose	FO, ME, TO	fall/winter	—
Rubiaceae	*Galium*	bedstraw, cleaver	—	summer/fall	FW
Solanaceae	*Nicotiana*	Indian tobacco	ME	fall	—
Typhaceae	*Typha latifolia*	cattail	FO, TE, BU, TO	summer/fall	HA, OW

[1] FO=food; ME=medicine; FU=fuel; TO=tool; TE=textile; BU=building material; FI=fiber; DY=dye.
[2] DR=drought resistant; FW=facultative wetland; HA=halophyte; FU=facultative upland; OW=obligate wetland; DA=drought adapted; OU=obligate upland.

(54 percent), Poaceae (31 percent), and *Achnatherum* (2 percent) seeds (Table S2). F.14-01 also contained bits of jackrabbit fur, unidentified animal hair, and feathers. Its morphology and contents suggest that it is the remains of a *Neotoma* midden.

MACROBOTANICAL DISCUSSION

Understanding traditional subsistence strategies has long been a goal of archaeological research in the northern Great Basin (Cressman 1940, 1942; Helzer 2001; Prouty 2004; Stenholm 1994; Wingard 2001). Documenting the presence of seeds, fruits, charcoal, and charred tissues allows researchers to extrapolate data about past ecology, vegetation, diet, subsistence, trade, land management, and seasonality (Pearsall 2016). Sampling cultural features may reveal past behaviors including the types of plants and animals that people gathered and hunted. Hearths in particular offer evidence of food processing. The charcoal they contain also reflects the types of wood that people used for fuel. Finally, hearths often provide clues about local vegetation communities (Behre and Jacomet 1991). Although potentially unrelated to cultural activities, column samples also provide critical data. Foremost, they limit sampling bias, provide longitudinal data related to changing environmental conditions and cultural behaviors, offer information related to intrasite spatial patterning, and increase the potential for recovering plant remains associated with medicines, handicrafts, and household goods. Tables 5.6 and S3 list the identified plant remains from both the cultural features and the column samples, as well as the manners in which people may have used them.

The N105E99 Column

Charcoal was ubiquitous but not abundant throughout the column. Each column sample contained charcoal weighing <0.5 g. (Table S4). Except for individual fragments of *Atriplex* and *Rhus* charcoal in Stratum II at a depth of 41–44 cmbd, *Artemisia* constituted all the fuel wood in the column samples.

The column samples also included fragments of softer charred plant tissues including fruity, starchy, and vitrified tissues. Strata II and V/VI contained negligible amounts of vitrified tissues. Kennedy recovered tiny amounts of charred fruity tissue from Strata VI/VII 128–131 cmbd and a fairly large piece of charred starchy tissue from Stratum II 44–46 cmbd.

Identified seeds in the column samples represent 10 taxa belonging to eight families (Table S5). Uncharred seeds (~83 percent) outnumbered charred seeds (~17 percent) by roughly four to one. Uncharred seed taxa included *Atriplex* (41 percent), cheno-am perisperms (28 percent), *Chenopodium* (20 percent), *Amsinckia* (5 percent), *Agrostis* (2 percent), and *Descurainia* (2 percent). Brassicaceae, *Eriogonum*, *Mentzelia*, *Leymus cinereus*, *Urtica dioica*, *Phacelia*, Poaceae, and *Typha latifolia* each contributed less than 1 percent to the uncharred assemblage.

Among the charred seeds in the N105E99 column, we identified *Chenopodium* (64 percent), *Descurainia* (12 percent), *Agrostis* (9 percent) and cheno-am perisperms (6 percent). *Eriogonum*, *Atriplex*, *Leymus cinereus*, *Mentzelia*, *Typha latifolia*, *Phacelia*, Poaceae each constitute less than 1 percent of the total charred seed assemblage. Finally, 8 percent of the charred seeds could not be identified to species.

The populations of charred and uncharred seed assemblages are differentially distributed in the column samples (χ^2=2002.653, df=14, p<0.01). This limits our ability to attribute uncharred seeds outside of features to human activity. The charred seeds both inside and outside the features are more indicative of cultural activity. Accordingly, we excluded uncharred seed taxa from our interpretations of human behaviors but included them in our discussion of past environments.

When the seed data from the column are normalized to account for volumetric differences in sample size,

the upper sediment package (Strata I–IV) contained the bulk of seeds (86 percent). Most seeds were found in Stratum II. We observed no seeds in Stratum I, which is mainly cattle dung that postdates ~AD 1850. The upper sediment package primarily contained members of the Chenopodiaceae family including cheno-am perisperms, and *Atriplex* and *Chenopodium* seeds, but it also contained numerous *Descurainia*, *Agrostis*, and *Mentzelia* seeds. The frequency of *Amsinckia* seeds increased below 61 cmbd in Strata III/IV.

Seeds were not abundant in the middle sediment package (Strata IV/V, V, the tephra band, and Strata V/VI). *Chenopodium* and *Descurainia* were more prevalent in Strata IV/V than in the other middle package samples. Apart from *Amsinckia*, which increased in prevalence below Stratum V, seeds were virtually absent from samples in Strata V and VI.

The distribution of seed taxa in the lower sediment package in Strata VI/VII generally mimicked those of the upper sediment package, but they occurred in much lower frequencies. One obvious exception is the lack of *Descurainia* seeds below 76 cmbd. *Amsinckia* was the only identified plant taxon in Stratum VIII.

Hearths

We examined the macrobotanical constituents from two Late Paleoindian hearths (F.13-01, F.13-02), six Middle Archaic hearths (F.11-05/15, F.11-06/14-04, F.11-07, F.11-19, F.14-02, F.14-03), and three Late Archaic hearths (F.11-14, F.14-07, F.14-08). We recovered charcoal and wood, seeds/fruits, leaves, stems, and charred plant tissues from those features. Charcoal was ubiquitous, but its abundance varied by feature. The two Late Paleoindian hearths (F.13-01 and F.13-02) contained very low densities of charcoal, while the three Middle Archaic hearths (F.11-06/14-04, F.14-02, F.14-03) contained very high densities. *Artemisia* was the primary charcoal taxon in all of the hearths, but we also identified *Atriplex* charcoal in one Middle Archaic hearth (F.14-02) and two Late Archaic hearths (F.11-14 and F.14-07). *Artemisia* was the favored fuel wood, which is not surprising given its ubiquity around LSP-1.

Both charred fruity and starchy tissues were present in the hearth samples. We identified small fragments of charred fruity edible tissues in every hearth except F.13-02 (Late Paleoindian), F.11-06/14-04 (Middle Archaic), and F.14-07 (Late Archaic). This suggests that visitors to LSP-1 consumed sugar-laden fruits throughout the Holocene. A charred rosehip in F.14-07 (Late Archaic) and charred *Juniperus*, *Rosa*, *Prunus*, and *Ribes* seeds in several Late and Middle Archaic hearths indicate that the fruity edible tissue may reflect consumption of these berries. Charred starchy tissues were absent in both Late Paleoindian hearths, present in two Middle Archaic hearths (F.11-05/15 and F.14-02), and ubiquitous in Late Archaic hearths. These results suggest that (1) Late Paleoindian visitors did not process roots (a topic to which we return in Chapter 9); and (2) roots were a more important food source for Middle and Late Archaic visitors.

We identified only *Chenopodium*, cheno-am perisperms, and *Agrostis* in the Late Paleoindian hearths. The frequencies of these taxa were very low, suggesting that early visitors did not prepare plant foods in large quantities. We did observe more uncharred *Amsinckia* seeds in the Late Paleoindian hearths than the Middle Archaic hearths, a pattern that is consistent with the Late Archaic hearths (see below).

The charred seed assemblages from the Middle Archaic hearths were dominated by *Chenopodium* (59 percent) and *Descurainia* (24 percent). Middle Archaic hearths featured greater amounts of charred and uncharred *Atriplex* and lower amounts of uncharred *Amsinckia* than Late Archaic hearths. There is some interesting variation in the content of Middle Archaic hearths. For example, charred *Descurainia* seeds were primarily identified in F.11-06/14-04 and far less so in other hearths from that period. Additionally, while charred *Agrostis* seeds (15 percent) contributed a relatively large percentage to the Middle Archaic samples, most came from just two hearths: F.11-06/14-04 and F.14-02.

Late Archaic hearths featured more charred seeds than Middle Archaic hearths. Like the Middle Archaic hearths, most were either *Chenopodium* and cheno-am perisperms (72 percent) or *Descurainia* (23 percent). This indicates a focus on processing these seed-bearing taxa, but a variety of other taxa, including *Juniperus*, Poaceae, *Agrostis*, *Eriogonum*, *Amsinckia*, *Rosa*, *Phacelia*, Brassicaceae, *Atriplex*, *Scirpus*, *Carex*, *Ribes*, *Mentzelia*, and Montiaceae were also present. These taxa grow in different habitats (wetlands vs. uplands). Their co-occurrence in hearths indicates that Late Archaic visitors consumed or otherwise used plants collected from different habitats together or over short intervals of time.

We can draw two general inferences from the macrofloral assemblages in Late Archaic hearths. First, most of the wetland indicator plant species (*Carex*, *Juncus*, *Scirpus/Schoenoplectus*, and *Typha latifolia*) came from the Late Archaic hearths. Similarly, *Juniperus* only appears in Late Archaic hearths. Together, these observations suggest wetter conditions in North Warner Valley after 2000 cal BP. Second, although uncharred, the presence of *Nicotiana* in both F.11-14 and F.14-08 suggests

that Late Archaic visitors used it medicinally and/or recreationally.

Overall, the macrobotanical assemblages from the LSP-1 hearths suggest higher ratios of charcoal-to-seed densities in the Middle Archaic hearths and lower ratios of charcoal-to-seed densities in the Late Archaic hearths. The macrobotanical data also demonstrate significant differences in the frequencies of charred *Chenopodium* and *Descurainia* seeds in Late Archaic hearths (more abundant) versus Middle Archaic and Late Paleoindian hearths (less abundant). This difference alone suggests that Late Archaic visitors intensified their seed gathering and processing efforts at the site. Late Archaic visitors appear to have collected a more diverse suite of taxa including some from disparate settings (e.g., uplands and wetlands).

Neotoma *Midden*

Macrobotanical elements in the *Neotoma* midden (F.14-01) were limited to small quantities of charcoal and uncharred *Chenopodium*, *Achnatherum*, and other Poaceae seeds. The charcoal density was quite low compared to the Late and Middle Archaic hearths but much higher than the column samples. The macrobotanical assemblage in the midden (primarily uncharred) was inconsistent with the macrobotanical constituents found in Late Archaic hearths (primarily charred).

PALEOCLIMATE TRENDS

Plant remains from the column and feature bulk sediment samples represent taxa generally associated with desert scrub communities. They span most of the Holocene and are consistent across time, suggesting that the vegetation communities that characterize North Warner Valley today were established soon after pluvial Lake Warner receded from the study area ~10,300 cal BP. The only wetland taxon identified outside of hearth features was a *Typha latifolia* seed in a column sample from Strata VI/VII. All other wetland taxa were identified in hearths, primarily F.11-14 (dug into Strata II/III), F.14-07 (dug into Stratum IV), and F.14-08 (dug into Stratum IV). Most of the wetland plants were valued as sources of raw material for textiles. Their presence indicates introduction into the shelter by people. Elevated frequencies of wetland taxa in the Late Archaic hearths may indicate marsh rejuvenation in the Warner Basin ~1300–900 cal BP, perhaps as far north as Bluejoint Lake.

Long-term trends in the LSP-1 data indicate that, at times, North Warner Valley fostered drought- and salt-tolerant plants. Both charred and uncharred seeds in the Middle Archaic hearths, especially F.14-02 (Stratum IV) and F.11-06/14-04 (Stratum IV), include higher numbers of *Agrostis*, *Atriplex*, and *Chenopodium* than we observed in the Late Paleoindian hearths. Hansen (1947) reported similar conditions for the middle Holocene, based on his pollen record from farther south in Warner Valley.

Macrobotanical remains from the column samples include elevated proportions of *Amsinckia* in the middle (Strata V and VI) and lower (Stratum VIII) sediment packages, which primarily date to the early Holocene. Its presence in the early Holocene deposits suggests drier conditions, while its absence in the late Holocene deposits suggests improved conditions later in time. Interestingly, the distribution of *Amsinckia* seeds in the hearths shows a different trend. Hearth samples from the upper and middle sediment packages contained numerous uncharred *Amsinckia* seeds, whereas no hearth samples from the lower sediment package contained *Amsinckia* seeds. *Amsinckia* is a ruderal forb associated with desert scrub communities and flourishes in disturbed contexts (Montalvo et al. 2010). *Amsinckia* seeds are heavy and lack the adaptation for long-distance dispersal (van Rheede van Oudtshoorn and van Rooyen 1999). We suspect that the *Amsinckia* seeds in hearths represent postdepositional fill. Millennia of human visitation likely provided ideal conditions for *Amsinckia* near the apron of the rockshelter. Despite nuanced climate fluctuations in North Warner Valley through the Holocene, *Amsinckia* may have thrived immediately around LSP-1 due to recurring disturbances by people. Its presence in the Middle and Late Archaic hearths may be due to the fact that people mostly constructed hearths near or on the shelter's apron, while its absence in the column samples from those periods may be because we collected the column sample toward the back of the shelter, too far from where the plants grew to accumulate seed rain.

HUMAN BEHAVIOR
Seasonality of Site Use
Macrobotanical remains from the hearths indicate that most visits to LSP-1 occurred during the autumn, predominately between late August and October (see Table 5.6). This is especially clear in the remains from the Late Archaic and Late Paleoindian hearths. Though not statistically significant, F.11-07 and F.14-02 (both Middle Archaic hearths) diverge from this trend. Most seeds in F.11-07 would have been available to harvest in the late fall and winter. Seeds in F.14-02 did not yield a clear seasonality pattern because the timings of seed maturity for the various taxa differ. F.11-06/14-04 (a Middle Archaic hearth) also contained a number of taxa whose seeds mature in August and September.

Seasonality data offered by the macrobotanical remains corroborate those offered by the faunal remains, which we discuss in the next chapter. The faunal assemblage is dominated by rabbits and hares probably collected during communal drives. Ethnographically, rabbit drives took place in the fall when the animals were fat, and their fur was ready to be used for blankets and robes (C. Fowler 1992; Lowie 1924; Steward 1933, 1941; Wheat 1967). As we noted above, the data from F.14-02 and F.11-06/14-04 are a little different and suggest that a few Middle Archaic visits took place earlier in the year before drives typically occurred. Of note, neither of those hearths contained *Lepus* or *Sylvilagus* bones, suggesting that people built them during visits when rabbit collecting was not a major focus.

Subsistence
Ethnographic accounts demonstrate the importance of small seed processing to both the Klamath and Northern Paiute (Coville 1897; I. Kelly 1932; Park and Fowler 1989; Ray 1963; Spier 1930; Steward 1933; Stewart 1941). Among the seed taxa we documented, *Achnatherum*, *Amaranthus*, *Atriplex*, *Chenopodium*, and *Mentzelia* were all key resources for Great Basin groups (C. Fowler and Rhode 2007). Here, we discuss what the LSP-1 features reveal about people's use of these and other plant foods across time.

Late Paleoindian Hearths
Late Paleoindian visitors collected and processed chenoams and, to a lesser extent, fruits and berries. The low frequencies of plant resources in the hearths suggest that plant foods did not constitute a significant portion of people's diet during the early Holocene. This finding is at odds with the high number (n=141) of groundstone tools in the Late Paleoindian component (see Chapter 9), though, as we discuss in later chapters, some of those tools may have been used to process other resources.

Middle Archaic Hearths
The Middle Archaic hearths yielded more macrobotanical remains than the Late Paleoindian hearths. Fuel loads in the Middle Archaic hearths were particularly high, signifying longer burning fires or persistent hearth reuse. Based on their abundances in hearths from both periods, cheno-ams continued to be a food source but no more so than during the early Holocene. Both F.11-06/14-04 and F.14-02 contained elevated quantities of *Agrostis* seeds, which were commonly harvested by the Klamath (Coville 1897; Spier 1930). Like *Amsinckia*, *Agrostis* thrives in disturbed contexts and may have grown on the shelter's apron. Middle Archaic hearths also contained fragments of charred, edible, starchy tissues, indicating that people consumed roots.

Though Middle Archaic visitors processed and consumed some plant foods, those foods were not abundant enough in the hearths to suggest that seeds or edible tissue were a major food source. This possibility is supported by the fact that, when adjusted for the volume of excavated sediment, the density of groundstone artifacts is lower in the Middle Archaic deposits (6.3/m³) than both the Late Paleoindian (11.8/m³) and Late Archaic deposits (8.1/m³; see Chapter 9). We suspect that the paucity of both plant foods and the tools used to process them in the Middle Archaic component may have something to do with who used the site and why—a topic to which we return in the coming chapters.

Late Archaic Hearths

Large increases in the number of charred *Chenopodium* and *Descurainia* seeds from Middle Archaic to Late Archaic contexts, coupled with decreases in charcoal densities, suggest that Late Archaic visitors intensified and diversified their plant-collecting and processing efforts. *Chenopodium* and *Descurainia*—again, ethnographic staples—were abundant in Late Archaic hearths. Both charred and uncharred cheno-am perisperms were more abundant in Late Archaic hearths, which, because the perisperms lacked seed coats, indicates that they were ground during meal preparation. A relatively high density of groundstone tools in the Late Archaic component supports this contention. We identified charred, starchy, edible tissues in all three Late Archaic hearths and charred fruity edible tissues in two. The Late Archaic hearths also contained several taxa absent in earlier hearths. These include both facultative upland plants (*Juniperus*, *Rosa*, and *Prunus*) and a facultative wetland plant (*Carex*). The diversity of these taxa suggests that Late Archaic visitors collected and consumed plant foods found in a range of settings beyond the immediate vicinity of LSP-1.

Nondietary Cultural Patterns

Artemisia constituted most of the fuel wood in hearths from all time periods. This is not surprising, given that sagebrush is ubiquitous in North Warner Valley today and likely was throughout the Holocene as well. The absence of other archaeologically documented fuel woods such as *Juniperus*, *Pinus*, *Amelanchier*, and *Cercocarpus* (Connolly et al. 2015; Helzer 2001; Prouty 2001) is also telling about local conditions across time. As is the case today, these taxa probably did not grow in any number in North Warner Valley during the Holocene.

We identified *Nicotiana* seeds (probably *Nicotiana attenuate*, or coyote tobacco) in two Late Archaic hearths (F.11-14 and F.14-08). *Nicotiana* propagates most readily in disturbed areas under hot and dry conditions, and people used its leaves and seeds for both medicine and recreational smoking (Kelly 1932; Train et al. 1941). The seeds were uncharred and may represent post-depositional seed rain rather than deliberate human use, though we did recover a smoking pipe fragment from Middle Archaic deposits (see Chapter 10). Regardless of whether it can be attributed to human activity, the *Nicotiana* seeds indicate that tobacco likely grew near LSP-1.

CONCLUDING REMARKS

Macrobotanical remains offer clues about when, how, and why people occupied archaeological sites. At LSP-1, they suggest that local conditions were fairly stable throughout the Holocene and characterized mostly by desert scrub vegetation. People periodically brought extralocal plants into the site. These include both upland and wetland taxa probably collected outside of the NWVSA. Some of the Middle Archaic hearths suggest prolonged or repeated use. But generally, most cooking and/or warming fires were probably short-lived. With few exceptions, the contents of the features point to autumn visits—a scenario supported by the site's faunal record and ethnographic accounts of rabbit drives (see chapters 2 and 6). The frequencies of seeds and other plant remains are relatively low. However, groundstone tools are relatively common, especially in the Late Paleoindian and Late Archaic assemblages. This divergence in plant remains and plant-processing tools suggests that people used the groundstone to process other resources possibly including roots, small game, and pigment. We explore this possibility in the next few chapters.

NOTES

1. The term *cheno-am* refers to plants of either the genus Chenopodium or Amaranthus (Adams and Murray 2004). The two genera were split into separate families: Cheno-podiaceae and Amaranthaceae, respectively. *Cheno-am* encompasses both families here.

6

Fauna

Bryan S. Hockett, Evan J. Pellegrini, Geoffrey M. Smith, and Erica J. Bradley

The dry caves and rockshelters of the Great Basin are renowned for their excellent preservation of organic remains, including animal bones that offer clues about human subsistence and local environmental conditions. This is certainly the case for LSP-1, where we recovered a robust and well-preserved faunal assemblage dominated by hares and rabbits. The assemblage provides a detailed view of people's prey acquisition and processing strategies that, in concert with the lithic assemblage we describe in later chapters, tells a compelling story about human behavior in North Warner Valley.

PREVIOUS RESEARCH

Pellegrini (2014) analyzed a sample of the LSP-1 fauna from Stratum V for his thesis research. Stratum V reflects two periods of intensive use: 9775–8875 and 8200–8000 cal BP. His sample included bones from units N102E99, N103E99, N104E99, and a subset of bones from Unit N105E99. Pellegrini's (2014: Table 4.1) sample consisted of ~9,500 identifiable bones and bone fragments. Within this sample, he identified 2,701 hare (*Lepus*), 983 cottontail (*Sylvilagus*), and 29 general leporid bone specimens. Leporid tibiae were the most common identified elements (Table 6.1), suggesting that at least 30 hares and 23 cottontails were represented in the sample. Pellegrini also identified lesser numbers of carnivores, artiodactyls, rodents, and birds. Among the carnivores, he identified grey wolf (*Canis lupus*), coyote (*Canis latrans*), kit fox (*Vulpes macrotis*), bobcat (*Lynx rufus*), and spotted skunk (*Spilogale gracilis*). Artiodactyls included bison (*Bison bison*), mule deer (*Odocoileus hemionus*), and

possibly elk (*Cervus canadensis*). Based on his taphonomic analysis of the faunal assemblage, which we summarize below, he concluded that most of the rabbits and hares were products of human activity, while both human and nonhuman agents likely introduced the other taxa. Pellegrini (2014:94) ultimately concluded:

> The fact that such taxa [leporids] dominate the LSP-1 sample and appear to have been processed in a standardized fashion at the site suggests that communal hunting may have been a primary means of capturing leporids on the valley floor below the rockshelter. Today, jackrabbits are abundant in northern Warner Valley, and this may have been the case in prehistory as well.

Our analysis here supplements but does not repeat Pellegrini's work, though our overall conclusions wholly support his major finding: people collected leporids en masse during the terminal early Holocene. In this regard, our updated analysis provides a larger sample size and offers a better estimate of how many leporids were processed during the early Holocene occupation of LSP-1. Our larger sample also updates the number of nonleporid specimens, focusing on the carnivores and artiodactyls that the site's occupants likely hunted. Finally, because our sample includes fauna from terminal early Holocene, middle Holocene, and late Holocene deposits, for the first time we explore if and how human hunting patterns changed over time in North Warner Valley.

TABLE 6.1. NISP by element for leporids from Pellegrini's Stratum V faunal sample

Element	Taxa			Element	Taxa		
	Lepus	*Sylvilagus*	Leporid		*Lepus*	*Sylvilagus*	Leporid
astragalus	6	3	—	metapodial	230	34	3
acetabulum	10	12	—	molar	198	12	—
angular process	2	3	—	nasal front orbital	1	—	—
axis	1	—	—	palatine	18	2	—
basisphenoid	1	—	—	parietal	8	—	—
bulla	19	2	—	phalange	43	11	—
calcaneus	10	5	1	patella	-	1	—
cervical vertebra	2	—	—	premolar	94	23	3
condyloid process	46	6	—	pubis	3	—	—
coronoid process	11	—	—	radius	111	66	1
cranium fragment	1	—	—	ramus	13	—	—
exoccipital	1	—	—	rib	47	2	4
femur	326	187	—	rostral supraorbital process	1	—	—
fibula	8	—	—	scapula	73	45	—
humerus	109	68	—	skull fragment	302	8	9
ilium	4	15	—	squamosal	2	—	—
incisive	55	18	—	terminal phalanx	4	—	—
incisor	50	19	—	thoracic vertebra	7	2	—
innominate	4	6	—	tibia	430	264	—
ischium	6	11	—	tooth	3	—	6
lumbar vertebra	2	—	—	ulna	64	44	—
mandible	243	91	—	vertebra	3	—	1
maxilla/maxillary	115	15	—	zygomatic process	14	8	—

TABLE 6.2. Units and levels or depths from which the analyzed fauna originated

Component	Unit and Elevation (cmbd) of Hand-Counted Fauna		Unit and Levels of Fauna Estimated by Weight	
Late Archaic	N106E98	0–56	—	—
	N107E98	0–56	—	—
	N102E99	0–31	—	—
	N103E99	0–31	—	—
	N104E99	0–51	—	—
Middle Archaic	N102E99	31–56	—	—
	N103E99	31–81	—	—
	N104E99	51–81	—	—
Late Paleoindian	N106E99	56–126	N106E99	Levels 15–22
	N107E98	56–126	N102E101	Levels 7–17
	N102E99	76–91	N104E101	Levels 2–10
	N103E99	81–91	N103E102	Levels 5–15
	N104E99	81–136	—	—
	N107E99	66–131	—	—
	N104E100	86–131	—	—
	N105E100	91–131	—	—

Are the LSP-1 Leporids the Product of Human or Nonhuman Agents?

Pellegrini considered several attributes to differentiate elements deposited by human and nonhuman agents including: (1) burning; (2) the abundance of long-bone diaphysis cylinders; (3) surface texture such as weathering, polishing, or pitting; (4) puncture marks; (5) cutmarks; and (6) the age profiles of the rabbits and hares. Of the nearly 3,700 analyzed leporid bones, he noted evidence of nonhuman modification on less than 1 percent. Conversely, over half of the bones were burned, cutmarked, polished, or broken in ways suggesting that people extracted marrow from them. Finally, most rabbit and hare bones represented mature animals, leading to his conclusion that most leporid bones were the product of human activity.

Based on his actualistic studies of leporid butchering and corresponding patterns in his faunal sample, Pellegrini outlined the leporid carcass processing techniques that people employed. People likely collected the animals during the fall or winter and brought them into the shelter. They skinned the carcasses and roasted some of the animals, often with their feet still attached. Sometimes they boiled the animals instead of roasting them. People snapped off the ends of many limb bones and removed the marrow, either by sucking it from the long-bone shafts directly or boiling them to render it. They discarded the animals' heads and limb bones inside the shelter and pulverized the bodies containing both the rib and vertebral elements for immediate consumption, drying in preparation for winter storage, and/or carried the carcasses elsewhere.

Methods

To augment Pellegrini's sample, we selected fauna for analysis from excavation units where radiocarbon dates and/or diagnostic projectile points provided consistent age estimates across excavated levels and where animal bones were abundant (Table 6.2). Due to the large number of bones recovered, it was not feasible to hand identify and count each specimen. Instead, we employed a combination of hand identification and counting, as well as estimates based on weight. For the units listed in Table 6.2, we separated nonleporid bones and identified them to at least the Order level. We hand counted and identified bones from 139 of the 620 excavated 5 cm levels (a 22 percent sample). If the levels where we separated small mammal bones to estimate their numbers based on their aggregated weight are included, the sample of analyzed fauna rises to ~28 percent (174 5 cm levels). Table 6.3 shows the units and associated depths

of the faunal samples that we separated by hand and physically identified and counted, excluding the small-mammal-sized fraction. The greatest number of bones recovered from any of the units consisted of unidentified small-mammal-sized fragments. The count for those fragments is based on the average weight of three samples of 100 fragments taken from the units and depths shown in Column 2 of Table 6.2. In other words, we counted 100 fragments from three different units and levels, weighed each 100-bone sample, and averaged the results. The average weight of the three samples of 100 bone fragments was 16 g. After separating the unidentified small-mammal-sized bone fragments from the rest of the bones from these units and depths, we weighed the sample, divided the weight by 16, and multiplied the resulting number by 100 to estimate the number of fragments recovered. As noted, we physically separated, identified, and counted the remainder of the bones from these units and depths, including the leporid and nonleporid bones, as well as the large-mammal-sized fragments.

Following that process, and to better gauge the number of leporid carcasses deposited in the shelter during the early Holocene (i.e., the Late Paleoindian component), we estimated numbers of leporid bones for the units and levels shown in Column 3 of Table 6.2. To do this, we physically separated, identified, counted, and weighed the leporid bones from Unit N103E102, Level 11 (111–116 cmbd). The bones from this 5-cm level collectively weighed 473 g. Within this 473 g of bone, we identified 198 *Lepus*, 128 *Sylvilagus*, 8 *Brachylagus*, and 94 general leporid bones. Based on the numbers of tibiae diaphysis cylinders and proximal mandibles present (consistently the two most frequently identified leporid body parts), we obtained Minimum Number of Elements (MNE) and Minimum Number of Individuals (MNI) based on those MNE values. This demonstrated that at least 13 hares, 10 cottontails, and 2 pygmy rabbits (25 total individuals) are represented in that single 5-cm level of Unit N103E102. In addition, to get a general estimate of the number of unidentified small- and large-mammal-sized bone fragments present in this level, we used the same 16 g/100 bones figure described above. This resulted in an estimate of 1,066 unidentifiable fragments present in the 5-cm level. With those metrics, we simply divided 198 *Lepus* bones by the 473 g of total weight to obtain a formula for estimating the number of hare bones present within a 5-cm sample of bone based on weight alone (e.g., 0.42 *Lepus* bones per g; Table 6.3). We did the same for the MNE values based on numbers of tibiae diaphysis cylinders and proximal mandibles

TABLE 6.3. Metrics used to estimate NISP, MNE, and MNI values for leporids and unidentified small- and large-mammal bones based on weight from the units and levels displayed in Column 3 of Table 6.2

Bone Count Estimates	Formula	Example
unidentified small-mammal bones	grams (unid. small mammal bone fragments) ÷ 16 × 100 = #bones	42 g ÷ 16 × 100 = 263 bones
leporid bones present in unprocessed 5-cm-level bag	grams (bone) × 0.42 = #*Lepus* bones grams (bone) × 0.27 = #*Sylvilagus* bones grams (bone) × 0.017 = #*Brachylagus* bones grams (bone) × 0.20 = #leporid bones grams (bone) × 2.25 = #unid. bone fragments (large and small mammals)	473 g × 0.42 = 198 *Lepus* bones 473 g × 0.27 = 128 *Sylvilagus* bones 473 g × 0.017 = 8 *Brachylagus* bones 473 g × 0.20 = 94 leporid bones 473 g × 2.25 = 1,066 unid. large and small mammal bones
leporid MNE estimates in unprocessed 5-cm-level bag	grams (bone) × 0.055 = #LTDCs[1] grams (bone) × 0.055 = #*Lepus* mandibles grams (bone) × 0.04 = #STDCs[2] grams (bone) × 0.032 = #*Sylvilagus* mandibles grams (bone) × 0.0085 = #*Brachylagus* mandibles	2,686 g × 0.055 = 148 LTDCs[1] 2,686 g × 0.055 = 148 *Lepus* mandibles 2,686 g × 0.04 = 107 STDCs[2] 2,686 g × 0.032 = 86 *Sylvilagus* mandibles 2,686 g × 0.0085 = 23 *Brachylagus* mandibles

[1] *Lepus* tibia diaphysis cylinders.
[2] *Sylvilagus* tibia diaphysis cylinders.

present for *Lepus*, *Sylvilagus*, and *Brachylagus* to estimate the number of elements and individuals that these bones represented (see Table 6.2).

RESULTS

Table 6.4 displays the NISP values for the fauna in our sample. A variety of terrestrial animals are represented. These include: (1) leporids including hare (*Lepus*), cottontail (*Sylvilagus*), and pygmy rabbit (*Brachylagus idahoensis*); (2) pika (*Ochotona princeps*); (3) artiodactyls including bison (*Bison bison*), mountain sheep (*Ovis canadensis*), and cf. elk (*Cervus canadensis*); (4) mustelids including badger (*Taxidea taxus*) and spotted skunk (*Spilogale gracilis*); (5) carnivores including gray wolf (*Canis lupus*), coyote (*Canis latrans*), kit fox (*Vulpes macrotis*), and bobcat (*Lynx rufus*); and (6) rodents including marmot (*Marmota flaviventris*). Most of these taxa were also reported by Pellegrini, but the pygmy rabbits, pika, mountain sheep, and badger are new identifications. Pellegrini also reported specific rodent and bird identifications from the Late Paleoindian component, including great horned owl (*Bubo virginianus*), sagebrush vole (*Lagurus curtatus*), and bushy-tailed woodrat (*Neotoma cinerea*).

Each of the taxa that we identified were present in the Late Paleoindian component of Stratum V. The Middle Archaic component only included hare, rabbit, and elk/bison. The Late Archaic component included lagomorphs as well as elk/bison, coyote, bobcat, and badger. Sample size may be a factor in the lower species diversity of both the Middle and Late Archaic components, either resulting from the loss of a sizable portion of the site's upper deposits or our heavy emphasis on fauna from the early Holocene deposits.

Despite these differences in species diversity, leporids are by far the most common taxa represented in the Late Paleoindian, Middle Archaic, and Late Archaic components. If we remove the unidentified small and large mammal fraction from the NISP counts listed in Table 6.4, leporids constitute 98.5 percent of the identified bones in the Late Paleoindian component (NISP=17,568), 97 percent in the Middle Archaic component (NISP=513), and 91 percent in the Late Archaic component (NISP=1,651). These numbers suggest that while there may have been a slight decline in leporid hunting across time, they more clearly suggest that rabbit and hare hunting remained consistently important in North Warner Valley.

HOLOCENE HUNTING PATTERNS IN NORTH WARNER VALLEY: THE VIEW FROM LSP-1

The Late Paleoindian Component

The number of leporid carcasses processed in LSP-1 from near the end of the early Holocene is impressive. Table 6.5 shows that within just the Stratum V levels from the units we analyzed a minimum of 760 individual animals are represented. If we analyzed the bones from the Stratum V levels for all of the units in the shelter, this number would likely total at least 1,000 rabbits and hares. As Pellegrini suggested, the most parsimonious explanation for the abundance of leporids is communal hunting near the shelter. Jackrabbits weigh an average of ~2 kg, cottontails weigh an average of ~1 kg, and pygmy rabbits weigh an average of ~0.5 kg. The numbers of these animals processed in the shelter would have provided huge quantities of meat (perhaps processed for future consumption), skins for clothing, and bones for tools and ornaments. Their abundance in North Warner

TABLE 6.4. Number of Identified Specimens (NISP) of fauna

Taxa	Component				Total
	Late Archaic	Middle Archaic	Late Paleoindian	Pre-Occupation	
Lepus sp.	210	244	6,458	53	6,965
Sylvilagus sp.	562	71	4,864	71	5,568
Brachylagus idahoensis	132	17	269	38	456
Leporidae	747	181	5,977	154	7,059
Ochotona princeps	1	—	—	5	6
Marmota sp.	2	—	2	—	4
Lagurus curtatus[1]	—	—	1	—	1
Dipodomys merriami[1]	—	—	1	—	1
Neotoma cinerea[1]	—	—	6	—	6
Neotoma lepida[1]	—	—	1	—	1
Perognathus longimembris[1]	—	—	1	—	1
Peromyscus[1]	—	—	2	—	2
Rodentia	118	11	187	69	385
Bubo virginianus[1]	—	—	1	—	1
Aves	34	—	18	79	131
Chiroptera[2]	—	—	—	—	—
rodent/leporid-sized mammals	2,954	1,369	41,377	965	46,665
badger/small artiodactyl-sized mammals	687	129	3,118	790	4,724
elk/bison-sized mammals	4	3	16	—	23
Bison bison	—	—	2	—	2
Ovis canadensis	—	—	2	—	2
cf. *Cervus canadensis*	—	—	1	—	1
Ovis/Odocoileus	—	—	1	—	1
Lynx rufus	1	—	10	—	11
Canis latrans	1	—	4	—	5
Canis lupus	—	—	1	—	1
Vulpes macrotis	—	—	1	—	1
cf. *Urocyon/Vulpes*	—	—	1	—	1
Spilogale gracilis	—	—	1	—	1
Taxidea taxus	5		5	1	11
Total	5,458	2,025	62,328	2,225	72,036

[1] Pellegrini (2014: Table 4.1).
[2] Bats were present in all four components but were not counted.

Valley may have supported relatively high human population levels, at least periodically, as the early Holocene drew to a close. The abundance of rabbits and hares in the late Holocene strata suggests that this was also the case later in time.

Early Holocene leporids include cottontails, jackrabbits, and pygmy rabbits, which tell us something about local conditions at that time. Cottontails generally prefer cooler and wetter habitats than black-tailed jackrabbits, and pygmy rabbits inhabit mature stands of sagebrush. The Stratum V sample is marked by a 54:46 ratio of hares to cottontails and contains at least 55 pygmy rabbits (see Table 6.5). This suggests relatively cool and moist conditions near the shelter between ~9775 and 8875 cal BP, and perhaps a few centuries later, when people discarded the bones. Two additional lines of

TABLE 6.5. Minimum Number of Elements (MNE) and Minimum Number of Individuals (MNI) of the leporids from the Late Paleoindian component in Stratum V

Leporid	Tibia Diaphysis MNE (MNI)	Proximal Mandible MNE (MNI)	MNI
Lepus	762 (381)	745 (373)	381
Sylvilagus	648 (324)	566 (283)	324
Brachylagus	—	110 (55)	55
Total leporids	1,410	1,421	760

evidence support this possibility. First, Pellegrini identified more bushy-tailed woodrats (*Neotoma cinerea*), which prefer cooler conditions than desert woodrats (*Neotoma lepida*), which prefer warmer conditions, in his early Holocene sample. Second, the ratios of hares to

FIGURE 6.1. Leporid long-bone diaphysis cylinders from LSP-1: (1–4) *Brachylagus* tibiae; (5–7) *Sylvilagus* tibiae; (8–10) *Lepus* tibiae; (11–13) *Sylvilagus* femora cylinders; (14–16) *Lepus* femora cylinders; (17–18) *Sylvilagus* humeri; and (19–20) *Lepus* humeri.

cottontails and pygmy rabbits in LSP-1's pre-occupation terminal Pleistocene and initial early Holocene deposits (Strata VIII–X)—a time that we know with some certainty was relatively cool and moist—are similar to those from the cultural Stratum V (43:57 hares to cottontails and an NISP of 38 for pygmy rabbits; see Table 6.4). Together, these data suggest some continuity in local conditions between the terminal Pleistocene and early Holocene. It is important to note that while we believe this was the case, the presence of five pika mandibles in the pre-occupation strata and none in Stratum V does suggest that conditions were even cooler and moister before ~9775 cal BP.

Pellegrini's work showed that 10 different taxa exhibited cutmarks. Cutmarks displayed parallel V-shaped

features on bone, often with shallower cutmarks paralleling deeper cuts. Some cutmarks exhibited feathering, interpreted as being produced by cortex on the stone tool scraping the bone when a cut is made (Hockett and Jenkins 2013). In Pellegrini's analysis of ~9,500 bones, *Lepus* tibiae (*n*=92) and femora (*n*=66) had the highest frequency of cutmarks; metapodials, radii, humeri, and ulnae all exhibited lower frequencies. He also observed this trend in his *Sylvilagus* sample, with tibiae (*n*=42) and femora (*n*=46) also exhibiting the highest frequency of cutmarks and metapodials, radii, humeri, and ulnae exhibiting lower frequencies.

Second, femora, tibiae, and humeri diaphysis cylinders are abundant in all three components (Figure 6.1). While raptors can produce this pattern (Hockett 1991),

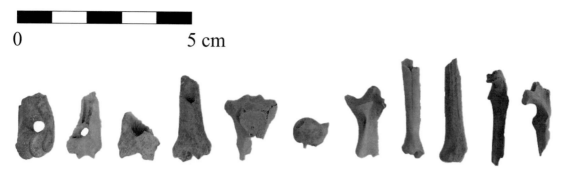

FIGURE 6.2. *Lepus* long-bone ends from LSP-1. All specimens were recovered from a single 5-cm level (Level 23) from Stratum V (Paleoindian) in Unit N107E98. Left to right: two distal humeri; two distal tibiae; proximal tibia; proximal femur; proximal scapula; proximal radius; distal radius; and two proximal ulnae.

it is uncommon compared to systematic marrow extraction by people documented in numerous clearly cultural contexts at sites across the Great Basin (see Hockett 1994, 1998, 2015; Schmitt and Lupo 2005). People created the cylinders by snapping, biting, or chewing off the ends of leporid long bones (Figure 6.2).

Third, leporid carcass processing created thousands of metapodial cylinders (Figure 6.3). Snapping the ends from leporid metapodials and using them as bone beads was common in the Great Basin (e.g., Hattori 1982), and we identified several such beads in our sample (see Chapter 10). We recognized them because they are polished, cutmarked, or both. Most leporid metapodial cylinders from LSP-1 are neither polished nor cutmarked. Whether people created those cylinders with the intention of stringing them onto necklaces or if they represent actual beads is unknown. Leporid metapodial beads lacking polish and/or cutmarks are known from some sites near Winnemucca Lake in western Nevada (Hattori 1982), so it is possible that some of the metapodial cylinders in our sample were strung onto necklaces at some point—or were intended to be.

Fourth, the ratios of appendicular-to-axial skeletal elements are consistent between the cultural components (Table 6.6). Axial skeletal elements are present in low frequencies in all three cultural components as well as in the preoccupation terminal Pleistocene deposits. Yet whereas the vertebral columns, represented by numbers of sacrae present in Table 6.6, are low throughout the shelter's deposits, cranial elements (primarily represented by mandibles and maxillae) are far more common in the cultural deposits than in the pre-occupation terminal Pleistocene deposits. These data again support the argument presented in this chapter that not only were leporids the preferred quarry near LSP-1, but the pattern of leporid carcass processing also remained consistent across time: people discarded the crania and limb bones and ground up the ribs and vertebrae and/or carried the bodies elsewhere for later consumption. Ethno-

graphically, the Northern Paiute sometimes pulverized dried rabbit carcasses—bones and all—for consumption (Gilmore 1953; Wheat 1967). Leporid fur and protein have also been noted on groundstone from a few archaeological contexts in the American West (Herzog and Lawlor 2016; Padilla 2017).

Smaller numbers of large and small artiodactyl bones are also present in the early Holocene fauna; taxa include bison, elk, mountain sheep, and mule deer. Bison remains have been recovered from other early Holocene contexts in the northwestern Great Basin, including the Black Rock Desert, the Connley Caves, Catlow Cave, Cougar Mountain Cave, and possibly Dirty Shame Rockshelter, Hanging Rock Shelter, and Fort Rock Cave. However, they were likely never common (Grayson 2011 and references therein). Elk remains have also been recovered at a few of those sites, although their early Holocene distribution is less well understood than that of bison (Grayson 2011). Several carnivores and mustelids are also present in the early Holocene fauna; these may have been hunted or trapped and brought into LSP-1.

The Middle Archaic Component

Following a terminal early Holocene florescence, groups all but abandoned LSP-1 and, more broadly, North Warner Valley (see Chapter 13). A few radiocarbon dates suggest that a very brief occupation occurred 8200–8000 cal BP, but, given the lack of Northern Side-notched points, we think that occupation more likely reflects the end of Late Paleoindian use of LSP-1—at least in terms of the dominant diagnostic artifact types. People did not return to the shelter until 4500 cal BP by which time they had adopted Middle Archaic projectile point types. Essentially, there is no recognizable Early Archaic component (8000–5750 cal BP) at LSP-1. The disappearance of Lake Warner and overall environmental deterioration in North Warner Valley were likely both contributing factors.

FIGURE 6.3. *Lepus* metapodial cylinders from Stratum V (Late Paleoindian) in Unit N107E98.
The cylinders do not show polishing or cutmarks but could have been intended for use as beads
(bone-bead blanks), fell from broken necklaces, or perhaps had bone marrow sucked from them.

Many of the patterns that we identified in the fauna from the Late Paleoindian component are present in the Middle Archaic component, although as we noted earlier rabbits and hares are slightly less abundant, proportionately speaking, and species diversity is somewhat lower. Interestingly, the ratio of hare (NISP=244) to cottontail (NISP=71) bones (77:23) is not complementary with the generally accepted date of 5000 cal BP for the onset of cooler and wetter conditions. Additionally, pygmy rabbit bones (NISP=17) are nearly absent. These trends are more suggestive of warmer and drier conditions.

There are at least two possible explanations for this incongruence: (1) the restructuring of the habitat and concomitant biogeography of North Warner Valley from the middle to late Holocene occurred somewhat later than other microhabitats in the region; or (2) groups altered their hunting strategies and started to take leporids individually rather than through communal drives; people preferentially took larger jackrabbits over smaller cottontails and pygmy rabbits. Regardless of how they were taken, based on the consistent body part representations, Middle Archaic groups appear to have processed leporid carcasses in a manner similar to that employed by earlier groups.

Middle Archaic groups also occasionally brought larger game into the shelter, as evidenced by the presence of a few elk or bison bones and some small artiodactyl-sized bone fragments. Pellegrini (2014) describes a large

TABLE 6.6. NISP for axial and appendicular leporid elements by component

Component	Element	*Lepus*	*Sylvilagus*	*Brachylagus*	Total
Late Archaic	Axial (26.5%)	41	142	62	245
	head	41	142	61	244
	sacrum	—	—	1	1
	Appendicular (73.5%)	164	437	80	681
	innominate	8	21	2	31
	femur	21	49	1	71
	tibia	37	166	43	246
	foot	20	19	3	42
	scapula	9	73	17	99
	humerus	38	50	9	97
	ulna	9	21	1	31
	radius	22	38	4	64
	Total	205	579	142	926
Middle Archaic	Axial (26.4%)	21	18	3	42
	head	21	18	3	42
	sacrum	—	—	—	—
	Appendicular (73.6%)	60	48	9	117
	innominate	1	3	—	4
	femur	10	4	2	16
	tibia	10	13	4	27
	foot	7	1	—	8
	scapula	7	3	1	11
	humerus	13	7	2	22
	ulna	3	3	—	6
	radius	9	14	—	23
	Total	81	66	12	159
Late Paleoindian	Axial (22.0%)	567	625	62	1,254
	head	565	625	62	1,252
	sacrum	2	—	—	2
	Appendicular (78.0%)	2,442	1,940	58	4,440
	innominate	111	129	1	241
	femur	353	229	3	585
	tibia	503	476	32	1,011
	foot	135	111	3	249
	scapula	223	216	1	440
	humerus	472	359	14	845
	ulna	201	141	—	342
	radius	444	279	4	727
	Total	3,009	2,565	120	5,694
Pre-Occupation	Axial (6.5%)	—	5	1	6
	head	—	5	1	6
	sacrum	—	—	—	—
	Appendicular (93.5%)	19	40	27	86
	innominate	0	4	1	5
	femur	2	7	—	9
	tibia	6	12	5	23
	foot	3	—	10	13
	scapula	3	—	1	4
	humerus	1	9	3	13
	ulna	2	6	3	11
	radius	2	2	4	8
	Total	19	45	28	92

bone flake from a bison femur that may have been used as a tool, and Smith et al. (2014) reported a radiocarbon date of 4010±25 ^{14}C BP (4525–4420 cal BP) obtained on a second bison femur fragment (see Table 4.2). Bison bones have been reported at a handful of other sites dating to around that time, including Nightfire Island, King's Dog, and the Connley Caves, but again, they were probably never common in the region (Grayson 2011). There are no identified carnivore remains in the Middle Archaic faunal sample.

The Late Archaic Component

The NISP counts for the different leporid taxa in the Late Archaic component indicate a relatively cool and moist climate between 2000 and 1000 cal BP. Cottontails (NISP=562) greatly outnumber jackrabbits (NISP=210), and pygmy rabbits are relatively common (NISP=132). The combination of hares, cottontails, and pygmy rabbits present in relatively large numbers—especially considering the amount of Late Archaic deposits destroyed by looters—suggests that communal rabbit drives may have remained the preferred leporid collection method in North Warner Valley. Leporid body-part representation in the Late Archaic sample is remarkably consistent with that of the Late Paleoindian and Middle Archaic samples, which again suggests some continuity in how groups processed rabbits and hares. Bison and/or elk remains are also present in very low numbers, as are the bones of smaller artiodactyls. Bison have been recovered from a few late Holocene contexts in the northern Great Basin, although they generally postdate 600 cal BP (Grayson 2011). By that time, LSP-1 had been abandoned for 300 years. Little is known about the distribution of elk in Oregon during Late Archaic times (Grayson 2011), although they occur in some of the mountain ranges near Warner Valley today. Finally, at least one lynx and one coyote are represented in the Late Archaic sample.

CONCLUDING REMARKS

LSP-1 is the third site in the Great Basin with compelling evidence for early Holocene communal rabbit drives. It joins 35Lk1881 and 35Lk2076, two open-air sites in the Fort Rock Basin that Oetting (1994a) interpreted as places where groups roasted large numbers of rabbits and hares collected via drives. Radiocarbon dates from those sites place them during the same general period as the first two pulses of occupation at LSP-1 (Oetting 1994a; Rosencrance 2019). At 35Lk1881, Oetting (1994a) reported ~10,000 leporid bones, most of which were hares. Stratum V in LSP-1 contained well over 20,000 leporid bones that we estimate represent ~1,000 animals. While traditional models of Paleoindian subsistence have emphasized the importance of big game hunting, LSP-1 and other recently excavated sites (e.g., Paisley Caves, Bonneville Estates Rockshelter) clearly show that small game was a critical component of early diets in the Great Basin (Blong et al. 2020; Hockett 2007; Hockett et al. 2017), just as they were during later periods including ethnographic times. Though far smaller than the Late Paleoindian sample, the samples of analyzed fauna from the Middle and Late Archaic components provide equally important clues about human subsistence during those periods. In the next few chapters, we discuss the stone tools that people used to hunt and process the small and large game remains found in LSP-1.

Flaked Stone Artifacts

Geoffrey M. Smith, Richard L. Rosencrance, and Daniel O. Stueber

We turn now to the flaked stone artifacts from LSP-1, focusing on where people obtained toolstone and the tool production and maintenance activities that they caried out at the site. We recovered 687 flaked stone tools and ~28,000 pieces of debitage from ~26 m³ of excavated deposits (Tables 7.1 and 7.2) and classified these artifacts using the typologies described below. While the destruction of much of the shelter's middle and late Holocene deposits by looters prevents us from comparing the absolute frequencies of tools and debitage among cultural components, their proportions allow us to consider how people's use of LSP-1 changed over time.

METHODS

We assigned tools recovered in situ and tools and flakes recovered from sifted sediment excavated in 5-cm levels to the shelter's Late Paleoindian, Middle Archaic, and Late Archaic components. Some tools and debitage came from mixed deposits (e.g., levels with conflicting radiocarbon dates, looters' backdirt, wall collapse and floor clean-up), which we report but do not discuss in detail or include in our comparisons. A few tools and flakes came from excavated levels deep in the deposits. We concluded they do not represent a pre-9775 cal BP occupation and suspect that those artifacts moved down from the lowest cultural levels. Thus, we assigned them to the Late Paleoindian component.

Because there is no standard typology based on objective criteria for early Holocene stemmed or foliate points, we instead used key attributes (e.g., edge grinding, basal facets, remnant platforms, collateral flaking,

general morphology) to identify them (Beck and Jones 2009, 2015; Ozbun and Fagan 2010). Stueber examined the stemmed and foliate points for macroscopic and microscopic use-wear to determine whether they served as projectiles or knives. We used the Monitor Valley Key to classify dart and arrow points, recognizing that their age ranges are not necessarily the same in the northern Great Basin as in the central Great Basin where Thomas (1981) developed the key. Radiocarbon dates from the shelter provide site-specific age ranges for the points, while regional chronologies help us place the points into a broader context (King 2016a; T. Largaespada 2006; Oetting 1994b; Rosencrance 2019).

We classified bifaces using four stages (2–5) based on the degree to which they were completed (see Andrefsky 2005), recognizing that people sometimes used bifaces as tools or cores at different stages along the reduction sequence. Many Stage 5 bifaces are likely projectile point fragments that lack notches and other defining attributes. *Biface fragments* are pieces that we did not assign to particular stages. We classified breaks on bifaces using eight categories: (1) *bipolar*; (2) *manufacture bending*; (3) *use bending*; (4) *perverse*; (5) *tranchet removal*; (6) *overshot removal*; (7) *impact burination*; and (8) *thermal*.

We classified flake tools using a typology based on the location and type of retouch. We recognize that terms such as *scraper, notch, drill,* and *graver* imply that we know the activities for which tools were used and, except for Van der Voort's analysis of some early Holocene flake tools (see Chapter 8), did not conduct a use-wear study of the flake tools. With that caveat in mind, our

TABLE 7.1. Flaked stone tool and debitage counts, percentages, and densities

Artifact Type and Raw Material	Component				Total
	Late Archaic	Middle Archaic	Late Paleoindian[1]	Mixed Deposits/ No Provenience	
Tools[2]					
obsidian	64	49	417	81	611
CCS[3]	1	4	17	2	24
FGV[4]	6	5	36	5	52
Debitage[5]					
obsidian	1,852	3,494	18,656	2,322	26,324
CCS	31	50	313	23	417
FGV	112	190	864	58	1,224
Volume of Deposits (m³)	3.2	1.9	11.9	2.4	25.8[6]
Tools/m³	22.2	30.5	39.5	36.7	—
Flakes/m³	623.4	1,965.3	1,705.6	1,001.3	—

[1] Includes four tools and 464 flakes from 6.4 m³ of excavated noncultural deposits (0.63 tools/m³ and 72.5 flakes/m³). We assume that these artifacts migrated downward from the lowest Late Paleoindian levels.

[2] Due to low expected frequencies for CCS and FGV tools, we combined those categories to compare them to obsidian. There is no significant difference in the frequencies of obsidian and other raw materials in the tools from different periods ($\chi^2 = 1.13$, $df = 2$, $p = .568$).

[3] Cryptocrystalline silicate.

[4] Fine-grained volcanic.

[5] There are significantly more FGV flakes in the Late Archaic sample than expected by chance. ($\chi^2 = 10.46$, $df = 4$, $p = .033$).

[6] Total includes 6.4 m³ of non-cultural deposits.

flake tool typology is standard and should convey the types of implements present.

Scrapers are flakes that possess steep and regular retouched edges sometimes featuring more than one generation of flake scars; *end scrapers* are flakes with retouched distal margins; and *side scrapers* are flakes with one or more retouched lateral margins. *Utilized flakes* are flakes that have minimal and sometimes discontinuous retouch along one or more margins; such retouch is typically a single generation of small flake scars. *Notches* are flakes with one or more concavities along their edges produced via margin retouch. *Drills* and *gravers* are unifacial, bifacial, and sometimes trifacial tools that possess one or more protruding and shaped bits. We distinguished these types based on the size and cross sections of the bits. *Choppers* are very large flakes possessing one or more unifacially or bifacially retouched margins. When possible, we noted the types of flakes on which flake tools are made. Finally, *cores* are nodules with one or more flake removals that presumably served as sources of blanks for tools. We measured the maximum linear dimension of cores and noted whether they retained cortex.

We analyzed all flakes from LSP-1, collecting both quantitative (e.g., weight, maximum linear dimension) and qualitative (e.g., platform type) data. We separated them into four size categories: (1) <¼ in; (2) ¼–½ in; (3) ½–1 in; and (4) >1 in. We also weighed each flake to the nearest 0.1 g (we recorded very small flakes weighing <0.1 g as 0.1 g). For flakes <⅛ in recovered from sifted sediment, we counted them, weighed them together, and calculated an average flake weight for each level. We recorded the presence/absence of cortex for each flake. Finally, we recorded each flake's striking platform morphology using four categories: (1) *cortical* (any cortex present); (2) *simple* (flat); (3) *complex* (faceted); and (4) *missing*.

Flake size (maximum linear dimension and weight) allows us to consider the basic kinds of reduction activities (e.g., tool production vs. tool maintenance) that people carried out. Platform types and the presence/absence of cortex also allow us to understand the types of tools that people produced and modified. We adopted a simplified version of the debitage typology that Elston (2005) employed for Camels Back Cave, Utah. We recognized seven debitage types. *Shatter* is angular pieces of debitage with no discernable ventral and dorsal surfaces that typically lack platforms. *Early core reduction flakes* possess cortical platforms. *Late core reduction flakes* possess simple platforms with or without cortex on the ventral surface (but not on the platform). *Biface thinning flakes* lack cortex and possess complex platforms. *Pressure flakes* are small, contain complex platforms, and are parallel sided to slightly contracting. Sometimes they retain a "propeller-like twist" (Elston 2005:100). *Very small flakes* are small flakes that lack

TABLE 7.2. Flaked stone tools

| Tool Type[1] | Component | | | | |
	Late Archaic	Middle Archaic	Late Paleoindian	Mixed Deposits/ No Provenience	Total
biface (by stage)					
2	3	1	25	3	32
3	3	4	25	8	40
4	3	1	21	6	31
5	3	3	26	7	39
fragment	3	5	45	3	56
projectile point	12	16	41	22	91
crescent	—	—	1	—	1
core	5	4	36	5	50
scraper	3	3	37	4	47
graver	2	—	5	1	8
notch	—	—	1	—	1
drill	—	—	4	1	5
chopper	1	—	—	1	2
utilized flake	33	21	203	27	284
Total	71	58	470	88	687

[1] The proportions of bifaces, flake tools, and cores do not vary significantly between the three components ($\chi^2=3.68$, $df=4$, $p=.451$).

sufficient characteristics to be called pressure flakes. Finally, *flake fragments* are flakes lacking platforms.

LITHIC RAW MATERIALS

Obsidian comprises 89 percent of the flaked stone tool assemblage and 94 percent of the debitage assemblage. Pebbles of glassy black Buck Spring obsidian are embedded within the shelter's walls and ceiling. They are small and contain vugs and other imperfections, rendering them generally unsuitable for larger tool production but suitable as sources of flake blanks for smaller tools. Although we did not source any debitage, we suspect that Buck Spring obsidian comprises the bulk of the flakes. Mahogany, opaque gray, and opaque black obsidian are also represented among the tools and debitage, as are a variety of CCS and FGV colors (cryptocrystalline silicate and fine-grained volcanic). Tan is the most common CCS color, with nine of 23 CCS tools made from that material. A few tools and flakes are also made from white, yellow, orange, red, and pink CCS. The sources of these materials are generally unknown, although the tan chert may be from the Eagle's Nest source in the Malheur Basin (Lyons et al. 2003). Tools and flakes made from FGV are generally gray. Some of these are made from Warner Valley FGV, with one source ~20 km southwest of LSP-1. Low cell counts preclude a chi-square comparison of tools made of obsidian, CCS, and FGV across components, but when CCS and FGV are combined and compared to obsidian the proportions of raw materials do not differ ($\chi^2=1.13$, $df=2$, $p=.568$). The proportions of raw materials do differ significantly in the debitage assemblage ($\chi^2=10.46$, $df=4$, $p=.033$), and FGV flakes are more common in the Late Archaic component than the Middle Archaic and Late Paleoindian components.

We submitted 166 obsidian and FGV tools and cores to the Northwest Research Obsidian Studies Laboratory for geochemical characterization (Table 7.3). One hundred fifty-one artifacts are made of 21 known obsidian and five known FGV types. Fifteen additional artifacts are made of 12 obsidian and FGV types whose source locations are unknown. Known sources of these materials range between 1 and 220 km from LSP-1 and are mostly located in southeastern and central Oregon, with a few also located in northwestern Nevada and northeastern California (Figure 7.1). Local Buck Spring ($n=63$; 38 percent) and nearby Beatys Butte obsidian ($n=24$; 14 percent) are the most common material types. Other obsidian and FGV types each comprise less than 5 percent of the sample.

FLAKED STONE TOOLS

Projectile Points

We recovered 91 projectile points and point fragments, 48 of which we assigned to five different series (Table 7.4). Table 7.5 shows the stratigraphic distribution of typed specimens.

TABLE 7.3. Source assignments for obsidian and FGV tools

Geochemical Type	Distance (km)	Late Archaic				Middle Archaic				Late Paleoindian				Total
		PPT	BIF	FLT	COR	PPT	BIF	FLT	COR	PPT	BIF	FLT	COR	
Alturas FGV	166	—	—	—	—	—	—	—	—	1	—	—	—	1
Badger Creek	119	—	—	—	—	—	—	—	—	—	1	—	—	1
Bald Butte	50	—	—	—	—	—	—	—	—	1	2	—	—	3
Beatys Butte	33	3	3	—	—	5	2	—	—	2	8	1	—	24
Big Stick	48	—	—	—	—	—	—	—	—	1	5	—	—	6
Buck Mountain	123	—	—	—	—	2	—	—	—	—	1	—	—	3
Buck Spring	1	1	1	3	5	4	2	4	3	1	11	6	22	63
Curtis Creek	119	—	—	—	—	—	—	—	—	—	1	—	—	1
Delintment Lake	79	—	—	—	—	—	—	—	—	—	—	—	1	1
Double O FGV	48	—	—	—	—	—	—	—	—	2	—	—	—	2
Glass Buttes (all varieties)	76	—	—	—	—	—	—	—	—	—	1	1	—	2
Horse Mountain	57	1	—	—	—	—	—	—	—	1	5	—	—	7
Hurley Spring	180	—	1	—	—	—	—	—	—	—	—	—	—	1
McComb Butte	55	—	—	—	—	—	—	—	—	1	2	—	—	3
Massacre Lake/ Guano Valley	64	—	—	—	—	—	—	—	—	2	1	—	—	3
Mosquito Lake	110	—	—	—	—	—	—	—	—	1	—	—	—	1
Paradise Valley	220	—	—	—	—	—	—	—	—	1	—	—	—	1
Silver Lake/ Sycan Marsh	98	—	—	—	—	—	—	—	—	1	—	—	—	1
Sugar Hill	128	—	—	—	—	—	—	—	—	—	2	—	—	2
Surveyor Spring	93	—	—	—	—	—	—	—	—	—	—	—	1	1
Tank Creek	48	1	—	—	—	1	1	—	—	2	2	1	—	8
Tucker Hill	115	—	—	—	—	—	—	—	—	1	—	—	—	1
Venator FGV	163	—	—	—	—	—	—	—	—	1	—	—	—	1
Wagontire	58	1	—	—	—	1	—	—	—	—	1	—	—	3
Warner Valley FGV	20	—	—	1	—	—	1	2	—	1	3	1	—	9
Yreka Butte	106	—	—	—	—	—	—	—	—	—	1	—	—	1
unknown obsidian	?	—	—	—	—	—	—	—	—	1	1	—	—	2
unknown obsidian 1	?	1	—	—	—	—	—	—	—	—	—	—	—	1
unknown obsidian A	?	—	—	—	—	—	—	—	—	—	1	—	—	1
unknown obsidian B	?	—	—	—	—	1	—	—	—	—	—	—	—	1
unknown obsidian C	?	—	—	—	—	—	—	—	—	—	—	1	—	1
unknown obsidian D	?	—	—	—	—	—	—	—	—	—	—	1	—	1
unknown obsidian E	?	—	—	—	—	—	—	—	—	—	1	—	—	1
unknown FGV	?	—	—	1	—	—	—	—	—	—	1	—	—	2
unknown FGV 1	?	—	1	—	—	—	—	—	—	—	—	—	—	1
unknown FGV 2	?	—	1	—	—	—	—	—	—	—	—	—	—	1
unknown FGV 3	?	—	1	—	—	—	—	—	—	—	1	1	—	3
Malheur Lake unknown FGV	?	—	—	—	—	—	—	—	—	—	1	—	—	1
Total		8	8	5	5	14	6	6	3	21	53	13	24	166
Mean PPT Transport (km)		37.6				40.1				74.5				
Average # of Sources (PPT)		6.0				4.5				7.4				

Note: PPT=projectile point; BIF=biface; FLT=flake tool; COR=core.

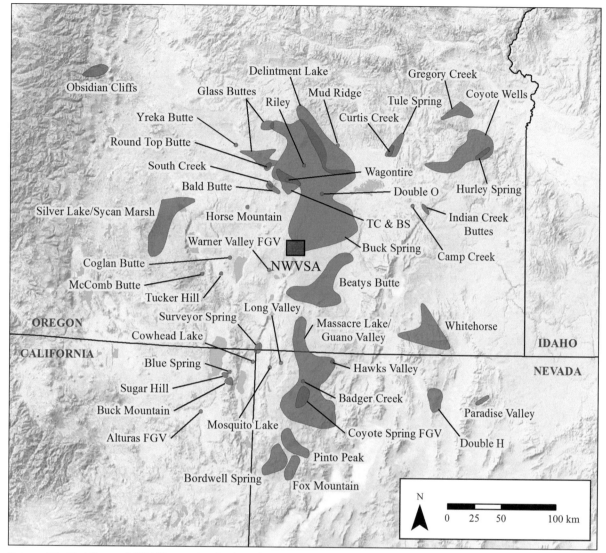

FIGURE 7.1. Obsidian and FGV (fine-grained volcanic) sources represented at LSP-1 and other North Warner Valley sites (see Chapter 13). Note: TC & BS = Tank Creek and Big Stick.

Western Stemmed Tradition and Foliate Points

Stemmed and foliate points are common in the northern Great Basin, and stemmed points are the oldest diagnostic artifacts in Oregon (Jenkins et al. 2012, 2013). Researchers recognize numerous subtypes such as Haskett, Cougar Mountain, Parman, and Windust (Beck and Jones 2009), but the lack of a standardized typology has traditionally limited their utility as fine-grained index fossils. Rosencrance (2019) recently redated several WST components in the Intermountain West and demonstrated that Haskett points date to the Younger Dryas, whereas Parman, Windust, and Cougar Mountain points mostly date to the early Holocene. At LSP-1, we recovered one complete and one broken Parman point (artifacts 791 and 1074; Figure 7.2) as well as two Windust points (artifacts 975 and 2291; see Figure 7.2) from deep in Stratum V. Nine other WST point frag-

ments are not complete enough to assign to subtypes, though they also came from Stratum V or Stratum VI. Based on use-wear, the stemmed points served as both knives and projectile tips (Table S6).

We recovered four foliate points from Strata IV (*n*=1), V (*n*=2), and VI (*n*=1) (Figure 7.3). Foliate points are poor time-markers (Oetting 1994b; Smith et al. 2012), but the deposits from which we recovered them primarily date to the terminal early Holocene. They co-occur with stemmed points in Strata V and VI, an association that Connolly and Jenkins (1999) reported for the roughly contemporary pre-Mazama components 1 and 2 at the Paulina Lake Site (35Ds34). Use-wear on the foliate points is limited and equivocal regarding their use.

Finally, we recovered four lanceolate points from Stratum V that we could not confidently assign to either the WST or foliate types (see Figure 7.3). In some cases,

TABLE 7.4. Typed projectile points

Acc. Art No.	Stratum	Attribute[1]											Material	Type[5]
		L_T	L_A	W_B	W_M	W_N	Thi.	PSA	DSA	NO	Wt.	BIR		
74	V/VI	55.3	54.3	15.5	17.4	n/a	7.1	n/a	n/a	n/a	7.4	.98	Venator FGV	WST
75	V/VI	—	—	—	20.8	n/a	8.9	n/a	n/a	n/a	—	—	Bald Butte OBS	FOL
118	V/VI	—	—	17.2	—	12.3	3.7	120	—	—	—	—	Beatys Butte OBS	ECN?
184	IV	—	—	20.7	—	14.2	5.0	110	—	—	—	—	unknown B OBS	ECN?
241	V	—	—	—	17.0	n/a	6.4	n/a	n/a	n/a	—	—	ML/GV[3] OBS	FOL/WST
303	IV	42.6	41.4	14.8	24.0	8.7	4.4	125	110	—15	3.2	.97	Tank Creek OBS	ECN
304	IV/V	52.8	52.8	8.4	14.2	n/a	7.8	n/a	n/a	n/a	4.9	1.0	McComb Butte OBS	FOL
368	II	—	—	—	14.4	7.0	3.4	—	160	—	—	—	Beatys Butte OBS	RG
428	IV	—	—	—	—	12.3	4.9	110	—	—	—	—	Beatys Butte OBS	EE
791	VI	90.9	90.9	14.2	22.7	14.2	7.6	90	210	120	12.6	1.0	Big Stick OBS	WST
882	LB[2]	—	—	—	23.4	14.1	4.9	120	160	40	—	—	Beatys Butte OBS	ES
885	LB[2]	21.0	21.0	—	10.7	4.5	2.2	120	160	40	.4	1.0	Wagontire OBS	RG
888	LB[2]	—	—	7.8	—	6.4	2.6	120	130	10	.3	—	Beatys Butte OBS	RG
889	LB[2]	30.7	30.7	8.9	16.0	7.2	4.0	110	—	—	—	1.0	unknown 1 OBS	RG
890	LB[2]	—	—	—	16.9	12.0	6.3	110	190	80	—	—	Buck Spring OBS	ECN
929	LB[2]	27.7	25.3	18.2	18.4	14.3	4.8	140	180	40	1.9	.91	Buck Mountain OBS	EE
963	V	39.2	39.2	9.0	14.5	n/a	6.8	n/a	n/a	n/a	4.0	1.0	CCS	WST
975	V	27.3	24.4	19.1	20.6	18.5	5.7	90	255	165	3.3	.89	Beatys Butte OBS	WST
998	V	—	—	22.2	—	17.6	8.1	110	230	120	—	—	ML/GV[3] OBS	SIDE-REM
999	V	—	—	—	18.2	—	7.0	n/a	n/a	n/a	—	—	SL/SM[4] OBS	FOL/WST
1074	V	—	—	9.2	—	16.4	6.5	80	210	130	—	—	Buck Spring OBS	WST
1093	V	44.7	43.6	10.7	18.3	n/a	7.9	n/a	n/a	n/a	5.4	.98	Beatys Butte OBS	FOL/WST
1135	V	51.9	51.9	12.1	17.6	n/a	8.8	n/a	n/a	n/a	6.6	1.0	Tank Creek OBS	FOL/WST
1239	V	—	—	14.3	22.7	n/a	7.5	n/a	n/a	n/a	—	—	Tank Creek OBS	WST
1309/1528	V	58.6	n/a	n/a	21.6	n/a	6.9	n/a	n/a	n/a	—	n/a	CCS	CRES
1563	V	—	—	15.4	—	—	6.6	—	—	n/a	—	—	Tucker Hill OBS	WST
1704	V	63.4	63.4	11.4	22.2	n/a	10.0	n/a	n/a	n/a	15.6	1.0	Warner Valley FGV	FOL
1778	V	44.5	43.6	12.7	17.6	n/a	8.4	n/a	n/a	n/a	6.7	.98	unknown OBS	WST
1779	V	55.3	55.3	7.7	18.1	n/a	7.6	n/a	n/a	n/a	7.1	1.0	Double O FGV	FOL
1780	V	—	—	—	20.4	11.2	7.2	n/a	n/a	n/a	—	—	Horse Mountain OBS	WST
2057	V	—	—	—	22.0	n/a	9.7	n/a	n/a	n/a	—	—	Alturas FGV	WST
2139	V	—	—	21.7	—	14.5	8.0	130	190	60	—	—	Mosquito Lake OBS	SIDE-REM
2170	V/VII	—	—	—	—	12.0	4.0	115	—	—	—	—	Beatys Butte OBS	ECN?

#[1]		LT	LA	WB	WM	WN	Thi	PSA	DSA	NO	BIR	Wt	Site	Type[5]
2196	IV	28.7	—	—	21.3	10.5	4.1	145	160	15	—	—	Buck Spring OBS	ES
2198	IV	—	40.3	14.0	26.4	11.1	4.8	115	125	10	3.3	.94	Beatys Butte OBS	ECN
2291	V	50.1	49.3	19.2	21.6	19.3	6.9	85	230	145	6.6	.98	Paradise Valley OBS	WST
2299	V	51.2	51.2	12.5	16.9	n/a	6.4	n/a	n/a	n/a	6.4	1.0	Double O FGV	WST
2369	IV	—	—	—	22.1	13.0	5.4	130	140	10	5.3	—	OBS	ES
2779	IV	38.1	33.7	22.0	30.6	12.0	6.8	145	150	5	4.2	.88	Buck Spring OBS	EE
2793	IV	—	—	19.8	—	13.7	5.5	110	—	—	—	—	Wagontire OBS	ECN?
2949	II	—	—	7.8	—	6.4	—	115	150	45	—	—	Tank Creek OBS	RG
2969	IV	45.5	42.1	—	21.6	9.8	5.5	120	150	30	—	.93	Horse Mountain OBS	EE
3025	IV/V	—	—	—	12.6	5.3	2.3	—	140	—	.5	—	Buck Spring OBS	RG
3132	II	—	—	—	12.7	6.0	2.5	—	150	—	—	—	OBS	RG?
3144	II	13.5	13.1	8.7	11.4	6.3	2.8	125	155	30	.2	.97	OBS	RG
3177	IV	27.9	22.4	—	19.4	11.2	3.4	140	150	10	—	.80	Buck Mountain OBS	EE
3180	IV	21.1	20.0	8.8	18.1	7.7	3.3	115	160	45	.9	.95	Beatys Butte OBS	RG
3431	IV	—	—	20.6	24.9	18.9	7.6	130	160	30	—	—	Buck Spring OBS	ES

[1] LT=total length; LA=axial length; WB=basal width; WM=maximum width; WN=neck width; Thi.=thickness; PSA=proximal shoulder angle; DSA=distal shoulder angle; NO=notch opening; Wt.=weight; BIR=basal indentation ratio.
[2] LB=looters' backdirt.
[3] ML/GV=Massacre Lake/Guano Valley.
[4] SL/SM=Silver Lake/Sycan Marsh.
[5] WST=Western Stemmed Tradition; FOL=foliate; SIDE-REM=Side-removed; ECN=Elko Corner-notched; EE=Elko Eared; ES=Elko Series; RG=Rosegate; CRES=crescent.

TABLE 7.5. Stratigraphic distribution of typed projectile points

| | Point Type | | | | | | | |
Stratum	Rosegate	Elko	Foliate	Foliate/WST	WST	Crescent	Side-Removed	Total
II	4	—	—	—	—	—	—	4
IV	1	10[1]	—	—	—	—	—	11
IV/V	1	1	1	—	—	—	—	3
V	—	—	2	4	10	1	2	19
V/VI	—	1[2]	1	—	1	—	—	3
VI	—	—	—	—	1	—	—	1
V/VII	—	1[2]	—	—	—	—	—	1
Unknown	3	3	—	—	—	—	—	6
Total	9	16	4	4	12	1	2	48

[1] Includes two basal fragments tentatively typed as Elko Corner-notched points.
[2] Basal fragments tentatively typed as Elko Corner-notched points.

this was because they were broken or lacked diagnostic attributes. In other cases, they were fairly complete but nevertheless defied easy classification. Use-wear indicates that three of the points primarily served as knives, which may have played a role in their generalized design or altered their original shapes through resharpening.

Although small, the early Holocene point sample is notable for its morphological diversity: two Parman points, two Windust points, one concave base WST point, one expanding stem WST point, and three foliate points come from Strata V or VI. We also recovered two robust "side-removed" points from deep in Stratum V that do fit comfortably within either the Northern Side-notched or Pinto point categories. This considerable diversity suggests that people using a variety of projectile point styles visited LSP-1 during the terminal early Holocene. Alternatively, the shelter's terminal early Holocene deposits record the transition from various stemmed point forms to foliate and, ultimately, incipient notched points, but in a manner that is not readily apparent in their vertical distribution. In any case, people stopped using LSP-1 near the onset of the middle Holocene before Northern Side-notched points became widespread in the region (Jenkins et al. 2004a).

Twenty-one sourced WST, foliate, and indeterminate lanceolate points are made of 16 different obsidian and FGV types mostly found in Oregon's Abert-Chewaucan, Fort Rock, and Malheur Lake basins but also northeastern California and northwestern Nevada. No more than two points are made of any one material type. The two side-removed points are made of Massacre Lake/Guano Valley and Mosquito Lake obsidian, both located in northwestern Nevada. The early Holocene sample of sourced projectile points is as diverse in its source profile as it is in its morphology. Based on this fact alone and for other reasons we discuss later, we suspect that the shelter witnessed repeated visits by small groups during the early Holocene.

Dart and Arrow Points

We recovered examples of two dart point series (side-removed and Elko) and one arrow point series (Rosegate). As we indicated, the two side-removed points came from Stratum V at the same depths as WST and foliate points (see Figure 7.3).

Elko points are more abundant, and both corner-notched and eared examples mostly come from Stratum IV, dated to the late Holocene and reflecting Middle Archaic occupations (Figure 7.4). We recovered two corner-notched point bases deep in Stratum V, one (Artifact 118) at the strata V/VI interface 106–116 cmbd, the other (Artifact 2170) at the strata V/VII interface 136–141 cmbd. The former came from a level that also produced two stemmed points and one foliate point. Artifact 2170 marks the deepest projectile point recovered at the site. Both fragments are thin relative to the side-removed points. They possess basal widths and proximal shoulder angles that fall firmly within the range of Elko points. The depths and ages of the deposits from which they originated suggest that they are from the early Holocene. Most Elko points date to the late Holocene in the northern Great Basin (Oetting 1994b; Smith et al. 2013b), although a few have been recovered in initial middle Holocene contexts. Smith and colleagues (2013b) obtained a date of 7785–7670 cal BP on sinew attached to an Elko point from Elephant Mountain Cave in northwestern Nevada. Wilde (1985) recovered Elko points below Mazama tephra at Skull Creek Dunes in nearby Catlow Valley (also see Saper et al. 2020), implying that they are older than ~7700 cal BP. Finally, Saper and colleagues (2020) reported Elko points from deposits dated to ~8500 cal BP at the Connley Caves. The two LSP-1 specimens are small fragments, but their basal morphology is wholly consistent with that of Elko points. The fact that they came from an early Holocene context supports the possibility that some Elko points, or at least a corner-notched point

0   5 cm

791 (V/VI)   1074 (V)   975 (V)   2291 (V/VII)

963 (V, CCS)   1778 (V)   74 (V/VI, FGV)   2299 (V, FGV)

1563 (V)   1780 (V)   1239 (V)   2057 (V, FGV)

FIGURE 7.2. Western Stemmed Tradition points from LSP-1. Artifacts are obsidian unless otherwise noted. Roman numerals denote the strata from which artifacts were recovered.

0   5 cm

75 (V/VI)   304 (IV/V)   1074 (V)   1779 (V, CCS)

241 (V)   1093 (V)   1135 (V/VII)   999 (V)

2139 (V)   998 (V)   1309/1528 (V, CCS)

FIGURE 7.3. Foliate points (*top row*), foliate/WST points (*middle row*), and side-removed points and crescent (*bottom row*) from LSP-1. Artifacts are obsidian unless otherwise noted. Roman numerals denote the strata from which artifacts were recovered.

type that many archaeologists call Elko points, are fairly old in the northern Great Basin.

Fourteen Elko points are made of six obsidian types; nine of those (64 percent) are made of the two closest sources, Buck Spring (1 km) and Beatys Butte (33 km).

The other five points are made of obsidian from the Buck Mountain (*n*=2), Tank Creek (*n*=1), Wagontire (*n*=1), and Unknown B sources[1] located southwest and north of LSP-1.

Rosegate points are the only arrow points at LSP-1

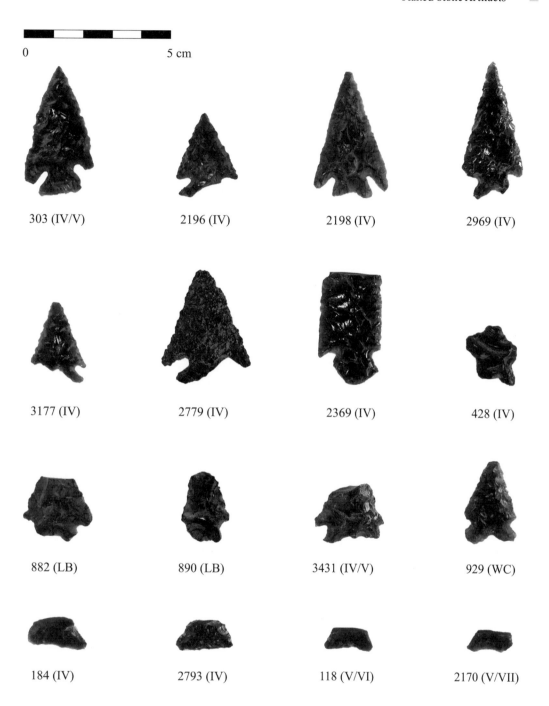

0   5 cm

303 (IV/V)   2196 (IV)   2198 (IV)   2969 (IV)

3177 (IV)   2779 (IV)   2369 (IV)   428 (IV)

882 (LB)   890 (LB)   3431 (IV/V)   929 (WC)

184 (IV)   2793 (IV)   118 (V/VI)   2170 (V/VII)

FIGURE 7.4. Elko points (*top three rows*) and corner-notched point bases tentatively typed as Elko points (*bottom row*) from LSP-1. All artifacts are obsidian. Roman numerals denote the strata from which artifacts were recovered. (LB = looters' backdirt; WC = wall cleaning).

(Figure 7.5). They may have appeared earlier and persisted longer in the northern Great Basin than other places (Delacorte 2008; Hildebrandt and King 2002; Oetting 1994b), but at LSP-1 most of them come from Stratum II, dated to 1300–900 cal BP and mark Late Archaic visits. That age range is consistent with Rosegate age ranges in the central and western Great Basin

(Thomas 1981). Sourced Rosegate points are made of Beatys Butte (*n*=3), Buck Spring (*n*=1), Horse Mountain (*n*=1), Tank Creek (*n*=1), Wagontire (*n*=1), and Unknown 1 obsidian found to the north and southeast.

The absence of Northern Side-notched, Gatecliff, Humboldt, and Desert series points at LSP-1 is telling. While the looters destroyed a sizeable portion of

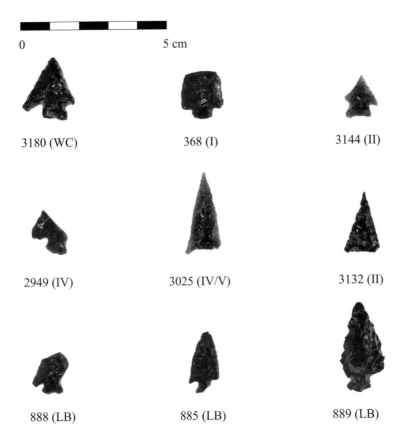

0   5 cm

3180 (WC)   368 (I)   3144 (II)

2949 (IV)   3025 (IV/V)   3132 (II)

888 (LB)   885 (LB)   889 (LB)

FIGURE 7.5. Rosegate points from LSP-1. All artifacts are obsidian. Roman numerals denote the strata from which artifacts were recovered. (LB = looters' backdirt; WC = wall cleaning).

the shelter's middle Holocene deposits, thereby potentially obliterating evidence of occupations dating to the period to which those types date, roughly half of our excavation units did contain intact middle Holocene deposits. Nor did we recover any Northern Side-notched, Gatecliff, or Humboldt points from them. As noted in Chapter 4, the absence of these points suggests that LSP-1 was largely abandoned during the middle Holocene—a possibility that is supported by the paucity of radiocarbon dates from that period. Similarly, the absence of Desert Series points in LSP-1 corresponds to a lack of Terminal Prehistoric dates from the shelter, suggesting that use of the site waned after 900 cal BP. These hiatuses are both evident in the survey data we present in Chapter 13.

The LSP-1 Crescent

Crescents occur at many WST surface sites including some in North Warner Valley (see Chapter 13). They are most often associated with relict wetlands (Sanchez et al. 2017). In 2012, we recovered most of a gray CCS crescent 87 cmbd in Stratum V (see Figure 7.3). Later

that summer, we found the rest of it ~111–116 cmbd in an adjacent excavation unit. Charcoal and bone from around the larger fragment returned a range of early and late Holocene dates (Smith et al. 2014), suggesting that it came from deposits disturbed by looting. Early Holocene dates on charcoal recovered at roughly the same depth as the smaller fragment in adjacent units indicate that the crescent dates to the early Holocene.

The crescent is burned and thermally fractured. The pot-lids interrupt its flake scars, suggesting that it was burned and broken after it was finished rather than during heat-treating. Given that crescents from well-dated contexts are rare, we submitted the larger fragment to Archaeological Investigations Northwest Inc. for Crossover Immunoelectrophoresis analysis. It produced a positive reaction for pronghorn, suggesting that the tool contacted that taxon during butchering or hafting activities. Sediment from around the crescent did not produce any positive reactions. Although artiodactyls possibly including pronghorn are present in the Stratum V fauna, they are greatly outnumbered by smaller game.

Bifaces

Next to utilized flakes (see below), bifaces are the most abundant constituent of the flaked stone tool assemblage. We recovered 198 bifaces in various stages of completion (Figure 7.6); if projectile points and the crescent are included that number rises to 290. Over half ($n=132$; 56 percent) of the staged bifaces ($n=235$) are finished tools (projectile points + stage 5 bifaces). The proportions of unfinished and finished bifaces made of obsidian (83 and 119), CCS (5 and 5), and FGV (15 and 8) do not differ significantly ($\chi^2=5.04$, $df=2$, $p=.081$). The proportions of unfinished and finished bifaces differ significantly between components ($\chi^2=7.01$, $df=2$, $p=.030$): finished bifaces are more common in the Middle and Late Archaic components, while unfinished bifaces are more common in the Late Paleoindian component.

Sixteen known and eight unknown obsidian and FGV types are represented among the 67 sourced bifaces. This high diversity is likely because some Stage 5 biface fragments are broken projectile points. Forty percent of the sourced bifaces come from the two closest sources, Buck Spring ($n=14$; 21 percent) and Beatys Butte ($n=13$; 19 percent). The rest are made of obsidian and FGV types found across central and southeastern Oregon. Unfinished bifaces made of nonlocal obsidian outnumber those made of local Buck Spring obsidian by almost 3 to 1, indicating that people brought numerous unfinished bifaces to LSP-1.

Eighty-five percent ($n=247$) of the 290 bifaces are broken (Table 7.6). Bifaces broken during production (evidenced by early, middle, and late-stage manufacturing bending breaks, overshot flake removals that produced breakage, tranchet flake removals, and perverse breaks) are most common ($n=130$; 45 percent). Bifaces broken during use ($n=61$; 21 percent) or broken to generate new working edges (evidenced by radial breaks, bipolar breaks, and intentional burin removals) are also present ($n=52$; 18 percent). Eighty-five percent ($n=52$) of bifaces broken during use are finished tools. We did not assign roughly half of the bifaces broken to generate new working edges to particular stages due to their fragmentary nature, so it is hard to say at which stage of production people recycled bifaces. However, our sense is that most unclassified fragments represent pieces of finished tools. If we are correct, then 37 of 51 recycled bifaces (73 percent) were finished tools when people broke them. The proportions of manufacturing, use, and recycling breaks do not vary significantly across time ($\chi^2=4.97$, $df=4$, $p=.290$).

The breakage types among the LSP-1 bifaces reflect a range of activities. Foremost, biface manufacturing was important, as evidenced by the numerous specimens broken during production and high proportions of biface thinning flakes at the site (see below). As noted, most unfinished bifaces are made of nonlocal obsidian and FGV. Of the 36 sourced bifaces broken during use, 30 (83 percent) are made of nonlocal raw materials, indicating that people discarded tools broken during transit upon arriving at the shelter. Interestingly, only six of the 30 sourced bifaces broken during production (20 percent) are made on Buck Spring obsidian, indicating that biface manufacturing mostly featured nonlocal materials. Finally, of the 18 sourced bifaces broken to produce new working edges, 13 (72 percent) are made with nonlocal raw materials. Again, some of these may have been broken during transit and discarded upon arrival. The biface breakage patterns, combined with the sourcing data, indicate that people brought unfinished bifaces—some of them perhaps already broken—to LSP-1 where they finished, used, and recycled before final discard. Visitors to the site were clearly aware of the limitations of the local Buck Spring pebbles and arrived with enough high-quality materials to maintain their inventory of bifacial tools.

Before we turn our attention to the other flaked stone tool types and debitage from LSP-1, four additional features of the bifaces warrant discussion because they are seldom recognized or described in the Great Basin: (1) burins; (2) radial breakage; (3) tranchet flaking; and (4) novice knapping. These features shed additional light on the activities that took place at LSP-1 and who may have carried them out.

Burins

Although burin technology is widely recognized in Old World assemblages (d'Errico et al. 1998; Nowell et al. 2016; Pitzer 1977; Shea et al. 2019; Venditti et al. 2016) and the North American Arctic (Giddings 1956; Potter et al. 2013; Tremayne 2010), researchers have rarely noted it in the Great Basin or Columbia Plateau (but see Estes 2009; Fagan 1974; Goebel et al. 2011; Rice 1972; Tuohy 1969). At this writing, Stueber (unpublished data) has recently observed both burins and burin spalls in other Paleoindian assemblages in Oregon, including the WST points from the Dietz Site, Paisley Caves, and Connley Caves.

Burin technology includes both the burinated piece (i.e., the core), which may be a flake, blade, biface, or biface fragment, and the burin spall (i.e., the flake). Both burinated pieces and burin spalls can serve as tools. To produce a burin, a toolmaker removes the spall from a prepared or existing platform at and along an edge of

0   5 cm

3324 (V, FGV)   23 (III, FGV)   2297 (V, FGV)

1353 (V)   17 (II)

34 (III/IV, CCS)   2055 (V)   1131 (V, CCS)   2290 (V)

FIGURE 7.6. Examples of bifaces from LSP-1: (3324) Stage 3 biface; (23) Stage 2 biface; (2297) Stage 3 biface; (1353) Stage 3 biface; (17) Stage 4 biface; (34) Stage 4 biface; (2055) Stage 4 biface; (1131) Stage 5 biface; and (2290) Stage 4 biface. Artifacts are obsidian unless otherwise noted. Roman numerals denote the strata from which artifacts were recovered.

TABLE 7.6. Biface breakage by type and component

Component and Biface Type	Comp.	Ind.	Manufacturing				Use	Recycling			Ther.	Total
			Bend.	Tran.	Perv.	Over.	Bend.	Bur.	Bip.	Rad.		
Late Archaic												
Stage 2	1	—	2	—	—	—	—	—	—	—	—	3
Stage 3	1	—	1	—	—	—	—	—	—	1	—	3
Stage 4	1	—	1	—	—	—	1	—	—	—	—	3
Stage 5	—	—	2	1	—	—	—	—	—	—	—	3
fragment	—	—	1	—	—	—	1	1	—	—	—	3
point	1	—	5	—	1	—	5	—	—	—	—	12
Total	4	—	12	1	1	—	7	1	—	1	—	27
Middle Archaic												
Stage 2	—	—	1	—	—	—	—	—	—	—	—	1
Stage 3	—	—	4	—	—	—	—	—	—	—	—	4
Stage 4	—	—	—	—	—	—	1	—	—	—	—	1
Stage 5	—	—	—	—	—	—	2	—	—	1	—	3
fragment	—	—	—	—	—	—	—	1	1	2	1	5
point	2	—	9	—	—	—	5	—	—	—	—	16
Total	2	—	14	—	—	—	8	1	1	3	1	30
Late Paleoindian												
Stage 2	8	1	13	—	1	—	1	1	—	—	—	25
Stage 3	6	—	12	—		1	—	1	—	5	—	25
Stage 4	3	—	6	—	2	1	3	2	—	4	—	21
Stage 5	1	—	6	1	—	—	10	2	—	6	—	26
fragment	—	—	23	1	—	2	—	10	—	9	—	45
point	13	—	11	—	1	—	16	—	—	—	—	41
crescent	—	—	—	—	—	—	—	—	—	—	1	1
Total	31	1	71	2	4	4	30	16	—	24	1	184
Mixed Deposits												
Stage 2	1	—	2	—	—	—	—	—	—	—	—	3
Stage 3	2	—	4	—	2	—	—	—	—	—	—	8
Stage 4	1	—	4	—	—	—	—	—	—	1	—	6
Stage 5	—	1	2	—	—	—	2	1	—	1	—	7
fragment	—	—	—	—	—	—	2	—	—	1	—	3
point	2	—	7	—	—	—	12	—	—	1	—	22
Total	6	1	19	—	2	—	16	1	—	4	—	49
Total	43	2	116	3	7	4	61	19	1	32	2	290

Note: Comp.=complete; Ind.=indeterminate; Bend.=bending; Tran.=tranchet; Perv.=perverse; Over.=overshot; Bur.=burin; Bip.=bipolar; Rad.=radial; Ther.=thermal.

a core using percussion or pressure flaking. The resulting 90° burinated edge of the core makes an excellent scraper plane. Burin spalls driven from bifacial edges retain their triangular cross section and, with slight modification, make excellent drills. Finally, two burin spalls driven from a core in opposite directions from a platform creates ideal gravers/chisels (see Inizan et al. 1999 for more information about burin technology).

We recorded 21 instances of burin technology including 19 burinated bifaces and two tools made on burin spalls. Most (17 of 21) of these come from the Late Paleoindian component, with burin technology proportionally more common in the Late Paleoindian component (~9 percent of all bifaces) than both the Middle and Late Archaic components (~3 and ~4 percent of all bifaces, respectively). The burinated bifaces were primarily made using biface fragments and ultimately drafted into use as scraper planes, gravers/chisels, and drills. The two burin spalls (artifacts 196 and 1158) are quite large and were modified into trifacial drills (Figure 7.7).

Microflaking and rounding use-wear were observed at 10× magnification on several of the burinated bifaces and both trifacial drills.

Radial Breakage

Radial break technology is a recycling strategy that has been identified in Paleoindian assemblages elsewhere in North America (Frison and Bradley 1980; McAvoy and McAvoy 2003; Root et al. 1999; Surovell 2009; Waters et al. 2011) but rarely in the Great Basin. Radial break technology has been compared to bipolar reduction technology (Amick 2007), but the only similarity between the two technologies is the use of an anvil and a hammerstone.

To accomplish bipolar technology, the core (a pebble, biface, or flake) is held firmly in place on an anvil and struck by a hard hammerstone with a downward blow. This causes a wedging initiation on the core that produces distinct, straight, flat flakes that lack full formation of a percussion bulb and display pronounced compression rings (Cotterell and Kaminga 1987).

To produce radial breaks, a flake, biface, or biface fragment is placed flat on an anvil stone and struck in the center using a hard hammer, causing bending and radial fractures (Jennings 2011). The resulting triangular pieces have acute-angled points and lateral edge angles of ~90°. These pieces are effective for working wood, bone, antler, and soft stone and are used in a similar manner to burin tools. Like burin tools, the presence of radially broken pieces indicates that detailed craftwork took place at a site.

The LSP-1 assemblage contains 30 biface fragments that were intentionally radially broken. Radially broken bifaces are more common in the Late Paleoindian component (n=24; 13 percent of bifaces) than in both the Middle Archaic (n=3; 10 percent of bifaces) and Late Archaic (n=1; 4 percent of bifaces) components. Many of the radially broken biface fragments show microflaking use-wear at 10× magnification. These pieces may have been used to manufacture some of the bone or shell tools and ornaments we describe in Chapter 10.

Tranchet Flaking

Tranchet technology entails removing one or more oblique flakes by percussion or pressure flaking from the distal or lateral edge of a biface or other tool. The result is a razor-sharp, unretouched transverse edge (Crabtree 1972; Inizan et al. 1999). Tools modified by tranchet flaking are excellent for butchering and other tasks that require extremely sharp but durable cutting edges.

Researchers have reported tranchet technology at sites across Eurasia (al-Nahar and Clark 2009; Claud

2015; Hosfield and Chambers 2009; McNabb and Rivett 2007; Rollefson et al. 1997; Shipton et al. 2013). In North America, it has been primarily reported as "chisel tips," or small square tips sometimes found on WST bifaces (Beck and Jones 2009, 2015; Duke et al. 2018; Green et al. 1998; Tuohy 1969). Toolmakers produced such tips using pressure flaking. Use-wear on a chisel-tipped WST point from Utah's Old River Bed led Duke et al. (2018) to postulate that it may have been used as a gouge for working leather.

The LSP-1 flaked stone assemblage contains two bifaces with tranchet flake removals (both from the Late Paleoindian component) and two tranchet flakes (one from the Late Archaic component and one from mixed deposits). The tranchets were made by percussion flaking and probably served as large cutting tools. Similar tools have been reported from Maya sites in Belize (Shafer 1983; Shafer and Hester 1983).

Novice Knapping

Burins, tranchets, and, to a lesser extent, radial break tools, are specialized technologies. Their presence at LSP-1 indicates that expert flintknappers intentionally produced certain types of tools used for specific tasks. As we discuss later, these tasks probably included making bone tools and ornaments.

In addition to this evidence of expert flintknappers, the lithic assemblage also contains evidence of novice knappers, probably children or adolescents. Flintknapping is a skill that can take years to master (Bamforth and Finlay 2008; Geribàs et al. 2010; Khreisheh 2013; Stout and Semaw 2006). Among traditional foraging societies, individuals likely started learning toolmaking at an early age (Dugstad 2010; Hildebrand 2012; Högberg 2008; Stapert 2007; Sternke and Sørensen 2007). Beginner knappers commonly make mistakes that accomplished knappers rarely, if ever, make. These errors are expressed in many ways: (1) bifaces with severe and often multiple hinge and step fractures; (2) stacks on bifaces (repeated striking of the same area with no flake release); (3) bifaces with sinuous edges; (4) attempted flake removals at incorrect angles and/or locations along biface margins; and (5) bifaces flaked with no clear outcome in mind (Dugstad 2010; Khreisheh 2013; Milne 2005; Sternke and Sørensen 2007). Although not widely reported in the Great Basin, evidence for novice knappers is probably present in many assemblages, especially those from domestic contexts.

Twenty-nine of the 290 LSP-1 bifaces (10 percent) possess one or more of novice knapping errors. Novice errors are highest in the Late Paleoindian bifaces (n=22; 12 percent) and Late Archaic bifaces (n=3; 11 percent)

and lowest in the Middle Archaic bifaces (n=1; 3 percent) and bifaces from mixed deposits (n=3, 6 percent). The fact that the assemblage contains bifaces with novice knapping errors tells us something about the people who visited the shelter. Foremost, the fairly high rates of mistakes in the Late Paleoindian and Late Archaic biface assemblages suggest that individuals who had yet to become accomplished knappers, probably children or adolescents, spent some time there. In contrast, the low rate of errors in the Middle Archaic biface assemblage suggests that visitors during that period were, in general, experienced toolmakers. Later, we discuss other aspects of the LSP-1 record that similarly suggest that group composition may have varied across the Holocene.

Flake Tools

We recovered 357 flake tools, including 323 from the three cultural components. Obsidian is the most common raw material among the flake tools from each component although a few are made of CCS and FGV. A large but uneven sample prevents us from using a chi-square test or Fisher's Exact test to determine whether toolstone proportions vary significantly between periods.

Scrapers (n=47) comprise ~7 percent of the lithic assemblage (Figure 7.7). Thirty possess one or more retouched lateral margins, 14 possess retouched distal ends, and three possess retouched lateral margins and distal ends. Of the 35 scrapers with recognizable blank types, roughly half (n=16) are made on early core reduction flakes, and roughly half (n=15) are made on late core reduction flakes (Table S7). This trend is consistent across raw material type. One end scraper (Artifact 1117) and one side scraper (Artifact 2425)—both from the Late Paleoindian component—are made on tabular pieces of tan chert. A bifacial knife (Artifact 1131; see Figure 7.7) and two utilized flakes (artifacts 344 and 849) from the Late Paleoindian component are also made from that material.

Utilized flakes are the most abundant lithic tools at the site (~41 percent). Over 90 percent of utilized flakes are obsidian. We identified blank type for roughly three-quarters (n=216) of the utilized flakes. Biface thinning flakes (n=106) are the most common type of utilized flakes, with late core reduction (n=56) and early core reduction flakes (n=53) used equally. In contrast, the scrapers, gravers, and notches from LSP-1 are predominantly made on larger early and late core reduction flakes. This difference is significant (χ^2=17.12, df=1, p<.001). Some utilized flakes have uniform and continuously retouched edges, suggesting that people modified them prior to use. Others have irregular and/or discontinuous retouched edges, suggesting that such edge wear

accrued during use. Finally, many utilized flakes possess edge damage barely visible to the naked eye, suggesting that they were used only briefly. As we discuss in the next chapter, some utilized flakes were used to process rabbit or hare carcasses while others were used to work harder materials such as bone or wood.

Other tool types including gravers, notches, choppers, and drills occur in low numbers (see Figure 7.7). Two drills (artifacts 1158 and 196) are made from trifacially flaked burin spalls driven from the lateral margins of large bifaces. One drill (Artifact 1777) is made from a recycled WST point. While we did not conduct use-wear analyses of these tools, their presence suggests that groups carried out a range of activities in the shelter including working bone, wood, and/or shell.

We sourced 23 flake tools (15 scrapers, 5 utilized flakes, 2 gravers, and 1 drill). Thirteen of the sourced tools are made of Buck Spring obsidian, most of which appear to have been made using pebbles from the shelter's walls. Other sourced flake tools are made of Warner Valley FGV (n=4), more distant obsidian sources (one each of Glass Buttes, Tank Creek, and Beatys Butte obsidian), or obsidian/FGV from unknown locations (n=3). The Glass Buttes obsidian tool (Artifact 1777) is the drill made from a recycled WST point. Most of the cortex-bearing utilized flakes are visually consistent with the local pebbles. As we discuss below, people probably used those pebbles as sources of flake blanks for expedient tools.

Cores

Cores (n=50) comprise 7 percent of the tool assemblage. Their relative abundances do not vary between components. They are exclusively made on obsidian. Of the 32 we sourced, all but two (one of Delintment Lake obsidian and one of Surveyor Spring obsidian) are made of Buck Spring obsidian. Cores average 42.4 mm in maximum linear dimension. Only three specimens are bigger than 70 mm. While generally small, most cores (n=41; 82 percent) retain cortex. Many display just a few flake removals, suggesting that they are not small because they were used to exhaustion but because they started out as pebbles. To reiterate, the pebbles are generally unsuitable for larger tool production but provided smaller flakes that could be used as cutting tools.

DEBITAGE

We analyzed all 27,965 pieces of debitage from LSP-1. Of these, 25,558 flakes came from deposits that we assigned to one of three cultural components. The majority (94 percent) of flakes are obsidian, with lesser numbers of CCS (2 percent) and FGV (4 percent) flakes. As we

Figure 7.7. Examples of flake tools from LSP-1: (354) drill; (1777) drill made from WST point; (1158) drill made on burin spall; (196) drill made on burin spall; (337) end scraper; (828) side scraper; (1065) end scraper; (2425) end scraper; (2465) utilized flake; and (1122) side scraper. Artifacts are obsidian unless otherwise noted. Roman numerals denote the strata from which artifacts were recovered.

noted earlier, the Late Archaic component contains significantly more FGV flakes than both the Middle Archaic and Late Paleoindian components.

Considered as a whole, the LSP-1 debitage includes significantly more small (<½ in) obsidian flakes and significantly more larger (>½ in) CCS and FGV flakes than chance would indicate (χ^2=170.73, df=6, p<.001; Table S8). The average weights of flakes by raw material (0.2 g for obsidian, 0.3 g for CCS, and 0.5 g for FGV) show a similar pattern. The Late Archaic component contains significantly fewer smaller flakes and significantly more larger flakes; the Middle Archaic component contains significantly more smaller flakes and significantly fewer larger flakes than would be expected by chance (χ^2=75.65, df=2, p<.001).

Cortex-bearing FGV flakes are significantly more common than cortex-bearing obsidian and CCS flakes in the debitage assemblage (χ^2=6.08, df=2, p=.048; Table S9). There are significantly more cortex-bearing flakes in the Late Archaic component and significantly fewer cortex-bearing flakes in the Middle Archaic component (χ^2=80.37, df=2, p<.001). Excluding flake fragments, biface thinning flakes are the most common flake type in the debitage made of each raw material; however, FGV core reduction flakes (early + late) are more common, and small FGV flakes (pressure + very small flakes) are less common than would be expected by chance (χ^2=126.32, df=6, p<.001; Table S10). Flake types also vary by component: the Late Archaic component contains more core reduction and fewer biface thinning flakes, the Middle Archaic component contains more small flakes and fewer biface thinning flakes, and the Late Paleoindian component contains more biface thinning flakes and fewer core reduction flakes and small flakes than chance would dictate (χ^2=270.73, df=4, p<.001).

In sum, small obsidian biface thinning flakes dominate the LSP-1 debitage sample, suggesting that later-stage obsidian biface production and/or tool maintenance were common activities throughout all time periods. The sample of sourced bifaces indicates that people carried many of those tools from other places. While this is also true for FGV and CCS tools to some extent, since there are no known local sources of those materials, the higher proportions of large FGV core reduction flakes relative to flake types of other materials indicates that either people did not reduce FGV bifaces to the same extent as obsidian bifaces or reduced them in a way that did not generate as many small flakes. We have noted that there is no significant relationship between earlier and later-stage bifaces and raw material type, but nevertheless there are proportionately more early-stage and fewer finished FGV bifaces than those

made of obsidian or CCS, suggesting that the former scenario may be more likely.

DIACHRONIC VARIABILITY IN LITHIC TECHNOLOGICAL ORGANIZATION AT LSP-1

The proportions of bifaces, flake tools, and cores do not vary significantly among the components (χ^2=3.68, df=4, p=.451), suggesting that basic technological activities (the types of tools that groups made, used, and discarded) remained consistent across time. With just a few exceptions, noted above and further discussed below, each component is dominated by small obsidian biface thinning flakes, utilized obsidian flakes, and later-stage bifaces including projectile points. People smashed bifaces, which were mostly made of nonlocal materials, to generate new working edges. Flake tools such as scrapers, gravers, drills, and notches are present but not abundant. Most are made of local obsidian pebbles. Against the backdrop of this general homogeneity, we highlight some of the more notable features of the three cultural components.

The Late Paleoindian Component

In terms of both flaked stone tools and debitage, the Late Paleoindian assemblage is the most substantial of the three. Chronologically and typologically, it straddles the late Fort Rock (12,000–9000 cal BP) and early Lunette Lake (9000–7600 cal BP) periods of northern Great Basin culture history (Jenkins et al. 2004a). Diagnostic artifacts include stemmed and foliate points, some of which appear to have served as knives, and a crescent. Near the end of the early Holocene, people stopped using LSP-1 before Northern Side-notched points became widespread.

Obsidian dominates both the tools and debitage (Table 7.7), although this is the case for all three components. But the high toolstone diversity sets the Late Paleoindian component apart: 34 obsidian and FGV types are represented among 111 tools, including 17 types among 21 projectile points. When adjusted for sample size, the Late Paleoindian projectile points are made from a significantly richer collection of obsidian and FGV than both the Middle Archaic (p<.001) and Late Archaic (p<.001) projectile points.[2] The average transport distance for Late Paleoindian points (74.5 km) is also substantially greater than that of both Middle Archaic (40.1 km) and Late Archaic points (37.6 km).[3] Most of the obsidian and FGV types occur within or near the Abert-Chewaucan, Fort Rock, and Malheur Basins. In terms of toolstone diversity, LSP-1's Late Paleoindian assemblage is very rich, suggesting recurrent but short-term visits.

Unfinished and finished bifaces occur in roughly equal frequencies and do not differ significantly by raw material. Toolmakers made bifaces using local obsidian and recycled exhausted bifaces made of exotic obsidian. Relative to the Middle Archaic component, novice knapping errors are common. The rest of the Late Paleoindian assemblage is fairly diverse, with nine tool types recognized. The crescent is unusual because it is one of only a handful found in caves or shelters (Smith et al. 2014). Utilized flakes are common and, as Van der Voort and Smith discuss in the next chapter, some of them were used to butcher hares and rabbits. Other tools such as gravers, notches, and drills may have been used to work bone into beads or tools. Cores tend to be small and made from local obsidian pebbles. Given their small size, people probably used them mostly to produce expedient cutting tools.

Relative to later components, biface thinning flakes are more common, but core reduction and small flakes are less common. This is likely because unfinished bifaces are also more common. There are more cortex-bearing FGV flakes than those made of obsidian or CCS, and large FGV flakes are more common than in both later components. These trends correspond well with the fact that FGV bifaces tend to be larger and in earlier stages of completion in the Late Paleoindian assemblage.

Taken together, these trends suggest that people repeatedly visited LSP-1, carrying with them finished stemmed and foliate points but also unfinished bifaces. While some core reduction and tool finishing/maintenance certainly occurred, later-stage biface production was a primary activity. When bifaces became unusable, people smashed them to produce new working edges, many of which show signs of being used. While these early Holocene visits produced more lithic detritus than later visits, as we will discuss, early-stage lithic reduction does not seem to have been a major activity. Late Paleoindian toolmakers also produced and used both expedient and formed flake tools using local Buck Spring obsidian.

The Middle Archaic Component

The density of tools in the Middle Archaic component (30.5/m³) is lower than the Late Paleoindian component (39.8/m³), but the density of flakes is higher (1965.3/m³ vs. 1,705.6/m³). Obsidian remained the preferred raw material for both tools and flakes, although the use of CCS and FGV for flake tools is roughly twice that of the Late Paleoindian and Late Archaic components (Table 7.8). Toolstone richness is low (seven obsidian and FGV types represented among 29 sourced tools), and when adjusted for sample size the Middle Archaic point

TABLE 7.7. The Late Paleoindian flaked stone assemblage

Tool Type	Obsidian	CCS	FGV	Total
Biface (by stage)[1]				
2	22	1	2	25
3	16	1	8	25
4	20	1	—	21
5	24	1	1	26
fragment	42	1	2	45
projectile point	34	1	6	41
crescent	—	1	—	1
core	36	—	—	36
flake tool				
scraper	27	4	6	37
graver	5	—	—	5
notch	1	—	—	1
drill	3	1	—	4
utilized flake	188	5	10	203
Total	417	17	36	470
Flake Type[2]				
early core reduction	765	11	63	839
late core reduction	387	6	30	423
biface thinning	7,590	162	351	8,103
pressure	1,493	19	14	1,526
fragment	6,000	87	367	6,454
shatter	478	3	8	489
very small flakes	1,943	25	31	1,999
Total	18,656	313	864	19,833
Flake Size[3]				
<¼ in	1,943	25	31	1,999
¼–½ in	12,511	188	556	13,255
½–1 in	3,597	83	227	3,907
>1 in	605	17	50	672
Total	18,656	313	864	19,833

[1] The proportions of early (stages 2–4) and finished (stage 5 + points) bifaces do not differ significantly by raw material ($p=.752$, Fisher's Exact test).

[2] The proportions of core reduction flakes (early + late), biface thinning flakes, and small flakes (pressure + very small flakes) differ significantly by raw material ($\chi^2=122.05$, $df=4$, $p<.001$). There are fewer small CCS and FGV flakes and more FGV biface thinning and core reduction flakes than would be expected by chance alone.

[3] The proportions of smaller flakes (< ½ in) and larger flakes (> ½ in) differ significantly by raw material ($\chi^2=56.35$, $df=2$, $p<.001$). There are significantly more larger CCS and FGV flakes and significantly fewer smaller FGV flakes than would be expected by chance alone.

sample is significantly less rich than the Late Paleoindian point sample ($p<.001$) but not the Late Archaic point sample ($p=.219$). Their average transport distance is also significantly less than the Late Paleoindian point sample ($p=.028$) but not the Late Archaic point sample

TABLE 7.8. The Middle Archaic flaked stone assemblage

Tool Type	Raw Material			Total
	Obsidian	CCS	FGV	
Biface (by stage)[1]				
2	1	—	—	1
3	3	—	1	4
4	—	1	—	1
5	2	—	1	3
fragment	4	1	—	5
projectile point	16	—	—	16
core	4	—	—	4
flake tool				
scraper	1	—	2	3
utilized flake	18	2	1	21
Total	49	4	5	58
Flake Type[2]				
early core reduction	97	1	7	105
late core reduction	108	3	20	131
biface thinning	1,195	22	83	1,300
pressure	359	2	5	366
fragment	1,109	17	68	1,194
shatter	101	-	3	104
very small flakes	525	5	4	534
Total	3,494	50	190	3,734
Flake Size[3]				
<¼ in	525	5	4	534
¼–½ in	2,317	34	123	2,474
½–1 in	578	9	52	639
>1 in	74	2	11	87
Total	3,494	50	190	3,734

[1] The proportions of early (stages 2–4) and finished (stage 5 + points) bifaces do not differ significantly according to raw material (p=.133, Fisher's Exact test).
[2] The proportions of core reduction flakes (early + late), biface thinning flakes, and small flakes (pressure + very small flakes) differ significantly by raw material (χ^2=61.64, df=4, p<.001). There are fewer small FGV flakes and more FGV core reduction and biface thinning flakes than would be expected by chance alone.
[3] The proportions of smaller flakes (<½ in) and larger flakes (>½ in) differ significantly by raw material (χ^2=24.39, df=2, p<.001). There are significantly fewer smaller FGV flakes and significantly more larger FGV flakes than would be expected by chance alone.

(p=.869). These trends correspond to a regional shift toward the use of fewer toolstone sources by Middle Archaic groups in the northwestern Great Basin (McGuire 2002; Smith 2010). For the people using LSP-1, Beatys Butte was one of those sources, and Buck Spring also remained important. This may be related to the large areas over which those sources occur. Other toolstone sources each represented by one or two tools are located north (Tank Creek, Wagontire) and southwest (Buck Mountain, Warner Valley FGV) of the shelter.

Elko points mark Middle Archaic visits to LSP-1. Together, projectile points (n=16) and finished bifaces (n=3) comprise a significantly higher proportion of the Middle Archaic biface assemblage than in the Late Paleoindian and Late Archaic assemblages (χ^2=7.01, df=2, p=.030). This difference suggests that Middle Archaic visitors focused more on biface finishing/maintenance than the earlier stages of biface production—a scenario that is supported by the debitage. It may also reflect a greater emphasis on large game hunting, although the faunal assemblage does not clearly demonstrate that possibility. Knapping errors are rare, which may indicate that fewer novice toolmakers visited the site than during the early Holocene. Instead, experienced hunters may have constituted the bulk of visitors.

Middle Archaic debitage is dominated by small flakes that lack cortex. Like the Late Paleoindian assemblage, relative to obsidian and CCS there are significantly fewer small FGV flakes and significantly more large FGV flakes (χ^2=24.39, df=2, p<.001), but there are fewer cortex-bearing FGV flakes than in the other components. Again, this may indicate that people used FGV more for early-stage biface production. The fact that only one FGV biface is present in the Middle Archaic assemblage may mean that people ultimately transported unfinished bifaces away from the shelter. Except for utilized flakes, which are slightly less common, the proportions of tool types are consistent with those from other periods.

The Late Archaic Component

Tool (22.2/m³) and especially flake (623.4/m³) density are relatively low in the Late Archaic component, suggesting that stone tool production and/or maintenance—and perhaps use of the shelter more broadly—was less intensive than during the preceding periods. Again, obsidian is common in both the tool and debitage samples but FGV use peaks (Table 7.9). Twelve obsidian and FGV types are represented among 26 tools. Sources of five of these material types (four FGV and one obsidian) remain unknown, suggesting that they are fairly localized. Beatys Butte obsidian remained important for biface production, while Buck Spring obsidian provided a source of flakes for both bifaces and flake tools. Other obsidian and FGV types represented mostly by single projectile points or bifaces are located north of LSP-1. When adjusted for sample size, the Late Archaic point sample is significantly less rich than the Late Paleoindian point sample (p<.001) but does not differ significantly from the Middle Archaic point sample (p=.219).

TABLE 7.9. The Late Archaic flaked stone assemblage

Tool Type	Raw Material			Total
	Obsidian	CCS	FGV	
Biface (by stage)[1]				
2	2	—	1	3
3	2	—	1	3
4	2	—	1	3
5	2	1	—	3
fragment	3	—	—	3
projectile point	12	—	—	12
core	5	—	—	5
flake tool				
chopper	—	—	1	1
scraper	2	—	1	3
graver	1	—	1	2
utilized flake	33	—	—	33
Total	64	1	6	71
Flake Type[2]				
early core reduction	152	2	6	160
late core reduction	94	6	21	121
biface thinning	627	10	32	669
pressure	89	—	3	92
fragment	576	8	45	629
shatter	47	1	2	50
very small flakes	267	4	3	274
Total	1,852	31	112	1,995
Flake Size[3]				
<¼ in.	267	4	3	274
¼–½ in	1,058	13	59	1,130
½–1 in	456	12	38	506
>1 in	71	2	12	85
Total	1,852	31	112	1,995

[1] The proportions of early (stages 2–4) and finished (stage 5 + points) bifaces differ significantly according to raw material (p=.042, Fisher's Exact test). Early stage FGV bifaces are more common than would be expected by chance alone.

[2] The proportions of core reduction flakes (early + late), biface thinning flakes, and small flakes (pressure + very small flakes) differ significantly by raw material (χ^2=25.31, df=4, p<.001). There are fewer small FGV flakes and more FGV core reduction flakes than would be expected by chance alone.

[3] The proportions of smaller flakes (<½ in) and larger flakes (>½ in) differ significantly by raw material (χ^2=16.92, df=2, p<.001). There are significantly more larger FGV flakes than would be expected by chance alone.

The average transport distance for Late Archaic points (37.6 km) is slightly lower than that for Middle Archaic points (40.1 km) but not significantly so (p=.869).

Rosegate points are the only point type present in the Late Archaic assemblage, and, as noted, the absence of Desert Series points corresponds to a lack of features and dated textiles younger than 900 cal BP. This suggests that LSP-1 fell into disuse in the final centuries before Euro-American contact—a topic we will return to in Chapter 13.

As is the case with earlier periods, the Late Archaic debitage sample is dominated by obsidian, and small biface thinning flakes lacking cortex remain the norm. Relative to CCS and obsidian, there are again significantly more large FGV flakes (χ^2=16.92, df=2, p<.001). Relative to other periods, there are significantly fewer small obsidian flakes and significantly more large obsidian flakes in the Late Archaic assemblage (χ^2=67.30, df=2, p<.001). This last trend may indicate that more early-stage biface production occurred compared to other periods. However, a comparison of unfinished and finished obsidian bifaces between periods shows that while their frequencies do differ significantly (χ^2=9.22, df=2, p=.010), unfinished obsidian bifaces are not overrepresented in the Late Archaic component. Slightly more early-stage obsidian biface production may certainly have occurred during the Late Archaic period, as the debitage data suggest, but, if so, either toolmakers discarded fewer broken examples or carried more of them away. Novice biface knapping errors are more common in the Late Archaic component than in the Middle Archaic component, suggesting that children or adolescents returned to the site. Flake tools and cores are present though not in high numbers.

SUMMARY

In terms of the tools present and the production and maintenance activities represented, the flaked stone assemblage is homogenous, considering that it spans much of the Holocene. Given the tremendous volume of rabbit and hare remains deposited by people, the lithic assemblage is modest. Utilized flakes are the most common tools in each component, and, as Van der Voort and Smith discuss in the next chapter, some of them were used to process leporids. Dart and arrow points—and the byproducts of their production and maintenance—are present but in low numbers, suggesting that groups both readied themselves for hunting trips and repaired or discarded tools upon returning. High incidences of novice knapping errors in the Late Paleoindian and Late Archaic components highlight the possibility that children or adolescents visited the site during those periods, while a low incidence of knapping errors in the Middle Archaic component suggests that this may not have been the case during that period. Finally, a range of other tool types such as drills, scrapers, and gravers are present though never common, suggesting that people carried out other activities beyond food processing.

Obsidian was always the favored raw material type,

and people used Buck Spring obsidian pebbles as a source of flakes. Visitors also brought obsidian and FGV from other sources throughout the northern Great Basin, ranging from the Cascade Front to the west and the Snake River to the east. A few raw materials from northwestern Nevada and northeastern California in the assemblage indicate that visitors occasionally originated from places to the south or interacted with the people who lived there. But as a whole, the source profile for LSP-1 is very much oriented to the north. Furthermore,

in terms of technology and chronology, the LSP-1 lithic assemblage is consistent with those from sites in the Abert-Chewaucan, Fort Rock, and Malheur basins (Jenkins et al. 2004a; Oetting 1989, 1990, 1994b). As such, the shelter probably lay within the socioeconomic sphere of the groups that called those basins home for much of the Holocene, although, as we have noted, it was not used during much of the middle Holocene or the centuries leading up to Euro-American contact.

NOTES

1. The unknown obsidian and FGV types we report here are lab-specific designations made by the Northwest Research Obsidian Studies Laboratory (NWROSL). They do not necessarily correspond to unknown designations made by other commercial labs. For example, the NWROSL's Unknown B obsidian type should not be confused with the Geochemical Research Laboratory's Unknown B obsidian type from Nevada's Black Rock Desert, which is today referred to as Buffalo Hills obsidian (Young 2002).

2. Because traditional measures of richness (in this case, source diversity) may be influenced by sample size, we calculated it using a bootstrapping routine. We bootstrapped larger samples (using 1,000 iterations) to directly compare source diversity among projectile points from different periods. We also followed this routine in Chapter 13 to compare source diversity among projectile points from open-air sites.

3. To compare artifact transport distances between periods, we bootstrapped the means by pooling all the values for projectile points from two periods, drawing samples of sizes n_1 and n_2 and comparing the difference between the new means. The two-tailed probability was calculated as the relative frequency of bootstrapped mean absolute differences greater than the absolute observed difference. We repeated this process to compare projectile points from all time periods. We also followed this procedure in Chapter 13 to compare transport distances for projectile points from open-air sites.

8

Early Holocene Leporid Processing

Madeline Ware Van der Voort and Geoffrey M. Smith

With its well-preserved faunal assemblage and numerous lithic tools, LSP-1 offered an opportunity to better understand how Late Paleoindians used small game. As many as 1,000 rabbits and hares are represented in the early Holocene fauna. We hypothesize that groups periodically held rabbit drives nearby and transported the carcasses into the shelter for processing and, in some cases, consumption.

Given the abundant leporid bones in the early Holocene strata, lithic tools from the Late Paleoindian component should show evidence of rabbit and hare butchering. We anticipated that large flakes should show use as cutting or skinning tools. Here, we present the major results of Van der Voort's (2016) use-wear analysis of flake tools from the lower levels of Stratum V. Her results, which suggest that people targeted leporids for both their meat and skins, help us to understand the range of activities that took place at LSP-1.

GENERAL TRENDS IN THE LEPORID ASSEMBLAGE

Pellegrini's (2014) analysis of the leporid remains, which was supplemented by our study of a larger sample, highlighted four general trends: (1) most remains represent adult individuals, suggesting that the animals were taken during the late fall or winter; (2) the prevalence of diaphysis cylinders signals long-bone marrow extraction; (3) cutmarks, burning, and polishing suggest that some individuals were skinned, butchered, and cooked (either roasted or boiled); and (4) a paucity of axial elements suggests that consumers ground those parts of the skeletons into bone meal or carried those portions of the carcasses elsewhere for consumption.

Because his analysis focused on how people processed and consumed rabbits and hares, Pellegrini devoted little attention to the potential ways that people used other parts of the carcasses, namely, the skins. Ethnographic accounts highlight the importance of rabbit skin blankets and robes (I. Kelly 1932; Lowie 1924; Steward 1938; Wheat 1967), and archaeological evidence indicates that Great Basin groups used rabbit skins for clothing during the TP/EH (Jenkins et al. 2016; Tuohy and Dansie 1997). Use-wear analysis of stone tools from the lowest levels of LSP-1 can demonstrate whether rabbit hide processing was a major activity during the Late Paleoindian occupations of the site—a question that the faunal remains by themselves cannot address.

THE LATE PALEOINDIAN FLAKE TOOL ASSEMBLAGE

Stratum V reflects two pulses of Late Paleoindian activity, 9775–8875 and 8200–8000 cal BP, but a few radiocarbon dates suggest that in places it also contains a Middle Archaic component. To ensure that the flake tools included in her analysis date to the early Holocene, Van der Voort examined only those specimens recovered from below ~100 cmbd where radiocarbon dates on shell beads, isolated charcoal and animal bones, and features consistently show that those deposits date to that period. Because Prasciunas (2007) demonstrated in her flake-cutting efficiency experiments that smaller flakes (<5 g and/or <7 cm²) make poor prehensile cutting tools, Van der Voort limited her sample to flakes that size or larger. While 172 flakes (all obsidian) from >100 cmbd matched those criteria, only 37 possessed

TABLE 8.1. Late Paleoindian flake tools examined for use-wear

Artifact No.	Max. Length (mm)	Max. Width (mm)	Weight (g)	Surface Area (cm²)	Excavation Unit	Elevation (cmbd)
78	44.7	45.7	16.3	14.9	N105E99	115
524	40.2	34.3	10.6	13.5	N104E99	102
733	67	37	10	16.6	N105E100	101
759	49.9	39.3	12.1	16.7	N105E100	111–116
819	44.5	33.4	9.9	10.2	N106E100	101
856	30.8	41.6	7.9	10	N106E100	117
983	40	33.3	6.9	12.1	N103E100	104
984[1]	27	32.1	6.6	6.5	N103E100	106
1019	45.5	30.7	11.9	7.3	N103E100	121
1030	56.1	27.6	14.4	11.6	N103E100	122
1375	78.4	35.6	31	20.9	N104E101	106
1393	41.1	33.4	5.8	9.9	N104E101	112
1507	35.9	24.6	12.3	6.4	N104E102	101–106
1597	43.5	36.1	12.4	9.2	N105E101	111
1608	44.6	28.4	4.8	9.4	N105E101	118
1611	37	50.1	8.8	13.2	N105E101	118
1630	40.5	29.8	10.8	10.9	N105E101	126
1705	63.3	36.8	16.5	16.1	N105E102	106
1737	39.7	21.8	5.4	7.5	N105E102	121–126
1787	32.7	45.3	26.4	13.7	N106E101	107
1951	48	31.9	5.2	11.9	N106E99	105
1958	28.5	56.2	11.8	7.8	N106E99	109
1982	43.3	35.2	10.4	9.5	N106E99	116.5
2127	51.3	34.7	15.8	12	N102E100	101
2142	46.5	37.2	8.2	13.5	N102E100	109
2292	47.6	25	8.1	10.4	N102E101	111
2427	40.6	32.8	5.1	9.9	N102E102	105
2446	47.6	27.5	16.4	12.1	N102E102	109
2455	54.4	40.8	11.3	16.5	N102E102	117
2465[1]	65.4	47.3	24.9	22	N102E102	121
2674	59.9	20.7	10.7	8.9	N104E102	115.5
2695	63.2	28.3	18.7	12.1	N104E102	126–131
2846	50.5	22.1	7.0	7.6	N106E98	101
2860	43.4	26.1	7.2	9.9	N106E98	109.5
3342	36.8	39.9	14.1	14.7	N107E100	111
3358	39.6	34.8	16.6	11.3	N107E100	125
3411	48	46.3	35.7	22.6	N102E102	110
Mean	46.4	34.7	12.6	12.1	—	—
Range	27–78.4	20.7–56.2	4.8–35.7	6.4–22.6	—	—

[1] Excluded from analysis.

evidence of macroscopic modification (intentional shaping or flaking generated through use). She ultimately excluded two of those from additional analysis because the poor quality of the toolstone made recognizing use-wear difficult. Table 8.1 presents basic metric data and provenience information for the early Holocene flake tools included in Van der Voort's study and discussed here.

THE REPLICATED TOOL ASSEMBLAGE

The most effective studies of stone tools from prehistoric contexts feature replicated implements manufactured using comparable raw materials used for specific activities (Greiser and Sheets 1979; Kononenko 2011). Researchers generally document the duration of use and conditions under which replicated tools were used. Toward that goal, Van der Voort obtained obsidian cobbles

TABLE 8.2. Tasks carried out during use-wear experiment

RT[1] No.	Major Activity	Task	Motion	Duration (minutes)
3	hide processing	defleshing hide	unidirectional transverse (scraping)	255
5	carcass processing	disjointing feet and legs	bidirectional longitudinal (sawing)	73
6	hide processing	defleshing hide	unidirectional transverse (scraping)	128
7	carcass processing	disjointing feet	bidirectional longitudinal (sawing)	10
8	hide processing	cutting hide into strips	bidirectional longitudinal (cutting)	21
9	hide processing	removing skin	unidirectional longitudinal (skinning)	41
10	hide processing	defleshing	unidirectional transverse (scraping)	7
11	carcass processing	disjointing legs	bidirectional longitudinal (sawing)	12
12	meat processing	deboning/cutting meat	bidirectional longitudinal (cutting)	40
13	meat processing	deboning/cutting meat	bidirectional longitudinal (cutting)	13
14	carcass processing	disjointing feet and tail	bidirectional longitudinal (sawing)	5
15	meat processing	deboning	bidirectional longitudinal (cutting)	37
16	carcass processing	disjointing all joints and cutting spinal cord	bidirectional longitudinal (sawing)	21
17	meat processing	cutting meat	bidirectional longitudinal (cutting)	24
18	meat processing	deboning/cutting meat	bidirectional longitudinal (cutting)	31

[1] Replicated tool.

from Glass Buttes, Oregon, ~75 km from North Warner Valley. Glass Buttes obsidian is favored among flintknappers today and has been widely used by Native American toolmakers since the terminal Pleistocene (Stueber and Skinner 2015). Tools made of Glass Buttes obsidian are present in both the Late Paleoindian component at LSP-1 and several open-air sites in North Warner Valley (see chapters 7 and 13).

Geoffrey Cunnar (Western Cultural Resources Management Inc.) and Timothy Van der Voort (Nevada BLM)—both experienced flintknappers—drove numerous flakes from the cobbles. Of these, Van der Voort selected 15 flakes that met Prasciunas's (2007) criteria for effective prehensile cutting tools as the replicated tool (RT) sample for her experiment. Wear generated on them during the controlled experiments guided her interpretations of use-wear on the early Holocene flake tools.

The RTs are on average slightly longer and heavier than the LSP-1 flake tools (Table S11). The ventral surface areas of the RTs are also on average larger than the LSP-1 tools. Two factors likely contribute to these differences. First, some of the LSP-1 artifacts are made on biface thinning flakes, which are generally smaller and lighter than the core reduction flakes that Van der Voort used as RTs. Second, some of the LSP-1 tools are broken, whereas all the RTs were intact.

Prior to use, Van der Voort photographed and measured each RT. She documented manufacturing wear patterns with digital images using both a Luxo Midas digital microscope at 40× magnification and an Olym-

pus BHM reflected light metallurgical microscope at 100× and 200× magnification. This ensured that she did not mistake existing features for use-wear.

THE LEPORID PROCESSING EXPERIMENT: GENERATING AND DOCUMENTING USE-WEAR

Van der Voort used the RTs to butcher three domesticated European rabbits (*Oryctolagus cuniculus*) comparable in body size and weight to the jackrabbits processed at LSP-1. Prior to butchering, she removed their heads and internal organs using a steel knife. During the butchering process, Van der Voort focused on three major activities: (1) *hide processing*, which included skinning, scraping, and slicing hides; (2) *carcass processing*, which included disarticulating the carcasses; and (3) *meat processing*, which included deboning the carcass and cutting the meat. She used five RTs to process hide in several different ways for a total of 452 minutes, using five RTs to process carcasses in several different ways for a total of 121 minutes, and five RTs to process meat in several different ways for a total of 145 minutes (Table 8.2). Some tasks initially took longer to complete (e.g., the first time skinning a carcass) but with practice she became more efficient.

Documenting the Use-Wear

Following Kononenko's (2011) protocol for documenting use-wear on obsidian flake tools, Van der Voort illustrated both sides of each RT on graph paper. She noted the RTs numbers and briefly described the activities for which each RT was used. Prior to examining the RTs under magnification, Van der Voort gently washed them with mild soap and water and patted them dry. She then wiped them with isopropyl alcohol on a cotton pad, rinsed them with plain water, and dried them again.

Van der Voort used the Olympus BHM microscope with 10×, 20×, and 50× infinity-corrected objectives to examine the ventral and dorsal edges of each RT. When she observed use-wear traces, she marked a photo point (PP) on the recording sheet corresponding to the examined edge and captured digital images of the wear using an Infinity 2 Lumenera microscope camera. Many PPs corresponded to several numbered photographs at 100×, 200×, and/or 500× magnification. Van der Voort followed this protocol when documenting use-wear on the early Holocene flake tools.

Classifying the Use-Wear

Van der Voort classified evidence of use-wear following Kononenko (2011) and Hurcombe (1992).

Edge damage, or scarring, refers to small flake scars that are sometimes visible macroscopically. Van der Voort classified these based on their termination type as well as their distribution, orientation, size, and shape. Termination types included *bending, feather, step,* and *hinge.* Size categories included small (< 2 mm), medium (2–3 mm), and microflaking (only visible under the microscope; Kononenko 2011).

Striations are important for determining tool use-motion (Kononenko 2011). Striations form when dust, grit, or tool fragments become trapped between the tool and worked material. Van der Voort recorded four types of striations: (1) *sleeks* had straight sides and smooth bottoms; (2) *rough bottom striations* had irregular bottom surfaces and straight or irregular sides; (3) *intermittent striations* were composed of small, round, distinct points of damage arranged linearly along the surface; and (4) *flaked striations* were associated with edge damage caused by flake removal from the edge of the tool (Hurcombe 1992; Kononenko 2011). She recorded individual linear use-wear features that did not fit easily into any of these categories. In addition to striation type, when necessary, she categorized striation orientation as parallel, perpendicular, or diagonal to the working edge.

Edge rounding, or attrition, refers to the degree of smoothing and dulling of the edge, which is exacerbated by the presence of grit or sand (Kononenko 2011). Obsidian is brittle and prone to this type of wear. Van der Voort recorded the degree using the following ordinal categories: (1) *slight* (dull but visible edge); (2) *medium* (dull and very rounded edge); and (3) *intensive* (flat-tened and abraded edge). She noted other distinct characteristics (e.g., edge irregularities) on a case-by-case basis.

Polish formation is the least understood process in use-wear analysis. Kononenko (2011:8) defines it as "surface alteration from abrasive roughening through smoothing to a highly reflective gloss." Fullagar (1991) described four stages of polish formation. *Stage 1* is a very light polish with slight edge stabilization and slight edge rounding with a rough, sugary texture, compared to a freshly fractured surface. *Stage 2* is a light polish consisting of an abraded surface with polished, leveled peaks, deepening cracks, and granular impaction in depressions. Material is physically removed from the tool surface. Most soft materials (e.g., meat) do not cause polish formation past this stage. *Stage 3* is a developed polish on higher peaks through an extensive, stable, polished surface, extension of subsurface cracks, and gradual removal of surface defects. It can be distinctive of worked material, such as wood, plants, bone, and hide. *Stage 4* is well-developed polish varying from an extensively polished surface to a completely polished, featureless surface. Van der Voort recorded the location, stage, and distribution of polish.

Finally, Van der Voort recorded the presence and type of residues on both the RTs and early Holocene flake tools. Non-use-related residues usually appear as isolated instances on the tool away from the edge, while residues related to use may be smeared on the surface or trapped in crevices near the tool's working edge (Kononenko 2011). Residues are often deposited slightly inward from the tool's edge and may include plant remains such as phytoliths and starches, animal remains such as blood, and inorganic remains such as ochre or hafting mastic (Kononenko 2011). Van der Voort recorded the presence and location of residues, along with a brief description of its visual characteristics. Table 8.3 recaps the types and descriptions of these use-wear attributes.

Experimental Use-Wear Results

Table 8.4 summarizes the use-wear that Van der Voort identified on the RTs after the rabbit butchering experiments described below.

Hide Processing

Hide-processing activities produced a suite of distinct attributes that includes discontinuous scarring (Figure 8.1A), sleek and rough bottom striations (Figure 8.1B), edge rounding (Figure 8.1C), and early polish stages (Figure 8.1d). The orientation of the striations reflected the direction of tool motion, with mostly parallel

TABLE 8.3. Descriptions of use-wear attributes

Attribute	Description	Types
edge damage/ scarring	small flake scars that are sometimes visible macroscopically	feather step bending hinge
striations	form when dust, grit, or tool fragments are trapped between tool and worked material	sleeks rough bottoms intermittent flaked
edge rounding/ attrition	degree of smoothing and dulling of edge	slight medium intensive
polish	surface alteration from abrasive roughening through smoothing to a highly reflective gloss	Stage 1 Stage 2 Stage 3 Stage 4
residues	residues related to use may accrue on surface or in crevices near tool's working edge	folded grainy particle band patchy spots

striations diagnostic of longitudinal cutting motions and dense perpendicular striations diagnostic of transverse scraping motions.

Carcass Processing

Carcass processing activities generated a pattern characterized by continuous feather-and-step scarring (Figure 8.1D), sleek and intermittent striations with edge rounding (Figure 8.1F), flaked striations (Figure 8.1G), and polish formation (Figure 8.1H). The presence of continuous scarring, intermittent striations, and Stage 3 polish, and the absence of rough bottom striations makes this pattern distinct from use-wear created during hide-processing activities. In addition, the frequency of both types of parallel striations (intermittent and flaked) reflects the longitudinal motion employed in carcass processing.

Meat Processing

Meat-processing activities generated yet another distinct pattern that included the presence of continuous feather or step scarring, all types of striations, a parallel residue band, and a lack of edge rounding or polish formation (Figure 8.1I). This suite of characteristics differs from carcass processing due to the lack of edge rounding and polish formation, presence of rough bottom striations, and more frequent occurrence of a residue band parallel to the working edge. These features are also distinct from those generated during hide processing due to

the occurrence of continuous rather than unpatterned scarring, frequent presence of intermittent striations, and lack of edge rounding and polish formation. The striation orientation on tools used for meat-processing activities was less indicative of use-motion than on tools used for carcass and hide processing.

Summary of Experimental Use-wear Results

Processing an animal carcass is a continuum of contacted materials and use-motions. Some of the RTs exhibited overlapping use-wear traces, and most accrued folded grainy particles (Figure 8.1J) and rough and shiny patchy residues (Figures 8.1K and 8.1L) on their working edges. Even though some RTs exhibited use-wear suggesting their use for more one activity, most possessed a diagnostic suite of characteristics when used for a single activity. These characteristics were distinct enough to identify some of the materials (e.g., hide, meat, bone) on which the early Holocene flake tools from LSP-1 were used, as well as the way they were used (e.g., sawing, cutting, scraping). Hide processing produced discontinuous feather-and-step scarring, sleek and rough bottom striations, edge rounding, and polish. Carcass processing produced continuous feather-and-step scarring, sleek, intermittent, and flaked striations, edge rounding, and polish. Meat processing produced continuous feather-and-step scarring, mixed striation types, parallel residue bands, and a lack of edge rounding and polish.

Table 8.4. Use-wear attributes on replicated tools

RT No.	Processing Task	Mode of Use	Duration (minutes)	Scarring 1	Scarring 2	Striations 1	Striations 2	Striations 3	Striations 4	Edge Rounding 1	Edge Rounding 2	Edge Rounding 3	Polish 1	Polish 2	Polish 3	Polish 4	Residues FGP	Residues Band	Residues Patchy	Residues Spots
5	carcass	saw	73	C		+		PL	+			+			+		+		+	+
16	carcass	saw	21		C	+		PL	+		+				+		+		+	+
11	carcass	saw	12	C		+		PL	+			+						+	+	
7	carcass	saw	10	C	C	PD		PL	+			+				+	+			+
14	carcass	saw	5	C	C			DG	+			+					+		+	+
3	hide	scrape	255	D	D	+	PD		+		+	+		+			+		+	+
6	hide	scrape	128	D	C	+	PD		+			+	+				+		+	+
10	hide	scrape	7	D		+		PD			+	+	+				+		+	+
9	hide	skin	41		D	+	+		+	+				+			+		+	+
8	hide	cut	21	C		+	PL										+		+	
12	meat	cut	40	C	C		PL	PD									+		+	
15	meat	cut	37	C	C		PL		+		+				+			+	+	+
18	meat	cut	31		C			PL	+								+			
17	meat	cut	24		C	+	PD		+									+	+	+
13	meat	cut	13	C			PD	PD											+	

Scarring: 1=feathered; 2=stepped; C=continuous; D=discontinuous. Striations: 1=sleeks; 2=rough bottoms; 3=intermittent; 4=flaked; PL=parallel; PD=perpendicular; DG=diagonal. Edge Rounding: 1=slight; 2=medium; 3=intensive. Polish: 1=stage 1; 2=stage 2; 3=stage 3; 4=stage 4. Residues: FGP=folded grainy particle.

THE LSP-1 FLAKE TOOL SAMPLE

Table 8.5 and Figure 8.2 summarize the analysis of early Holocene flake tools from LSP-1, including their use-wear attributes and inferred activities. Twenty-two of the 35 tools possess use-wear consistent with that generated on the RT sample. Eight (Artifacts 733, 983, 1030, 1507, 1597, 1611, 1787, and 3342) possess attributes consistent with hide processing. Four (Artifacts 856, 1737, 2446, and 2846) possess attributes consistent with carcass processing. Only one (Artifact 2142) shows clear evidence of use for meat processing. Finally, nine (Artifacts 78, 759, 1375, 1393, 1958, 2127, 2292, 2455, and 2674) appear to have been used for more than one type of processing. Among the remaining 13 flake tools, 11 exhibit wear that does not match the wear generated during Van der Voort's experiment (we classified such wear as *other*). One appears to have been unused, and one was used too lightly to definitively identify any activities (we classified the wear as *inconclusive*). These tools may have been used for activities not included in her experiment.

In addition to identifying the materials they were used to process, the flake tools offer clues about the ways in which they were used. Of the 22 flake tools used to process leporids, roughly one-third appear to have only been used to process hides; these include two tools used longitudinally, four tools used transversely, and two tools used both longitudinally and transversely. These motions suggest that hides were both scraped and cut. Four tools possess only carcass processing wear; three of these were used longitudinally and one was used transversely. These motions suggest that carcasses were disarticulated, and, in one instance, bone tools were produced (see below). The lone artifact used solely to process meat was employed with a longitudinal motion, which suggests cutting. Four tools were used for carcass and hide processing, including one that employed both longitudinal and transverse motions, two that were used with a transverse motion, and one that was used with a longitudinal motion. Two tools were used for carcass and meat processing with longitudinal motions. Three tools were used for hide and meat processing: two with both longitudinal and transverse motions and one with longitudinal motions only.

EARLY HOLOCENE RABBIT AND HARE PROCESSING

The Stratum V fauna indicate that leporids were an important resource during the early Holocene. Based on his faunal analysis, Pellegrini (2014) concluded that groups processed the carcasses, consumed many animals onsite, ground the axial elements into bone meal, and used the skins and bones to make clothing and tools.

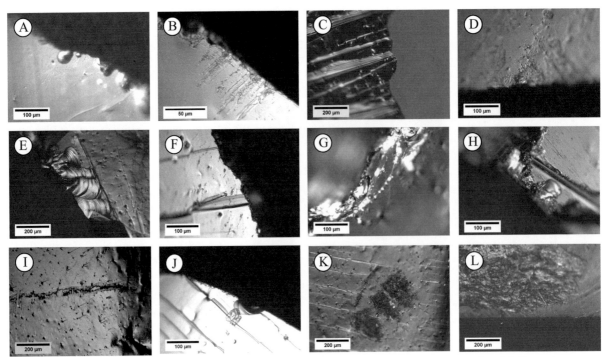

FIGURE 8.1. Use-wear on replicated tools (RTs). Top row, generated during hide processing activities: (A) discontinuous scarring on RT 6; (B) sleeks and rough bottom striations on RT 3; (C) medium edge rounding on RT 10; (D) stage 1 polish on RT 10. Middle row, generated during carcass processing activities: (E) continuous scarring on RT 11; (F) sleek and intermittent striations with intensive edge rounding on RT 5; (G) flaked striations on RT 14; (H) late-stage polish and parallel intermittent striations on RT 16. Bottom row, additional examples of use-wear: (I) parallel residue band generated during meat processing on RT 12; (J) folded grainy particle on RT 5 (found on most replicated tools regardless of activity); (K) rough, patchy residue on RT 9 (found on most replicated tools regardless of activity); (L) shiny patchy residue on RT 10 (found on most replicated tools regardless of use activity).

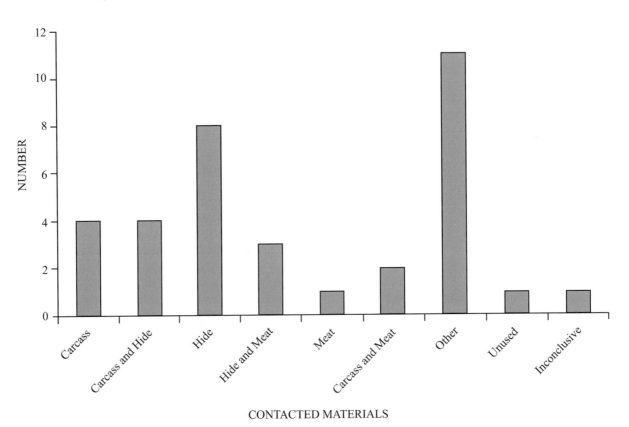

FIGURE 8.2. Frequencies of Late Paleoindian flake tools used to contact different materials.

TABLE 8.5. Use-wear attributes on Late Paleoindian flake tools

Art. No.	Scarring 1	Scarring 2	Striations 1	Striations 2	Striations 3	Striations 4	Edge Rounding 1	Edge Rounding 2	Edge Rounding 3	Polish 1	Polish 2	Polish 3	Polish 4	FGP	Band	Patchy	Spots	Unid.	Worked Material	Motion
78	C	C	+	PL/PD	+	+			+		+					+		+	carcass, hide	long., trans.
524	C	D	+	+				+					+						other	—
733	C	C	+	PL				+	+			+		+		+		+	hide	long.
759	C	C	+	PL/PD	+				+			+		+	+	+			meat, hide	long., trans.
819	D			+	DG			+	+	+	+		+	+		+		+	other	—
856	C		+		PL				+					+					carcass	long.
983		C	+	PL					+					+		+		+	hide	long.
1019	C		+	PD	PD				+				+						other	—
1030	D		+	PD					+				+	+		+			hide	trans.
1375	C		+	PD	DG				+		+			+			+		carcass, hide	trans.
1393	D	C		+	PD	+			+		+		+	+		+	+		carcass, hide	trans.
1507	D/C		+	PD	PL			+	+			+		+		+	+		hide	long., trans.
1597	C		+	PD/PL	+			+	+		+			+			+		hide	long., trans.
1608	D		DG	+	+			+	+		+			+			+	+	other	—
1611	D		DG	PD					+				+	+			+		hide	trans.
1630	D		+																used	—
1705	C		+	PD/PL	PD				+				+	+		+	+		other	—
1737	D		+	PD	PD				+			+		+		+	+	+	carcass	trans.
1787	D		+	PD		+			+		+			+			+		hide	trans.
1951	D	C	+	DG				+	+				+	+					other	—
1958	C		+	PD	PL				+			+			+	+			carcass, meat	long.
1982	D		+	DG	+				+									+	other	—
2127	C		PL	PL					+					+			+		meat, hide	long.
2142		C	+						+			+		+		+	+		meat	long.
2292	C/D		+	PD/PL	+				+			+		+		+	+		carcass, hide	long.
2427	D			PD										+		+	+		unknown	—
2446	C		+	PL	PD	+			+		+			+		+	+		carcass	long.
2455	D/C	C	+	PD/DG	+				+	+				+			+	+	hide, meat	long., trans.
2674	C/D	C	+	PD	PL			+	+		+				+	+	+		carcass, meat	long.
2695	C		DG					+				+		+			+	+	other	—
2846	C		+	PD	PL							+		+		+	+		carcass	long.
2860	C	D	DG			+	+		+			+	+	+		+	+		other	—
3342	D		+	PD				+	+		+			+		+	+		hide	trans.
3358	C/D	D		PD					+				+			+	+		other	—
3411	C/D		+	DG	PL				+			+							other	—

Scarring: 1=feathered; 2=stepped; C=continuous; D=discontinuous. Striations: 1=sleeks; 2=rough bottoms; 3=intermittent; 4=flaked; PL=parallel; PD=perpendicular; DG=diagonal

Edge Rounding: 1=slight; 2=medium; 3=intensive. Polish: 1=stage 1; 2=stage 2; 3=stage 3; 4=stage 4. Residues: FGP=folded grainy particle; Unid.=unidentified.

Use-wear on LSP-1's early Holocene flake tools supports these interpretations and suggests that people used the implements for a range of activities. Roughly one quarter of the tools appear to have only been used to process hides/skins. These include implements employed for scraping, cutting, or both. While we did not recover any direct evidence that the tools were used to manufacture rabbit-skin clothing, the fact that they were used solely to process skins may reflect that activity indirectly. Ethnographically, rabbit-skin blanket production involved cutting each hide into a long, furred strip and twisting it into a rope, which was then woven with up to 100 additional hides to make a single blanket (Wheat 1967). Among the Northern Paiute, this work was carried out by both men and women (Fowler 1989; I. Kelly 1932). Rabbit-skin blankets made using this technique have been recovered from Gypsum Cave in southern Nevada, Butte Creek Cave in northeastern Oregon, and Spirit Cave in western Nevada (Cressman 1950; Harrington 1933; Tuohy and Dansie 1997). Spirit Cave contained Burial No. 2, which consisted of an individual (known as the Spirit Cave Mummy) interred with a woven rabbit-skin blanket/robe dated to ~10,600 cal BP (Tuohy and Dansie 1997). Traditionally, rabbit-skin blankets were the only clothing woven using mammal hides, perhaps because the specialized technique allowed the fur strips to hold still air within the blanket, thus providing excellent insulation (Yoder et al. 2005).

Finally, whereas we have only indirect evidence of rabbit-skin blanket/robe production, we recovered tools and ornaments made of rabbit and hare bones (see Chapter 10). The Northern Paiute used leporid bones to make fishhooks, needles, beads, and pins (C. Fowler and Bath 1981; I. Kelly 1932; Riddell 1978). The co-occurrence of leporid bone artifacts and flakes used to work bone suggests that the occupants of LSP-1 targeted rabbits and hares for more than just meat. As we discuss later, the way groups processed and consumed game is consistent with other lines of evidence about who used the rockshelter and why.

9

Ground- and Burned-Stone Artifacts

Geoffrey M. Smith and Denay Grund

The ground- and burned-stone artifacts from LSP-1 are significant for three reasons. First, groundstone tools are especially common in the Late Paleoindian component, which sets LSP-1 apart from most other early Holocene sites in the Great Basin. Second, while groundstone was rather abundant in the early Holocene strata, economically important seeds were not (see Chapter 5), suggesting that people used the tools to process other resources including perhaps roots or small game. Finally, fire-affected rock was fairly abundant in the early Holocene strata but not closely associated with the two Late Paleoindian hearths. Instead, it was mostly concentrated along the southeastern edge of our excavation block near the shelter's apron. This fact may reflect the presence of a large thermal feature such as a roasting pit at LSP-1.

GROUNDSTONE ARTIFACTS

We recovered 203 groundstone artifacts (manos, metates, pestles, anvils, palettes, and indeterminate fragments) from LSP-1 (Table 9.1 and Figure 9.1). Most implements are made of loaf-shaped vesicular basalt cobbles (n=137; 67 percent) or blocks or rounded cobbles of welded tuff (n=57; 28 percent). The remaining ones are made of rhyolite (n=8; 4 percent) and andesite (n=1; <1 percent) blocks. These materials either occur in the rimrock into which the shelter is cut or along the Pleistocene shorelines immediately below the shelter. With few exceptions, the groundstone tools appear to be local. When adjusted for the volume of excavated deposits, groundstone is most abundant in the Late Paleoindian component (11.8 artifacts/m³), followed by the Late Archaic component (8.1/m³) and the Middle Archaic (6.3/m³) component.[1] The proportions of manos and metates

do not differ significantly among components (χ^2=1.5, df=2, p=.472).

Metates

We recovered 92 metates, roughly two thirds of which are made of vesicular basalt and one third of which are made of tuff. One specimen is made of rhyolite and one specimen is made of andesite. Most metates are unifacial, but six are bifacial; thus, we examined 98 total faces. Faces with light use-wear (minimal abrasion or polish, many remaining surface irregularities) and medium use-wear (most surface irregularities are removed) occur in about the same frequency (n=42 and n=43). Faces with heavy use-wear (all surface irregularities are removed, pecking may be present) are less common (n=12). Most surfaces are flat (n=84) or concave (n=11), with just a few being convex (n=3). Seven surfaces show striations and four surfaces are pecked. Two faces contain red ochre staining, and one contains a black residue (see Figure 9.1).

Only four metates show clear evidence of shaping, although most are small fragments and we could not effectively assess shaping for half of them. Basalt metate fragments average ~10 cm in maximum linear dimension, while tuff metate fragments average ~19 cm. Two thirds of the metate fragments possess breaks that are consistent with thermal fractures (Neubauer 2018), and all but five of those are vesicular basalt.

Manos

We recovered 51 manos, 30 of which are vesicular basalt, 17 of which are tuff, and 4 of which are rhyolite. Unifacial (n=26) and bifacial (n=25) manos occur in roughly equal numbers and together contain 76 used faces. Faces with

TABLE 9.1. Stratigraphic distribution of groundstone and fire-affected rock

| Stratum | Groundstone Type | | | | | | Total | F.A.R.[1] |
	Mano	Metate	Pestle	Anvil	Palette	Indet.		
I/II	—	—	—	—	—	—	—	1
II	5	3	—	—	—	5	13	5
II/III	3	5	—	—	—	1	10	9
III	—	—	—	—	—	1	1	—
III/IV	1	1	—	—	—	1	3	40
IV	2	10	—	—	—	3	15	—
IV/V	2	2	—	—	—	1	5	11
V	34	61	—	1	1	39	136	217
V/VI	1	—	—	—	—	—	1	—
V/VI/VII	—	1	—	—	—	—	1	—
V/VII	—	2	—	—	—	1	3	—
Unknown	3	7	1	—	—	4	15	4
Total	51	92	1	1	1	57	203	287
Component[2, 3]								
Late Paleoindian	34	65	—	1	1	40	141	213
Middle Archaic	3	6	—	—	—	3	12	35
Late Archaic	8	10	—	—	—	8	26	25
Mixed deposits	6	11	1	—	—	6	24	4

[1] F.A.R.=Fire-affected rock.

[2] When adjusted for the volume of deposits assigned to each component, the densities of groundstone artifacts are: (1) 11.8/m³ for the Late Paleoindian component; (2) 6.3/m³ for the Middle Archaic component; (3) 8.1/m³ for the Late Archaic component; and (4) 10.0/m³ for mixed deposits/no provenience.

[3] When adjusted for the volume of deposits assigned to each component, the densities of fire-affected rock are: (1) 17.9/m³ for the Late Paleoindian component; (2) 18.4/m³ for the Middle Archaic component; (3) 7.8/m³ for the Late Archaic component; and (4) 1.7/m³ for mixed deposits/no provenience.

light (n=34) and medium (n=31) use-wear are common, while faces with heavy use-wear are less so (n=11). Most worn surfaces are flat (n=57), but a few are convex (n=13) or concave (n=6). Six specimens are pecked, three contain striations visible to the naked eye, and one is battered. Eight specimens are stained with red ochre and one contains traces of a black residue (see Figure 9.1).

Just six manos show clear evidence of having been shaped. Roughly 60 percent of manos are broken, and a disproportionate number of those are made of vesicular basalt. Basalt mano fragments average ~8 cm in maximum linear dimension while tuff mano fragments average ~9 cm. Twenty-five manos possess thermal fractures, and the proportions of broken basalt and tuff manos are roughly the same.

Indeterminate Fragments

Indeterminate fragments—broken pieces that show at least one worn face that we could not confidently classify as manos or metates—comprise a third groundstone type. We recovered 57 indeterminate fragments, most of which are vesicular basalt (n=41) or tuff (n=13). Three fragments are made of rhyolite. Thirteen fragments are

worn on both faces; thus, we recorded attributes for 70 faces. Thirty-eight (54 percent) show light use-wear, 22 (31 percent) show medium use-wear, and 10 (15 percent) show heavy use-wear. Flat faces (n=54) are most common, followed by convex faces (n=14) and concave faces (n=2). All but four fragments possess thermal fractures. The average sizes of basalt, tuff, and rhyolite fragments are each ~6 cm. We did not observe residues on any of the indeterminate fragments.

Miscellaneous Groundstone Artifacts

We recovered single examples of three additional groundstone tool types. Artifact 2353 is the midsection of a shaped basalt pestle. It measures 6 × 7 × 4 cm and is thermally fractured both across and along the long axis of the tool. We recovered it 59 cmbd from mixed deposits. Artifact 2685 is part of a bifacial tuff anvil that measures 14 × 16 × 4 cm. One face is heavily ground and pecked in its center. The other face is lightly ground. We recovered it 117 cmbd in deposits assigned to the Late Paleoindian component. Artifact 1251 is a vesicular basalt palette with light polish on one face. It measures

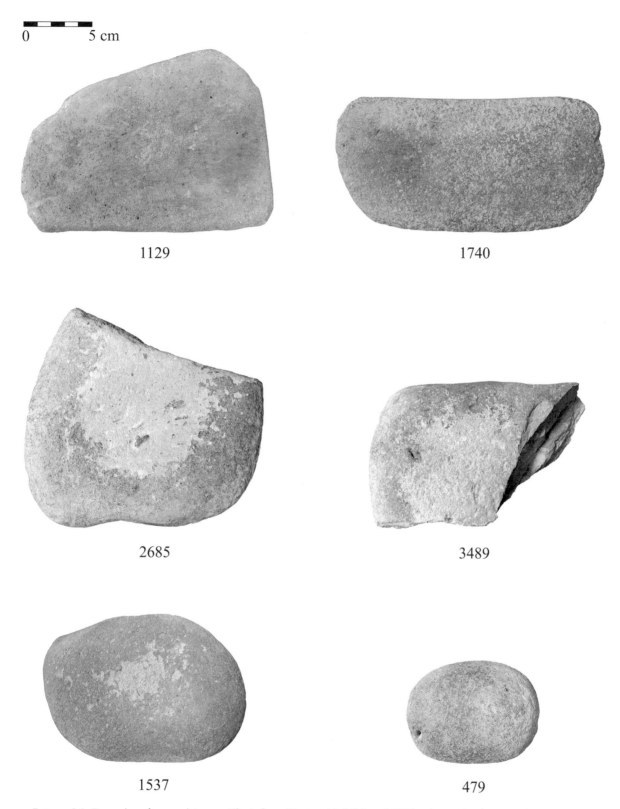

FIGURE 9.1. Examples of groundstone artifacts from Stratum V: (1129 and 1740) ocher-stained manos; (2685) anvil with pecking; (3489) metate fragment with pecking; (1537) mano with pecking; (479) mano with black residue.

15 × 12 × 2 cm and is heavily stained with red ochre on the polished face. We recovered it 107 cmbd and assigned it to the Late Paleoindian component.

FIRE-AFFECTED ROCK

We recorded 287 pieces of fire-affected vesicular basalt cobbles (see Table 9.1). We logged their rough dimensions and locations on level records but did not collect them. Some of the pieces may be unrecognizable manos or metate fragments. When adjusted for the volume of deposits assigned to each component, the densities of fire-affected rock are 17.9/m³ for the Late Paleoindian component, 18.4/m³ for the Middle Archaic component, and 7.8/m³ for the Late Archaic component. The high number of burned rock pieces (including manos and metates) in the Late Paleoindian component is not consistent with the low number and ephemeral nature of the early Holocene hearths. As we discuss further in Chapter 12, most of the fire-affected rock was concentrated in the southeastern quadrant of our excavation block. Given its abundance there, we suspect that additional early Holocene hearths or other thermal features may be located south of our excavation block toward the shelter's apron. Ethnographically, people sometimes roasted rabbits in hot coals or ashes (C. Fowler 1992; Lowie 1924), and, given the volume of leporid bones in the early Holocene deposits, it is possible that additional cooking features are present in unexcavated portions of the site.

SUMMARY

Both groundstone and fire-affected rock were surprisingly abundant, given the shelter's modest size. Groundstone implements are mostly made of local cobbles and blocks and in general do not appear to have been heavily used. This may reflect the local abundance of vesicular basalt and tuff, the short-term nature of occupations at the site, and/or the tasks for which people used manos and metates (a topic to which we return below). Almost 80 percent of groundstone tools possess thermal fractures, and some of the fire-affected rock pieces are probably unrecognizable groundstone fragments.

The high number of groundstone fragments in the early Holocene deposits is notable given their age. Regionally, people began using groundstone tools in greater numbers ~9500 cal BP (Jones and Beck 2012), which is around the time that people first visited LSP-1. Researchers have generally interpreted this shift as evidence that people began to consume lower-ranked seeds (Grayson 2011; Madsen 2007; Simms 2008). This may have been the case at some sites, but, ethnographically, people also used groundstone to process roots and

tubers (Couture et al. 1986; C. Fowler 1990b; Stewart 1942), small game (Gilmore 1953; Wheat 1967), and pigment (Schroth 1996; Steward 1933). Herzog and Lawlor (2016) have identified leporid hair and geophyte starch grains on early Holocene groundstone at Hogup Cave. Louderback and Pavlik (2017) reported wild potato (*Solanum jamesii*) starch grains on groundstone from the early Holocene deposits at North Creek Shelter in southern Utah. Closer to LSP-1, Connolly and Jenkins (1999) recovered a pigment-stained mano from early Holocene deposits at 35Ds34 in Newberry Crater, Oregon. These observations indicate that people used groundstone to process a range of materials in the more distant past as well.

Although groundstone tools are abundant at LSP-1, economically important seeds are rare in the early Holocene hearths (see Chapter 5). Some of the Late Paleoindian groundstone was clearly used to process pigments: 11 tools are ochre-stained, and we recovered hematite fragments in several early Holocene levels. There are over 300 documented sources of hematite in southeastern and south-central Oregon, including a location in Coleman Valley at the south end of the Warner Basin (Nancy Pobanz, personal communication, 2020). Thus, people could have collected the pigment from any number of places prior to visiting LSP-1.

Some of the early Holocene groundstone may also have been used to process roots, the soft tissues of which do not preserve as well as seeds or other macrobotanical remains (Herzog and Lawlor 2016). This seems likely during the Middle and Late Archaic periods because we recovered charred starchy tissue from hearths dating to those periods (see Table 5.3). We did not recover any starchy tissue in the Late Paleoindian hearths, but, to more fully address the possibility that early visitors processed roots, at this writing we are conducting starch-grain analysis of the groundstone.

Some of the Late Paleoindian groundstone may also have been used to process small mammals including the abundant rabbits and hares whose bones littered the early Holocene deposits. We are currently evaluating this possibility through protein residue analysis of the manos and metates.

The relative scarcity of groundstone in the Middle Archaic component corresponds to the fact that seeds and starchy edible tissues were not especially abundant in the hearths dating to that period. It also runs counter to recent data collected during the Ruby Pipeline project in northern Nevada that show milling equipment density peaked during the Middle Archaic period (McGuire et al. 2016), though this difference is perhaps not surprising given that the Ruby data are mostly derived from open-air sites located in different settings. If the frequencies of tools such as projectile points and groundstone tell us anything about how people used sites, then, as we proposed in Chapter 7 and reiterate here, visitors to LSP-1 may have focused more on hunting during the Middle Archaic period than either the Late Paleoindian or Late Archaic periods. The Middle Archaic flaked stone assemblage reflects projectile point manufacturing and repair, carried out by more experienced flintknappers, and more so than either the Late Paleoindian or Late Archaic assemblages. Thus, LSP-1 may have seen more visits by hunters and fewer visits by families during the first part of the late Holocene.

Finally, groundstone density is higher in the Late Archaic deposits than the Middle Archaic deposits, which is the opposite of McGuire and colleagues' (2016) findings for northern Nevada. The abundance of groundstone is matched by an abundance of seeds and root/fruity tissues in the Late Archaic features. Although there are a few larger metates, most groundstone pieces are smaller and lightly worn, which may reflect generally shorter-term visits to the shelter.

NOTES

1. We elected to calculate groundstone density using artifact counts rather than artifact weight because the presence of a few very large pieces would substantially skew the results.

Stone, Bone, and Shell Ornaments and Tools

Geoffrey M. Smith and Bryan S. Hockett

During our excavations, we recovered a handful of stone, bone, and shell ornaments and tools that are mostly unrelated to food procurement and processing (Table 10.1 and Figures 10.1 and 10.2). Because these items reflect a range of activities, evidence for which generally does not preserve at most sites, and because they help us to place LSP-1 into a broader social, behavioral, and chronological context, we briefly discuss them here.

STONE ORNAMENTS AND TOOLS

Steatite Bead

Artifact 43 is a complete, biconically drilled steatite disc bead. It has an exterior diameter of 10.5 mm, an interior diameter of 2.7 mm, and a thickness of 2.3 mm. It weighs 0.4 g. It has a small black dot on one face that measures 2.1 mm in diameter. We recovered the bead in screened sediment from 66–76 cmbd and assigned it to the Middle Archaic component. Similar, though generally smaller, steatite disc beads have been recovered from Middle Archaic contexts at the DJ Ranch and, to a lesser extent, other sites in the Fort Rock Basin (Jenkins et al. 2004b). Jenkins and colleagues posit that the quarries from which the stone for those beads originated may be located either on the Columbia Plateau or southern California. However, steatite sources are also found closer to LSP-1 in Jackson County in southern Oregon (Peterson 1978) and Humboldt and Trinity counties in northern California (Heizer and Treganza 1944).

Spindle Whorl

Artifact 2113 is a spindle whorl made of volcanic tuff. It is roughly circular, with a diameter of 41.2 mm and a thickness of 4.7 mm. It has a biconically drilled hole with a diameter of 5.7 mm. It weighs 7.7 g. We recovered the whorl 92 cmbd and assigned it to the Late Paleoindian component. Although similar whorls have been reported from other sites in the Intermountain West (Hilbish 2019), to the best of our knowledge the LSP-1 whorl is the oldest example in the Great Basin (Gene Hattori, personal communication 2020). While we did not recover any early Holocene textiles, the presence of the whorl suggests that Late Paleoindian visitors processed fibers inside the shelter.

Possible Awl

Artifact 2241 is a small piece of tuff ground into a rod with a rounded tip. It measures 18 × 12 × 6 mm and weighs 1.2 g and appears to be the broken tip of a longer tool, perhaps an awl. We recovered it 85 cmbd in Late Paleoindian deposits.

Rod Fragment

Artifact 2636 is a small piece of a partially fossilized bone rod. We identified the material using long- and short-wave Fourier-transform infrared spectroscopy in the UNR Shared Instruments Lab. The material contains spectra consistent with calcite and dolomite carbonates and less pronounced bioapatite peaks, all suggesting carbonate bone diagenesis (Beasley et al. 2014). It produced distinct peaks and troughs associated with bioapatite, shifted CO_3, and carbonates—common compounds in bone (Beasley et al. 2014; Dal Sasso et al. 2016; Pothier Bouchard et al. 2019).

The piece measures 14 × 13 × 7 mm and weighs 2.4 g. It was shaped by grinding and appears to be the midsection of a rod that is planoconvex in cross section. We

TABLE 10.1. Stone, bone, and shell ornaments

| Artifact and Material | Component | | | | Total |
	Late Archaic	Middle Archaic	Late Paleoindian	Mixed Deposits	
stone					
bead	—	1	—	—	1
whorl	—	—	1	—	1
awl	—	—	1	—	1
rod	—	—	1	—	1
pipe bowl	—	—	—	1	1
incised	1	—	—	—	1
net weight	1	—	—	—	1
Total	2	1	3	1	6
bone					
bead	9	1	7	1	18
awl	3	—	2	—	5
flaker	—	—	1	—	1
utilized flake	—	—	1	—	1
gaming/jewelry	1	—	—	—	1
indeterminate	1	—	4	1	6
Total	14	1	15	2	32
Shell					
Haliotis pendant	1	—	—	—	1
Haliotis bead	—	1	—	—	1
Olivella bead	—	—	7	2	9
disc bead	—	—	1	—	1
Total	1	1	8	2	12
Total	17	3	26	5	51

recovered it 142 cmbd near the bottom of the artifact-bearing deposits and assigned it to the Late Paleoindian component. Charcoal and bone from the same elevation in other parts of the shelter returned both early Holocene and terminal Pleistocene radiocarbon dates (see Table 4.2). Given its small size and the fact that it is broken, we do not know what kind of ornament or tool it represents.

Pipe Bowl

Artifact 301 is a ground tuff pipe-bowl fragment. It measures 29 × 22 × 15 mm and weighs 8.1 g. When complete, the bowl would have possessed an outside diameter of ~50 mm and an interior diameter of 15–20 mm. The inner surface of the bowl is burned. We recovered it 60–65 cmbd in mixed deposits that contain both Middle Archaic and Late Paleoindian artifacts. We recovered tobacco seeds (*Nicotiana attenuata*) from F.11-14, a late Holocene hearth dated to 975–805 cal BP (see Chapter 5). Ethnographically, the Northern Paiute smoked tobacco recreationally and used it for medicinal purposes (I. Kelly 1932).

Incised Stone

Artifact 2976 is a fragment of an incised stone recovered from sifted sediment excavated 41–46 cmbd and assigned it to the Late Archaic component. It measures 27 × 17 × 9 mm and is rough/broken on all sides except the incised face, which is naturally or ground flat. Two parallel 1-mm wide and 1-mm deep V-shaped incised lines are spaced 5 mm apart and run across the flat face. The artifact is made of a soft rock type, possibly limestone. It is too fragmentary to compare to those that Thomas (2019) recently reported.

Net Weight

Artifact 25 is a large, flat flake made of FGV from an unknown source. We recovered it 54 cmbd in N105E99 and assigned it to the Late Archaic component. It measures 104 × 83 × 15 mm and weighs 148.6 g. The artifact shows continuous flake removals around its margins on its dorsal surface, which shaped the artifact and produced large notches on opposing lateral margins. Its ventral surface is minimally flaked. Cannon (1993) noted identical

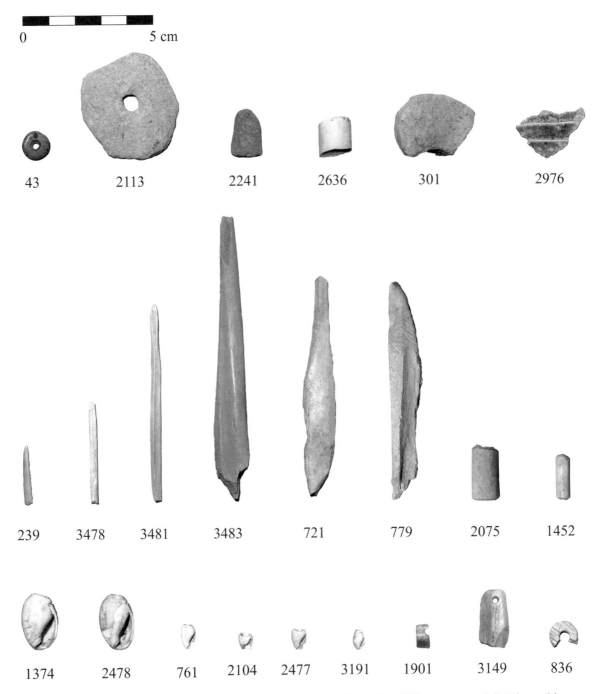

FIGURE 10.1. Examples of stone, bone, and shell tools and ornaments from LSP-1: (43) steatite bead; (2113) possible spindle whorl; (2241) possible tuff awl; (2636) stone rod; (301) tuff pipe bowl; (2976) incised stone; (239–721) bone needles/awls; (779) bone flaker; (2075 and 1452) bone beads; (1374–3191) *Olivella* beads; (1901) *Haliotis* bead; (3149) *Haliotis* pendant; (836) shell disc bead.

objects from excavated sites and surface contexts around the Warner Lakes. Tuohy (1990) reported similar artifacts from Pyramid Lake. Both researchers interpreted them as fishing-net weights. Warner Valley supports four species of native fish: (1) tui chub; (2) dace; (3) redband trout; and (4) Warner sucker. The presence of net weights around the Warner Lakes, including in some cases on the dry lakebeds themselves, suggests that people used weighted nets to either capture tui chub or larger fish in those lakes. Chub and sucker vertebrae are present in low numbers throughout LSP-1's early Holocene deposits (Butler 2012), but we did not identify any in the late Holocene deposits from which we recovered the net weight.

0   5 cm

11

3013

25

3254   1084   1413   225   974

grooves

FIGURE 10.2. Miscellaneous stone and pumice tools: (3013) percussor; (11) hammerstone; (25) net weight; (3254 and 1084) battered cobbles; (1413–974) pumice abraders/shaft straighteners. Note the multiple grooves on Artifact 974.

Hammerstones and Percussors

We recovered just four hammerstones and a large flake percussor, which is surprising given the volume of lithic detritus in the shelter. Artifact 11 is an andesite cobble from the Late Archaic component that measures 89 × 75 × 41 mm and weighs 287 g. It was shaped by removing several large flakes. A few of its arrises are polished, and its margins are heavily battered. Artifact 1084 is a small, elongated tuff cobble from the Late Paleoindian component that measures 73 × 31 × 25 mm and weighs 66 g. One end is heavily battered and marked by stepped flake scars aligned to the long axis, suggesting that it may have been used to resurface worn metate surfaces by pecking rather than as a hammerstone used to produce flaked stone tools. Artifact 3254 is also a small, elongated cobble made of andesite, also from the Late Paleoindian component. It measures 68 × 35 × 26 mm and weighs 78 g. Like Artifact 1080, one of its ends is battered and flake scarred, and it may have been used in a similar manner. Artifact 2379 is a spall from a quartzite hammerstone that measures 68 × 36 × 21 mm and weighs 51 g. It is the only quartzite artifact in the LSP-1 assemblage and as such is probably not made from local material. It bears few signs of use other than the prominent negative flake scar that marks its removal from the cobble, which would have required a considerable amount of force. We assigned it to the Late Paleoindian component. Artifact 3013 is a large andesite flake that measures 153 × 93 × 35 mm and weighs 411 g. Both lateral margins have had flakes removed to shape the artifact, and the distal margin shows both heavy rounding and stepped flaking. We assigned it to the Late Paleoindian component.

Abraders and Other Pumice Tools

We recovered seven pumice artifacts, six of which we assigned to the Late Paleoindian component. Two pieces, artifacts 403 and 1240, are too small and fragmentary to infer their possible function, but both show possible shaping along their edges. Three larger pieces show clear evidence of modification and/or use. Artifact 505 is a rounded pumice cobble that shows light wear along one margin. Artifact 2592 is a rectangular piece that shows heavy polish on one end and was shaped to a point at the other end, giving it a wedge-shaped appearance in cross section. Artifact 1334 shows rounded and battered arrises on one end. Two final pieces, artifacts 225 and 974, are likely shaft straighteners. Artifact 225 is an elongated piece with an 11 mm wide and 5 mm deep groove running the length of one of its faces. One end appears to have been ground at an angle. Artifact 974 is an irregular piece that has four grooves worn into it. Three are on one face: the most prominent measures 11 mm wide

by 5 mm deep, while two lesser ones run parallel to one another and each measure 7 mm by 2 mm deep. On the piece's opposite face, a deep groove measures 11 × 5 mm.

Tools and other artifacts made of pumice are known from other TP/EH contexts in the northern Great Basin. Jenkins and colleagues (2013) reported a pumice abrader from the Younger Dryas-aged Botanical Lens. Donham and colleagues (2019) also reported a pumice abrader from Younger Dryas deposits at the Connley Caves. Finally, Connolly and Jenkins (1999) reported a shaped piece of pumice from an early Holocene component at the Paulina Lake Site. Farther afield, Labelle and Newton (2020) analyzed grooved abraders in early Holocene assemblages from the Plains and Rocky Mountains and concluded that these likely represent dart shaft straighteners. The U-shaped grooves in their sample average 11 mm in width—the same as three of the grooves on the two possible shaft straighteners from LSP-1. Given the similarities in the shape and size of Cody and Windust points (Amick 2013; Hartman 2019), it is possible that the wooden or bone foreshafts to which those point types were hafted were roughly the same size.

BONE ORNAMENTS AND TOOLS

We recovered 32 pieces of worked bone consisting of 18 beads, five awls (including one piece that may be a needle), one possible flaker, one utilized bison bone flake, one broken gaming or jewelry piece, and six pieces of unknown function. Sixteen of the 18 beads are made from leporid metapodials, and two are made from medium-sized animal (possibly canid) long bones. Some of the leporid metapodial beads had ends that were scored and snapped from the shaft while others had their ends simply snapped or broken off, leaving more jagged ends. We identified the specimens with snapped or broken ends because they are extensively polished, suggesting that they were once strung on a necklace and became polished by wear. Hattori (1982: Figure 18) recovered similar minimally modified leporid metapodial beads still strung on complete necklaces at Falcon Hill in western Nevada. The awls, gaming or jewelry piece, flaker, and most pieces of unknown function are made of shaped, small artiodactyl (pronghorn, mountain sheep, or mule deer) long-bone fragments. One of the unidentified pieces is made of antler.

We recovered the worked bone artifacts in roughly equal numbers from Late Paleoindian (*n*=15) and Late Archaic (*n*=14) deposits, with a few also coming from Middle Archaic (*n*=1) and mixed (*n*=2) deposits. Bone beads—the most common type of bone artifact—were also equally distributed in Late Paleoindian (*n*=7) and

Late Archaic (*n*=9) deposits, whereas other bone arti-facts were slightly more common in the Late Paleoin-dian (*n*=8) deposits than the Late Archaic (*n*=5) deposits (though this is probably because we excavated more early Holocene deposits). Given that Hockett and col-leagues only analyzed the fauna from one third of the excavated levels (see Chapter 6), there are almost cer-tainly additional worked-bone artifacts in the unana-lyzed level bags. Nevertheless, our sample of bone tools and ornaments provides some insight into human be-havior in the shelter.

Foremost, the production of bone beads made of leporid elements suggests that people carried out a range of activities beyond simply processing and con-suming foods. Similarly, the broken awls and possible needle suggest that people made or maintained baskets, sandals, clothing, or other fiber items at the site, even though we did not recover such items in some of the components. Finally, the possible gaming piece suggests that people may have enjoyed recreational activities in the shelter.

SHELL ORNAMENTS

We recovered 12 marine shell ornaments from the three cultural components, including one *Haliotis* pendant, one *Haliotis* bead, nine *Olivella* beads, and one clam-shell disc bead.

Haliotis *Pendant*

We recovered one tear-drop shaped pendant (Artifact 3149) made of iridescent abalone (*Haliotis* sp.) shell. It measures 21 × 11 × 2 mm, is mostly complete, and was shaped by grinding. One face, recovered from Late Ar-chaic deposits, appears to have some remnants of red pigment embedded in it. The diameter of the pendant's hole is 2 mm. Tipps (1998) reported similar pendants from 35Lk2927, a pair of small rockshelters near the Coyote Hills that produced a radiocarbon date of ~625 cal BP but also glass trade beads, and 35Lk734, a large multicomponent site on the shore of Crump Lake that produced radiocarbon dates of ~300 cal BP, ~400 cal BP, and ~425 cal BP. She did not report the specific taxa from which those pendants are made, and it is unclear whether they are made of abalone. A similar abalone shell pendant from the Bergen Site in the Fort Rock Basin was dated to ~5600 cal BP (L. Largaespada 2006).

Haliotis *Bead*

Artifact 1901 is a broken rectangular *Haliotis* shell bead that measures 9 × 5 × 1 mm. Part of the biconical hole is intact and measures 2 mm. We recovered the bead from Middle Archaic deposits. Similar square and rectangular

abalone beads mostly come from Middle Archaic con-texts in the Fort Rock Basin (L. Largaespada 2006).

Olivella *Beads*

We recovered nine *Olivella* shell beads consisting of two A1a (small, simple, spire-lopped) beads, two probable A1b (medium, simple, spire-lopped) beads, two A2a (small, oblique, spire-lopped) beads, two A2c (large, oblique, spire-lopped) beads, and one unidentified bead fragment (Bennyhoff and Hughes 1987) (Table S12). Seven beads came from early Holocene deposits and two came from mixed deposits. Given their strati-graphic position deep in the deposits, we submitted seven of the beads for AMS dating and isotopic analysis to determine age and origin. Because *Olivella* snails live up to 15 years, their shells form over multiple seasons and years during which time ocean temperature and upwelling can vary (Eerkens et al. 2005). Furthermore, individual snail shells may possess variable ^{14}C content in different growth bands (Culleton et al. 2006; Hadden and Cherkinsky 2015). To account for these fluctuations in ocean conditions, we sampled each bead at different points along the shell's growth rings and in two cases (Artifacts 1374 and 2478) dated the same bead multiple times (see Smith et al. 2016a for more information about our sampling methodology). Five beads returned early Holocene dates and one bead returned a late Holocene date (see Table 4.2). Their isotope signatures generally indicate that the beads came from north of Point Con-ception, California, probably along the Oregon or Wash-ington coast (Smith et al. 2016a: Table 4 and Figure 4).

Excavations at sites around the Warner Lakes have produced a handful of *Olivella* shell beads from two sites, though from much later contexts. 35Lk121 is un-dated but produced a range of projectile point types. Radiocarbon dates from 35Lk2579 indicate that it dates to after 700 cal BP (Tipps 1998). Several of the *Olivella* beads from LSP-1 are the oldest directly dated marine shell beads in the northern Great Basin and among the oldest dated shell beads in the western United States. They support claims of early Holocene marine shell bead use in the Oregon desert, based on less secure asso-ciations between beads and dated features of strata (Jen-kins et al. 2004b). Together with obsidian from inland sources at coastal sites in Oregon (Davis et al. 2004), the LSP-1 beads suggest that coastal and interior groups established exchange networks fairly early.

Finally, the fact that the early Holocene beads from LSP-1 consistently originated along the northern Cali-fornia, Oregon, or Washington coasts sets them apart from middle and late Holocene *Olivella* beads from the northern Great Basin. In the Fort Rock Basin, middle

Holocene beads appear to have originated at multiple areas along the Pacific Coast, while late Holocene beads mainly originated in southern California (Bottman 2006). These differences hint at changes in coastal-interior exchange throughout the Holocene.

Shell Disc Bead

We recovered a disc bead made of shell from an unknown bivalve, probably a clam. Artifact 836 measures 11 mm in diameter and 2 mm thick. It has a biconical drilled hole with a diameter of 4 mm. We recovered it from sifted sediment from 101–106 cmbd and assigned it to the Late Paleoindian component. The bead is larger than similar clam shell disc beads from late Holocene contexts in the Fort Rock Basin (L. Largaespada 2006), and we are unaware of comparable specimens from early Holocene contexts in the northern Great Basin.

SUMMARY

Bone, stone, and shell ornaments and tools like those from LSP-1 generally do not preserve at open-air sites. They offer glimpses of daily life that in some cases are not directly related to food acquisition: basketry or clothing production; personal adornment; recreation; and ties to distant groups. The presence of hammerstones and abraders indicate that people made and maintained the organic and inorganic components of weapons. The presence of bone awls/needles—traditionally women's tools—supports our belief that families visited LSP-1, at least near the end of the early Holocene and latter part of the late Holocene. Lastly, the marine shell beads reveal that visitors to the shelter participated in broader socio-economic systems that also included groups living along the Pacific Coast.

Fiber Artifacts

Anna J. Camp, Pat Barker, and Eugene M. Hattori

The fiber artifacts from LSP-1, though the assemblage is small and in generally poor condition, still contribute to broader discussions of technology and human population histories in the northern Great Basin. The assemblage consists of 15 cordage fragments, two net fragments, three Catlow Twine basketry wall fragments, two other basketry fragments, five incomplete woven sandals, one large sagebrush fiber bundle, and five small fiber fragments. The sandal fragments, a Catlow Twine wall fragment, and the large sagebrush bundle originated in pit feature F.14-10.

METHODS

We analyzed the basketry using Adovasio's (1977) methods. We assigned the sandals to recognized types using attributes outlined by Connolly and Barker (2004) and, in one case, ethnographic information (Barrett 1910). Finally, we classified the cordage using procedures and terminology following Hurley (1979) and classified knots following Shaw (1972).

BASKETRY

Table 11.1 summarizes the metric data and radiocarbon dates for the LSP-1 basketry. Three fragments (artifacts 2926, 2927, and 3434) represent Catlow Twine, a basketry type found across the northern Great Basin beginning ~9400 cal BP and continuing into the ethnographic period with Klamath–Modoc basketry (Camp 2017; Connolly 1994; Connolly et al. 2016; Cressman 1942; C. Fowler and Hattori 2011, 2012) and referred to by Adovasio (1977) as Type 1 basketry. Catlow Twine is a semi-flexible, close simple twined basketry type manufactured using a Z-twist (down-to-the-right) weft and a two-ply,

S-spun, Z-twist (Zss) cordage warp. It is typically made from split tule cordage warp and split tule weft. The largest piece of Catlow Twine (Artifact 3434) likely represents a fragment of a large bowl or tray (Figure 11.1).

The remaining two basketry fragments are also manufactured from tule but are not demonstrably Catlow Twine. The first (Artifact LSP-1-NP-1) is a flexible, diagonally twined piece with a Z-twist weft direction made from tule. It has two weft rows that terminate, exposing the Zss cordage warp. This is likely a decorative element in the wall of the basket. There is visible overlay of cane (*Phragmites*) in the weft rows. This type of flexible diagonally twined basketry with a cordage warp co-occurs with Catlow Twine at some sites in the northern and western Great Basin (Connolly et al. 2016). It contrasts with the rigid, diagonally twined, peeled willow rod ethnographic Numic basketry (C. Fowler 1994). The second (Artifact 923) is likely a piece from the selvage of a tule basket where the cordage warps were folded and incorporated into the final weft row. It is unclear whether the basket is Catlow Twine, although the fragment does contain a tule cordage warp with the same spin and twist as Catlow Twine (Zss). Two Catlow Twine baskets from Chewaucan Cave in the nearby Abert-Chewaucan Basin have selvages similar to Artifact 923 from LSP-1 (Kallenbach 2013).

We directly dated four basketry fragments (see Tables 4.2 and 11.1). The calibrated age ranges of three pieces—two recovered from the rat midden (F.14-01) and one recovered from the looters' backdirt—overlap for the period between 1175 and 1065 cal BP, which falls within LSP-1's final occupation period of 1300–900 cal BP. We recovered the fourth piece from the F.14-10

TABLE 11.1. Basketry and sandals

Basketry	Artifact No.				
	2926	2927	3434	LSP-1-NP-1	923
type	Catlow Twine	Catlow Twine	Catlow Twine	Diagonally Twined	braided cordage
construction	close simple	close simple	close simple	close diagonal	n/a
dimensions (cm)	1 × 1	2 × 2	7 × 5.5	3 × 2	2 × 1
^{14}C lab number	UGA-16860	UGA-16859	UGA-18235	AA-103861	n/a
^{14}C date	1160±20	1200±20	1790±20	1230±35	n/a
cal BP, 95.4% confidence	1175–990	1180–1065	1815–1625	1265–1065	n/a

Sandals	Artifact No.				
	3435	3436	3437	3439	3438
type	spiral weft	Klamath style	Multiple Warp	unknown	unknown
twining	close simple	open simple	open simple	unknown simple	open simple
no. of warps	5	12	9	10+	3+
heel pocket	+	+	?	?	?
toe flap	—	?	—	?	?
start location	center	heel	heel	?	?
dimensions (cm)	13 × 8 × 2	19 × 11 × 1	18 × 8 × 1	—	—
^{14}C lab number	UGA-18236	UGA-18238	UGA-18239	UGA-18240	—
^{14}C date	1860±20	1300±20	1760±20	1880±20	—
cal BP, 95.4% confidence	1865–1730	1285–1185	1720–1610	1880–1735	—

Note: +=present; —=absent; ?=indeterminate.

pit that also contained the sandals. It returned an age of 1815–1625 cal BP, which overlaps with three of the sandal dates (see below) and marks an earlier, Late Archaic occupation.

SANDALS

The five LSP-1 sandals have been previously published in detail (Smith et al. 2016b). Here, we simply reiterate their important aspects and place them into what we have learned about LSP-1 since that article was published. The sandals are all made from sagebrush bark and all came from the F.14-10 storage pit. There is no evidence of toe flaps, decoration, or repair, although the sandals are fragmented and in poor condition. Two (Artifacts 3438 and 3439) are in such bad condition that we could not assign them to particular types and do not discuss them further. Stich slant for all sandals is down-to-the-right (Zss). While the sandals from LSP-1 were well-worn, they were intentionally cached in a storage pit rather than just discarded (see Chapter 5). Used sandal caching in caves and rockshelters in the northern Great Basin has a long history, extending back to the TP/EH (Connolly and Barker 2004, 2008).

Multiple Warp Sandal

F.14-10 included a fragmented Multiple Warp type sandal (Artifact 3437). Multiple Warp sandals (Connolly and Barker 2004, 2008; Cressman 1942) are close twined from heel to toe with warps running parallel to the axis of the foot. They have an even number of warps, typically more than eight. Instead of a flat sole, Multiple Warp sandals have an integral twined heel pocket and an untwined or open twined toe flap made with shredded warps. Warps are typically unspun skeins of sagebrush bark or tule shoots. At the toe, one selvage warp is converted to twined cordage to make a lace. Weft loops are paired on either side of the sole. Artifact 3437 is a typical Multiple Warp sandal instep sole fragment that lacks either a heel or toe (Smith et al. 2016b). It returned an age of 1720–1610 cal BP.

Spiral Weft Sandal

F.14-10 also contained a Spiral Weft type sandal (Artifact 3435). Spiral Weft sandals are made with warps running perpendicular to the axis of the foot and wefts twined in a spiral pattern from the centerline of the foot (Connolly and Barker 2004, 2008; Cressman 1942). At the edge of the sole, warp loop bindings are made by converting the warp to two-ply cordage that is then looped out and back to the sole. Warp loops are offset on alternating sides of the sole. Artifact 3435 is a Spiral Weft sandal sole fragment with a heel pocket, warp loop bindings, and no toe flap. In contrast to most Spiral Weft sandals, its warps are two-ply, Zss cordage. This sandal is also atypical because it has an attached heel pocket. It returned an age of 1865–1730 cal BP.

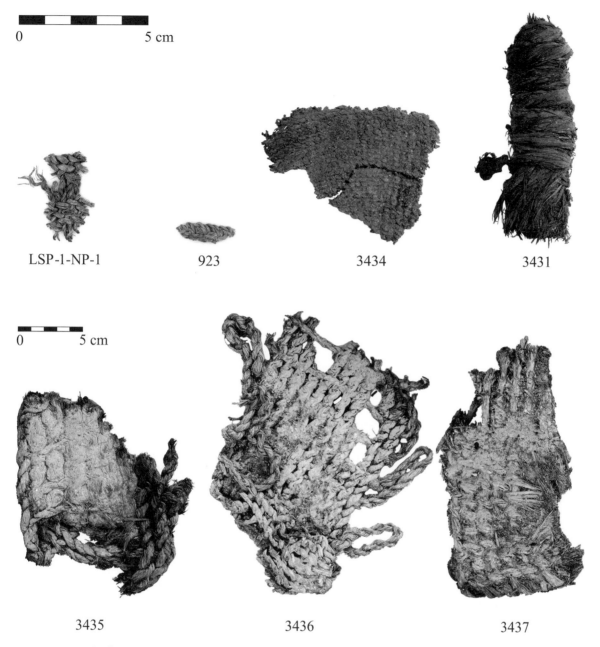

0   5 cm

LSP-1-NP-1   923   3434   3431

0   5 cm

3435   3436   3437

FIGURE 11.1. Textiles from LSP-1. Top row: (LSP-1-NP-1) diagonally twined basketry fragment; (923) basketry selvage (923); (3434) Catlow Twine basketry from F.14-10; and (3431) sagebrush bark bundle. Bottom row: (3435) Spiral Weft sandal; (3436) Klamath style sandal; and (3437) Multiple Warp sandal. Note the different scales for items in the top and bottom rows.

Klamath Style Sandal

Artifact 3436 is technically a Multiple Warp sandal, although it is markedly different than Artifact 3437, described above. It is a sole fragment with part of a heel pocket but no toe flap. The sole was made with open simple twining. The warps are 2-Zss cordage, and the wefts are Z-twined down to the right. Artifact 3436's bindings, cordage warps, "ladder" heel pocket, and very open twining are more like ethnographic Klamath sandals (Barrett 1910) than other Multiple Warp sandals

recovered from archaeological contexts. It returned an age of 1285–1185 cal BP.

CORDAGE

Traditionally, people made cordage by rolling damp fiber strands with the palm of a hand along the thigh, either toward or away from the body to form a single twisted ply or strand. Paired strands were then twisted together in the opposite direction of the single ply to make a two-ply cord. Pushing first away from the body produced two-ply s-spun Z-twist cord and pulling first toward the body resulted in a two-ply z-spun S-twist cord (Eiselt 1997b; C. Fowler 1989, 1992; I. Kelly 1932; Wheat 1967). Spin and twist are the opposite of what is described above for a left-handed cordage maker.

Excavation produced 15 cordage fragments from LSP-1 (Table 11.2). Eleven are Szz two-ply cords, three are one-ply z-twist strands from two-ply Szz cords, and one is a two-ply Zss cord. Materials include dogbane (*n*=7), probable dogbane (too crusted to identify; *n*=2), milkweed (*n*=1), sagebrush (*n*=1), and tule (*n*=4). The cordage assemblage includes two net fragments each consisting of two Szz cords joined by a weaver's knot. Both fragments are dogbane stained with red ochre. Unfortunately, they are too small to determine use. A single piece of cordage recovered from F.14-02 (a hearth from Stratum IV) dates to 4520–4415 cal BP, but it was destroyed before we had an opportunity to describe it. As such, we do not include it in our discussion here. The other cordage pieces remain undated, and, with two exceptions (Artifacts 2539 and 2545, both from Late Archaic deposits) all originated within or adjacent to F.14-01 (the rat midden). As such, we cannot confidently assign them to any of the cultural components without directly dating them. The cordage may represent pieces of degraded nets used to capture some of the leporids from the site, though given their small size we cannot be certain.

In sum, the LSP-1 cordage assemblage is typical of those from northern Great Basin sites. It is generally consistent with C. Fowler's (1994) observation that cordage in archaeological or ethnographic contexts is predominantly two-ply S-spun Z-twist, except that the two netting fragments do not conform to her observation that netting is predominantly two-ply Z-spun S-twist. If both fragments were made by the same spinner, then this discrepancy could be due to handedness.

MISCELLANEOUS MATERIALS

The textile assemblage includes a large sagebrush bark bundle (Artifact 3431) found in feature F.14-10 along with five small tule fragments and one small piece of shredded sagebrush bark. The sagebrush bark bundle dates to 1300–1190 cal BP. It is difficult to know what the bundle's function was, although elsewhere (Smith et al. 2016b) we suggested it may have served as a source of raw material for fiber artifacts—a possibility in line with our suggestion that F.14-10 contained a cache of textiles that, although well-worn, could nevertheless provide cordage with which to repair existing items. Five very small fiber fragments were also recovered from LSP-1, but none possessed any diagnostic attributes.

DISCUSSION

The LSP-1 textile assemblage is small and came mostly from two late Holocene features: F.14.01 (the rat midden) and F.14.10 (a storage pit). Given that we recovered a spindle whorl and several awls in the early Holocene deposits, Late Paleoindian groups probably also made and used fiber artifacts at LSP-1, though we did not recover any baskets, sandals, or cordage from that period. It is possible that the crack in the ceiling, which periodically admits water to the shelter, has contributed to poorer organic preservation in LSP-1's lower strata. The general absence of fiber artifacts in the Middle Archaic component may also be explained by poorer preservation, although the absence of awls and whorls from that period may indicate that Middle Archaic visitors did not emphasize textile production.

Though fragmentary, the LSP-1 textiles contribute to our understanding of how and when people used the site and, at a broader scale, the history of the northern Great Basin. In terms of site use, the ages of the textiles mostly correspond to the final major occupation period (1300–900 cal BP). During that period, visitors to the site made and used Rosegate points, used groundstone implements to process seeds and other resources, and discarded numerous rabbit and hare carcasses. They also excavated a pit and filled it with well-worn textiles.

The date for the Spiral Weft sandal overlaps the date for the unidentified sandal fragment. The Multiple Warp sandal and the Catlow Twine fragment are ~60 years younger. However, the Klamath Style sandal and bark bundle dates overlap and are significantly younger. It is difficult to explain the bimodal distribution of dates from of the cache. Well-worn sandals were commonly but inexplicably cached in caves, while Catlow Twine baskets and trays were not (Connolly and Barker 2004, 2008). The twine fragment may be intrusive, while the sandals and the bark bundle could have been cached for later use, possibly as tinder for fire starting.

At a broader scale, the LSP-1 textiles may speak to Penutian and Numic use of Warner Valley during the Late Archaic and Terminal Prehistoric periods. The presence of Catlow Twine basketry dated to 1815–1625, 1180–1065, and 175–990 cal BP in LSP-1 suggests that Penutian groups visited the shelter during the Late Archaic period. The 1285–1185 cal BP date on the Klamath Style sandal supports this scenario. Although LSP-1 fell into disuse after ~900 cal BP, other sites in Warner Valley have produced Catlow Twine basketry with even later dates (Camp 2017 and references therein). Two pieces from South Warner Cave (35Lk94) returned dates of 920–465 cal BP and 760–550 cal BP. One piece from the Peninsula Site (35Lk2579) returned a date of 255–0

TABLE 11.2. Cordage

Artifact No.	Type	Ply	Twist/ Spin	Turns per cm	Length (mm)	Diameter (mm)	Material	Remarks
131	cordage	2	Szz	4.5	70.2	1.9	*Apocynum*	
135.1	cordage	2	Szz	4.0	38.9	2.1	*Apocynum?*	Weaver's knot? Too crusted to identify material and knot; has two cords.
135.2	cordage	2	Szz	8.0	35.3	1.7	*Apocynum?*	Weaver's knot? Too crusted to identify material and knot; has two cords.
136	cordage	2	Szz	5.5	60.6	1.1	*Apocynum*	
141	cordage	2	Szz	5.0	54.4	1.5	*Apocynum*	
155.1	cordage	2	Szz	9.0	34.6	1.7	*Asclepias*	overhand knot; has two cords
155.2	netting	2	Szz	thick 4.7 thin 5.1	thick 46.4 thin 32.4	thick 2.2 thin 1.2	*Apocynum*	Net with thick and thin cordage; weaver's knots; red ocher stain; sagebrush bark skein overhand knot on thick cord.
157	cordage	2	Szz	4.5	45.2	2.0	*Schoenoplectus*	
159	cordage	2	Szz	8.0	24.8	1.3	*Apocynum*	overhand knot
922.1	cordage	2	Szz	5.5	58.0	1.7	*Schoenoplectus*	has two cords
922.2	netting	2	Szz	6.0	101.7	2.0	*Apocynum*	weaver's knots; red ocher stain
978	cordage	2	Zss	thick 3.0 thin 4.5	180.6	thick 1.8 thin 1.1	*Apocynum*	variable diameter
2089	cordage	2	Szz	9.0	13.8	1.4	*Schoenoplectus*	
2503	cordage	1	Z	4.5	47.5	3.0	*Artemisia* bark	½ of 2-ply cord
2539	cordage	1	Z	7.0	14.6	1.3	*Apocynum*	½ of 2-ply cord
2545	cordage	1	Z	2.7	54.8	1.5	*Schoenoplectus*	crusted
2925	cordage	2	Szz	5.0	70.8	1.6	*Apocynum*	

cal BP–Present, suggesting that it may mark an ethnohistoric occupation.

These late dates on putative Penutian textiles do not correspond with ethnographic accounts that identified Warner Valley as Northern Paiute Territory (Barrett 1910; C. Fowler and Liljeblad 1986; I. Kelly 1932; Spier 1930; Stern 1998). The late dates may indicate either that the Northern Paiute did not start visiting Warner Valley until just prior to the historic period, or that the area saw shared use by Penutian and Numic groups during the Terminal Prehistoric period. We return to this topic in Chapter 13.

12

Site Structure and Occupation Duration

Erica J. Bradley, Geoffrey M. Smith, and Christopher S. Jazwa

Site structure is a common theme in archaeological research in other parts of the world, but it has not traditionally been a focus of Great Basin cave and rockshelter studies. Certainly, some excellent work has been done; for example, Thomas's (1983) work at Gatecliff Shelter and Schmitt and Madsen's (2005) work at Camels Back Cave. Work at those sites benefited in part from the separation of many of the cultural layers by sterile deposits, which helped excavators isolate short-term "living surfaces." In our opinion, the way that the Gatecliff and Camels Back Cave records were reported is the gold standard for Great Basin cave and rockshelter archaeology.

Unfortunately, sites like Gatecliff and Camels Back Cave are rare. Most Great Basin cave and rockshelter records are messy due to recurrent human use and post-depositional processes. LSP-1 falls into this category. People visited the site several times during the twilight of the early Holocene, depositing a huge volume of leporid bones, fire-affected rock, and other artifacts that quickly formed a thick layer of detritus. They then abandoned the site for most of the middle Holocene, during which time very little sediment accumulated in the shelter. People returned to LSP-1 at the beginning of the late Holocene when the shelter floor was probably still littered with the remains of the final early Holocene visits. Thus, although the LSP-1 record features a long hiatus, it lacks a band of sterile sediment separating the early Holocene from late Holocene deposits.

The challenge of teasing apart this more-or-less continuous vertical distribution of artifacts was compounded by the fact that some bioturbation occurred over the course of the Holocene. Some out-of-sequence radiocarbon dates suggest that minor mixing occurred in places. These are mostly on isolated charcoal fragments or small macrobotanical remains along the Strata IV/V contact. We addressed this issue by assigning each 5 cm excavation level to three cultural components (Late Paleoindian, Middle Archaic, and Late Archaic). We excluded cases where we could not confidently assign a level to one of these components because conflicting radiocarbon dates or diagnostic artifacts suggested disturbance or mixing. The three cultural components do not reflect single visits to the site; rather, as we argue below, the site probably witnessed repeat visits during each period. As such, the components are best conceived as aggregates that reflect the sum of different activities carried out by different people at different times. A final obstacle was the destruction of much of the site's Middle and Late Archaic occupations by looters. This made tracking the different strata across the shelter's interior difficult though not impossible. In our discussions of those periods, we focus on excavation units that contained intact Middle and Late Archaic deposits.

Despite these challenges, investigating site structure at LSP-1 was warranted. Understanding how people organized their space in caves and shelters can offer insight into group size and composition—two aspects of hunter-gatherer archaeology that have not been adequately explored in the Great Basin. Here, we outline what we know about site structure and occupation span in LSP-1. We begin with the Late and Middle Archaic periods, the records of which are both limited due to the looting event, and conclude with the Late Paleoindian

TABLE 12.1. Late and Middle Archaic artifact densities (artifacts/m³)

Excavation Unit	Excavated Volume (m³)		Flaked Tools		Groundstone		Debitage	
	Late Archaic	Middle Archaic	Late Archaic	Middle Archaic	Late Archaic	Middle Archaic	Late Archaic	Middle Archaic
N102E99	.25	.20	16	35	16	10	252	700
N103E99	.25	.25	16	0	8	0	196	632
N104E99	.45	.30	13.3	26.7	2.2	0	364.4	2,390
N105E99	.45	.30	15.6	20	4.4	0	508.9	1,300
N106E99	.25	.175	12	16.7	20	0	740	1,850
N107E99	.315	—	60.7	—	12	—	949.2	—

Note: Because there were no Middle Archaic deposits in N107E99, that unit is not included in our discussion of site structure.

record, which offers a more complete picture of early Holocene lifeways. We focus on understanding whether people used some parts of the shelter more than others and whether the early Holocene deposits contained spatially discrete depositional areas (*sensu* Carr 1984).[1]

To address these questions, we draw primarily upon Thomas's (1983) discussion of site structure at Gatecliff Shelter and, to a lesser extent, Schmitt and Madsen's (2005) work at Camels Back Cave. We also rely upon the limited ethnographic data regarding cave and rockshelter use (see Galanidou 2000 and references therein). Thomas divided the floor of Gatecliff Shelter into three segments: (1) the *interior*, or the area between the rear wall and mean hearthline (the average position of hearths relative to the wall); (2) the *hearth zone*, or the area between the average hearthline and shelter's dripline; and (3) the *outside*, or the area beyond the dripline. He used these zones to examine the distribution of artifacts across each horizon. Because our excavation block did not extend beyond LSP-1's dripline, we instead divided the floor into two zones: (1) the *interior*, a ~23 m² area carved into the welded tuff and andesite rimrock; and (2) the *apron*, a roughly equivalent area between the base of the rimrock and the dripline. Table 12.1 lists the excavation units that we included in our limited analysis of Late and Middle Archaic site structure.

Thomas also developed an *exogene cave model*, which is essentially Binford's (1978) refuse-disposal model adapted for rockshelters. He retained the idea of *drop zones* (areas surrounding hearths where food remains, tools, and other refuse accumulates) and *toss zones* (areas where people throw larger items). The model predicts that larger debris will be concentrated between a shelter's hearths and opening. Though the relationship between Gatecliff's rear wall, hearths, and dripline changed across time, the distribution of detritus generally conformed to this model. Using the exogene cave model and a basic distinction between LSP-1's interior and apron, we turn our attention to Late and

Middle Archaic site structure using flaked and groundstone tools as well as debitage densities from the six excavation units that comprised the E99 Trench (see Table 12.1). Later, we examine Late Paleoindian site structure more thoroughly using a larger sample and more sophisticated approaches.

THE LATE ARCHAIC COMPONENT

The Late Archaic component was restricted to the western part of the shelter, where we excavated the 6 × 1 m E99 Trench and two additional 1 × 1 m units in its northwest quadrant, and the front of the shelter just behind the dripline, where we excavated most of a 5 × 1 m east–west line of units along the southern edge of the looters' pit.

We cannot know how Late Archaic groups used much of the shelter's interior because looting destroyed those deposits, but we can say a few things about site structure during that period. First, LSP-1 never offered a large living space and, in the millennia leading up to Euro-American contact, it would have been smaller than the preceding periods due to sediment accumulation. Roughly 45 m² would have been available behind the dripline and ~23 m² in the interior, although the ceiling would have been barely high enough for people to stand. In the southwest quadrant, the floor would have sloped up to the west due to the debris cone that brought material into the shelter. Based on the size of the shelter and estimates derived from various sources (e.g., Cook 1972; Porčić 2012), our best guess is that six or seven people could have occupied LSP-1 at any given time if they only used the shelter's interior. If people also worked and slept on the shelter's apron, then the site could have probably accommodated twice that number.

Late Archaic visitors built a hearth (F.11-14) in the excavation block's southwest quadrant and a storage pit (F.14-10) in its southeast quadrant (see Figure 5.1). Three undated hearths (F.14-06, F.14-07, and F.14-08) dug into Stratum IV in the southeast quadrant are also likely Late Archaic in age, given their stratigraphic position. The F.11-14 hearth was located ~3 m from the back wall, ~2 m from the west wall, and ~5 m behind the dripline. The pit and the other three hearths clustered ~1 m from the east wall and ~3 m behind the dripline. F.11-14 was the northernmost hearth, and, while we do not know whether Late Archaic groups also built fires in the northeast quadrant, we know they did not do so in the northwest quadrant where we excavated intact Late Archaic deposits. This is not surprising as fires in the back of the shelter would have quickly filled the space with smoke, given the shelter's low ceiling and relatively small interior. Furthermore, it would have reduced the amount of heated space suitable for sleeping (Thomas 1983). Heated space would have been especially important if people visited LSP-1 during the autumn, which the animal and plant remains suggest. Finally, the position of the hearths near the mouth of the shelter is consistent with ethnographic data regarding caves and shelter use that show people tend to conduct most cooking activities on the aprons (Walthall 1998 and references therein).

Artifact density in the E99 Trench does not clearly conform to the exogene cave model: flaked and groundstone tools as well as debitage are generally more common toward the interior than they are toward the apron. Moreover, artifact density is not notably higher in units immediately adjacent to the F.11-14 hearth (i.e., the drop zone). One possible explanation for these trends is that if people occupied LSP-1 during the autumn, then they may have conducted some activities behind the hearth where it would have been relatively warm.

The F.11-14 hearth dates to 975–805 cal BP, which is younger than the F.14-10 pit. The pit contained two fiber artifacts whose age ranges overlap between 1285 and 1190 cal BP, and four fiber artifacts dated to between 1880–1735 cal BP and 1720–1610 cal BP. As such, it marks two periods of Late Archaic use. We have argued in earlier chapters that the bimodal age of the pit's contents may reflect later visitors collecting fiber artifacts left behind by earlier visitors, possibly for reuse later. Finally, we collected three small pieces of basketry whose age ranges overlap between 1175 and 1065 cal BP from the rat midden and the looters' backdirt. Together, these six dates on artifacts and features indicate that Late Archaic groups used the site between ~1900–1600 cal BP and ~1300–900 cal BP. The calibrated age ranges of the younger items from the pit and the scattered basketry fragments only overlap in one case, suggesting that they mark separate visits. The dated hearth postdates the directly dated Late Archaic artifacts. Thus, within the broader periods during which Late Archaic groups used LSP-1, there were likely at least three separate visits.

Late Archaic groups made and discarded stone tools, processed large numbers of rabbits and hares, and ground seeds and perhaps other resources using manos and metates. They discarded broken ornaments and worn-out sandals and baskets. At least one flintknapper made novice errors typical of children or adolescents. Finally, visitors lost or discarded bone awls and needles. Together, these trends suggest that families—probably no more than one or two at a time, given the shelter's small size—were the most frequent visitors to LSP-1 during the Late Archaic period.

THE MIDDLE ARCHAIC COMPONENT

The horizontal extent of excavated Middle Archaic deposits is roughly the same as that of the Late Archaic deposits; therefore, we faced the same challenges in interpreting Middle Archaic site structure. Because the Late Archaic deposits were shallow, the usable area inside the shelter was not significantly greater during the Middle Archaic period. Visitors would have faced the same space constraints as later groups, though there would have been more room to stand during the Middle Archaic period.

Middle Archaic hearth positioning strategies seem to have been like Late Archaic strategies. The northernmost Middle Archaic hearth (F.11-19) was built in essentially the same spot as a Late Archaic hearth (F.11-14), ~3 m from the back wall. It dates to 3160–2960 cal BP. A second Middle Archaic hearth (F.11-05/15) lay ~1 m to the west but postdates F.11-19 by at least a few centuries (F.11-05/15 dates to 2725–2475 cal BP). Four other Middle Archaic hearths lay a few meters closer to the dripline: F.14-06 was 1 m from the east wall and ~3 m inside the dripline. It dates to 3450–3270 cal BP and thus predates both interior features. Three hearths (F.11-06/14-04, F.14-02, and F.11-07) were clustered in the southwest quadrant of the shelter, 1–2 m closer to the dripline than the ones described above. Those hearths each date to the same time, 4520–4415 cal BP, suggesting either that people repeatedly visited the shelter during that interval or built more than one hearth per visit. Those hearths mark the earliest Middle Archaic occupation of the site and people's return to the shelter after a lengthy middle Holocene hiatus.

The distribution of Middle Archaic artifacts is different from that of Late Archaic artifacts in the E99 Trench. Whereas flaked and groundstone tools as well as debitage were densest toward the back of the shelter in the Late Archaic deposits, flaked stone tools and groundstone were both densest toward the shelter's opening in the Middle Archaic deposits. Like the Late Archaic debitage, Middle Archaic debitage is densest toward the shelter's back wall. The abundance of Middle Archaic flaked and groundstone tools toward the front of the shelter is probably related to the cluster of hearths in that area and may reflect people using and dropping tools around the fires. The abundance of flakes behind the hearths may mark places where people flint-knapped deeper inside shelter, which again makes sense if they used the site during the colder months.

As is the case with the Late Archaic component, the age ranges of several Middle Archaic features do not overlap, which suggests that people visited LSP-1 at least four times during that period. Because the area behind the dripline was not significantly different from the Late Archaic period, our estimate for how many people used the site at one time remains unchanged: probably no more than six to seven.

The Middle Archaic assemblage contains a diverse suite of artifacts including projectile points, manos and metates, personal ornaments, and bone tools. In that regard, it is like the Late Archaic assemblage, though with a few differences. For example, groundstone is less common, projectile points and finished bifaces are more common, and there are fewer instances of novice knapping errors. Large mammal bones are slightly more abundant. Seeds and other plant resources are present but not abundant. Together, these differences suggest that Middle Archaic visitors focused more on hunting large game than later or, as we explain below, earlier visitors. Expert hunters/toolmakers may have constituted a greater proportion of those groups than during either the Late Archaic or Late Paleoindian periods.

The Late Paleoindian Component

Our understanding of Middle and Late Archaic site structure is limited by the loss of much of the deposits dating to those periods. Future studies of artifact distribution may help to identify finer-grained patterns of human behavior beyond simple hearth positioning strategies and coarse-grained trends in artifact density, though even then the view may remain narrow because intact deposits from those periods are limited. Fortunately, Stratum V, which dates to the end of the early Holocene and was the main artifact-bearing stratum in LSP-1, largely escaped destruction. We carefully excavated ~23 m² of Stratum V across the shelter's interior, making it ideal for examining how people used LSP-1. Because the stratum accumulated very rapidly, in part due to a brief but intense period during which people discarded ~1,000 rabbit and hare carcasses, we focused on two questions: (1) how many visits occurred during the terminal early Holocene? and (2) did people carry out different activities in different parts of the shelter?

Materials

The Late Paleoindian component included 470 flaked stone tools, 143 groundstone tools, ~20,000 flakes, ~62,000 faunal elements, and a handful of stone, bone, and shell ornaments and tools recovered from 11.9 m³ of excavated deposits. Of these, we recorded 303 flaked stone tools and 116 groundstone tools in situ. We recovered the rest of the stone tools (167 flaked stone and 27 groundstone tools) and all the flakes and animal bones from sifted sediment excavated mostly in 5-cm levels. We also recorded the positions of 212 pieces of fire-affected rock. We recorded one hearth (F.13-01) dated to 9735–9550 cal BP and a smaller hearth (F.13-02). Both are located ~3 m from the shelter's rear wall.

We recovered these artifacts from Strata V and VI, and, in places, the lowest levels of Stratum IV and the upper levels of Stratum VII. Because the looters' pit had an irregular floor, the thickness of the Late Paleoindian deposits varied. In some excavation units, the deposits spanned 70 cm; in others, they spanned just 20 cm. Here, we focus on the Stratum V deposits from 86 to 126 cmbd to examine Late Paleoindian site structure at LSP-1. Those deposits provided an optimal sample for several reasons. First, they totaled ~8.7 m³, or 82 percent of the Late Paleoindian deposits. Second, 26 of the 29 excavation units (90 percent) contained Late Paleoindian deposits in that elevation range; those that did not were small, wedge-shaped units located against the shelter walls. Third, they contained most of the Late Paleoindian assemblage: ~77 percent of the flaked stone tools (n=360); ~85 percent of the groundstone tools (n=121); ~75 percent of the debitage (n=14,841); and 80 percent of the fire-affected rock (n=169). In short, the 86–126 cmbd deposits offered a horizontally expansive and artifact-rich sample of a standardized volume with which to examine human behavior near the end of the early Holocene.

Methods

Establishing the Age of the 86–126 cmbd Deposits

We developed a stratigraphic model of radiocarbon dates from the lower strata of LSP-1 with two goals: (1) refine the precision of the age range for the 86–126 cmbd deposits; and (2) assess whether those deposits are consistent with a single occupation event or multiple periods of occupation. This proved difficult because of some overlap in dates from Strata IV–VIII, which likely reflects some mixing from recurrent human use and/or natural processes. To address this issue, we removed dates from the model that prevented agreement for 86–126 cmbd when creating a stratigraphic model in the OxCal 4.3 calibration software. These decisions produced a well-constrained age range for those deposits that is also conservative for occupation during this period. Samples dating to the very beginning or end of the range are the most likely to be excluded because they were most frequently the ones mixed with earlier or later strata, which are temporally distinct.

To establish this model, we assumed that: (1) the base of Stratum VIII, represented by samples from 141 and 155 cmbd, predates the 86–126 cmbd deposits of interest; and (2) the boundary between Strata IV and V, represented by samples from 71–76, 56–61, and 51–56 cmbd, postdate the 86–126 cmbd deposits. We combined the samples from each of the strata of interest into phases that we in turn placed into a sequence in Oxcal 4.3. The phase for the 86–126 cm deposits consisted of 14 dates (three from marine shell samples and 11 from terrestrial samples) that were temporally consistent with the model. This yielded a modeled range of 9655–9555 cal BP for the beginning age of the 86–126 cmbd level and a modeled range of 9380–9235 cal BP for the ending age of the 86–126 cmbd level. These modeled ranges suggest that the 86–126 cmbd Stratum V deposits took between 175 and 420 years to accumulate, or between 0.23 and 0.09 cm per year. Overlap in dates between those deposits and the overlying and underlying strata, along with other dates from mixed layers, indicates that the age range for the 86–126 cmbd level is a minimum estimate. The actual range may extend beyond this span, but our estimate represents a range of those dates that can be definitively associated with this occupation.

Examining the Horizontal Distribution of Artifacts

A major question about Stratum V was whether we could identify different depositional areas (i.e., artifact clusters) that mark places where individuals carried out specific tasks (e.g., biface production, core reduction, novice knapping, pigment production, secondary refuse disposal). Toward that goal, we used the R statistical environment to determine: (1) whether in situ artifacts were clustered; (2) the number and locations of clusters; (3) whether the depths of the clusters differed; (4) whether the contents of the clusters differed; and (5) whether the distribution of flaked stone tools and debitage differed across the shelter floor. We employed ArcGIS 10.7.1 to help visualize these analyses. We included in situ artifacts and/or those from sifted sediment, depending on their applicability to analytical techniques we describe here.

To determine whether the in situ flaked stone tools (projectile points, bifaces, flake tools, and cores) were clustered or randomly distributed, we used the spatstat package in R (Baddeley et al. 2015). We first calculated the L-function estimate (Besag's [1977] transformation of Ripley's K [Ripley 1977]) for their planar coordinates.[2] We then generated 99 Monte Carlo-simulated random point patterns and obtained their L-function estimates. Finally, we performed a Maximum Absolute Deviation (MAD) test (Baddeley et al. 2014) to evaluate whether significant differences exist between the observed L-function estimate and the estimates obtained through simulations.

The MAD test indicated that the plotted tools were not randomly distributed ($p = 0.01$); therefore, we used the NbClust package (Charrad et al. 2014) to identify the optimal number of clusters.[3] Subsequently, we applied a k-means clustering algorithm to assign each tool to a cluster.[4] We then compared the proportions of raw material types among tools and debitage, bifaces and flake tools, early- and late-stage bifaces, and bifaces with novice knapping errors. We also compared flake types and flake size among clusters using debitage collected from one excavation unit within the center of each cluster (N106E99, N105E101, N103E100, and N102E102). To assess the contemporaneity of the clusters and the groundstone, we compared their mean depths.

In addition to these statistical analyses, we created maps to visualize the distributions of both plotted and screened artifacts. For plotted artifacts, we used the Kernel Density tool in ArcGIS to produce density maps with smoothly tapered surfaces.[5] We generated one for flaked stone tools and one for groundstone tools plus fire-affected rock. For screened artifacts, we calculated the artifact densities for each excavation unit using their counts (including both plotted artifacts when available) divided by their excavation volumes and symbolized unit densities using graduated colors. To avoid inflated artifact densities, we multiplied them by 0.4, reflecting the modal volume of excavated deposits in each unit (0.4 m³). In addition, we produced separate maps for flakes smaller than 1 in and flakes larger than 1 in to explore the possibility of size-sorting. Finally, using the calculated tool density and debitage density by unit, we applied Pearson's correlation coefficient to determine if there is a relationship between where debitage and tools accumulated in the rockshelter.

Results

General Patterns

LSP-1 possesses fairly steep walls, which means that while earlier visitors would have enjoyed more headroom than later visitors they would not have had much more floorspace. As we outlined earlier, the shelter's small size would also have limited the number of people who could use it at one time. Again, both ethnographic and archaeological data suggest that number is six or seven individuals if people only used the interior, or twice that number if they also used the apron. Despite the volume of rabbit and hare bones in Stratum V, we do not think that the shelter ever housed large numbers of people. There simply was not enough room. As we have argued in earlier chapters, families were probably the primary social unit to visit LSP-1 during the terminal early Holocene. The lithic and faunal assemblages suggest that these stays were generally brief, and we suspect that the materials from 86–126 cmbd accumulated as the result of recurrent autumn visits, a topic we will explore further.

Like later visitors, the first people to visit LSP-1 did not build fires in the back of the shelter. The two early Holocene hearths were positioned 2–3 m from the shelter's back wall, a distance consistent with that of Middle and Late Archaic hearths in the western half of the shelter. We also have a clear picture of how flaked stone tools, groundstone and burned rock, and debitage were distributed across the shelter's interior. Figure 12.1 shows the densities (number of artifacts/0.4 m³ of sediment) of various artifact types recovered both in situ and from screened sediment. The assemblage was primarily concentrated in the eastern half of the shelter (Figure 12.1, upper left). That area enjoys sunlight longer than the shelter's western half. This would have offered two benefits. First, it would have provided more hours of daylight for people to work. Second, and perhaps more importantly, if people visited LSP-1 during the autumn, as we believe, then it would have stayed warmer for longer, and the wall would have continued to radiate heat after sunset. Artifact density was generally higher between the rear wall and the two hearths, which is consistent with ethnographic accounts of people living and working behind cooking or warming fires (Walthall 1998 and references therein). Again, that would make sense if people visited LSP-1 during the autumn. We found no clear evidence of hearth-centered activities (i.e., drop zones) around either F.13-01 or F.13-02. Nor was there clear evidence of regular disposal of lithic debris toward the shelter's front (i.e., a toss zone).

Debitage density (Figure 12.1, lower left) is consistent with that of the lithic assemblage as a whole, which is to be expected given that flakes are by far the most common artifact type. Larger flakes (>1 in) are more common than smaller flakes in excavation units along the eastern wall, perhaps because they were gradually pushed aside as people moved about inside the rockshelter (Binford 1983; Stevenson 1991).

The density of flaked stone tools across the shelter's interior was somewhat consistent, with 16 of 26 units containing 18 or fewer tools (Figure 12.1, upper right). Units with more than 18 tools were mostly located in the shelter's northeast quadrant between the rear wall and the hearths. While we found no evidence of drop zones around the hearths, as we will discuss, the flaked stone tools were not randomly distributed across the shelter's interior. The densities of flaked stone tools and debitage are not negatively correlated ($r=0.139$, $p=0.500$) as might be the case if there were discrete tool production areas (areas with lots of flakes but few tools) or tool-use areas (areas with some tools but few flakes).

The distribution of groundstone was more patterned than either the debitage or flaked stone tools (Figure 12.1, lower right; Figure 12.2). Most fragments—especially those that are fire-affected—came from the southeast quadrant of the excavation block near the two hearths. The distribution of fire-affected rocks was generally the same as the groundstone (see Figure 12.2). The abundant burned rock is inconsistent with the ephemeral nature of the two hearths. We suspect that additional early Holocene hearths or perhaps some sort of roasting feature may lie immediately south of our excavation block. Thus, while people may have mostly made and used flaked stone tools within the shelter's interior, they seem to have concentrated their cooking activities near its apron. This pattern is in accordance with ethnographic accounts of groups who separate their tool maintenance and sleeping areas from cooking areas and conducted the latter just inside the dripline (Galanidou 2000).

In sum, over approximately 175–420 years, groups built warming and/or cooking fires 2–3 m from the back of the shelter. They tended to produce and discard flaked stone tools in the eastern half of the shelter, which would have remained lit by the afternoon and evening sun and remained warm once the sun set. We found no clear evidence of hearth-centered activity areas. However, given that the 86–126 cmbd deposits accumulated over several centuries, those short-term events may simply be obscured by longer-term trends. Groundstone and fire-affected rock mostly accumulated in the southeast quadrant. Its abundance there may signal the presence of additional hearths or other thermal features toward the shelter's apron.

Flaked Stone Tool Clusters

Beyond these general trends in the horizontal distributions of flaked and groundstone tools, fire-affected rock, and debitage, there was some finer-grained patterning in the distribution of flaked stone tools. Plotted Late Paleoindian tools were not randomly distributed across the shelter, and most clustering indices suggest that four is the optimal number of clusters. The k-means clusters

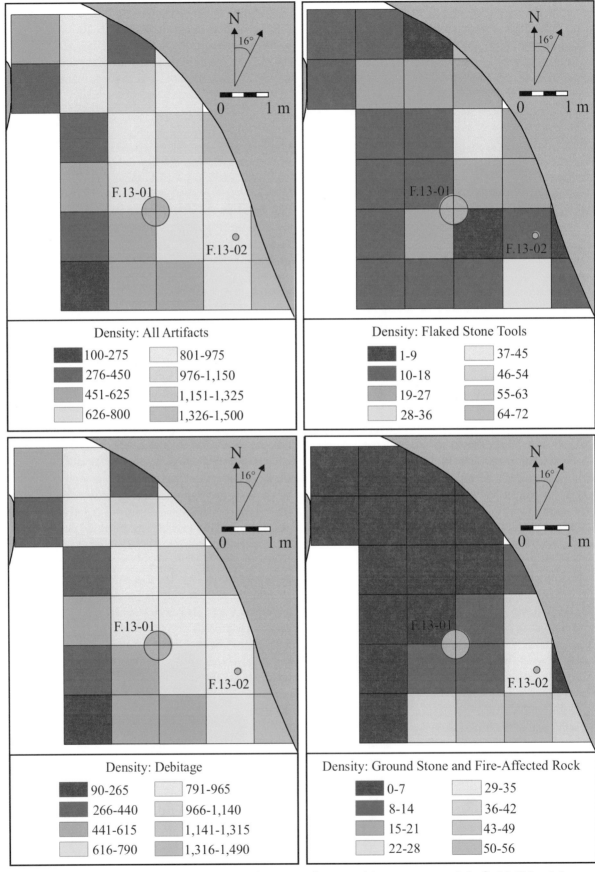

FIGURE 12.1. Late Paleoindian artifact densities (both in situ and recovered from screens per 0.4 m³), 86–126 cmbd.

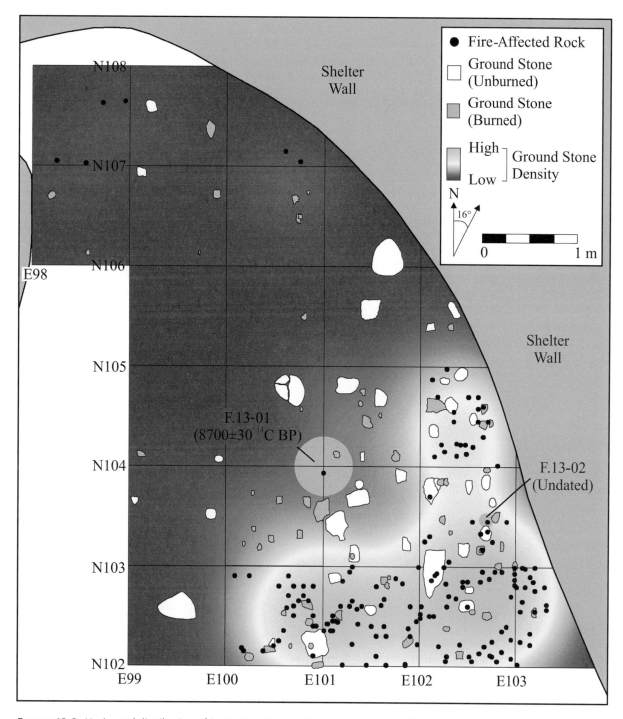

FIGURE 12.2. Horizontal distribution of in situ Late Paleoindian groundstone and fire-affected rock, 86–126 cmbd.

are each 2–3 m in diameter and possess similar tool densities: (1) Cluster 1 contains 59 tools (~11 tools/m²); (2) Cluster 2 contains 68 (~17 tools/m²); (3) Cluster 3 contains 59 (~13 tools/m²); and Cluster 4 contains 47 (~15 tools/m²; Figure 12.3). We did not include ground-stone or fire-affected rock in the cluster analysis but, as noted, it was concentrated in the shelter's southeast quadrant where Cluster 4 is also located.

Again, we do not view these flaked clusters as spatially or temporally discrete areas where individuals carried out specific tasks over short intervals. Rather, we think they mark places within the shelter that saw more use than others during different visits. There is some support for this idea. First, the mean elevations of the clusters differ slightly. Cluster 2 is the deepest (110 cmbd ± 10 cm), Cluster 3 is the shallowest (104 cmbd ± 10 cm),

TABLE 12.2. Late Paleoindian artifact cluster attributes

Attribute	Cluster 1	2	3	4
Tools				
obsidian	53	59	41	42
CCS	—	2	7	1
FGV	6	7	1	4
Debitage				
obsidian	775	795	512	697
CCS	8	25	7	8
FGV	44	34	30	38
Bifaces				
Stage 2	4	11	4	0
Stage 3	4	6	6	3
Stage 4	4	2	5	4
finished	3	5	4	1
fragment	4	1	1	3
projectile point	1	3	7	4
flake tools	38	37	25	26
cores	1	3	7	6
Novice Knapping Errors (bifaces)				
present	4	6	4	3
absent	16	22	23	12
Debitage				
core reduction	66	66	33	39
biface thinning	297	336	287	266
pressure	157	137	51	146
shatter	4	5	35	0
fragment	303	310	143	292
Flake Size				
<1 in	797	816	533	720
>1 in	30	38	16	23

and clusters 1 and 4 possess essentially the same elevations (107 cmbd ± 10 cm and 106 cmbd ± 11 cm). The mean elevation of the groundstone concentration in the southeast quadrant (103 cmbd ± 10 cm) is roughly the same as Cluster 3. The elevation of Cluster 2 differs significantly from that of both Cluster 3 and the groundstone concentration ($F = 3.99$, $df = 4$, $p = .004$). These differences suggest that the clusters accumulated during separate short-term visits within the modeled 175–420-year period rather than during one longer-term occupation (something that the modeled age range itself suggests).

Second, although dates on charcoal and bone from within the different clusters do not unambiguously demonstrate that they are separated in time, perhaps because of mixing, directly dated *Olivella* beads from within clusters 2, 3, and 4 do date to different periods

(see Table 4.2).[6] Cluster 3 (the shallowest cluster) contained Artifact 2104, dated to 8260–7970 cal BP, while Cluster 2 (the deepest cluster) contained artifacts 761 and 1374, dated to 9435–9120 and 9475–9230 cal BP, respectively. Cluster 4 (whose elevation falls between clusters 2 and 3) contained two beads, Artifact 2478 dated to 9140–8765 cal BP, and Artifact 2477 dated to 9815–9490 cal BP. While Artifact 2477 is aberrantly old, given its stratigraphic position, the age of Artifact 2478 is consistent with the elevation of Cluster 4 (intermediate between clusters 2 and 3). The 95.4 percent (i.e., 2σ) age ranges of the beads generally do not overlap, indicating that people discarded them during different visits.

Third, although there are some minor differences in the kinds of flakes in the clusters (e.g., Cluster 2 contained more CCS flakes than the other clusters, Cluster 3 contains more biface thinning flakes and fewer pressure flakes than the other clusters, and Cluster 4 contains more pressure flakes than the other clusters), they are far more alike than they are different (Table 12.2). Neither the proportions of early-stage and finished bifaces ($\chi^2 = 1.89$, $df = 3$, $p = .596$), bifaces and flake tools ($\chi^2 = 3.97$, $df = 3$, $p = .265$), raw materials from which tools are made ($\chi^2 = 0.5$, $df = 3$, $p = .919$), nor proportions of tools exhibiting novice knapping errors ($p = .916$) differ significantly. None of the clusters appear to represent spaces dedicated to specific tasks, as might be expected with longer-term occupations (Kent 1991, 1993; O'Connell 1993). Instead, the intracluster heterogeneity and intercluster homogeneity are more consistent with shorter-term occupations (Simek 1987).

Finally, although there is a fair amount of overlap in the obsidian types represented in the different clusters, there are a few subtle differences that suggest they mark the arrival of people from different places. For example, Cluster 2 is the only cluster containing artifacts made of obsidian from sources in the Abert-Chewaucan Basin. Similarly, Cluster 3 is the only cluster containing artifacts made of obsidian from sources in Nevada's High Rock Country. Perhaps not coincidentally, Cluster 3 contains the only side-removed projectile points from the Late Paleoindian component (Artifacts 998 and 2139; see Figure 7.3).

SUMMARY

The destruction of portions of the Late and Middle Archaic deposits prevents us from fully understanding how people used LSP-1 during the late Holocene, but intact deposits within the E99 Trench offer some clues. Visitors built hearths no closer than ~3 m to the shelter's rear wall, probably to provide a warm area to work and sleep and to limit the amount of smoke that would have

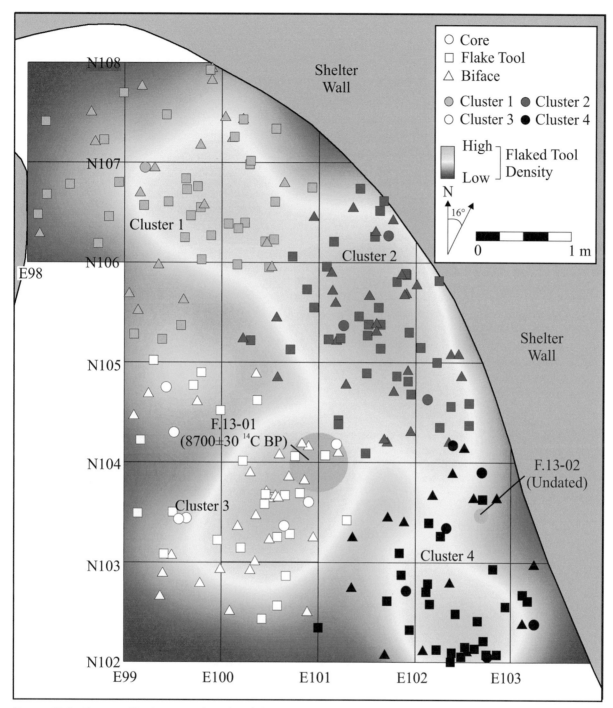

FIGURE 12.3. Clusters of in situ Late Paleoindian flaked stone tools, 86–126 cmbd.

filled the shelter. They also built hearths a few meters inside the dripline, perhaps for cooking. Thus, Late and Middle Archaic site structure at LSP-1 corresponds well with both ethnographic and archaeological accounts of hearth positioning (Thomas 1983; Walthall 1998). Late Archaic visitors mostly made and discarded stone tools toward the back of the shelter, perhaps to take advantage of the warmer area. Middle Archaic groups prob-

ably also did this to some extent, but most flaked and groundstone tools were discarded closer to the dripline around several hearths. These patterns are amalgams of at least three to four different visits during each period.

More extensive early Holocene deposits provide a clearer picture of Late Paleoindian site structure. Stratum V deposits between 86 and 126 cmbd contained flaked stone tool clusters, a groundstone concentration, one hearth dated to 9735–9550 cal BP, and a second smaller undated hearth. The clusters are consistent in some ways. For example, tool types, raw material types, early- versus late-stage bifaces, and novice knapping errors. Each cluster also contains at least one *Olivella* shell bead. This suggests that they do not necessarily mark areas where people conducted different activities during the same occupation(s). Instead, we suspect that they mark different parts of the shelter that saw greater use during separate visits that took place over a few centuries.

NOTES

1. Carr (1984) defines depositional areas as clusters of tools and debris that form through various behavioral, geological, and biological processes. In contrast, activity areas are clusters of tools and debris that were specifically produced and/or used together. Simply put, the concept of depositional areas addresses the numerous ways that artifact aggregations can develop.

2. Ripley's K determines whether a point pattern deviates from complete spatial randomness at a given distance (Ripley 1977). The L-function is a transformation of Ripley's K-function that stabilizes the variance (Besag 1977). We applied Ripley's isotropic correction (Ripley 1988) to reduce bias from the edge effect.

3. The NbClust package uses 30 different indices to identify the optimal number of clusters (Charrad et al. 2014). Identifying the optimal number of clusters is a prerequisite to implementing a k-means algorithm because the user defines the number of clusters.

4. K-means clustering algorithms assign every observation in a dataset to a cluster such that the sum of the squared distance between the observation and its assigned cluster center is minimized. We used Hartigan and Wong's (1979) algorithm.

5. The Kernel Density tool calculates the magnitude per unit area from point features using the quartic kernel function (Silverman 1986). This function spreads the point location value outward to each cell within the search radius (defined here as 1 m), creating a surface with the highest value at the point location and the lowest value at the search radius boundary. The values of the individual surfaces are summed for each output cell.

6. We associated each of the 14 dates from the 86–126 cm level in our model with the clusters in which we recovered the dated samples. We modeled each of the clusters as a separate phase twice, first within the larger sequence and then independent of the other strata. In both cases, the start and end age ranges of the clusters overlap substantially. This indicates that we cannot reliably distinguish them as separate temporally discrete occupations using the available dates. The clusters may represent contemporary activity areas, or perhaps more likely, we are simply asking too much of the radiocarbon dates.

PART III

North Warner Valley
Settlement-Subsistence Patterns

13

Survey Results

Geoffrey M. Smith, Teresa A. Wriston, and Donald D. Pattee

In Part II (chapters 4–12), we focused on the LSP-1 rock-shelter. The site is significant because it contains a record of human use that spans much of the Holocene. Its stone, bone, fiber, and shell artifacts speak to a range of topics including subsistence, seasonality, technology, mobility, trade, site structure, and group composition. The diversity of the assemblage exemplifies the important contribution that dry caves have made to Great Basin archaeology: the excellent organic preservation that they often afford provides a more complete picture of past lifeways than most open-air sites, where preservation is generally poor and only lithic artifacts remain.

Still, it is important to recognize that single sites tend to provide narrow views of the past. Moreover, caves and rockshelters often record behaviors that differ from open-air sites, which may reflect the specialized manners in which people used them (Wriston 2016). To effectively reconstruct the past, researchers should carry out cave and rockshelter excavations and regional surveys in tandem (e.g., Aikens and Jenkins 1994; Aikens et al. 1982; Thomas 1970, 1983, 1988).

The NWVSA presented us with such an opportunity, and in Part III we present the salient results of three seasons of pedestrian survey. Two questions drove our survey work: (1) what were the general demographic and settlement-subsistence patterns in North Warner Valley? and (2) from where and how did groups procure and use toolstone? To address these questions, we focused on the distribution of sites and isolated resources containing time-sensitive projectile points and how people used the lithic raw materials found at those sites.

THE SAMPLE

Archaeological Sites and Isolated Resources

We recorded 114 archaeological sites in the NWVSA, all of which contain precontact components. Of those, 69 contained one or more projectile points that we used to assign the sites to cultural periods (Table 13.1). We also recorded 355 isolated resources. Of those, 55 contained one or more typed projectile points (Table 13.2). For more information about each of these sites, we direct interested readers to Smith and Wriston (2018), the contract report that we submitted to the BLM Lakeview Resource Area Office. Here, we discuss only the most important examples from each period.

Projectile Points

Two hundred and sixty projectile points inform our understanding of when groups visited North Warner Valley (Tables 13.3 and 13.4). We discuss diachronic variability in settlement patterns later in this chapter. Here, we highlight some of the more notable aspects of the NWVSA projectile points and emphasize the Paleo-indian types that comprise over half of the sample.

Fluted Points

The NWVSA contains one of the few locales with multiple fluted points in Oregon; others include the Dietz Site in the nearby Alkali Basin, Sheep Mountain and Sage Hen Gap sites in the Harney Basin, and Trout Creek Paleo Camp in the Alvord Desert (Smith and Barker 2017 and references therein). While we recorded it as several smaller sites for management purposes,

TABLE 13.1. Archaeological sites containing typed projectile points

Site No.	Site Area (m²)	Period(s)[1]	No. of Tools	Tool Types	Features	Site No.	Site Area (m²)	Period(s)[1]	No. of Tools	Tool Types	Features
35Ha4702	4,496	PI	10	P, B, FT	—	35Ha4680	1,148	MA	4	P, B, FT	—
35Ha4695	8,456	PI, LA	14	P, B, FT	—	35Ha4681	2,720	PI	11	P, B, FT	—
35Ha4696	11,518	PI	15	P, B, C, FT	—	35Ha4682	4,620	PI	11	P, B	—
35Ha4697	6,231	MA	6	P, B, C, FT	—	35Ha4686	3,952	PI	1	P	—
35Ha4621[2]	2,000	LA	3	P, B	—	35Ha4687	3,837	MA	2	P, FT	—
35Ha4622	12,548	MA	10	P, B, GS	—	35Ha4690	2,454	PI	1	P	—
35Ha4623	1,600	MA, TP	5	P, B	—	35Ha4691	5,494	PI	8	P, B, FT	—
35Ha4632	3,000	MA	1	P	—	35Ha4693	1,744	PI	16	P, B, FT	—
35Ha4633	3,200	MA	6	P, B, FT	—	35Ha4694	3,008	PI	5	P, B, FT	—
35Ha4634	140,000	MA, LA	19	P, B, GS	—	35Ha4714	5,850	LA	6	P, B, FT, GS	—
35Ha4635	3,600	LA	3	P, B	—	35Ha4711	17,290	PI, TP	6	P, B	—
35Ha4637	750	MA, LA	4	P, B, C	—	35Ha4712	3,904	PI	3	P, FT	—
35Ha4639	1,600	MA	1	P	—	35Ha4708	7,139	PI, EA, MA	7	P, B, FT, GS	—
35Ha4645	18,069	PI	19	P, B, FT	—	35Ha4709	8,262	PI	9	P, FT	—
35Ha4646	9,300	MA	8	P, B, FT	—	35Ha4710	1,158	PI	4	P, B, FT	—
35Ha4648	12,245	MA, LA	15	P, B, FT	—	35Ha4685	925	MA	1	P	—
35Ha4650	2,890	PI, LA	2	B, FT	—	35Ha4715	2,732	PI	28	P, B, C, FT	—
35Ha4651	19,100	PI	4	P, B	—	35Ha4716	4,630	PI	10	P, B, FT	—
35Ha4653	10,264	PI, MA	12	P, B, C, FT	—	35Ha4729	4,238	PI, MA	16	P, B, FT	—
35Ha4654	13,142	PI	6	P, B	—	35Ha4730	1,562	PI	5	P, B	—
35Ha4655	50,663	PI	5	P, B, FT	—	35Ha4717	2,594	PI	6	P, B, FT	—
35Ha4656	43,570	MA	18	P, B, FT, GS	3 hearths	35Ha4731	17,729	PI	18	P, B, FT, GS	—
35Ha4658	3,467	EA	5	P, B, FT, T	—	35Ha4718	3,838	PI, MA	5	P, FT	—
35Ha4659	4,500	PI, MA	12	P, B, C, FT	—	35Ha4732	3,838	PI	5	B, FT	1 hearth
35Ha4660	3,368	LA	1	P	—	35Ha4720	8,962	PI	6	P, B, FT	—
35Ha4662	641	MA	1	P	—	35Ha4721	14,568	PI	11	P, B, FT	—
35Ha4666	12,826	PI, MA	14	P, FT	—	35Ha4722	3,041	PI, LA	2	P	—
35Ha4667	421	LA	1	P	—	35Ha4723	6,356	MA	5	P, B, FT	—
35Ha4522	12,100	LA, TP	50+	P, B, FT	2 hearths	35Ha4724[2]	2,779	MA	6	P, B, FT, GS	—
35Ha4669	4,350	MA	6	P, B, FT	—	35Ha4725	1,187	MA	5	P, GS	—
35Ha4670	3,360	PI	5	B, FT	—	35Ha4733	38,202	EA, MA, LA	43	P, B, C, FT, GS	—
35Ha4672	4,970	PI	4	P, FT	—	35Ha4726	4,139	MA, LA	4	P, B	—
35Ha4676	7,420	TP	3	P, B, FT	—	35Ha4734	75,913	PI, MA	67	P, B, FT	—
35Ha4678	9,504	PI	2	P	—	35Ha4728	2,269	MA	6	P, B, FT	—
35Ha4679	6,960	PI	3	P, FT	—						

[1] PI=Paleoindian; EA=Early Archaic; MA=Middle Archaic; LA=Late Archaic; TP=Terminal Prehistoric; P=projectile point; B=biface; C=core; FT=flake tool; GS=groundstone.

[2] Projectile points neither collected nor included in Table 13.4.

most of the fluted points (9 of 11; Figure 13.1) in North Warner Valley came from what probably represents a single campsite located along a small drainage.

Researchers continue to debate the place of fluted point technology in the Intermountain West. Some (e.g., Beck and Jones 2010, 2013; Davis et al. 2012; Grayson 2016; Smith and Goebel 2018) have argued that fluted points originated east of the Rocky Mountains and spread later to other regions. A lack of well-dated fluted point sites in the Great Basin has hindered attempts to resolve this debate, although there does appear to be some quantitative and qualitative difference in fluted points from the Intermountain West and Clovis points from the Southwest and Plains (Beck and Jones 2010, 2013; Davis et al. 2012; Taylor 2003). Beck and colleagues (2019) recently outlined criteria for distinguishing the two. While they are generally broken and/or reworked, with one exception (35Ha4711-6, a badly damaged and heavily reworked point), the NWVSA fluted points possess most of the characteristics of Clovis points (Table

TABLE 13.2. Isolated resources containing typed projectile points

IR No.	Description	Period(s)
AIF-2	obs. Rosegate point	LA
AIF-10	obs. Humboldt point	MA
AIF-15	obs. crescent	PI
AIF-16	obs. Rosegate point	LA
AIF-18	obs. Gatecliff Split Stem point	MA
AIF-22	obs. Gatecliff Split Stem point	MA
AIF-23	obs. foliate point	EA
AIF-24	obs. Humboldt point	MA
AIF-30	obs. Elko Eared point	MA
AIF-40	obs. WST point	PI
AIF-41	obs. WST point	PI
CIF-52	obs. Rosegate point; 2 obs. flakes	LA
CIF-65	obs. Rosegate point	LA
GIF-5	obs. Elko Eared point	MA
GIF-8	2 obs. WST points; 6 obs. flakes	PI
GIF-9	FGV WST point	PI
GIF-20	obs. Rosegate point; 3 obs. flakes; FGV flake	LA
GIF-28	2 obs. WST points	PI
GIF-31	obs. fluted point	PI
GIF-41	obs. Elko Corner-notched point; 2 metates; 3 manos; obs. biface	MA
GIF-44	obs. Desert Side-notched point	TP
GIF-45	obs. Gatecliff Split Stem point	MA
GIF-50	1 CCS Gatecliff Contracting Stem point; 2 obs. Elko Corner-notched points; 2 obs. point fragments	MA
GIF-51	1 obs. Gatecliff Contracting Stem point; 2 obs. projectile point fragments; CCS flake	MA
GIF-53	obs. Gatecliff Split Stem point	MA
GIF-54	3 obs. Gatecliff Split Stem points	MA
GIF-55	obs. foliate point	EA
GIF-65	obs. WST point	PI
GIF-91	obs. Northern Side-notched point; obs. flake	EA
GIF-92	obs. Humboldt point	MA
GIF-110	obs. WST point	PI
GIF-111	obs. Gatecliff Split Stem point	MA
GIF-116	FGV WST point; 7 obs. flakes	PI
GIF-123	FGV WST point	PI
GIF-124	obs. crescent	PI
GIF-125	CCS crescent	PI
GIF-126	obs. Gatecliff Split Stem point	MA
PIF-2	obs. Elko Eared point	MA
PIF-25	obs. Northern Side-notched point; obs. flake	EA
PIF-41	obs. WST point	PI
PIF-51	obs. WST point	PI
TIF-5	obs. Northern Side-notched point	EA
TIF-9	obs. Rosegate point	LA
TIF-29	obs. WST point	PI
TIF-30	FGV WST point	PI
TIF-54	obs. WST point	PI
TIF-59	obs. fluted point	PI
TIF-73	obs. Rosegate point	LA
TIF-76	obs. Northern Side-notched point	EA
TIF-78	obs. WST point	PI
TIF-85	obs. Elko Eared point; obs. stage 3 biface; 2 obs. flakes	MA
TIF-86	obs. Elko Corner-notched point; 3 bifaces	MA
TIF-95	obs. Rosegate point	LA
TIF-96	obs. Elko Eared point	MA
TIF-97	obs. WST point	PI

Note: PI=Paleoindian; EA=Early Archaic; MA=Middle Archaic; LA=Late Archaic; TP=Terminal Prehistoric.

TABLE 13.3. Counts and time-adjusted frequencies of typed projectile points

Period and Point Type	Within Sites	Isolated Resources	Total	% of Points in NWVSA	Time-Adjusted Frequency (Points/Years)
Paleoindian (*n*=145)				55.8	.029
fluted	9	2	11	4.2	
WST	103	18	121	46.6	
Black Rock Concave Base	2	—	2	0.8	
crescent	8	3	11	4.2	
Early Archaic (*n*=10)				3.8	.004
foliate	—	2	2	0.8	
Northern Side-notched	4	4	8	3.1	
Middle Archaic (*n*=65)				25.0	.017
Humboldt Series	13	3	16	6.2	
Gatecliff Series	20	12	32	12.3	
Elko Series	8	9	17	6.5	
Late Archaic (*n*=21)				8.1	.015
Rosegate Series	13	8	21	8.1	
Terminal Prehistoric (*n*=19)				7.3	.042
Desert Series	18	1	19	7.3	
Total	198	62	260	100.0	

13.5; also see Table 13.4). We found most of them just above the 1,390 m asl Lake Warner shoreline (see Figure 3.6), which dates between 14,760–14,100 cal BP and 12,575–12,095 cal BP. This broad range encompasses the Clovis Era and offers indirect support for our contention that most of the North Warner Valley fluted points are Clovis.

Western Stemmed Tradition Points

WST points are the most common projectile type in North Warner Valley, which likely reflects the degree to which Paleoindians used the area and our emphasis on beach ridge parcels during survey. Due to ambiguities in current typological schemes and the fact that most of the points are broken, we did not assign them to subtypes (e.g., Parman, Haskett, Cougar Mountain), although such examples are certainly present (Figures 13.2 and 13.3). Stemmed points are distributed between ~1,363 m asl (the lowest point in the NWVSA) and 1,417 m asl, with high numbers found at 1,363–1,370 m asl (*n*=36), 1,391–1,400 m asl (*n*=32), and 1,401–1,410 m asl (*n*=35: see Figure 3.6). Points found below 1,390 m asl must necessarily postdate 14,760–14,100 cal BP, while those found on the valley floor probably do not predate 10,300 cal BP (the time by which Lake Warner had receded southward and out of the NWVSA).

Like the fluted points found at the same elevation, WST points at or just above 1,390 m asl may date to sometime between 14,760–14,100 cal BP and 12,575–

12,095 cal BP if the people who discarded them camped adjacent to the lake. Interestingly, most (8 of 11) sites that produced long-stemmed Haskett points lie within ~5 m of the dated 1,390 m asl shoreline. Elsewhere in the northern and eastern Great Basin, Haskett points consistently date to the Younger Dryas (Rosencrance 2019). Based on their association with the 1,390 m asl shoreline, this may also be the case in North Warner Valley.

A final Paleoindian point type from North Warner Valley—well-made, square-base points—warrants some discussion (Figure 13.4). They occurred as isolates and at a handful of sites, the most notable being 35Ha4682. Similar points are called Windust on the Columbia Plateau (D. Rice 1972; H. Rice 1965) and Alberta/Cody on the Plains (Knell and Muñiz 2013). Amick (2013) suggests that researchers too often use Windust as a catchall name for early Holocene square-base points in the Intermountain West. He notes that square-base points from northwestern Nevada and southeastern Oregon are consistent in shape, size, and manufacturing technique with Cody Complex points from the Plains and suggests that square-base points from the northwestern Great Basin should be called Cody. Amick posits that square-base points in Oregon and Nevada mark incursions by Late Paleoindian bison hunters from the Plains. In Oregon, bison are known from early Holocene contexts in Connley, Fort Rock, and Cougar Mountain Caves (Cowles 1960; Grayson 1979). In Nevada's Black Rock Desert, square-base points were found with a bison skeleton

0   5 cm

35Ha4690-1   35Ha4711-6   35Ha4717-1   35Ha4717-3

35Ha4717-5   35Ha4720-3   35Ha4731-4   35Ha4731-17

35Ha4731-18   GIF-31-1   TIF-59-1

FIGURE 13.1. Fluted points from North Warner Valley.

dated to ~11,200 cal BP (Amick 2013; Dansie and Jerrems 2004). Square-base points seem to grow more common as one moves east from Warner Valley into Guano Valley (Reaux et al. 2018), Hawksy Walksy Valley (Christian 1997), and the Alvord Desert (Pettigrew 1984). The Snake River, which extends west from the Rocky Mountains to the Oregon-Idaho border, is a likely corridor along which Plains groups could have accessed southeastern Oregon's lake basins (Hartman 2019).

Table S13 presents key measurements of those square-base points from North Warner Valley (*n*=10) that most closely resemble Cody points. The majority comes from 35Ha4682; most are basal fragments, so our dataset is small. Nevertheless, in every attribute the North Warner Valley points are within a few millimeters

of Cody points from the Plains (Table S14). In general, the NWVSA points are slightly larger, but this is also the case for other square-base points from the northwestern Great Basin (Amick 2013: Table 8.5). Amick suggests that this difference indicates that square-base points from the far West are generally less refined than those from the Plains. The NWVSA sample supports that idea.

Crescents

We recorded 11 crescents including examples of Tadlock's (1966) type I, II, and III variants (Figure 13.5 and Table 13.6). Almost half are made of CCS, which is consistent with other collections (Beck and Jones 2009; Jew et al. 2015). Some are large, well-made bifacial implements, while others are small and flaked mostly on one

TABLE 13.4. Metric and sourcing data for typed projectile points

Site No.	FS	Frag. Type[1]	LT (mm)	LA (mm)	WB (mm)	WM (mm)	WN (mm)	Thi. (mm)	PSA (°)	DSA (°)	NO (°)	BIR	Wt. (g)	Raw Mat.	Geochemical Type
Fluted (n=11)															
35Ha4690	1	P-M	—	—	26.4	—	n/a	7.8	n/a	n/a	n/a	—	—	OBS	Horse Mountain B
35Ha4711	6	P-M	—	—	20.5	—	n/a	7.6	n/a	n/a	n/a	—	—	OBS	Beatys Butte
35Ha4717	1	P	—	—	—	—	n/a	6.5	n/a	n/a	n/a	—	—	FGV	Double O
35Ha4717	3	P	—	—	—	—	n/a	8.2	n/a	n/a	n/a	—	—	OBS	Beatys Butte
35Ha4718	5	P-M	—	—	—	—	n/a	8.1	n/a	n/a	n/a	—	—	FGV	Camp Creek
35Ha4720	3	P	—	—	—	—	n/a	5.0	n/a	n/a	n/a	—	—	FGV	unknown 1
35Ha4731	4	P	—	—	—	—	n/a	6.6	n/a	n/a	n/a	—	—	FGV	Double O
35Ha4731	17	P	—	—	—	—	n/a	5.4	n/a	n/a	n/a	—	—	OBS	Beatys Butte
35Ha4731	18	P-M	—	—	—	—	n/a	7.5	n/a	n/a	n/a	—	—	OBS	Buck Spring
GIF-31	1	P-M	—	—	—	35.9	n/a	8.6	n/a	n/a	n/a	—	—	OBS	Buck Spring
TIF-59	1	P-M	—	—	26.1	—	n/a	8.6	n/a	n/a	n/a	—	—	OBS	McComb Butte
Black Rock Concave Base (n=2)															
35Ha4645	1	P	—	—	26.6	n/a	n/a	6.0	n/a	n/a	n/a	—	—	OBS	Beatys Butte
35Ha4712	1	P	—	—	20.0	—	n/a	4.7	n/a	n/a	n/a	—	—	OBS	Coglan Buttes
Western Stemmed Tradition (n=121)															
35Ha4645	3	M-D	—	—	—	21.8	n/a	9.8	n/a	n/a	n/a	—	—	OBS	Double H/Whitehorse
35Ha4645	5	P-M	—	—	—	—	—	9.1	—	—	—	—	—	OBS	Horse Mountain
35Ha4645	10	P	—	—	19.8	—	—	6.8	—	—	—	—	—	OBS	Hawks Valley
35Ha4645	18	M	—	—	—	—	—	4.9	—	—	—	—	—	OBS	—
35Ha4651	1	P	—	—	—	—	—	7.0	—	—	—	—	—	OBS	Big Stick
35Ha4651	3	M	—	—	—	—	16.9	7.0	90	200	110	—	—	OBS	Bald Butte
35Ha4653	2	P	—	—	—	—	—	8.0	—	—	—	—	—	FGV	unknown
35Ha4653	5	P	—	—	—	18.9	15.0	5.6	80	200	120	—	—	OBS	Riley
35Ha4653	7	P-M	—	—	—	—	—	10.5	—	—	—	—	—	OBS	South Creek
35Ha4653	11	D	—	—	—	23.4	17.4	6.5	85	190	105	—	—	OBS	Riley
35Ha4654	1	D	—	—	—	—	—	7.6	—	—	—	—	—	OBS	Beatys Butte
35Ha4654	3	C	43.9	43.9	—	19.0	14.3	6.6	80	210	130	1.0	4.7	OBS	Glass Buttes Variety 3
35Ha4655	5	M	—	—	—	—	—	10.4	—	—	—	—	—	OBS	—
35Ha4659	4	P	—	—	—	—	—	4.9	—	—	—	—	—	FGV	Warner Valley
35Ha4659	5	M	—	—	—	—	—	6.2	—	—	—	—	—	OBS	Buck Spring
35Ha4659	6	C	35.2	35.2	5.7	15.8	n/a	5.9	n/a	n/a	n/a	1.0	3.0	OBS	Buck Spring
35Ha4659	7	C	37.5	37.5	11.2	16.1	n/a	6.9	n/a	n/a	n/a	1.0	4.0	OBS	Horse Mountain

Catalog No.	No.	Type												Source	Location
35Ha4659	10	D	—	—	—	—	—	7.6	—	—	—	—	—	OBS	Buck Spring
35Ha4666	9	P	—	—	—	—	—	5.9	—	—	—	—	—	OBS	Horse Mountain
35Ha4666	11	P	—	—	—	8.5	—	6.0	—	—	—	—	—	OBS	Horse Mountain
35Ha4666	14	P	—	—	—	—	—	5.8	—	—	—	—	—	OBS	Horse Mountain
35Ha4672	1	D	—	—	—	—	—	6.2	—	—	—	—	—	OBS	Silver Lake/Sycan Marsh
35Ha4678	1	C	76.8	76.8	—	18.1	11.6	8.2	95	235	140	10.5	1.0	OBS	Bald Butte
35Ha4678	2	D	—	—	—	—	—	6.9	—	—	—	—	—	OBS	—
35Ha4679	3	D	—	—	—	—	—	5.3	—	—	—	—	—	OBS	Wagontire
35Ha4681	2	P	—	—	—	—	—	4.5	—	—	—	—	—	OBS	Big Stick
35Ha4681	3	P	—	—	16.2	—	—	5.4	—	—	—	—	—	OBS	Long Valley
35Ha4681	4	P	—	—	—	—	—	5.7	—	—	—	—	—	OBS	Tucker Hill
35Ha4681	5	P	—	—	—	—	—	6.1	—	—	—	—	—	OBS	Buck Spring
35Ha4681	6	P	—	—	16.8	15.7	13.1	4.3	85	230	145	—	—	OBS	Beatys Butte
35Ha4681	8	M	—	—	—	—	—	4.3	—	—	—	—	—	OBS	Big Stick
35Ha4681	9	P	—	—	13.5	—	—	5.5	90	—	—	—	—	OBS	Glass Buttes Variety 3
35Ha4681	10	P	—	—	15.2	—	—	4.2	—	—	—	—	—	OBS	Badger Creek
35Ha4681	11	C	40.6	40.6	13.2	21.2	17.1	5.3	90	220	130	5.3	1.0	FGV	Wagontire
35Ha4682	1	P	—	—	20.0	—	—	4.1	90	—	—	—	—	OBS	unknown 1
35Ha4682	3	P	—	—	20.5	25.2	21.1	5.0	90	180	90	—	—	OBS	Yreka Butte
35Ha4682	4	P	—	—	—	—	—	6.8	—	—	—	—	—	FGV	Glass Buttes Variety 4
35Ha4682	5	M-D	—	—	21.1	—	—	9.2	90	—	—	—	—	OBS	Horse Mountain
35Ha4682	6	D	—	—	20.1	—	—	10.4	85	—	—	—	—	OBS	Horse Mountain
35Ha4682	7	P	—	—	23.9	—	—	6.0	90	—	—	—	—	OBS	Horse Mountain
35Ha4682	8	P	—	—	21.8	—	—	6.6	90	—	—	—	—	OBS	Horse Mountain
35Ha4682	9	P	—	—	20.1	—	21.4	6.8	90	108	90	1.0	—	FGV	Double O
35Ha4682	10	P	—	—	14.8	—	—	5.6	—	—	—	—	—	OBS	Beatys Butte
35Ha4682	11	P-M	—	—	—	—	—	6.1	—	—	—	—	—	OBS	Horse Mountain
35Ha4686	1	M	—	—	—	—	—	8.1	—	—	—	—	—	OBS	Beatys Butte
35Ha4691	1	D	—	—	—	—	—	9.7	—	—	—	—	—	OBS	Horse Mountain
35Ha4691	2	L	—	—	—	—	—	8.5	—	—	—	—	—	OBS	ML/GV[2]
35Ha4691	3	D	—	—	—	—	—	10.0	—	—	—	—	—	OBS	ML/GV[2]
35Ha4691	4	D	—	—	—	—	—	9.0	—	—	—	—	—	OBS	Horse Mountain
35Ha4691	8	P	—	—	—	—	—	7.2	—	—	—	—	—	OBS	Beatys Butte
35Ha4693	2	P	—	—	—	—	—	7.4	—	—	—	—	—	OBS	—
35Ha4693	4	P	—	—	—	—	—	5.4	—	—	—	—	—	OBS	—
35Ha4693	15	P	—	—	12.1	—	—	4.7	—	—	—	—	—	CCS	—
35Ha4693	16	C	38.7	38.7	11.7	16.8	15.2	6.1	90	220	130	4.3	1.0	OBS	—
35Ha4694	1	P	—	—	—	—	—	6.5	—	—	—	—	—	OBS	—

TABLE 13.4. (cont'd.) Metric and sourcing data for typed projectile points

Site No.	FS	Frag. Type[1]	LT (mm)	LA (mm)	WB (mm)	WM (mm)	WN (mm)	Thi. (mm)	PSA (°)	DSA (°)	NO (°)	Wt. (g)	BIR	Raw Mat.	Geochemical Type
35Ha4694	3	P-M	—	—	8.3	—	—	7.9	—	—	—	—	—	OBS	—
35Ha4695	2/3	P-M	—	—	—	—	—	9.9	—	—	—	—	—	OBS	Beatys Butte
35Ha4695	4	P	—	—	—	—	—	6.4	—	—	—	—	—	OBS	Glass Buttes Variety 1
35Ha4695	8	M	—	—	—	—	—	7.3	—	—	—	—	—	OBS	Buck Spring
35Ha4695	14	P	—	—	—	—	—	6.7	—	—	—	—	—	OBS	Beatys Butte
35Ha4696	1	P-M	—	—	15.5	21.5	n/a	6.4	n/a	n/a	n/a	—	—	OBS	Glass Buttes Variety 1
35Ha4702	1	P	—	—	—	—	—	9.5	—	—	—	—	—	OBS	Mosquito Lake
35Ha4708	7	M	—	—	—	—	—	10.7	—	—	—	—	—	OBS	—
35Ha4709	1	P	—	—	13.3	—	—	5.8	—	—	—	—	—	OBS	Buck Mountain
35Ha4709	3	P	—	—	12.3	—	—	5.9	—	—	—	—	—	OBS	Tank Creek
35Ha4709	7	M	—	—	—	21.1	—	7.0	—	—	—	—	—	OBS	Mosquito Lake
35Ha4709	8	P	—	—	7.4	—	—	6.5	—	—	—	—	—	OBS	—
35Ha4709	9	C	46.3	45.6	22.5	27.2	21.3	10.9	90	180	90	12.0	0.98	FGV	Alturas
35Ha4710	1	P	—	—	25.9	—	31.9	5.4	85	—	—	—	—	CCS	—
35Ha4711	2	P	—	—	14.8	28.2	—	4.4	—	—	—	—	—	OBS	—
35Ha4715	1	P-M	—	—	—	—	n/a	12.0	n/a	n/a	n/a	—	—	OBS	Horse Mountain B
35Ha4715	2	P-M	—	—	9.5	—	—	8.4	—	—	—	—	—	OBS	Beatys Butte
35Ha4715	3	P	—	—	—	—	—	6.3	—	—	—	—	—	OBS	ML/GV[2]
35Ha4715	5	P	—	—	—	—	—	6.6	—	—	—	—	—	OBS	Beatys Butte
35Ha4715	26	P	—	—	—	—	—	8.7	—	—	—	—	—	OBS	Beatys Butte
35Ha4715	27	P	—	—	—	—	—	9.1	—	—	—	—	—	OBS	Beatys Butte
35Ha4715	28	P	—	—	—	—	—	6.9	—	—	—	—	—	OBS	Sugar Hill
35Ha4716	10	P-M	—	—	—	—	—	9.9	—	—	—	—	—	OBS	Horse Mountain
35Ha4718	1	P	—	—	19.0	—	—	8.8	—	—	—	—	—	OBS	Gregory Creek
35Ha4720	7	P	—	—	—	—	—	4.3	—	—	—	—	—	OBS	—
35Ha4721	8	P	—	—	15.2	—	—	5.3	—	—	—	—	—	OBS	Horse Mountain
35Ha4721	9	P	—	—	10.8	—	12.2	5.4	90	—	—	—	—	OBS	Tank Creek
35Ha4721	10	L	—	—	—	—	—	8.5	—	—	—	—	—	OBS	Beatys Butte
35Ha4722	2	C	50.5	50.5	10.2	18.4	12.3	7.6	90	180	90	6.2	1.0	OBS	—
35Ha4729	12	P	—	—	11.5	—	—	6.0	—	—	—	—	—	OBS	—
35Ha4729	13	M	—	—	—	—	—	7.3	—	—	—	—	—	OBS	ML/GV[2]
35Ha4729	14	P	—	—	17.6	—	—	7.7	—	—	—	—	—	OBS	Glass Buttes Variety 4
35Ha4729	15	P	—	—	7.7	—	—	5.6	—	—	—	—	—	OBS	Tank Creek
35Ha4730	3	M	—	—	—	26.8	—	10.6	—	—	—	—	—	OBS	Gregory Creek

Sample	No.	Type												OBS/FGV	Location
35Ha4731	1	L	—	—	—	—	—	6.9	—	—	—	—	—	OBS	Wildhorse Canyon
35Ha4734	1	P-M	—	—	—	—	n/a	10.3	n/a	n/a	n/a	—	—	FGV	Warner Valley
35Ha4734	4	C	60.0	60.0	10.3	18.8	15.0	8.1	90	210	120	8.7	1.0	OBS	Beatys Butte
35Ha4734	13	P-M	—	—	—	—	n/a	10.5	n/a	n/a	n/a	—	—	OBS	Glass Buttes Variety 3
35Ha4734	14	P	—	—	—	—	—	6.4	—	—	—	—	—	OBS	Glass Buttes Variety 9
35Ha4734	17	P	—	—	25.5	—	21.9	8.4	105	—	—	—	—	OBS	Bald Butte
35Ha4734	21	M	—	—	—	—	—	9.7	—	—	—	—	—	OBS	Glass Buttes Variety 3
35Ha4734	24	P	—	—	—	—	—	4.8	—	—	—	—	—	OBS	Tank Creek
35Ha4734	25	P	—	—	—	—	—	5.9	—	—	—	—	—	OBS	BS/PP/FM [3]
35Ha4734	26	P	—	—	—	—	—	5.1	—	—	—	—	—	OBS	Cowhead Lake
35Ha4734	40	M-D	—	—	—	—	—	8.6	—	—	—	—	—	FGV	—
35Ha4734	41	P-M	—	—	—	33.0	17.1	7.8	80	190	110	—	—	OBS	Beatys Butte
35Ha4734	42	P	—	—	14.9	—	—	5.4	—	—	—	—	—	OBS	Coglan Buttes
35Ha4734	51	M	—	—	—	19.6	13.5	6.4	—	185	—	—	—	OBS	Beatys Butte
AIF-40	1	M	—	—	—	—	—	6.7	—	—	—	—	—	OBS	—
AIF-41	1	P	—	—	—	—	14.7	6.5	—	—	—	—	—	OBS	—
GIF-8	1	M-D	—	—	—	23.5	20.2	8.9	105	240	135	—	—	OBS	Double O
GIF-8	2	M-D	—	—	—	21.1	15.0	6.8	90	190	100	—	—	OBS	Mud Ridge
GIF-9	1	P	—	—	18.0	—	—	4.8	—	—	—	—	—	FGV	—
GIF-28	2	L	—	—	—	—	—	13.3	—	—	—	—	—	OBS	Beatys Butte
GIF-30	1	M-D	—	—	—	25.5	13.2	6.9	100	180	80	—	—	OBS	Buck Mountain
GIF-65	1	P-M	—	—	24.1	41.0	23.4	10.4	100	170	70	—	—	OBS	Big Stick
GIF-110	1	M-D	—	—	—	23.0	—	8.7	—	—	—	—	—	OBS	Tucker Hill
GIF-116	1	P-M	—	—	22.6	25.4	20.3	8.4	95	210	115	—	—	FGV	Yreka Butte
GIF-123	1	C	27.1	27.1	19.4	19.9	n/a	6.8	n/a	n/a	n/a	3.7	1.0	FGV	—
PIF-41	1	C	43.4	43.4	10.2	17.0	11.2	8.0	85	240	155	5.0	1.0	OBS	—
PIF-51	1	P	—	—	—	—	—	6.9	—	—	—	—	—	OBS	—
TIF-29	1	P	—	—	16.7	—	—	4.5	—	—	—	—	—	OBS	Indian Creek Buttes
TIF-30	1	M	—	—	—	—	—	10.1	—	—	—	—	—	FGV	—
TIF-54	1	C	85.5	85.5	10.5	29.2	n/a	9.4	n/a	n/a	n/a	22.4	1.0	OBS	Blue Spring
TIF-78	1	P-M	—	—	—	24.0	16.8	8.9	95	180	85	—	—	OBS	Buck Spring
TIF-97	1	P	—	—	—	—	—	7.1	—	—	—	—	—	OBS	Beatys Butte

Foliate (n=2)

Sample	No.	Type												OBS/FGV	Location
AIF-23	1	C	40.7	40.7	7.3	14.2	n/a	6.0	n/a	n/a	n/a	2.8	1.0	OBS	—
GIF-55	1	C	77.3	77.3	9.4	20.5	n/a	7.9	n/a	n/a	n/a	12.1	1.0	OBS	ML/GV [2]

TABLE 13.4. (cont'd.) Metric and sourcing data for typed projectile points

Site No.	FS	Frag. Type[1]	LT (mm)	LA (mm)	WB (mm)	WM (mm)	WN (mm)	Thi. (mm)	PSA (°)	DSA (°)	NO (°)	Wt. (g)	BIR	Raw Mat.	Geochemical Type
Northern Side-notched (n=8)															
35Ha4658	5	P-M	—	—	23.0	23.0	16.0	4.0	170	180	10	—	—	OBS	Tank Creek
35Ha4708	4	C	25.8	20.4	18.7	18.7	10.5	5.0	170	190	20	1.7	0.79	OBS	Surveyor Spring
35Ha4733	1	P-M	—	—	22.2	22.2	13.4	6.2	160	160	0	—	—	OBS	Cowhead Lake
35Ha4733	33	P-M	—	—	—	19.0	12.2	6.4	160	170	10	—	—	OBS	Tucker Hill
GIF-91	1	L	—	—	19.9	—	12.1	8.1	160	180	20	—	—	OBS	Beatys Butte
PIF-25	1	P-M	—	—	—	19.9	10.3	6.4	150	180	30	—	—	OBS	—
TIF-5	1	P-M	—	—	—	—	10.4	5.9	180	210	230	—	—	OBS	Double O
TIF-76	1	P-M	—	—	21.8	21.8	15.5	5.0	160	180	20	—	—	OBS	Cowhead Lake
Gatecliff Contracting Stem (n=4)															
35Ha4622	4	M-D	—	—	—	24.6	8.8	6.4	85	160	75	—	—	OBS	McComb Butte
35Ha4622	8	P-M	—	—	—	16.8	8.9	4.7	90	160	70	—	—	OBS	Beatys Butte
GIF-50	4	C	59.9	59.9	13.6	16.2	13.5	6.9	95	220	125	6.8	1.0	CCS	—
GIF-51	3	C	53.8	53.8	17.2	17.2	15.4	6.0	95	200	105	4.6	1.0	OBS	—
Gatecliff Split Stem (n=28)															
35Ha4622	10	P-M	—	—	—	—	11.9	4.9	100	160	60	—	—	OBS	Double H/Whitehorse
35Ha4633	3	P-M	—	—	9.6	18.6	11.6	5.3	80	170	90	—	—	OBS	Beatys Butte
35Ha4634	10	P-M	—	—	9.9	15.6	8.5	5.6	100	190	90	—	—	OBS	Beatys Butte
35Ha4639	1	P-M	—	—	13.1	22.5	13.1	5.6	95	180	85	—	—	OBS	Tank Creek
35Ha4646	3	C	45.2	43.7	15.0	19.7	17.4	4.7	85	210	125	5.2	0.97	OBS	Round Top Butte
35Ha4648	12	C	42.7	41.4	11.0	17.5	14.7	6.0	80	190	110	2.9	0.97	OBS	Mosquito Lake
35Ha4662	1	P-M	—	—	—	22.9	15.2	5.2	85	200	115	—	—	OBS	Beatys Butte
35Ha4666	1	C	49.1	46.6	10.9	23.2	16.2	7.2	85	200	115	6.6	0.95	OBS	Beatys Butte
35Ha4666	5	P-M	—	—	13.2	—	13.3	4.9	90	180	90	—	—	OBS	Beatys Butte
35Ha4666	6	P-M	—	—	14.1	27.0	15.8	6.3	80	180	100	—	—	FGV	Warner Valley
35Ha4666	7	P-M	—	—	—	18.7	10.2	5.1	95	190	95	—	—	OBS	Indian Creek Buttes
35Ha4666	8	P-M	—	—	9.9	19.2	12.8	6.2	85	200	115	—	—	OBS	Buck Spring
35Ha4669	1	P-M	—	—	15.3	24.0	14.3	6.8	95	210	115	—	—	OBS	Beatys Butte
35Ha4687	1	C	44.6	41.0	13.1	23.1	16.2	6.0	85	235	150	4.9	0.92	OBS	ML/GV[2]
35Ha4708	1	P	—	—	13.8	—	13.1	6.6	90	—	—	—	—	OBS	—
35Ha4733	42	P-M	—	—	14.1	31.7	15.3	8.6	90	160	70	—	—	OBS	Beatys Butte
35Ha4734	29	P-M	—	—	—	20.7	15.3	5.7	90	210	120	—	—	OBS	Delintment Lake
35Ha4734	68	P-M	—	—	9.3	21.0	9.5	5.1	105	190	85	—	—	OBS	Beatys Butte

AIF-18	1	C	48.8	45.2	18.2	13.6	13.0	5.8	90	200	110	3.9	0.93	OBS	Horse Mountain
AIF-22	1	P	—	—	—	11.5	9.9	4.7	105	190	85	—	—	OBS	—
GIF-45	1	P-M	—	—	25.1	16.7	15.6	5.1	95	190	85	—	—	OBS	Big Stick
GIF-53	1	P-M	—	—	22.1	16.1	16.2	7.3	85	200	115	—	—	OBS	Beatys Butte
GIF-54	1	M	—	—	26.8	—	16.7	7.6	85	200	115	—	—	OBS	Beatys Butte
GIF-54	2	C	85.1	80.9	26.5	14.3	14.8	7.8	90	170	80	13.9	0.95	OBS	Indian Creek Buttes B
GIF-54	3	C	53.9	51.6	21.8	13.4	13.2	7.1	95	220	125	7.5	0.96	FGV	Double O
GIF-111	1	P-M	—	—	—	16.7	14.8	5.2	100	180	80	—	—	OBS	Beatys Butte
GIF-126	1	P-M	—	—	17.2	—	—	5.3	95	180	85	—	—	OBS	Buck Spring
PIF-51	1	P	—	—	—	—	11.1	7.0	—	—	—	—	—	OBS	—
Humboldt (n=16)															
35Ha4623	1	C	37.6	31.8	16.7	16.7	n/a	5.3	n/a	n/a	n/a	2.8	0.85	OBS	Beatys Butte
35Ha4634	13	P	—	—	—	16.6	n/a	8.6	n/a	n/a	n/a	—	—	OBS	Beatys Butte
35Ha4653	3	P-M	—	—	12.8	10.0	n/a	4.6	n/a	n/a	n/a	—	—	OBS	Tucker Hill
35Ha4656	6	P	—	—	—	—	n/a	3.7	n/a	n/a	n/a	—	—	OBS	—
35Ha4659	12	P	—	—	—	12.0	n/a	5.6	n/a	n/a	n/a	—	—	OBS	Buck Spring
35Ha4680	2	P	—	—	—	16.5	n/a	3.8	n/a	n/a	n/a	—	—	FGV	Obsidian Cliffs
35Ha4685	1	P	—	—	—	9.5	n/a	4.8	n/a	n/a	n/a	—	—	OBS	—
35Ha4697	4	P	—	—	—	16.2	n/a	5.0	n/a	n/a	n/a	—	—	FGV	Beatys Butte
35Ha4723	1	P-M	—	—	19.4	9.0	n/a	6.2	n/a	n/a	n/a	—	—	OBS	Beatys Butte
35Ha4725	1	P-M	—	—	—	13.6	n/a	5.6	n/a	n/a	n/a	—	—	OBS	Cowhead Lake
35Ha4729	9	P	—	—	—	11.9	n/a	4.1	n/a	n/a	n/a	—	—	OBS	Beatys Butte
35Ha4733	5	P	—	—	—	11.5	n/a	5.3	n/a	n/a	n/a	—	—	OBS	Buck Mountain
35Ha4733	43	P	—	—	—	16.0	n/a	6.8	n/a	n/a	n/a	—	—	OBS	Beatys Butte
AIF-10	1	C	28.7	27.0	16.2	14.6	n/a	5.1	n/a	n/a	n/a	2.2	0.94	OBS	Beatys Butte
AIF-24	1	P-M	—	—	15.9	9.4	n/a	6.2	n/a	n/a	n/a	—	—	OBS	—
GIF-92	1	—	—	—	16.4	16.4	n/a	5.6	n/a	n/a	n/a	—	—	OBS	Tule Spring
Elko Corner-notched (n=6)															
35Ha4632	1	P-M	—	—	20.1	14.9	11.3	5.0	140	160	20	—	—	OBS	Blue Spring
35Ha4637	2	P-M	—	—	—	—	11.3	5.0	110	150	40	—	—	FGV	Yreka Buttes
GIF-41	6	P-M	—	—	23.8	10.4	17.8	7.8	130	190	60	—	—	OBS	Cowhead Lake
GIF-50	2	M	—	—	—	—	10.2	3.9	110	200	90	—	—	OBS	—
GIF-50	5	M-D	—	—	—	—	10.6	3.8	110	210	100	—	—	OBS	—
TIF-86	4	P-M	—	—	18.6	18.6	12.4	7.6	125	200	75	—	—	OBS	Buck Spring
Elko Eared (n=9)															
35Ha4622	7	M	—	—	22.8	—	13.4	4.8	130	160	30	—	—	OBS	—
35Ha4708	2	C	35.9	33.3	17.3	16.5	8.9	3.7	140	180	40	1.5	0.93	OBS	—

TABLE 13.4. (cont'd.) Metric and sourcing data for typed projectile points

Site No.	FS	Frag. Type[1]	LT (mm)	LA (mm)	WB (mm)	WM (mm)	WN (mm)	Thi. (mm)	PSA (°)	DSA (°)	NO (°)	Wt. (g)	BIR	Raw Mat.	Geochemical Type
35Ha4718	3	P-M	—	—	19.1	19.1	13.8	4.6	130	210	80	—	—	OBS	Gregory Creek
35Ha4733	12	P-M	—	—	20.8	20.8	14.5	8.9	130	180	50	—	—	OBS	Mosquito Lake
AIF-30	1	P-M	—	—	16.0	—	12.0	4.2	125	160	35	—	—	OBS	—
GIF-5	1	P-M	—	—	17.7	—	12.6	6.4	110	180	70	—	—	OBS	Beatys Butte
PIF-2	1	P-M	—	—	18.5	29.3	16.6	7.3	120	170	50	—	—	OBS	—
TIF-85	1	C	33.8	31.6	19.6	21.9	13.9	5.5	130	180	50	2.7	0.93	OBS	unknown 1
TIF-96	1	P-M	—	—	15.0	25.4	13.6	5.7	110	170	60	—	—	OBS	Beatys Butte
Elko Series (*n*=2)															
35Ha4726	2	P	—	—	—	24.7	14.7	4.7	110	160	50	—	—	OBS	—
35Ha4728	4	M-D	—	—	—	—	—	5.8	110	160	50	—	—	OBS	—
Rosegate (*n*=21)															
35Ha4522	15	M-D	—	—	—	—	6.0	3.3	—	160	—	—	—	OBS	Tank Creek
35Ha4634	3	M	—	—	—	—	6.4	3.6	90	170	80	—	—	OBS	Buck Mountain
35Ha4634	4	P-M	—	—	6.0	16.4	5.3	2.7	95	140	45	—	—	OBS	Beatys Butte
35Ha4635	3	C	21.9	21.9	6.1	15.5	5.4	2.8	110	160	50	0.5	1.0	OBS	Riley
35Ha4637	1	C	17.7	16.1	7.8	17.2	5.8	2.7	120	120	0	0.4	0.91	OBS	Beatys Butte
35Ha4648	11	P-M	—	—	6.1	20.0	5.6	3.9	100	140	40	—	—	OBS	Buck Mountain
35Ha4660	1	C	28.2	28.2	5.7	12.3	4.7	3.2	90	170	80	0.7	1.0	OBS	Beatys Butte
35Ha4667	1	C	21.2	21.2	5.8	8.2	5.4	4.8	100	240	140	0.8	1.0	OBS	Buck Spring
35Ha4695	6	C	20.2	20.2	7.5	—	5.9	2.6	120	170	50	—	1.0	OBS	Buck Spring
35Ha4714	5	P-M	—	—	7.2	—	6.4	4.2	110	—	—	—	—	OBS	—
35Ha4722	1	P-M	—	—	5.8	12.3	5.3	3.3	100	170	60	—	—	OBS	Cowhead Lake
35Ha4726	1	C	21.9	21.9	6.3	—	4.6	2.9	110	170	60	—	1.0	OBS	Beatys Butte
35Ha4733	36	C	19.5	19.5	7.1	—	5.8	3.3	110	130	20	—	1.0	OBS	Buck Spring
AIF-2	1	P-M	—	—	7.6	18.3	6.6	3.1	120	150	30	—	—	OBS	Cowhead Lake
AIF-16	1	P-M	—	—	—	15.5	9.1	4.9	125	160	35	—	—	OBS	—
CIF-52	1	P-M	—	—	6.9	17.6	6.2	5.1	110	160	50	—	—	FGV	Venator
CIF-65	1	P-M	—	—	8.1	15.5	5.4	2.8	110	150	40	—	—	OBS	Buck Mountain
GIF-20	1	C	31.9	31.2	8.9	23.0	14.0	10.9	120	150	30	2.5	0.98	OBS	—
TIF-9	1	M	—	—	—	—	6.2	3.6	90	170	80	—	—	OBS	—
TIF-73	1	C	14.0	14.0	7.3	10.8	5.3	2.7	120	170	50	0.3	1.0	OBS	Beatys Butte
TIF-95	1	P-M	—	—	10.0	15.3	9.5	4.9	100	180	80	—	—	OBS	ML/GV[2]

Desert Side-notched (n=12)

Site	No.	Portion[1]												Material	Source
35Ha4522	2	P	—	—	—	—	14.9	2.8	180	230	50	—	—	OBS	Glass Buttes Variety 1
35Ha4522	4	P-M	—	—	12.2	12.2	—	2.4	180	240	60	—	—	OBS	Glass Buttes Variety 3
35Ha4522	8	L	—	—	—	—	—	3.0	160	240	80	—	—	OBS	Glass Buttes Variety 1
35Ha4522	10	C	27.3	24.2	14.7	14.7	9.2	3.2	180	190	10	1.0	0.89	OBS	Horse Mountain
35Ha4522	18	P	—	—	14.2	—	9.7	2.2	180	180	0	—	—	OBS	Glass Buttes Variety 2
35Ha4522	29	P-M	—	—	13.8	13.8	11.3	2.7	150	200	150	—	—	OBS	Tule Spring
35Ha4522	31	P-M	—	—	11.1	11.1	9.0	1.6	180	180	0	—	—	CCS	—
35Ha4522	371	P-M	—	—	14.2	14.2	10.6	3.1	170	180	10	—	—	OBS	Double H/Whitehorse
35Ha4522	372	C	16.1	12.9	12.5	12.5	—	2.7	180	205	25	0.5	0.80	OBS	Riley
35Ha4676	1	C	28.6	25.5	17.6	17.6	9.2	2.6	170	200	30	1.3	0.89	OBS	Beatys Butte
35Ha4711	1	P-M	—	—	12.1	12.1	8.9	2.6	170	190	20	—	—	CCS	—
GIF-44	1	M-D	—	21.1	—	13.6	10.3	3.1	—	190	—	—	—	OBS	—

Cottonwood Triangular (n=7)

Site	No.	Portion[1]												Material	Source
35Ha4522	1	L	—	—	—	—	n/a	3.4	n/a	n/a	n/a	—	—	OBS	Glass Buttes Variety 1
35Ha4522	3	C	32.2	31.3	16.6	16.6	n/a	3.4	n/a	n/a	n/a	1.6	0.97	OBS	Glass Buttes Variety 3
35Ha4522	16	C	37.2	37.2	17.5	17.5	n/a	4.8	n/a	n/a	n/a	2.8	1.0	CCS	—
35Ha4522	27	P-M	—	—	17.5	17.5	n/a	3.7	n/a	n/a	n/a	—	—	OBS	Glass Buttes Variety 1
35Ha4522	30	P-M	—	—	13.4	13.4	n/a	2.4	n/a	n/a	n/a	—	—	CCS	—
35Ha4623	2	C	23.8	23.5	13.5	13.5	n/a	2.1	n/a	n/a	n/a	0.5	0.99	OBS	Horse Mountain
35Ha4623	5	P-M	—	—	14.8	14.8	n/a	3.2	n/a	n/a	n/a	—	—	OBS	Horse Mountain

[1] C=complete; P=proximal; M=medial; D=distal; L=lateral.

[2] ML/GV=Massacre Lake/Guano Valley.

[3] BS/PP/FM=Bordwell Spring/Pinto Peak/Fox Mountain.

TABLE 13.5. Additional attributes of fluted points

Specimen (Site-FS)	BCD[1] (mm)	BCD/ BW	Max. Flute Length (mm)	Edge Grinding[2]	Flutes per Face	Flute Scratches[3]	Guide Scars[3]	Base Shape[4]	Determination
35Ha4690-1	1.5	0.06	>21.0	B, L	1, 1	—	—	arced	Clovis
35Ha4711-6	2.8	0.14	>23.9	B, L	1, 0	—	—	recurved	indeterminate
35Ha4717-1	1.0	—	>27.4	B, L	1, 1	—	—	arced	Clovis
35Ha4717-3	1.5	—	>18.5	L	1, 1	—	+	arced	Clovis
35Ha4718-5	>1.7	—	36.6	B	1, 2	—	—	N.M.	Clovis
35Ha4720-3	1.8	—	n/a	B, L	1, 1	—	+	arced	Clovis
35Ha4731-4	3.0	—	>29.4	B, L	1, 2	—	—	arced	Clovis
35Ha4731-17	>2.2	—	n/a	B, L	1, 1	—	+	arced	Clovis
35Ha4731-18	n/a	—	>22.5	L	1, 0	~	~	N.M.	Clovis
GIF-31-1	5.2	—	19.5	B, L	1, 1	+	+	arced	Clovis
TIF-59-1	1.3	0.05	>33.4	B, L	1, 1	—	+	arced	Clovis

[1] BCD=basal concavity depth.
[2] B=base; L=lateral margin.
[3] +=present; —=absent; ~=indeterminate.
[4] N.M.=not measurable.

face. Most possess edge-grinding and a minority possess damaged tips. Here, the North Warner Valley crescents are again consistent with those from other collections (Beck and Jones 2009; Jew et al. 2015).

Crescents mark Paleoindian occupations in the northwestern Great Basin (Smith and Barker 2017), and we typically found them at sites that also contained WST points. Two sites, 35Ha4720 and 35Ha4731, contained crescents along with WST and fluted points. A handful of sites across the Intermountain West and California have produced crescents in dated contexts. Their ages range between ~12,150 and ~8450 cal BP (Smith et al. 2014 and references therein). As noted in Chapter 7, we recovered a grey CCS crescent from Stratum V in LSP-1. It dates no earlier than ~9775 cal BP. Some of the crescents we recorded on survey may date to around this time, but those found at sites along the 1,390 m asl shoreline (35Ha4670-4, 35Ha4720-4, 35Ha4731-5, and 35Ha4732-1) may be older. Conversely, those found on the valley floor (35Ha4734-22, 35Ha4734-27, GIF-124-1, GIF-125-1) may be younger. One specimen, 35Ha4650-2, could be much younger. We found it together with a large biface made of obsidian from Glass Mountain, California, and a handful of flakes. The Glass Mountain obsidian flow formed ~1000 cal BP, which means that the biface must postdate that time. The crescent is made of obsidian from the Beatys Butte source. The ephemeral nature of 35Ha4650 suggests that the two artifacts mark the same short-term occupation, though it is also possible that Late Archaic or Terminal Prehistoric people collected the crescent from a nearby Paleoindian site before discarding it along with the biface made of Glass Mountain obsidian.

Archaic Dart and Arrow Points

More than half of the NWVSA projectile points date to the TP/EH. The remainder consist of various types that possess varying age ranges; these include Northern Side-notched, foliate, Gatecliff, Elko, Rosegate, and Desert Series points (Figures 13.6–13.10). Because Desert Series points date to the final centuries before Euro-American contact in the northwestern Great Basin (Delacorte 2008), they serve as excellent time markers. In contrast, Humboldt and foliate points were used for several millennia and are poor time markers (Oetting 1994b).

These point types occur in varying frequencies. We interpret their abundances as a coarse-grained reflection of the degree to which groups visited North Warner Valley during the middle and late Holocene (see Table 13.3). A paucity of Northern Side-notched points (~3 percent of the sample) suggests that groups did not occupy the area to any great degree during the middle Holocene, while an abundance of Gatecliff points (~12 percent of the sample) suggests that North Warner Valley witnessed fairly heavy use, at least by hunters, during the terminal middle Holocene and initial late Holocene. Finally, a dearth of Desert Series points may be evidence for broader ethnolinguistic shifts in the northern Great Basin in the centuries prior to Euro-American contact. We explore these topics in greater detail below.

SETTLEMENT AND SUBSISTENCE

What can our survey data tell us about how people used North Warner Valley? Here, we focus on their mobility strategies, how they positioned themselves relative to potential food sources, and how their settlement and subsistence strategies changed across time.

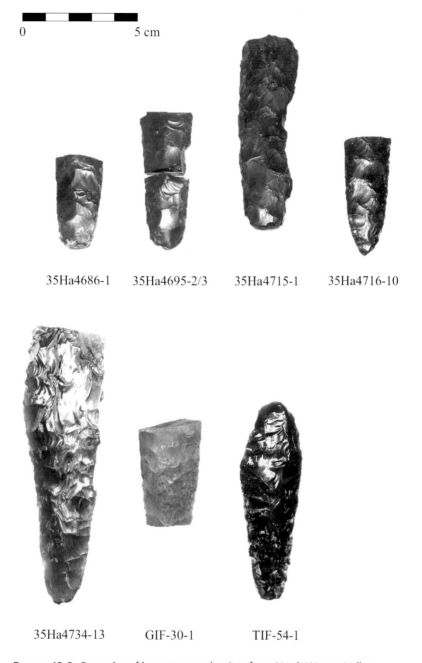

0   5 cm

35Ha4686-1   35Ha4695-2/3   35Ha4715-1   35Ha4716-10

35Ha4734-13   GIF-30-1   TIF-54-1

FIGURE 13.2. Examples of long-stemmed points from North Warner Valley.

The Paleoindian Period (pre-8000 cal BP)

Paleoindian artifacts, including Clovis points, Black Rock Concave Base points, WST points, and crescents, comprise ~56 percent of the time-sensitive artifacts in our sample. To account for the different amounts of time represented by our cultural periods (e.g., the Paleoindian period covers 5,000 years, while the Terminal Prehistoric period covers just 450 years), following Bettinger (1999), we calculated time-adjusted point frequencies by dividing the number of points representing a particular period by the number of years within that period. The results imply that, except for the Terminal Prehistoric period (which is essentially represented by a single site), there was a greater human presence in North Warner Valley before ~8,000 years ago than at any time afterward. Projectile point frequencies from the NWVSA and nearby study areas indicate that North Warner Valley may have been one of the more heavily populated parts of the northwestern Great Basin during the TP/EH (Table 13.7).

Paleoindian points occurred as isolates less often than would be expected by chance relative to points

0   5 cm

35Ha4654-3   35Ha4681-11   35Ha4722-2   35Ha4734-4

35Ha4734-41-1   GIF-28-1   PIF-41-1   TIF-78-1

FIGURE 13.3. Examples of short-stemmed WST points from North Warner Valley.

0   5 cm

35Ha4645-10   35Ha4682-1   35Ha4682-4   35Ha4682-7

35Ha4682-8   35Ha4682-9   35Ha4682-10   35Ha4682-11

GIF-116-1   35Ha4709-9   GIF-123-1   TIF-29-1

FIGURE 13.4. Examples of square-based points from North Warner Valley.

TABLE 13.6. Quantitative and qualitative data for crescents

Specimen (Site-FS)	Length (mm)	Width (mm)	Thick. (mm)	Wt. (g)	Edge Grinding	End Damage	Raw Mat.	Geochemical Type
35Ha4650-2	35.8	12.6	5.2	2.5	+	+	OBS	Beatys Butte
35Ha4670-4	—	19.7	5.7	—	—	—	OBS	—
35Ha4716-7	45.7	20.0	6.9	8.2	+	—	CCS	—
35Ha4720-4	—	16.8	6.7	—	—	—	CCS	—
35Ha4731-5	44.9	18.5	9.1	8.3	+	—	CCS	—
35Ha4732-1	38.4	13.6	4.8	2.9	—	+	CCS	—
35Ha4734-22	43.6	16.9	5.8	4.7	+	+	FGV	Coyote Spring
35Ha4734-27	—	18.3	4.9	—	—	+	OBS	Horse Mountain
AIF-15-1	—	20.3	7.1	—	—	—	OBS	Tucker Hill
GIF-124-1	38.6	14.0	6.6	4.1	+	—	OBS	—
GIF-125-1	43.7	12.4	6.5	3.6	+	—	CCS	—

Note: + = present

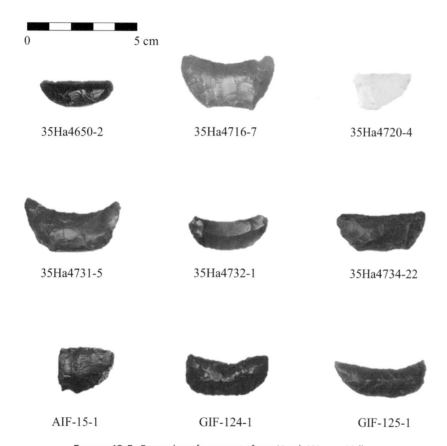

0   5 cm

35Ha4650-2   35Ha4716-7   35Ha4720-4

35Ha4731-5   35Ha4732-1   35Ha4734-22

AIF-15-1   GIF-124-1   GIF-125-1

FIGURE 13.5. Examples of crescents from North Warner Valley.

from other periods ($\chi^2 = 22.27$, $df = 4$, $p < .001$), suggesting a residentially mobile pattern in which people tended to stay together. Most sites are small and contain high tool-to-debitage ratios. We did not observe features or other evidence of longer-term occupations. Paleoindian sites and isolated projectile points occur primarily along the prominent beach ridges that crosscut North Warner Valley or on the valley bottom below, which could reflect

people's focus on near-shore resource patches such as back bar lagoons. We did not encounter any early artifacts or sites in the surrounding uplands/canyons.

As we have outlined, the association between many Paleoindian sites and the 1,390 m asl Lake Warner shoreline provides some degree of chronological control. The fact that most fluted points occurred along the early Younger Dryas or older shoreline suggests that they

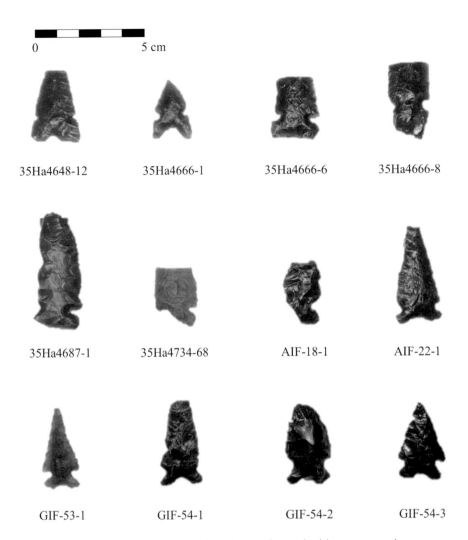

0   5 cm

35Ha4648-12   35Ha4666-1   35Ha4666-6   35Ha4666-8

35Ha4687-1   35Ha4734-68   AIF-18-1   AIF-22-1

GIF-53-1   GIF-54-1   GIF-54-2   GIF-54-3

FIGURE 13.6. Examples of Northern Side-notched (*top two rows*) and Elko Series (*bottom row*) points from North Warner Valley.

mark Clovis occupations. This possibility is additionally supported by overlap between the obsidian types represented in the North Warner Valley fluted points (see below) and other Clovis assemblages in the region, namely the Dietz Site (O'Grady et al. 2012). Pinson (2011) has suggested that Clovis foragers ranged through the lake basins of southeastern Oregon, including Warner Valley and the Dietz Basin. Our data fit her model.

Stemmed points occurred at a wider range of elevations above, at, and below the 1,390 m asl shoreline. Prior to 12,575–12,095 cal BP, elevations lower than 1,390 m asl were inundated. Therefore, stemmed points below 1,390 m asl should postdate that time. Because the valley floor had likely become dry by 10,300 cal BP, stemmed points there may date to that time or slightly later. The LSP-1 rockshelter was first occupied by people using stemmed points ~9775 cal BP, indicating that visitors to North Warner Valley still used them at that time.

The WST points associated with the 1,390 m asl shoreline may be roughly contemporary with the fluted points found there, if one accepts the premise that the users of both technologies (whether members of the same or different groups) camped along Lake Warner's shores. Elsewhere, we have argued that because both point types cluster along the shoreline they were probably used during the same general period (Smith et al. 2015b; Wriston and Smith 2017). Our coarse estimate for when Lake Warner paused at 1,390 m asl prevents us from knowing whether fluted-point users camped along the lakeshore a few centuries before WST point users, vice versa, or around the same time.

The elevational distributions of WST and fluted points alone cannot tell us anything definitive about their temporal relationship, but their horizontal distributions suggest that people probably did not discard them in the same locations at the same time. Although

0   5 cm

35Ha4623-1   35Ha4634-13   35Ha4653-3   35Ha4685-1

35Ha4697-4   35Ha4723-1   35Ha4725-1   35Ha4729-9

35Ha4733-5   AIF-10-1   AIF-24-1   GIF-92-1

FIGURE 13.7. Examples of Humboldt points from North Warner Valley.

most fluted points came from sites that also contained WST points, they occurred 54–264 m from the nearest WST points. On average, the point types were separated by 117 m (Smith et al. 2015b). This horizontal separation suggests that fluted and WST points were not simply different kinds of tools (e.g., projectiles and knives) used by the same people (contra Tuohy 1974). Differences in the obsidian types represented in the fluted and WST samples further suggest that this was not the case (Smith et al. 2015b).

Most Paleoindian sites are small and possess high tool-to-debitage ratios, suggesting that while early groups frequented North Warner Valley, they relocated

their camps often. There are a few notable exceptions that warrant discussion. The first is a cluster of four sites (35Ha4717, 35Ha4731, 35Ha4718, and 35Ha4720) containing fluted points that, although recorded separately, are likely a single locus. Whether it marks a single longer-term occupation or a place to which fluted point-users periodically returned remains unknown.

Site 35Ha4734 is also noteworthy because it is the second-largest site in the NWVSA and possessed a sizeable and diverse artifact assemblage. Located on the valley floor, it necessarily postdates 12,575–12,095 cal BP, probably closer to 10,300 cal BP. We recorded 67 tools including various types of WST points, bifaces, and

0   5 cm

35Ha4648-12   35Ha4666-1   35Ha4666-6   35Ha4666-8   35Ha4669-1

35Ha4687-1   35Ha4734-68   AIF-18-1   AIF-22-1   GIF-45-1

GIF-53-1   GIF-54-1   GIF-54-2   GIF-54-3   GIF-111-1

FIGURE 13.8. Examples of Gatecliff Split Stem points from North Warner Valley.

flake tools within a ~75,000 m² area. Numerous raw material types are represented among the thousands of flakes, suggesting that the location either saw prolonged occupation or was revisited several times. Either way, 35Ha4734 stands apart from the other Paleoindian sites. Subsurface testing revealed that artifacts are confined to the ground surface with little potential for buried deposits (Smith and Wriston 2018).

A final Paleoindian site, 35Ha4682, is notable not for its size or location but because it contains 10 well-made square-base points (see Figure 13.4). These points are generally not found at other sites in North Warner Valley, and, as we outlined above, they fit Amick's (2013) model of Plains bison hunters crossing the Rocky Mountains.

Since the Paleoindian record is essentially a surface one, we are left largely to speculate about the subsistence strategies of early groups. The association between fluted and WST sites and the 1,390 m asl shoreline suggests that Paleoindians positioned themselves close to the lakeshore to target wetland resources. The confluence of a drainage and Lake Warner appears to have been especially attractive before 12,575–12,095 cal BP and may have offered drinking water, waterfowl, fish, small mammals, and cattail and tule in protected back bar lagoons. The creek and marshes may have also attracted large game (Elston et al. 2014).

As Lake Warner receded after 12,575–12,095 cal BP, people appear to have followed it southward and downslope. WST sites occur as low as 1,363 m asl (the lowest elevation in our study area). For a time, people likely

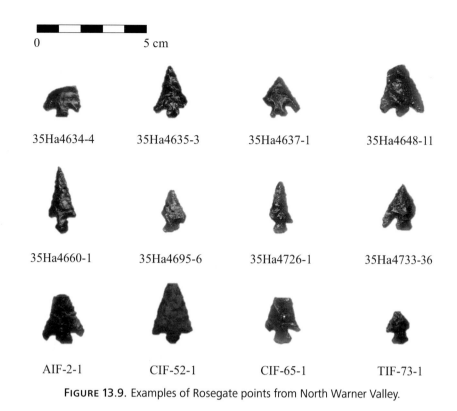

0   5 cm

35Ha4634-4	35Ha4635-3	35Ha4637-1	35Ha4648-11
35Ha4660-1	35Ha4695-6	35Ha4726-1	35Ha4733-36
AIF-2-1	CIF-52-1	CIF-65-1	TIF-73-1

FIGURE 13.9. Examples of Rosegate points from North Warner Valley.

0   5 cm

35Ha4522-4	35Ha4522-10	35Ha4522-18	35Ha4522-31
35Ha4522-371	35Ha4522-372	35Ha4676-1	35Ha4711-1
35Ha4522-1	35Ha4522-3	35Ha4522-30	35Ha4623-2

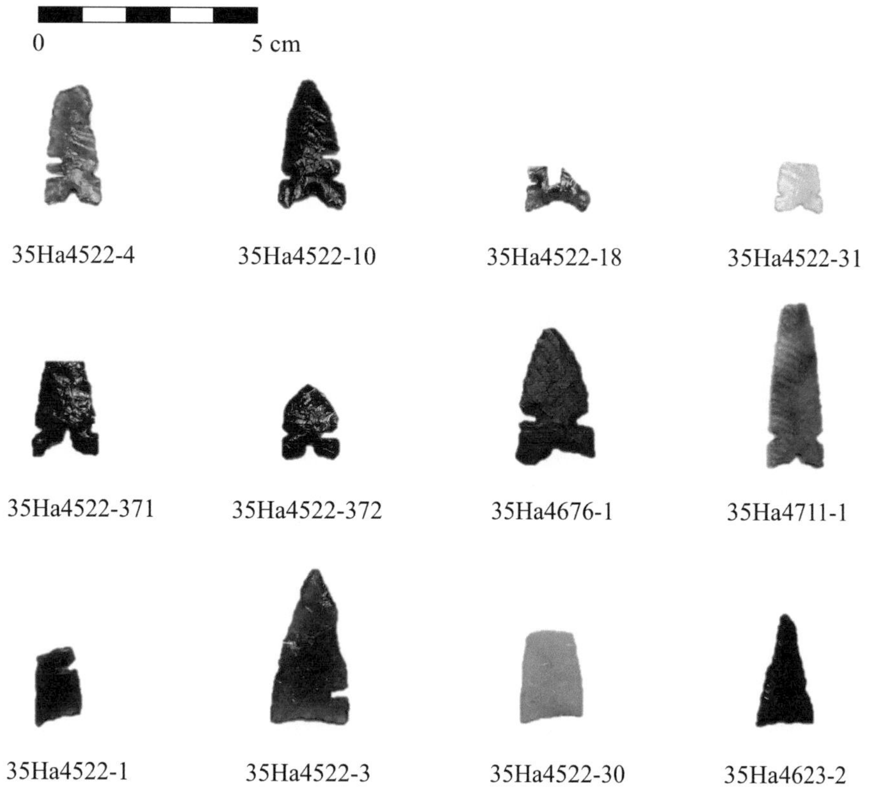

FIGURE 13.10. Examples of Desert Side-notched (*top two rows*) and Cottonwood Triangular (*bottom row*) points from North Warner Valley.

TABLE 13.7. Paired comparisons of projectile point frequencies for the NWVSA and nearby study areas

Comparisons of Study Areas	Period				
	Paleoindian	Early Archaic	Middle Archaic	Late Archaic	Terminal Prehistoric
NWVSA, OR	145 (+12.5)	10 (−0.6)	65 (−1.9)	21 (−7.7)	19 (+0.9)
Fort Rock Basin, OR	52 (−7.6)	35 (+0.4)	237 (+1.2)	335 (+4.7)	38 (−0.6)
$\chi^2=302.59$, $df=4$, $p<.0001$					
NWVSA, OR	145 (+10.4)	10 (−3.4)	65 (−1.8)	21 (−6.5)	19 (+3.1)
Abert-Chewaucan Basin, OR	29 (−7.8)	67 (+2.5)	161 (+1.4)	196 (+4.9)	7 (−2.4)
$\chi^2=272.44$, $df=4$, $p<.0001$					
NWVSA, OR	145 (+19.2)	10 (−3.5)	65 (−5.4)	21 (−4.8)	19 (+1.3)
Steens Mountain, OR	12 (−10.0)	122 (+1.8)	522 (+2.9)	247 (+2.5)	47 (−0.7)
$\chi^2=551.97$, $df=4$, $p<.0001$					
NWVSA, OR	145 (+7.6)	10 (−1.6)	65 (−4.2)	21 (−2.3)	19 (−0.6)
Massacre Lake, NV	5 (−7.9)	22 (+1.7)	144 (+4.4)	46 (+2.4)	23 (+0.6)
$\chi^2=174.22$, $df=4$, $p<.0001$					

Note: numbers in parentheses represent standardized residuals. Projectile point frequencies for each study area are derived from Bettinger (1999).

continued to target wetland resources, which may have grown more abundant as the deep lake became a broad marsh, but by 10,300 cal BP North Warner Valley had become dry. The abundant leporids in LSP-1's early Holocene deposits and the systematic way people processed them suggests that people captured the animals via communal drives on the valley floor.

Site locations relative to different landscape features provide indirect evidence of human subsistence strategies: earlier Paleoindians probably targeted wetland resources; later Paleoindians probably targeted leporids. Although a few economically important seeds in early Holocene features at LSP-1 suggest that early visitors consumed some plant resources, we know little about the role of plants at open-air sites. The frequency of two basic artifact classes—bifaces (all stages including finished points) and groundstone (manos and metates)—may provide a general understanding (McGuire et al. 2016) because bifaces offer a measure of hunting and groundstone offers a measure of plant processing. Following McGuire and colleagues, we calculated the density of bifaces and groundstone for each period by dividing the number of each tool type found at sites and as isolated resources by the number of components representing those time periods. High densities of bifaces imply a hunting-focused strategy; high densities of groundstone imply a plant-focused strategy, perhaps also indirectly implying the presence of nearby residential bases because plants are generally not worth transporting very far (Rhode 2011). High densities of both tool types imply intensified subsistence strategies and, likely, the presence of nearby residential bases (McGuire et al. 2016). Figure 13.11 and Table S15 show that, except

for the Terminal Prehistoric period, the Paleoindian period contains the highest density of bifaces and the lowest density of groundstone. This suggests a low reliance on plant resources requiring intensive processing, though maybe not a lack of Paleoindian residential camps in the area because, as noted, isolated Paleoindian points were rare.

The Early Archaic Period
(8000–5750 cal BP)

Three seasons of survey produced just 10 Early Archaic points. Both the absolute and time-adjusted frequencies of Early Archaic points suggest that groups visited the area infrequently between 8000 and 5750 cal BP. The LSP-1 rockshelter record paints a similar picture: after recurrent visits during the terminal early Holocene the shelter fell into disuse for several millennia. It is especially clear just how infrequently Early Archaic groups visited North Warner Valley when the frequencies of time-sensitive points are compared to neighboring areas. High numbers of Northern Side-notched points near Steens Mountain and the Abert-Chewaucan Basin suggest that Early Archaic groups refocused their settlement systems there. Of course, the drop in this measure of human use coincides with the onset of the middle Holocene, which was especially hot and dry 9000–6300 cal BP (Rhode 2016). Regionally, people seem to have responded to deteriorating local conditions by abandoning caves and rockshelters that were no longer adjacent to wetlands (Ollivier 2016) or vacating certain areas for a time (Grayson 2011). Both scenarios apparently played out in North Warner Valley.

While all signs point to a substantial reduction in

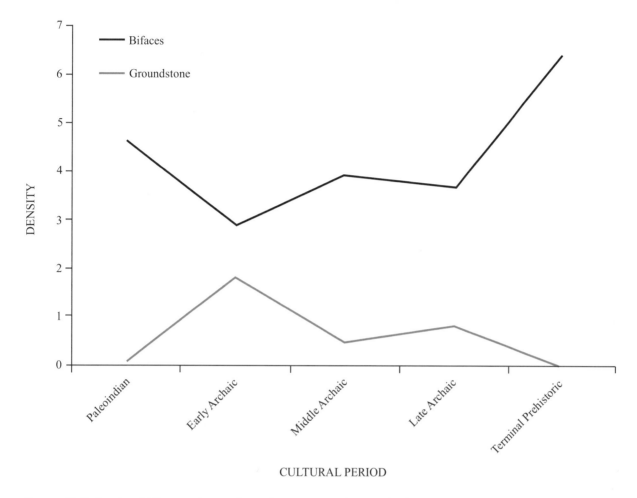

FIGURE 13.11. Density of bifaces and groundstone by component (sites and isolated resources) per period in North Warner Valley. Multicomponent sites counted once for each period represented at those sites (PI=Paleoindian; EA=Early Archaic; MA=Middle Archaic; LA=Late Archaic; TP=Terminal Prehistoric).

use, the handful of Early Archaic projectile points in North Warner Valley may tell us something about changes in settlement and subsistence. A greater proportion of Early Archaic points occurred on the valley bottom than Paleoindian points, and we only recorded an isolated Northern Side-notched point in the uplands. In the absence of wetlands, groups may have expanded their land-use strategies. Just over half of the Early Archaic points occurred as isolates, which is more often than would be expected by chance. Although our dataset is small, this could reflect increased logistical hunting from residential bases. The densities of bifaces (low) and groundstone (high) in the few Early Archaic components is consistent with this possibility. Site 35Ha4722 may be one of those residential bases. At ~38,000 m², it is among the largest sites that we recorded. Although Humboldt, Gatecliff, Elko, and Rosegate points were also present, indicating that it was periodically reoccu-

pied, 35Ha4722 is the only site in North Warner Valley where we recorded two Northern Side-notched points. We recorded 41 other tools including at least 19 manos and metates, cores of various raw materials, and bifaces and flake tools. Several groundstone implements are thermally fractured, suggesting that they served as boiling stones.

The Middle Archaic Period (5750–2000 cal BP)

Beginning ~4500 cal BP, Middle Archaic groups returned to LSP-1, revisiting it several times during the first half of the late Holocene. At surface sites, both the absolute (*n*=65; 25 percent) and time-adjusted (0.17) frequencies of Middle Archaic points rise sharply from Early Archaic lows. This implies that local conditions improved, and people may have reintegrated the area into broader settlement-subsistence systems. Still, a comparison of projectile point frequencies in North Warner Valley and adjacent regions suggests that it remained somewhat peripheral to Steens Mountain and the Fort Rock, Abert-Chewaucan, and Massacre Lake Basins (see Table 13.7).

Given their proximity to our study area, the Abert-Chewaucan Basin and the Warner Lakes may be especially critical to understanding how Middle Archaic groups used North Warner Valley. In the Abert-Chewaucan Basin, Oetting (1989, 1990) reported a persistent village pattern that began 4500 cal BP and intensified after 3300 cal BP. Sites were centered on the Chewaucan River and southern edge of Lake Abert. Near the Warner Lakes, substantial habitation sites appeared ~2900 cal BP (Tipps 1998; also see Aikens et al. 2011), around the same time that use of the Abert-Chewaucan Basin increased. In both cases, longer-term residential stays would have necessitated increased logistical trips to collect large and small game. North Warner Valley may have been one of the places to which groups traveled.

Like Early Archaic points, Middle Archaic points occurred more often as isolates than expected by chance, which is consistent with this scenario. So too are the densities of bifaces (high) and groundstone (low) in Middle Archaic components. In these regards, the survey and rockshelter data align remarkably well: both point to an emphasis on hunting. If North Warner Valley was a destination for hunters, then it fits well within the broader pattern of increased residential stability and logistical big-game hunting that occurred in the Great Basin and California during the Middle Archaic period (Hildebrandt and McGuire 2002; Hildebrandt et al. 2016; McGuire and Hildebrandt 2005). Large mammals were probably not the only draw for people in North Warner Valley though, as leporid carcasses continued to accumulate in high numbers at LSP-1.

Middle Archaic sites and isolated points occurred mostly around the beach ridges and on the valley floors. Most sites are small, but a few contain large and diverse lithic assemblages suggesting that they served as bases. Located on the valley floor among low dunes and covering ~44,000 m², 35Ha4656 is one of the larger sites in North Warner Valley. It is one of seven sites that, while recorded separately, probably represent a single locus. Obsidian, FGV, and CCS flakes are abundant and occur at varying densities. We recorded 18 tools including obsidian and CCS bifaces, flake tools, manos, and a metate. A single projectile point—probably a Humboldt—suggests that the site dates to the Middle Archaic period. Many artifacts are centered on three concentrations of thermally fractured rock and groundstone fragments that probably represent deflated hearths. Among all the sites from North Warner Valley, 35Ha4656 possesses the best evidence for a longer-term occupation. Site 35Ha4722, described above, is consistent with our expectations for a residential base and contains several Middle Archaic points.

The Late Archaic Period
(2000–600 cal BP)

While the absolute number and proportion of Late Archaic points are lower than Middle Archaic points, their time-adjusted frequency (.015) is essentially unchanged, implying that people continued to visit North Warner Valley somewhat consistently. The fact that Middle and Late Archaic radiocarbon dates from LSP-1 occur in roughly equal numbers suggests that this was also the case, although, as we have outlined, families may have once again become the primary social unit to use the shelter after 2000 cal BP. Comparisons of projectile point frequencies from different areas in the northwestern Great Basin imply that North Warner Valley remained undervisited during the Late Archaic period.

Late Archaic projectile points occurred mostly around the beach ridges and on the valley floor. They also occurred more often as isolates than expected by chance but less so than points from other periods. The density of bifaces in Late Archaic components is slightly lower than in Middle Archaic components, while the density of groundstone is slightly higher. These trends track the Late Archaic pattern at LSP-1 rather well and again suggest a return of family groups to North Warner Valley. However, there are no single-component Late Archaic sites that might represent longer-term residential bases. The only sites that may mark longer-term Late Archaic occupations (35Ha4634 and 35Ha4722) also contain projectile points from earlier periods. South of the project area, near the Warner Lakes and farther south where Honey Creek and other drainages provided reliable water, large residential sites mostly postdating 1000 cal BP and probably representing winter villages (Aikens et al. 2011) may have served as bases from which groups traveled north to hunt and gather. Young (1998) has made a similar argument for Late Archaic settlement-subsistence patterns in the Rabbit Basin, located just southwest of North Warner Valley. This is essentially the same pattern that Kelly (1932) noted during ethnographic times.

The Terminal Prehistoric Period
(600–150 cal BP)

The centuries leading up to the arrival of Euro-Americans were a time of significant change. The possible migration of Numic speakers is probably the most significant event, although researchers remain divided about how and when it occurred (Aikens and Witherspoon 1986; Bettinger and Baumhoff 1982; Lamb 1958;

Madsen and Rhode 1994). Unfortunately, our dataset is poorly equipped to address questions about Terminal Prehistoric settlement and subsistence and how they may be related to the arrival of the Northern Paiute. We only recorded three sites and one isolated resource containing Desert Series projectile points, which researchers generally attribute to the Numa (Bettinger and Baumhoff 1982; Delacorte 2008; Delacorte and Basgall 2012). The youngest hearth in LSP-1 dates to 975–805 cal BP; we found no Desert Series points in the rockshelter. As Camp and colleagues discussed in Chapter 11, the youngest directly dated artifacts from LSP-1 are Catlow Twine basketry and a Klamath Style sandal.

Due to the scant Terminal Prehistoric record in North Warner Valley, we elected to not compare projectile point counts, point frequencies at sites and isolated resources, or the densities of bifaces and groundstone (the latter of which there are none) to those from earlier periods or adjacent study areas. Instead, we focus here on 35Ha4522. Site 35Ha4522 is significant because it is one of the denser sites from any period in North Warner Valley but more so because it exemplifies a pattern that Scott Thomas (Burns District BLM, retired) has recognized in southeastern Oregon. Thomas (2014; also see Lyons et al. 2001) has attributed sites possessing Desert Series points, often made on distant obsidian types or white CCS from the Tosawihi quarry in northern Nevada, large blades that provided blanks for arrow points, bison bone, and, occasionally, ceramics to the Shoshone Complex. He has identified roughly a dozen such sites in the region, including the Lost Dune Site (35Ha792) in nearby Blitzen Valley. The Lost Dune Site dates to ~450 cal BP. Thomas has argued that it and others like it reflect incursions by Shoshone bison hunters from the Snake River Plain into territory held by the Northern Paiute and, before them, the Klamath. Except for ceramics, 35Ha4522 possesses each of these attributes, including bovid tooth enamel fragments and a bovid long-bone fragment dated to 490–320 cal BP (360±15 ^{14}C BP) (Scott Thomas, personal communication, 2018). Two fire-affected rock scatters indicate that people built a few fires.

Given that it is only one site, 35Ha4522 cannot effectively address broader questions of Terminal Prehistoric settlement or subsistence. Instead, its value lies in its ability to inform our understanding of one of many trends that together comprised an increasingly complex social landscape. Sites containing both putative Numic (35Ha4522) and Penutian (South Warner Cave and the Peninsula Site) artifact types dated to the centuries leading up to Euro-American contact suggest that the Warner Basin saw shared use by Klamath, Northern Paiute, and, perhaps occasionally, Shoshone groups.

Summary of Settlement and Subsistence Patterns

During the terminal Pleistocene and continuing into the initial early Holocene, North Warner Valley was a major draw for early populations. Groups using fluted and WST points arrived from the north and west, perhaps stopping in North Warner Valley as part of broader annual or longer rounds (Pinson 2011). While we do not know precisely when such visits occurred, the association between early Paleoindian sites and the dated Lake Warner shoreline implies that they were most frequent at the onset of the Younger Dryas. As the lake receded, later Paleoindians followed it downslope while probably continuing to collect wetland resources. With the lake gone and the valley floor exposed ~10,300 cal BP, WST-using people started to target rabbits and hares. For roughly a millennium, they processed leporid carcasses inside LSP-1, probably during repeated short-term visits.

During the middle Holocene, deteriorating environmental conditions or other factors led populations away from the area. People visited North Warner Valley infrequently and probably came from residential bases located to the south near the Warner Lakes or perhaps to the southwest in the Abert-Chewaucan Basin. Logistical big-game hunting may have taken place but so too did plant processing. These behaviors continued through the Middle and Late Archaic periods, albeit on a more frequent basis. Substantial sites that might have served as residential bases or field camps are uncommon. Rabbits and hares were probably always available, and the LSP-1 record, which shows that people returned beginning ~4500 cal BP, attests to those animals' continued importance to Middle and Late Archaic groups. The scant Terminal Prehistoric record makes it difficult to know how North Warner Valley fit into local and regional patterns although it was not a primary focus after 600 cal BP.

LITHIC PROCUREMENT AND PRODUCTION

Procurement

More than 90 percent of the survey sample artifacts are made of obsidian. We submitted 197 projectile points and 130 flakes for geochemical characterization. We also conducted a basic analysis of tools and debitage at sites to understand how groups conveyed toolstone into North Warner Valley (e.g., as unmodified cobbles, partially reduced cores or bifaces, or finished tools). These efforts allow us to address questions related to lithic procurement and production. In particular, to what extent did groups rely on local raw materials; from where did groups obtain nonlocal toolstone and what can that tell us about mobility, land use, and exchange; and what types of technological activities occurred at sites in the study area?

TABLE 13.8. Obsidian and FGV types represented in the NWVSA projectile point sample

Geochemical Type	Distance to Source	Direction to Source	Period					Total
			PI	EA	MA	LA	TP	
Alturas FGV	166 km	SW	1	—	—	—	—	1
Badger Creek	119 km	SE	1	—	—	—	—	1
Bald Butte	50 km	NW	3	—	—	—	—	3
Beatys Butte	33 km	SE	20	1	20	5	—	46
Big Stick	48 km	NW	4	—	1	—	—	5
Blue Spring	126 km	NW	1	—	1	—	—	2
BS/PP/FM[1]	161 km	SW	1	—	—	—	—	1
Buck Mountain	123 km	SW	2	—	1	3	—	6
Buck Spring	1 km	various	8	—	4	3	—	15
Camp Creek FGV	110 km	NE	1	—	—	—	—	1
Coglan Buttes	59 km	SW	2	—	—	—	—	2
Cowhead Lake	104 km	SW	1	2	2	2	—	7
Coyote Spring FGV	122 km	SE	1	—	—	—	—	1
Delintment Lake	79 km	NE	—	—	1	—	—	1
Double O[2]	48 km	NE	4	1	1	—	—	6
DH/WH[3]	129 km	SE	1	—	1	—	1	3
Glass Buttes[4]	76 km	NW	9	—	—	—	7	16
Gregory Creek	177 km	NW	2	—	1	—	—	3
Hawks Valley	100 km	SE	1	—	—	—	—	1
Horse Mountain[5]	57 km	NW	16	—	1	—	3	20
Indian Creek Buttes[6]	118 km	NE	1	—	2	—	—	3
Long Valley	104 km	SW	1	—	—	—	—	1
McComb Butte	55 km	NW	1	—	1	—	—	2
ML/GV[7]	64 km	SE	4	1	1	1	—	7
Mosquito Lake	110 km	SW	2	—	2	—	—	4
Mud Ridge	99 km	NE	1	—	—	—	—	1
Obsidian Cliffs	236 km	NW	—	—	1	—	—	1
Riley	81 km	NE	2	—	—	1	1	4
Round Top Butte	76 km	NW	—	—	1	—	—	1
SL/SM[8]	98 km	NW	1	—	—	—	—	1
South Creek	57 km	NW	1	—	—	—	—	1
Sugar Hill	128 km	SW	1	—	—	—	—	1
Surveyor Spring	93 km	SW	—	1	—	—	—	1
Tank Creek	48 km	SW	4	1	1	1	—	7
Tucker Hill	115 km	SW	3	1	1	—	—	5
Tule Spring	120 km	NE	—	—	1	—	1	2
Venator FGV	163 km	NE	—	—	—	1	—	1
Wagontire	58 km	NW	2	—	—	—	—	2
Warner Valley FGV	20 km	SW	2	—	1	—	—	3
Wildhorse Canyon	745 km	SE	1	—	—	—	—	1
Yreka Butte	106 km	NW	2	—	1	—	—	3
unknown FGV	?	—	2	—	—	—	—	2
unknown obsidian	?	—	1	—	1	—	—	2
Total	—	—	111	8	48	17	13	197

[1] BS/PP/FM=Bordwell Spring/Pinto Peak/Fox Mountain.
[2] Obsidian and FGV combined.
[3] DH/WH=Double H/Whitehorse.
[4] All varieties combined.
[5] Horse Mountain/Horse Mountain B combined.
[6] Indian Creek Buttes/Indian Creek Buttes B combined.
[7] ML/GV=Massacre Lake/Guano Valley.
[8] SL/SM=Silver Lake/Sycan Marsh.

Projectile Points

Forty different known obsidian and FGV types, one unknown FGV type, and one unknown obsidian type are represented in the projectile point sample (Table 13.8). These include two local types (Buck Spring obsidian and Warner Valley FGV) and 38 extralocal types found 33–745 km from North Warner Valley (see Figure 7.1). Although Buck Spring obsidian is represented among projectile points from all periods except the Terminal Prehistoric, Beatys Butte obsidian (33 km) dominates each period and accounts for roughly one quarter of all sourced points. Horse Mountain (57 km) and Glass Buttes obsidian (76 km) are also common and account for ~10 percent and ~8 percent of all sourced points, respectively. The other local toolstone type, Warner Valley FGV, is only represented by three points. The most unexpected toolstone type is obsidian from Utah's Wildhorse Canyon, located ~745 km away. A WST point fragment that we could not assign to a subtype is made on that material. Collectively, the source profile indicates that visitors to North Warner Valley either ranged throughout a territory that stretched from the Cascade Mountains to the west, the Blue Mountains to the north, the Snake River to the east, and the Black Rock Desert to the south, or possessed ties to groups who lived in those areas.

The relationship between distance to source and the frequencies of toolstone types resembles a typical fall-off curve. The only major departures are Buck Spring, which is underrepresented probably due to its small package sizes and poor quality, and Beatys Butte, which is overrepresented. Beatys Butte obsidian is high-quality material and after Buck Spring is the closest obsidian source to the NWVSA. At ~33 km from North Warner Valley, it lies beyond the 20 km radius that many researchers (e.g., Smith 2011; Surovell 2009) consider local (meaning that groups could travel to the source and back in a single day). However, people could have easily acquired it on overnight trips. In fact, the four most common obsidian types present in the projectile point sample (Beatys Butte [23 percent], Horse Mountain [10 percent], Glass Buttes [8 percent], and Buck Spring [8 percent]) all lie within the 88 km radius that marks the average one-way distance that ethnographic groups are known to have traveled logistically on multiday trips (R. Kelly 2011 and references therein).

When grouped by period, the projectile points do not exhibit significantly different transport distances (Table 13.9), which many researchers (Jones et al. 2003, 2012; Smith 2010) use as a proxy for foraging territories or exchange networks. This lack of change is notable given that similar studies have shown that obsidian

TABLE 13.9. Mean transport distance and adjusted richness for projectile points by period

Period	Mean Transport Distance (km)[2]	Adjusted Richness[3]
Paleoindian (PI)[1]	64.1	6.4
Early Archaic (EA)	76.1	7.0
Middle Archaic (MA)	62.9	5.4
Late Archaic (LA)	64.8	5.3
Terminal Prehistoric (TP)	79.5	5.3

[1] The WST point made on Wildhorse Canyon obsidian, the source of which lies 745 km from Warner Valley, is an obvious outlier. We excluded it from comparisons of toolstone transport distances and richness.

[2] Two-tailed p values for comparisons of mean transport distance: PI vs. EA=.416; PI vs. MA=.867; PI vs. LA=.948; PI vs. TP=.177; EA vs. MA=.452; EA vs. LA=.562; EA vs. TP=.772; MA vs. LA=.898; MA vs. TP=.249; LA vs. TP=.325.

[3] Two-tailed p values for comparisons of adjusted richness: PI vs. EA=.509; PI vs. MA=.560; PI vs. LA=.061; PI vs. TP=.053; EA vs. MA<.001; EA vs. LA=.006; EA vs. TP=.018; MA vs. LA=.126; MA vs. TP=.044; LA vs. TP=.282.

conveyance did vary diachronically. Regionally, transport distances are typically high for Paleoindian points, low for Early and Middle Archaic points, and high for Late Archaic and Terminal Prehistoric points (Connolly 1999; King 2016b; McGuire 2002; Smith 2007, 2010).

In terms of source diversity, although small, when adjusted for sample size, the Early Archaic point sample is significantly richer than the Middle Archaic, Late Archaic, and Terminal Prehistoric samples. The Middle Archaic sample is also significantly richer than the Terminal Prehistoric sample. Researchers generally interpret high toolstone richness to reflect a more mobile settlement pattern and increased access to more raw material sources; low toolstone richness reflects a less mobile settlement pattern and reliance on fewer raw material sources (McGuire 2002; Smith 2010, 2011). In the case of the NWVSA, there is little evidence for Early Archaic residential bases. Thus, we suspect that the high richness in the Early Archaic point sample may instead reflect the short-term nature of visits during the middle Holocene.

Despite this general consistency in transport distance and source diversity, there are a few notable differences in toolstone use between periods. First, Beatys Butte appears to have been especially important during the Paleoindian and Middle Archaic periods but less so at other times. Second, Horse Mountain and Glass Buttes obsidian are well represented in the Paleoindian sample. Again, this trend is consistent with Pinson's (2011) model of early movements through southeastern Oregon's lake basins, including the Alkali Basin (near Horse Mountain), the Harney Basin (near Glass Buttes),

TABLE 13.10. Obsidian and FGV types represented in the NWVSA debitage samples

Geochemical Type	Distance to Source	Direction to Source	PI (*n*=2)	MA (*n*=1)	LA (*n*=1)	TP (*n*=1)	Total
Beatys Butte	33 km	SE	17	17		3	37
BS/PP/FM[1]	161 km	SW				1	1
Buck Mountain	123 km	SW		1	1		2
Buck Spring	1 km	various	2	4	23		29
Cowhead Lake	104 km	SW	2			1	3
Double O[2]	48 km	NE	2				2
Glass Buttes[3]	76 km	NW	3	1		16	20
Gregory Creek	177 km	NW				2	2
Horse Mountain[4]	57 km	NW	8	1		7	16
McKay Butte	183 km	NW	1				
ML/GV[5]	64 km	SE	7				7
Quartz Mountain	145 km	NW	2				2
SL/SM[6]	98 km	NW	1		1		2
Tank Creek	48 km	SW	1				1
Tucker Hill	115 km	SW	2				2
Unknown Obsidian	?	—		1		2	3
Total	—	—	48	25	25	32	130

Note: PI=Paleoindian; MA=Middle Archaic; LA=Late Archaic; TP=Terminal Prehistoric.

[1] BS/PP/FM=Bordwell Spring/Pinto Peak/Fox Mountain.
[2] Obsidian and FGV combined.
[3] All varieties combined.
[4] Horse Mountain/Horse Mountain B combined.
[5] ML/GV=Massacre Lake/Guano Valley.
[6] SL/SM=Silver Lake/Sycan Marsh.

and Warner Valley (our study area). Both Horse Mountain and Glass Buttes obsidian are also well represented in the Terminal Prehistoric sample, which is derived largely from a single site, 35Ha4522. The people who created that site may have retooled at those sources shortly before traveling to North Warner Valley. Finally, there is no clear directionality in the obsidian sources used to manufacture projectile points. This suggests that North Warner Valley witnessed visits by groups traveling from a variety of distances and directions starting during the terminal Pleistocene and continuing until the final centuries before Euro-American contact.

Debitage

Debitage from Paleoindian (*n*=2), Middle Archaic (*n*=1), Late Archaic (*n*=1), and Terminal Prehistoric (*n*=1) sites provides a similar picture of toolstone procurement (Table 13.10). Beatys Butte obsidian is common in both the Paleoindian and Middle Archaic samples. Horse Mountain is also well represented in the Paleoindian sample. The Late Archaic debitage sample is dominated by Buck Spring obsidian, which is inconsistent with the Late Archaic projectile point sample, where <20 percent of points are made from it. Finally, the Terminal Pre-

historic sample derived from 35Ha4522 is rich in Glass Buttes and Horse Mountain obsidian.

Production

Source provenience data can tell us only from where groups in the NWVSA originated, the locations to which they traveled, or areas where the people with whom they traded for toolstone lived. Lithic technological data provide a better sense of how people used toolstone in North Warner Valley, which in turn offers additional insight into settlement and subsistence strategies beyond those offered by site location and character.

Table 13.11 lists the numbers of cores, bifaces by reduction stage, projectile points, and flake tools at each site. Projectile points are the most common tool type, comprising roughly 40 percent of the sample. Stage 4 and 5 bifaces and flake tools are also common. Cores and stage 2 and 3 bifaces are present but rare. The proportions of early-stage products (cores and stage 2 + 3 bifaces), late-stage products (stage 4 + 5 bifaces and projectile points), and flake tools do not differ significantly among periods (χ^2=3.76, *df*=4, *p*=.440). Fewer earlier-stage tools and more later-stage tools suggests that people generally transported partially finished tools

TABLE 13.11. Flaked and groundstone tools at NWVSA sites

Site No.	Period(s)	Cores	Biface Stage 2	3	4	5	Points	Flake Tools	Ground Stone	Total
35Ha4702	PI	—	—	1	—	—	1	8	—	10
35Ha4695	PI, LA	—	—	1	2	1	6	4	—	14
35Ha4696	PI	1	—	2	—	—	1	8	—	12
35Ha4697	MA	1	1	—	—	1	1	2	—	6
35Ha4621	LA	—	—	1	1	—	1	—	—	3
35Ha4622	MA	—	—	2	—	2	5	—	1	10
35Ha4623	MA, TP	—	—	2	—	—	3	—	—	5
35Ha4632	MA	—	—	—	—	—	1	—	—	1
35Ha4633	MA	—	—	—	2	1	1	2	—	6
35Ha4634	MA, LA	—	2	3	2	3	4	—	2	16
35Ha4635	LA	—	2	—	—	—	1	—	—	3
35Ha4637	MA, LA	1	—	—	1	—	2	—	—	4
35Ha4639	MA	—	—	—	—	—	1	—	—	1
35Ha4645	PI	—	—	4	3	1	8	3	—	19
35Ha4646	MA	—	—	1	—	3	1	3	—	8
35Ha4648	MA, LA	—	—	—	2	1	2	10	—	15
35Ha4650	PI, LA	—	—	—	—	1	1	—	—	2
35Ha4651	PI	—	—	—	—	2	2	—	—	4
35Ha4653	PI, MA	1	—	—	1	1	5	4	—	12
35Ha4654	PI	—	—	2	2	—	2	—	—	6
35Ha4655	PI	—	—	1	—	1	1	2	—	5
35Ha4656	MA	—	—	1	5	4	1	3	3	17
35Ha4658	EA	—	—	—	1	—	2	1	—	4
35Ha4659	PI, MA	1	—	—	2	—	6	3	—	12
35Ha4660	LA	—	—	—	—	—	1	—	—	1
35Ha4662	MA	—	—	—	—	—	1	—	—	1
35Ha4666	PI, MA	—	—	—	—	—	11	3	—	14
35Ha4667	LA	—	—	—	—	—	1	—	—	1
35Ha4522	LA, TP	—	1	2	1	1	16	—	—	21
35Ha4669	MA	—	—	—	—	—	1	4	—	5
35Ha4670	PI	—	—	1	—	1	1	2	—	5
35Ha4672	PI	—	—	1	—	—	1	2	—	4
35Ha4676	TP	—	—	1	—	—	1	1	—	3
35Ha4678	PI	—	—	—	—	—	2	—	—	2
35Ha4679	PI	—	—	—	—	—	1	2	—	3
35Ha4680	MA	—	—	—	1	—	1	2	—	4
35Ha4681	PI	—	—	—	—	—	9	1	—	10
35Ha4682	PI	—	—	1	—	—	10	—	—	11
35Ha4686	PI	—	—	—	—	—	1	—	—	1
35Ha4687	MA	—	—	—	—	—	1	1	—	2
35Ha4690	PI	—	—	—	—	—	1	—	—	1
35Ha4691	PI	—	—	—	1	1	5	1	—	8
35Ha4693	PI	—	1	—	1	—	6	8	—	16
35Ha4694	PI	—	—	—	1	—	2	2	—	5
35Ha4714	LA	—	—	—	1	—	2	2	1	6
35Ha4711	PI, TP	—	—	—	—	—	3	—	—	3
35Ha4712	PI	—	—	—	—	—	2	1	—	3
35Ha4708	PI, EA, MA	—	—	1	—	—	4	1	1	6
35Ha4709	PI	—	—	—	—	—	6	3	—	9

TABLE 13.11. (cont'd.) Flaked and groundstone tools at NWVSA sites

Site No.	Period(s)	Cores	Biface Stage 2	3	4	5	Points	Flake Tools	Ground Stone	Total
35Ha4710	PI	—	—	—	1	—	2	1	—	4
35Ha4685	MA	—	—	—	—	—	1	—	—	1
35Ha4715	PI	2	—	1	3	6	7	8	—	27
35Ha4716	PI	—	—	6	1	1	2	—	—	10
35Ha4729	PI, MA	—	1	—	3	4	6	2	—	16
35Ha4730	PI	—	—	1	2	1	1	—	—	5
35Ha4717	PI	—	—		1	1	2	2	—	6
35Ha4731	PI	—	3	—	3	—	5	4	2	17
35Ha4718	PI, MA	—	—	—	—	—	3	2	—	5
35Ha4732	PI	—	—	2	1	—	1	1	—	5
35Ha4720	PI	—	—	3	—	—	3	1	—	7
35Ha4721	PI	—	—	1	3	2	3	1	—	10
35Ha4722	PI, LA	—	—	—	—	—	2	—	—	2
35Ha4723	MA	—	—	—	—	—	2	2	—	4
35Ha4724	MA	—	—	—	—	—	2	1	2	5
35Ha4725	MA	—	—	—	—	—	1	—	—	1
35Ha4733	EA, MA, LA	4	2	1	2	—	10	3	15	37
35Ha4726	MA, LA	—	—	2	—	—	2	—	—	4
35Ha4734	PI, MA	—	—	2	11	2	22	27	—	64
35Ha4728	MA	—	—	—	1	2	1	2	—	6
Total		11	13	47	62	44	227	146	27	577

Note: PI-Paleoindian; EA=Early Archaic, MA=Middle Archaic; LA=Late Archaic; TP=Terminal Prehistoric.

rather than unmodified cobbles into North Warner Valley. Studies of quarry assemblages, including some utilized extensively by Paleoindians, have shown that if the distance between quarries and associated residential sites was great people manufactured Stage 3 bifaces at the quarries and carried them back to camp (Beck et al. 2002; Elston 1992). Doing so would have removed most of the low-utility cortex and ensured that transported stone tools retained only the high-utility portions (Beck et al. 2002). Additionally, catastrophic manufacturing failures tend to occur early in biface production (Johnson 1979). Such failures would be less costly if they occurred at quarries than if they occurred at residential camps far from toolstone sources.

Debitage from NWVSA sites offers support for these interpretations. Table 13.12 lists the relative amounts of primary (>50 percent cortex), secondary (<50 percent cortex and simple platforms), and tertiary (complex platforms, i.e., biface thinning and small retouch chips) flakes at each site. At 51 of the 69 sites that we assigned to one or more periods, tertiary flakes are dominant. Conversely, primary flakes are the dominant debitage type at just one site. This trend does not vary between the Paleoindian, Middle Archaic, and Late Archaic periods ($p = .742$, Fisher's Exact test). Although our ordinal cate-

gories provide a coarse-grained picture of lithic reduction, the pattern is nevertheless clear: primary reduction (probably biface staging) mostly occurred outside of the NWVSA; tool production (probably maintenance and/or repair) mostly occurred within the NWVSA.

Summary of Lithic Procurement and Production Patterns

Together, source provenience and technological data provide a picture of behavior that complements site distribution and character. People's go-to sources varied somewhat between cultural periods. For example, Beatys Butte was important during the Paleoindian and Middle Archaic periods but less so at other times. Throughout the terminal Pleistocene and much of the Holocene, groups seem to have either ranged throughout the same general areas of southeastern Oregon, northwestern Nevada, and northeastern California or possessed ties to groups that lived there. The sources of the obsidian and FGV found at North Warner Valley sites occur in alluvial fans along pluvial basin margins and at higher elevations in mountain ranges and tablelands, suggesting that people visited variable ecosystems to acquire toolstone or, more likely, food. There is no clear directionality in the source profiles for different

TABLE 13.12. Debitage types at NWVSA sites

Site No.	Period(s)	Flake Type		
		Primary (decortication)	Secondary (core reduction)	Tertiary (BTF[1]/retouch)
35Ha4702	PI	—	rare	dominant
35Ha4695	PI, LA	rare	common	dominant
35Ha4696	PI	rare	common	dominant
35Ha4697	MA	rare	rare	dominant
35Ha4621	LA	—	—	dominant
35Ha4622	MA	rare	dominant	common
35Ha4623	MA, TP	—	common	dominant
35Ha4632	MA	—	—	dominant
35Ha4633	MA	rare	rare	dominant
35Ha4634	MA, LA	common	rare	dominant
35Ha4635	LA	common	—	common
35Ha4637	MA, LA	dominant	common	—
35Ha4639	MA	rare	—	dominant
35Ha4645	PI	common	common	common
35Ha4646	MA	common	common	rare
35Ha4648	MA, LA	rare	common	dominant
35Ha4650	PI, LA	—	rare	dominant
35Ha4651	PI	rare	common	common
35Ha4653	PI, MA	rare	common	common
35Ha4654	PI	rare	common	common
35Ha4655	PI	rare	common	common
35Ha4656	MA	rare	common	common
35Ha4658	EA	common	rare	dominant
35Ha4659	PI, MA	rare	—	dominant
35Ha4660	LA	rare	—	dominant
35Ha4662	MA	common	—	common
35Ha4666	PI, MA	rare	rare	dominant
35Ha4667	LA	rare	dominant	rare
35Ha4522	LA, TP	rare	common	dominant
35Ha4669	MA	rare	rare	dominant
35Ha4670	PI	—	—	dominant
35Ha4672	PI	rare	rare	dominant
35Ha4676	TP	—	rare	dominant
35Ha4678	PI	common	rare	dominant
35Ha4679	PI	rare	—	dominant
35Ha4680	MA	common	common	common
35Ha4681	PI	—	—	dominant
35Ha4682	PI	rare	rare	dominant
35Ha4686	PI	rare	common	dominant
35Ha4687	MA	—	rare	dominant
35Ha4690	PI	—	rare	dominant
35Ha4691	PI	rare	common	dominant
35Ha4693	PI	rare	common	rare
35Ha4694	PI	rare	—	dominant
35Ha4714	LA	rare	rare	dominant
35Ha4711	PI, TP	rare	common	dominant
35Ha4712	PI	—	—	dominant
35Ha4708	PI, EA, MA	—	common	dominant

TABLE 13.12. (cont'd.) Debitage types at NWVSA sites

| | | Flake Type | | |
Site No.	Period(s)	Primary (decortication)	Secondary (core reduction)	Tertiary (BTF[1]/retouch)
35Ha4709	PI	rare	rare	dominant
35Ha4710	PI	rare	common	dominant
35Ha4685	MA	common	common	dominant
35Ha4715	PI	—	dominant	common
35Ha4716	PI	rare	rare	dominant
35Ha4729	PI, MA	rare	rare	dominant
35Ha4730	PI	rare	common	common
35Ha4717	PI	rare	common	common
35Ha4731	PI	—	rare	dominant
35Ha4718	PI, MA	rare	rare	dominant
35Ha4732	PI	rare	rare	dominant
35Ha4720	PI	rare	rare	dominant
35Ha4721	PI	rare	common	dominant
35Ha4722	PI, LA	common	rare	dominant
35Ha4723	MA	rare	—	dominant
35Ha4724	MA	—	—	dominant
35Ha4725	MA	rare	dominant	rare
35Ha4733	EA, MA, LA	common	common	dominant
35Ha4726	MA, LA	common	rare	dominant
35Ha4734	PI, MA	—	rare	dominant
35Ha4728	MA	common	common	dominant

Note: PI=Paleoindian; EA=Early Archaic, MA=Middle Archaic; LA=Late Archaic; TP=Terminal Prehistoric.
[1] BTF=biface thinning flake.

periods, which suggests that North Warner Valley fell within the annual or lifetime ranges of populations that also called central Oregon, northern California, and northwestern Nevada home.

Technological data strongly point to a gearing-up strategy in which groups partially reduced toolstone nodules into later-stage bifaces before traveling to North Warner Valley. Doing so would have minimized the chance of production failures and maximized the utility of transported toolstone. The trends exhibited in the tools and debitage suggest that groups generally provisioned individuals, rather than places, with toolstone (*sensu* Kuhn 1995), a finding that is in line with our interpretations of settlement and subsistence. With few exceptions, sites in North Warner Valley appear to represent shorter-term occupations.

PART IV

Synthesis and Conclusions

14 A Natural and Cultural History of North Warner Valley

Geoffrey M. Smith

Five years of fieldwork in North Warner Valley combined pedestrian survey, rockshelter excavations, and backhoe trenching. These efforts were aimed at addressing six questions about the natural and cultural history of North Warner Valley: (1) when did Lake Warner's highstand occur? (2) did Lake Warner rise during the Younger Dryas? (3) when did the basin floor become free of surface water? (4) when did people first visit the area? (5) when did they occupy LSP-1? and (6) how did people's use of the area change across time? In this final chapter, I bring together our major findings, organized by the environmental and cultural periods that we defined in Chapter 2. While there is still much to learn, our work—especially the excavations at LSP-1—has established a foundation for our current and future understanding of the natural and cultural history of North Warner Valley.

A NATURAL AND CULTURAL HISTORY OF NORTH WARNER VALLEY

The Terminal Pleistocene/Early Holocene

The Terminal Pleistocene (15,000–11,500 cal BP)
Lake Warner probably reached its terminal Pleistocene highstand of 1,454 m asl ~17,000–16,100 cal BP. As it receded, it cut numerous shelters into the bases of Steamboat Point and Little Steamboat Point. LSP-1 is the largest of these. As the lake receded, it left behind a thick layer of coarse black sand in the shelter. A few thousand years later, gravity and water brought larger andesite and tuff blocks from the surrounding rimrock into the shelter.

Below LSP-1, Lake Warner continued to recede, though it paused long enough for prominent beach ridges to form at 1,390 m asl. This pause took place sometime between 14,760–14,100 cal BP and 12,575–12,095 cal BP, probably during the latter half of this range, given that sites containing Clovis and Haskett points rest along the beach ridges. Though sites containing fluted and stemmed points occur along the same shoreline, those point types generally do not occur together, suggesting two possibilities: (1) Clovis and WST points mark sequential periods of occupation that we currently cannot tease apart; or (2) people using Clovis and stemmed points visited North Warner Valley during the same general period but did not use both point types at the same time in the same place.

These sites, which mark the period of heaviest use in North Warner Valley, represent the earliest visits to the area. Although the lake was still expansive and deep, a narrow ring of marshes likely stretched along its northern shore. A creek may have brought freshwater into the lake and provided a good place to camp. The obsidian and FGV types at those sites indicate that early visitors came primarily from central and southeastern Oregon. Overlap in the toolstone source profiles of the North Warner Valley Paleoindian sites and other typologically and, presumably, chronologically similar sites in the nearby Alkali Basin suggests that people ranged through Oregon's lake basins. The character of the Clovis and WST sites suggests that people periodically returned to North Warner Valley as part of a seasonal or longer round but did not remain there for extended periods. We can only speculate about the diets of these first visitors, although the association between sites and shorelines suggests that marsh resources, and perhaps the large animals that frequent wetlands, were important.

Although it was available for use, people did not visit LSP-1 during the terminal Pleistocene. In other parts of the United States, researchers have noted that early populations rarely used caves or shelters, suggesting that this reflects the settling-in process and an incomplete knowledge about the landscape (R. Kelly and Todd 1988), or settlement-subsistence strategies that did not require people to use such places (Walthall 1998). Early populations may also simply have had a cultural aversion to such places (Anderson 2007). Fluted point occupations in caves and shelters in the northwestern Great Basin are absent, perhaps for these or other reasons, but Younger Dryas stemmed point occupations are not (Smith et al. 2020 and references therein). LSP-1 is visible from the valley floor today and would have been even more so before it started to fill with sediment, so I do not believe that people were simply unaware of its existence. Instead, I suspect that the first visitors to North Warner Valley did not practice a settlement-subsistence regime that warranted using LSP-1, which may have been just a little too far removed from the lake's edge where people clearly spent much of their time.

The Early Holocene (11,500–9000 cal BP)

The first millennium of the Holocene saw Lake Warner recede to the south, and by 10,300 cal BP the floor of North Warner Valley was dry. Although Bluejoint Lake refilled periodically during the Holocene, and some of the smaller pans in the study area may have occasionally held water, North Warner Valley was free of a large lake or wetland beginning before the end of the early Holocene. The LSP-1 strata record this transition. After the lake deposited black sand at the end of the Pleistocene, blocks of andesite and welded tuff began to accumulate along the base of the rimrock and fill the shelter, as debris cones formed on both sides of its opening. Subsequently, beginning ~9775 cal BP—a few centuries after the valley floor was exposed for the first time—windblown silt started to fill the shelter. That process continued for more than 5,000 years.

Within the NWVSA, early Holocene groups using WST points tracked the receding lake south and continued to camp near its shores. Sites located below the 1,390 m asl shoreline and extending out onto the valley floor range in age between 11,500 and 9000 cal BP (the time around which stemmed points fell out of use). Most sites are small, contain high tool-to-debitage ratios, and lack features, suggesting that occupations continued to be brief. Site 35Ha4734, a large WST site, does not fit this pattern. Its assemblage features a range of tool types made of a diverse suite of raw materials, along with abundant debitage. It may represent a longer-term camp on the valley floor.

People began to visit LSP-1 ~9775 cal BP, which is roughly coincident with the appearance of WST sites on the valley floor. This may have been prompted by a more comfortable living surface provided by the wind-blown silt, which quickly buried the andesite and tuff blocks that had accumulated atop the black sand at the end of the Pleistocene. Or, perhaps Lake Warner's disappearance prompted a reorganization of settlement-subsistence strategies. The shelter's interior was never a large space and likely never accommodated more that six or seven people at once, perhaps twice that number if people also lived and worked on the apron.

Early Holocene visitors constructed two hearths inside the shelter, one of which dates to 9735–9550 cal BP. They made, used, recycled, and discarded flaked and groundstone tools. Novice knapping errors suggest that families visited the site. The toolstone types represented in the early Holocene assemblage, many of which are also represented at contemporary sites on the valley floor, suggest that people mostly came from central and southeastern Oregon. *Olivella* shell beads from the northern California, Oregon, or Washington coast also indicate that they had connections with more distant populations. Clusters of flaked stone tools at slightly different elevations and ages suggest that LSP-1 saw recurrent visits over a few centuries, but people generally did not stay for long periods. Moreover, these visits mostly took place in the autumn.

The LSP-1 faunal assemblage offers a clear picture of human subsistence at the end of the early Holocene and may explain why people continued to frequent North Warner Valley after the lake disappeared. Visitors discarded ~1,000 rabbit and hare carcasses inside the shelter, and while some of the animals may have been captured individually most were likely harvested during communal drives. People processed the animals in a systematic manner, using obsidian flakes and perhaps stemmed and foliate points to remove their heads and lower limbs. They then ground up the bodies, processed them in another manner that destroyed the axial elements, or carried the bodies elsewhere for later consumption. The high number of burned groundstone fragments and fire-affected rock in the southeastern quadrat of our excavation block is inconsistent with the two early Holocene hearths, both of which were small and unlined. It is possible that some of the carcasses were roasted in thermal features closer to the apron. People made tools and ornaments from a few of the bones and, perhaps, robes or blankets from the hides. They also ground ochre on some of the milling stones.

In sum, North Warner Valley saw dramatic environmental and cultural changes between ~13,000 and 9000 cal BP. Initially, people moving through the lake basins of the northern Great Basin were probably drawn to Lake Warner, but as conditions grew warmer and drier the lake gradually shrank. People continued to visit the lakeshore for a time, but once the valley floor was dry two things happened. First, small groups of people— probably families—started to visit LSP-1, never staying for long periods. Second, people started to collect rabbits and hares, probably communally. These changes reflect broader patterns that occurred in northwestern Nevada and southeastern Oregon near the end of the early Holocene.

The Middle Holocene

The notion of hard times is a recurrent theme in Great Basin archaeology (Elston 1982), and the legacy of Antevs's (1948) Altithermal, or Long Drought, has been hard to shake. An improved paleoenvironmental record for the northwestern Great Basin has revealed that the middle Holocene was not uniformly hot and dry. Having said that, in terms of climate, the interval between 9000 and 6300 cal BP was probably one of the hardest times that people endured in the region.

Researchers often point to gaps in the occupation histories of specific sites or regional declines in time-sensitive artifacts or radiocarbon dates as evidence that human populations declined. I have used those same data sources—the LSP-1 radiocarbon record and a paucity of Northern Side-notched points in the shelter and at surface sites—to make such an argument throughout this volume and repeat it here. Of the 89 radiocarbon assays for LSP-1, just nine date to between 9000 and 5000 cal BP. We did not recover any Northern Side-notched points in the shelter. Only eight of the 260 typed points we recorded at surface sites are Northern Side-notched points. Together, these trends suggest that people visited North Warner Valley less frequently than during earlier or later periods.

So where did the descendants of the people who camped along Lake Warner's shores during the terminal Pleistocene and processed rabbits and hares in the LSP-1 during the early Holocene go? Radiocarbon date frequencies for both the Lahontan Basin to the south and Fort Rock Basin to the northwest show troughs during the middle Holocene, which at face value implies that there were fewer people on the landscape (Louderback et al. 2010). This may have been the case, but most radiocarbon dates come from caves and rock-shelters where preservation is good. As such, rises and falls in regional radiocarbon frequencies may tell us more about how people used caves and shelters than broader demographic trends. In addition to perhaps using caves less (see Ollivier et al. 2016), Early Archaic groups may have changed how they used the landscape

in a way that gives the appearance of reduced populations, including perhaps aggregating around the remaining well-watered areas. This appears to have been the case in the Fort Rock Basin (Jenkins et al. 2004a and references therein), where middle Holocene residential sites containing Northern Side-notched points tend to be found near water sources. Closer to North Warner Valley, the Abert-Chewaucan Basin may have seen heavier use by Early Archaic groups, since Northern Side-notched points are more common there relative to North Warner Valley. Northern Side-notched points are also uncommon around the Warner Lakes (Eisele et al. 1993), which may not be surprising given that Young (2000) showed that the lakes were probably dry for an extended period leading up to 7800 cal BP. This suggests that the same factor that led people away from North Warner Valley—a lack of lakes and wetlands—also affected people farther south in the Warner Basin. In sum, while I am not wholly convinced that middle Holocene populations experienced hard times in all parts of the northwestern Great Basin, it certainly appears to have been the case in Warner Valley.

The Late Holocene

Near the onset of the late Holocene, people returned to North Warner Valley and predominantly used Elko points. At LSP-1, this happened ~4500 cal BP. The shelter's Middle Archaic lithic assemblage suggests a greater emphasis on projectile point maintenance, which may indicate that groups focused more on big game hunting than earlier or later groups. A lower frequency of groundstone may indicate that the shelter was used more by hunters and less by families. A paucity of novice knapping errors in the Middle Archaic biface assemblage supports this possibility. Rabbits and hares were still important though, as evidenced by their abundant remains in the late Holocene strata. People consumed some seeds and roots, but these do not appear to have been a major food source. Gaps in the age ranges of the Middle Archaic hearths suggest that LSP-1 saw several periods of use, most but not all of which took place in the autumn.

Middle Archaic sites in open-air settings provide a similar picture of North Warner Valley: bifaces tend to be more common and groundstone tends to be less common than Early Archaic sites. Projectile points occur more often as isolates than within sites, and most sites are small and lack evidence of longer-term occupations. Middle Archaic groups clearly visited North Warner Valley but may not have situated longer-term residential sites there.

The Late Archaic period in North Warner Valley was in some ways a continuation of the Middle Archaic trends. At LSP-1, people continued to visit the site mostly in the autumn and processed leporids. Dates on features and fiber artifacts suggest recurrent visits and generally short stays. There are some notable differences though. Foremost, people deposited more groundstone, at least some of which was used to process seeds and other plant foods. Novice knapping errors are also more common in the Late Archaic bifaces than the Middle Archaic bifaces, suggesting that families returned to LSP-1. Visitors made and discarded bone and shell beads and pendants and buried well-worn sandals and part of a basket, perhaps as a cache of cordage and other plant fiber to be used during later visits.

Late Archaic surface sites are marked by slightly lower proportions of bifaces and slightly higher proportions of groundstone, which could signal a return of more families to North Warner Valley. However, Late Archaic points still occur more often as isolates, and most sites do not appear to represent longer-term camps. The Fort Rock, Abert-Chewaucan, Massacre Lake, and Steens Mountain areas all contain more Rosegate points than the NWVSA, suggesting that people left villages in those basins and traveled to North Warner Valley periodically—perhaps to collect rabbits. The Late Archaic residential sites that UNR identified around the Warner Lakes in the 1980s and 1990s (Tipps 1998; Young 2000) may also have served as bases from which groups traveled to North Warner Valley to hunt and gather.

After 1000 cal BP, people visited North Warner Valley less often than during earlier periods or did so in a way that is less visible archaeologically. The Warner Lakes seem to have been more of a focus during that time, and there is some evidence for longer-term occupations (Eiselt 1997b; Tipps 1998). For researchers seeking evidence of the Numic Spread, our project area is not a good place to look. Late Archaic dates on Catlow Twine basketry and a Klamath Style sandal from LSP-1, and Terminal Prehistoric dates on Catlow Twine basketry from sites farther south in Warner Valley, suggest that Penutian speakers continued to visit the basin up to and perhaps during the historic period. Site 35Ha4522 and ethnographic accounts suggest that Numic speakers visited the North Warner Valley during the Terminal Prehistoric and historic periods. Beyond those data points, we know little about whether, how, and when those groups interacted in our study area.

DATA GAPS AND FUTURE RESEARCH

A decade of fieldwork and analysis has taught us a great deal about a remote part of the northern Great Basin. No single site can tell us everything about the past, and in the tradition of other long-term research programs in Oregon (e.g., the Northern Great Basin Prehistory Project and, before that, the Steens Mountain Prehistory Project), we brought a range of methodological approaches to bear on basic questions of culture history and people's decisions about when and why to use a particular place. We have answered most of those questions to one degree or another, at least as well as the data and my intellectual capacity have permitted.

But of course this study has raised new questions. First, there is only indirect evidence of the tasks for which the groundstone tools from LSP-1 were used. We did not conduct starch grain or protein residue analysis due to time and financial constraints, but the assemblage—especially the 100+ pieces from the Late Paleoindian component—offers ample additional opportunities to study early Holocene subsistence. The next phase of our research includes residue analyses of the groundstone. This should help us to understand whether people ground leporid carcasses or roots with those tools.

Second, our estimate of ~17,000–16,100 cal BP for the timing of pluvial Lake's Warner 1,454 m asl highstand is just that—an estimate. We based it in part on the terminal Pleistocene highstands of better-dated pluvial lakes in nearby basins (see Wriston and Smith 2017). A date of 14,485–14,025 cal BP on rabbit bone from Stratum X in LSP-1 (1,449 m asl) provides a limiting age for the event, meaning that the 1,454 m asl highstand must have occurred prior to that time. Future work to date it will require exploration deeper into Harney County, beyond the northern boundary of the NWVSA.

Third, while buried terminal Pleistocene sites proved to be elusive along the Younger Dryas shoreline, there may be some potential for buried early Holocene sites along the eastern edge of North Warner Valley where sediment blowing off the valley floor has accumulated since 10,300 cal BP. There, large blocks of rimrock have fallen from the nearby cliff and created small shelters and overhangs that may contain buried archaeological deposits. These places sit beyond our study area; thus, we did not investigate them during our time in North Warner Valley. Other terminal early Holocene sites may lie buried in the dune cores around the northernmost Warner Lakes. If they can be found, such sites will be important to understanding how people responded to the increased aridity that marked the beginning of the middle Holocene.

Finally, we conclude our research in North Warner Valley with a limited understanding of late Holocene environmental conditions. Cooler and wetter conditions may have brought renewed lakes into or very close to the southern edge of the NWVSA. At this point, we do not really know. Future research to address this possibility should take place closer to the Warner Lakes. A key goal should be to identify decade-or-longer wet and dry cycles like those that have taken place during the historic period (Cannon 1993). Those oscillations, which have periodically caused some of the Warner Lakes to dry completely, may have played a role in the pulses of human activity recorded at LSP-1.

CONCLUDING REMARKS

People have visited North Warner Valley for 13,000 years or more. In that time, the landscape has undergone tremendous transformations, shifting from one covered by a deep-water lake to one dominated by a barren playa to one enveloped by sagebrush, greasewood, and other desert vegetation. Against the backdrop of these major changes, countless yet unrecognized annual and decadal fluctuations must have also occurred. This variability—both over the long and short-term—played a role in people's decisions about when and why to visit North Warner Valley. The first generations of people were drawn to the marshes that ringed Lake Warner. Within a few millennia, people shifted to rabbit and hare hunting. Though big game hunting took place from time to time, it was the smaller animals that provided the primary food source. Families periodically congregated on the basin floor—likely during autumns—for communal rabbit drives, much as in ethnographic times. There is little evidence of long-term camps or villages in North Warner Valley, and people may have let the area lie fallow for a time after each successful drive.

Small groups—probably one or two families—sometimes carried their share of the bounty upslope to LSP-1, where they camped for short periods in the shadow of the Steamboat, processing the rabbits and hares for fur and meat in preparation for the coming winter. Novices tried their hand at flintknapping, honing a critical skill that would serve them well later in life. From time to time, especially during the initial late Holocene, hunters in search of pronghorn, bighorn sheep, or mule deer also visited North Warner Valley and LSP-1. Like the families, their visits were also brief.

The transitory nature of LSP-1 and the numerous open-air sites indicates that people frequented North Warner Valley but never stayed for long. In that regard, the place has always been part of a bigger story. It is tied to the Warner Lakes and the Abert-Chewaucan Basin, to Beatys Butte in Guano Valley, and to Glass Buttes in the Harney Basin. It is connected to Nevada's High Rock Country, to Oregon's Fort Rock Basin, and to Idaho's Snake River Plain. Finally, it is linked to the Pacific Coast, the Great Plains, and the Columbia Plateau. Our study has provided only a general picture of the interconnection of these places and how North Warner Valley fit into it all. Continued work in the area and those that surround it—work that better incorporates the traditional knowledge and perspectives of the Klamath and Northern Paiute—will bring that picture further into focus.

References

Adams, K. D.
2003   Age and Paleoclimatic Significance of Late Holocene
        Lakes in the Carson Sink, NV, USA. *Quaternary
        Research* 60(3):294–306.

Adams, K. D., and S. G. Wesnousky
1998   Shoreline Processes and the Age of the Lake Lahon-
        tan Highstand in the Jessup Embayment, Nevada.
        Geological Society of America Bulletin 110(10):
        1318–1332.

Adams, K. D., T. Goebel, K. E. Graf, G. M. Smith, A. J. Camp,
R. W. Briggs, and D. Rhode
2008   Late Pleistocene and Early Holocene Lake-Level Fluc-
        tuations in the Lahontan Basin, Nevada: Implications
        for the Distribution of Archaeological Sites. *Geoar-
        chaeology* 23(5):608–643.

Adams, K. R., and S. S. Murray
2004   Identification Criteria for Plant Remains Recovered
        from Archaeological Sites in the Central Mesa Verde
        Region. Electronic document, http://www.crow
        canyon.org, accessed July 30, 2016.

Adovasio, J. M.
1977   *Basketry Technology: A Guide to Identification and
        Analysis.* Aldine, Chicago.

Aikens, C. M.
1994   Adaptive Strategies and Environmental Change in the
        Great Basin and Its Peripheries as Determinants in
        the Migrations of Numic-Speaking Peoples. In *Across
        the West: Human Population Movement and the
        Expansion of the Numa*, edited by D. B. Madsen and
        D. Rhode, pp. 35–43. University of Utah Press, Salt
        Lake City.

Aikens, C. M., and D. L. Jenkins (editors)
1994   *Archaeological Researches in the Northern Great
        Basin: Fort Rock Archaeology since Cressman.*
        University of Oregon Anthropological Papers No. 50.
        University of Oregon Museum of Natural and Cul-
        tural History, Eugene.

Aikens, C. M., and Y. T. Witherspoon
1986   Great Basin Numic Prehistory: Linguistics, Archaeol-
        ogy, and Environment. In *Anthropology of the Desert
        West: Essays in Honor of Jesse D. Jennings*, edited by
        C. J. Condie and D. D. Fowler, pp. 9–20. University of
        Utah Anthropological Papers No. 115. University of
        Utah Press, Salt Lake City.

Aikens, C. M., D. K. Grayson, and P. J. Mehringer Jr.
1982   *Final Report to the National Science Foundation on
        the Steens Mountain Prehistory Project*, Part 3, Tech-
        nical Description of Project and Results. University of
        Oregon, Eugene. Submitted to the National Science
        Foundation, Washington, D.C.

Aikens, C. M., T. J. Connolly, and D. L. Jenkins
2011   *Oregon Archaeology.* Oregon State University Press,
        Corvallis.

Amick, D. S.
2007   Investigating the Behavioral Causes and Archaeologi-
        cal Effects of Lithic Recycling. In *Tools versus Cores:
        Alternative Approaches to Stone Tool Analysis*, edited
        by S. P. McPherron, pp. 223–252. Cambridge Scholars,
        Newcastle.
2013   Way Out West: Cody Complex Occupations from the
        Northwestern Great Basin. In *Paleoindian Life-
        ways of the Cody Complex*, edited by E. J. Knell and
        M. P. Muñiz, pp. 215–245. University of Utah Press,
        Salt Lake City.

Anderson, D. T.
2007   *Prehistoric Rockshelter Utilization in the Paint Rock
        Canyon Archaeological Landscape District.* Master's
        thesis, Department of Anthropology, University of
        Wyoming, Laramie.

Andrefsky, W. J., Jr.
2005   *Lithics: Macroscopic Approaches to Analysis.*
        Cambridge University Press, Cambridge.

Antevs, E.
1948   Climatic Changes and Pre-White Man. The Great
        Basin, with Emphasis on Postglacial Times. *Bulletin
        of the University of Utah* 38(20):168–191.

Baddeley, A., P. J. Diggle, A. Hardegen, T. Lawrence,
R. K. Milne, and G. Nair
2014   On Tests of Spatial Pattern Based on Simulation
        Envelopes. *Ecological Monographs* 84(3):477–489.

Baddeley, A., E. Rubak, and R. Turner
2015   *Spatial Point Patterns: Methodology and Applications
        with R.* Chapman and Hall/CRC, London.

Bamforth, D. B., and N. Finlay
2008   Archaeological Approaches to Lithic Production Skill
        and Craft Learning. *Journal of Archaeological Method
        and Theory* 15(1):1–27.

Barker, P.
2016   Ethnographic Background. In *Prehistory of Nevada's
        Northern Tier: Archaeological Investigations along the
        Ruby Pipeline*, edited by W. Hildebrandt, K. McGuire,
        J. King, A. Ruby, and D. C. Young, pp. 95–112. Anthro-
        pological Papers of the American Museum of Natural
        History Vol. 101. New York.

2018   V-twined Sandals as Archaeological Markers for Numic Populations in the Northern Great Basin. *In Situ* 22(3):5–8.

2019   What We Knew Then and What We Know Now: Thirty Years of CRM Archaeology in the Great Basin. In *Cultural Resources Management in the Great Basin, 1986–2016*, edited by A.M. Baldrica, P.A. DeBunch, and D.D. Fowler, pp. 79–94. University of Utah Anthropological Papers No. 131. University of Utah Press, Salt Lake City.

Barrett, S.A.

1910   The Material Culture of the Klamath Lake and Modoc Indians of Northeastern California and Southern Oregon. *University of California Publications in American Archaeology and Ethnography* 5(4):239–292.

Baumhoff, M.A., and R.F. Heizer

1965   Postglacial Climate and Archaeology in the Desert West. In *The Quaternary of the United States*, edited by H.E. Wright Jr. and D.G. Frey, pp. 697–708. Princeton University Press, Princeton, NJ.

Beasley, M.M., E.J. Bartelink, L. Taylor, and R.M. Miller

2014   Comparison of Transmission FTIR, ATR, and DRIFT Spectra: Implications for Assessment of Bone Bioapatite Diagenesis. *Journal of Archaeological Science* 46:16–22.

Beck, C., and G.T. Jones

2009   *The Archaeology of the Eastern Nevada Paleoarchaic, Part I, The Sunshine Locality.* University of Utah Anthropological Papers No. 126. University of Utah Press, Salt Lake City.

2010   Clovis and Western Stemmed: Population Migration and the Meeting of Two Technologies in the Intermountain West. *American Antiquity* 75(1):81–116.

2013   Complexities of the Colonization Process: A View from the North American West. In *Paleoamerican Odyssey*, edited by K.E. Graf, C.V. Ketron, and M.R. Waters, pp. 273–291. Texas A&M University Press, College Station.

2015   Lithic Analysis. In *The Paleoarchaic Occupation of the Old River Bed Delta*, edited by D.B. Madsen, D.N. Schmitt, and D. Page, pp. 97–208. University of Utah Anthropological Papers No. 128. University of Utah Press, Salt Lake City.

Beck, C., G.T. Jones, and A.K. Taylor

2019   What's Not Clovis? An Examination of Fluted Points in the Far West. *PaleoAmerica* 5(2):109–120.

Beck, C., A.K. Taylor, G.T. Jones, C.M. Fadem, C.R. Cook, and S.A. Millward

2002   Rocks Are Heavy: Transport Costs and Paleoarchaic Quarry Behavior in the Great Basin. *Journal of Anthropological Archaeology* 21(4):481–507.

Bedwell, S.F.

1970   *Prehistory and Environment of the Pluvial Fort Rock Lake Area of Southcentral Oregon.* PhD dissertation, Department of Anthropology, University of Oregon, Eugene.

1973   *Fort Rock Basin: Prehistory and Environment.* University of Oregon Press, Eugene.

Behre, K.E., and S. Jacomet

1991   The Ecological Interpretation of Archaeobotanical Data. In *Progress in Old World Paleoethnobotany: A Retrospective View on the Occasion of 20 Years of the International Work Group for Palaeoethnobotany*, edited by W. Van Zeist, K. Wasylikowa, and K.E. Behre, pp. 81–108. A.A. Balkema, Rotterdam.

Bennyhoff, J.A., and R.E. Hughes

1987   *Shell Bead and Ornament Exchange Networks between California and the Western Great Basin.* Anthropological Papers of the American Museum of Natural History Vol. 64, Pt. 2. New York.

Benson, L.V., J.P. Smoot, M. Kashgarian, A. Sarna-Wojcicki, and J.W. Burdett

1997   Radiocarbon Ages and Environments of Deposition of the Wono and Trego Hot Springs Tephra Layers in the Pyramid Lake Subbasin, Nevada. *Quaternary Research* 47(3):251–260.

Benson, L.V., M. Kashgarian, R. Rye, S. Lund, F. Paillet, J. Smoot, C. Kester, S. Mensing, D. Meko, and S. Lindström

2002   Holocene Multidecadal and Multicentennial Droughts Affecting Northern California and Nevada. *Quaternary Science Reviews* 21:659–682.

Benson, L.V., E.M. Hattori, J. Southron, and B. Aleck

2013a   Dating North America's Oldest Petroglyphs, Winnemucca Subbasin, Nevada. *Journal of Archaeological Science* 40(12):4466–4476.

Benson, L.V., J.P. Smoot, S.P. Lund, S.A. Mensing, F.F. Foit, and R.O. Rye

2013b   Insights from a Synthesis of Old and New Climate-Proxy Data from the Pyramid and Winnemucca Lake Basins for the Period 48 to 11.5 cal ka. *Quaternary International* 310:62–82.

Besag, J.E.

1977   Discussion of Dr. Ripley's Paper. *Journal of the Royal Statistical Society Series B* 39(2):193–195.

Bettinger, R.L.

1999   What Happened in the Medithermal. In *Models for the Millennium: Great Basin Anthropology Today*, edited by Charlotte Beck, pp. 62–74. University of Utah Press, Salt Lake City.

Bettinger, R.L., and M.A. Baumhoff

1982   The Numic Spread: Great Basin Cultures in Competition. *American Antiquity* 47(3):485–503.

Binford, L.R.

1978   Dimensional Analysis of Behavior and Site Structure: Learning from an Eskimo Hunting Stand. *American Antiquity* 43(3):330–361.

1983   *In Pursuit of the Past: Decoding the Archaeological Record.* Thames and Hudson, New York.

Blong, J.C., M.E. Adams, G. Sanchez, D.L. Jenkins, I.D. Bull, and L.M. Shillito

2020   Younger Dryas and Early Holocene Subsistence in the Northern Great Basin: Multiproxy Analysis of Coprolites from the Paisley Caves. *Archaeological*

and Anthropological Sciences 12(224). DOI:10.1007
/s12520-020-01160-9.

Bottman. T. C.

2006 *Stable Isotope Analysis to Determine Geographic
Provenience of* Olivella biplicata *Shell Beads Exca-
vated from Archaeological Sites in the Northern Great
Basin: Implications for Reconstructing Prehistoric
Exchange.* Master's thesis, Department of Anthropol-
ogy, University of Oregon, Eugene.

Bradley, E. J., G. M. Smith, and T. A. Wriston

2020 Possible Paleoindian Geophyte Use in Hawksy
Walksy Valley, Oregon. *Journal of California and
Great Basin Anthropology* 40(2):129–143.

Bronk Ramsey, C.

2009 Bayesian Analysis of Radiocarbon Dates. *Radiocarbon* 51(1):337–360.

Broughton, J. M., D. A. Byers, R. A. Bryson, W. Eckerle, and
D. B. Madsen

2008 Did Climatic Seasonality Control Late Quaternary
Artiodactyl Densities in Western North America?
Quaternary Science Reviews 27(19–20):1916–1937.

Burch, J. B.

1972 *Freshwater Sphaeriacean Clams (Mollusca: Pele-
cypoda) of North America.* Biota of Freshwater
Ecosystems, Identification Manual No. 3. U.S.
Environmental Protection Agency, Water Pollution
Control Research Series No. 18050 ELD03/72. Wash-
ington, D.C.

1982 *Freshwater Snails (Mollusca: Gastropoda) of North
America.* Environmental Monitoring and Support
Laboratory, Office of Research and Development, U.S.
Environmental Protection Agency, Cincinnati, OH.

Burch, J. B., and J. L. Tottenham

1980 *North American Freshwater Snails: Species List,
Ranges, and Illustrations.* Society for Experimental
and Descriptive Malacology, University of Michigan,
Ann Arbor.

Butler, V. L.

2012 *Report on a Sample of Fish Vertebrae from LSP-1.*
Letter Report on File, Department of Anthropology,
University of Nevada, Reno.

Calflora

2020 Information on Wild California Plants. Electronic
document, http://www.calflora.org, accessed July 30,
2020.

Camp, A. J.

2017 *Catlow Twine Basketry through Time and Space:
Exploring Shifting Cultural Boundaries through
Prehistoric and Ethnographic Basketry Technology
in the Northwestern Great Basin.* PhD dissertation,
Department of Anthropology, University of Nevada,
Reno.

2018 Catlow Twine Basketry in the Western Great Basin:
Use and Reuse in the Archaeological Record. *Quaternary International* 446(B):318–323.

Cannon, W. J.

1993 Utilization of Fish and Shellfish. In *Archaeological*

*Investigations in Warner Valley, Oregon, 1989–1992:
An Interim Report,* edited by D. D. Fowler, pp. 81–89.
Technical Report No. 93-1. Department of Anthropol-
ogy, University of Nevada, Reno.

Cannon, W. J., and M. F. Ricks

1986 The Lake County Oregon Rock Art Inventory:
Implications for Prehistoric Settlement System and
Land Use Patterns. In *Contributions to the Archae-
ology of Oregon 1983–1986,* edited by Kenneth M.
Ames, pp. 1–23. Association of Oregon Archaeologists
Occasional Papers No. 3. Eugene.

1999 Rock Art as an Indicator of Site Age in the Northern
Great Basin. Paper presented at the 64th Annual
Meeting of the Society for American Archaeology,
Chicago.

2019 How's Business? A Review of Forty Years of
CRM and the Used Site Business. In *Cultural
Resource Management in the Great Basin,
1986–2016,* edited by A. Baldrica, P. DeBunch, and
D. Fowler, pp. 72–78. University of Utah Anthro-
pological Papers No. 131. University of Utah Press,
Salt Lake City.

Cannon, W. J., C. C. Creger, D. D. Fowler, E. M. Hattori, and
M. F. Ricks

1990 A Wetlands and Uplands Settlement-Subsistence
Model for Warner Valley, Oregon. In *Wetland Adap-
tation in the Great Basin,* edited by J. C. Janetski and
D. B. Madsen, pp. 173–182. Brigham Young University
Museum of Peoples and Cultures Occasional Papers
No. 1. Provo, UT.

Cappers, R. T. J., R. Neef, and R. M. Bekker

2009 *Digital Atlas of Economic Plants.* Groningen Archaeological Studies 9. 3 vols. Barkhuis, Eelde.

Carpenter, K. L.

2002 Reversing the Trend: Late Holocene Subsistence
Change in Northeastern California. In *Bound-
ary Lands: Archaeological Investigations along
the California-Great Basin Interface,* edited by
K. R. McGuire, pp. 49–59. Nevada State Museum
Anthropological Papers No. 24. Carson City.

Carr, C.

1984 The Nature of Organization of Intrasite Archaeologi-
cal Records and Spatial Analytic Approaches to their
Investigation. *Advances in Archaeological Method and
Theory* 7:103–222.

Charrad, M., N. Ghazzali, V. Boiteau, and A. Niknafs

2014 NbClust: An R Package for Determining the Relevant
Number of Clusters in a Data Set. *Journal of Statistical Software* 61(6):1–36.

Christian, L. J.

1997 *Early Holocene Typology, Chronology, and Mobility:
Evidence from the Northern Great Basin.* Master's
thesis, Department of Anthropology, University of
Nevada, Reno.

Claud, E.

2015 The Use of Biface Manufacturing Flakes: Functional
Analysis of Three Middle Palaeolithic Assemblages

from Southwestern and Northern France. *Quaternary International* 361(10):131–141.

Connolly, T. J.

1994   Prehistoric Basketry from the Fort Rock Basin and Vicinity. In *Archaeological Researches in the Northern Great Basin: Fort Rock Archaeology since Cressman*, edited by C. M. Aikens and D. L. Jenkins, pp. 63–83. University of Oregon Anthropological Papers No. 50. University of Oregon Museum of Natural and Cultural History, Eugene.

1999   *Newberry Crater: A Ten-Thousand Year Record of Human Occupation and Environmental Change in the Basin Plateau Borderlands.* University of Utah Anthropological Papers No. 121. University of Utah Press, Salt Lake City.

Connolly, T. J., and P. Barker

2004   Basketry Chronology of the Early Holocene in the Northern Great Basin. In *Early and Middle Holocene Archaeology of the Northern Great Basin*, edited by D. L. Jenkins, T. J. Connolly, and C. M. Aikens, pp. 241– 250. University of Oregon Anthropological Papers No. 62. University of Oregon Museum of Natural and Cultural History, Eugene.

2008   Great Basin Sandals. In *The Great Basin: People and Place in Ancient Times*, edited by C. S. Fowler and D. D. Fowler, pp. 68–73. School for Advanced Research, Santa Fe.

Connolly, T. J., and D. L. Jenkins

1997   Population Dynamics on the Northwestern Great Basin Periphery: Clues from Obsidian Geochemistry. *Journal of California and Great Basin Anthropology* 19(2):241–250.

1999   The Paulina Lake Site (35Ds34). In *Newberry Crater: A Ten-Thousand-Year Record of Human Occupation and Environmental Change in the Basin-Plateau Borderlands*, edited by T. J. Connolly, pp. 86–127. University of Utah Anthropological Papers No. 121. University of Utah Press, Salt Lake City.

Connolly, T. J., C. L. Ruiz, D. L. Jenkins, and D. Deur

2015   *This Place is Home: Exploring Heritage and Community of the Klamath Tribes at the Beatty Curve Site (35KL95).* University of Oregon Museum of Natural and Cultural History Report No. 2015-006, Eugene.

Connolly, T. J., P. Barker, C. S. Fowler, E. M. Hattori, D. L. Jenkins, and W. J. Cannon

2016   Getting Beyond the Point: Textiles of the Terminal Pleistocene/Early Holocene in the Northwestern Great Basin. *American Antiquity* 81(3):490–514.

Connolly, T. J., J. B. Finley, G. M. Smith, D. L. Jenkins, P. E. Endzweig, B. L. O'Neill, and P. W. Baxter

2017   Return to Fort Rock Cave: Assessing the Site's Potential to Contribute to Ongoing Debates about How and When Humans Colonized the Great Basin. *American Antiquity* 82(3):558–573.

Cook, S. F.

1972   *Prehistoric Demography.* McCaleb Module in Anthropology No. 16. Addison Wesley, Reading, PA.

Cotterell, B., and J. Kamminga

1987   The Formation of Flakes. *American Antiquity* 52(4): 675–708.

Couture, M. D.

1978   *Recent and Contemporary Foraging Practices of the Harney Valley Paiute.* Master's thesis, Department of Anthropology, Portland State University, Portland, OR.

Couture, M. D., M. F. Ricks, and L. Housley

1986   Foraging Behavior of a Contemporary Northern Great Basin Population. *Journal of California and Great Basin Anthropology* 8(2):150–160.

Coville, F. V.

1897   Notes on Plant Use by the Klamath Indians of Oregon. *Contributions from the United States National Herbarium* 5(2):87–108.

Cowles, J.

1960   *Cougar Mountain Cave in South Central Oregon.* Daily News Press, Rainier, OR.

Crabtree, D. E.

1982   *An Introduction to Flintworking.* Idaho Museum of Natural History Occasional Papers No. 28. Pocatello.

Craven, G. F.

1991   *The Tectonic Development and Late Quaternary Deformation of Warner Valley South of Hart Mountain, Oregon.* Master's thesis, Department of Geology, Humboldt State University, CA.

Cressman, L. S.

1937   *Petroglyphs of Oregon.* University of Oregon Monographs, Studies in Anthropology No. 2. Eugene.

1940   Studies on Early Man in South Central Oregon. *Carnegie Institution of Washington Year Book* 39: 300–306.

1942   *Archaeological Researches in the Northern Great Basin.* Carnegie Institution of Washington Publication No. 538. Washington, D.C.

1950   Archaeological Research in the John Day Region of North Central Oregon. *Proceedings of the American Philosophical Society* 94(4):369–385.

Cressman, L. S., H. Williams, and A. D. Kreiger

1940   *Early Man in Oregon: Archaeological Studies in the Northern Great Basin.* University of Oregon Monographs, Studies in Anthropology No. 3. Eugene.

Culleton, B., D. J. Kennett, B. L. Ingram, and J. M. Erlandson

2006   Intrashell Radiocarbon Variability in Marine Mollusks. *Radiocarbon* 48(3):387–400.

Cummings, L. S.

1989   *Manual for Pollen, Phytolith, and Macrofloral Sampling.* Paleo Research Laboratories, Golden, CO.

Currey, D. R.

1990   Quaternary Palaeolakes in the Evolution of Semidesert Basins, with Special Emphasis on Lake Bonneville and the Great-Basin, USA. *Palaeogeography, Palaeoclimatology, Palaeoecology* 76(3–4):189–214.

Dal Sasso, G., M. Lebon, I. Angelini, L. Maritan, D. Usai, and G. Artioli

2016   Bone Diagenesis Variability among Multiple Burial

Phases at Al Khiday (Sudan) Investigated by ATR-FTIR Spectroscopy. *Palaeogeography, Palaeoclimatology, Palaeoecology* 463:168–179.

Dansie, A. J., and W. J. Jerrems

2004   Lahontan Chronology and Early Human Occupation in the Western Great Basin: A New Look at Old Collections. In *New Perspectives on the First Americans*, edited by B. T. Lepper and R. Bonnichsen, pp. 50–63. Texas A&M University Press, College Station.

Davis, L. G., M. L. Punke, R. L. Hall, M. Fillmore, and S. C. Willis

2004   A Late Pleistocene Occupation on the Southern Coast of Oregon. *Journal of Field Archaeology* 29(1–2):7–16.

Davis, L. G., S. C. Willis, and S. J. MacFarlan

2012   Lithic Technology, Cultural Transmission, and the Nature of the Far Western Paleoarchaic/Paleoindian Co-Tradition. In *Meetings at the Margins: Prehistoric Cultural Interactions in the Intermountain West*, edited by D. Rhode, pp. 47–64. University of Utah Press, Salt Lake City.

Davis, L. G., A. J. Nyers, and S. C. Willis

2014   Context, Provenance, and Technology of a Western Stemmed Tradition Artifact Cache from the Cooper's Ferry Site, Idaho. *American Antiquity* 79(4):595–615.

Davis, L. G., D. B. Madsen, L. Becerra-Valdivia, T. Higham, D. A. Sisson, S. M. Skinner, D. Stueber, et al.

2019   Late Upper Paleolithic Occupation at Cooper's Ferry Idaho, USA, ~16,000 Years Ago. *Science* 365:891–897.

Davis, L. W.

1993   *Weed Seeds of the Great Plains: A Handbook for Identification*. University of Kansas Press, Lawrence.

Delacorte, M. G.

2008   Desert Side-Notched Points as a Numic Population Marker in the Great Basin. In *Avocados to Millingstones: Papers in Honor of D. L. True*, edited by G. Waugh and M. E. Basgall, pp. 111–136. Monographs in California and Great Basin Anthropology No. 5. California State University, Sacramento.

Delacorte, M. G., and M. E. Basgall

2012   Great Basin-California/Plateau Interactions along the Western Front. In *Meeting at the Margins: Prehistoric Cultural Interactions in the Intermountain West*, edited by D. Rhode, pp. 65–91. University of Utah Press, Salt Lake City.

Delorit, R. J.

1970   *Illustrated Taxonomy Manual of Weed Seeds*. Agronomy Publications, River Falls, WI.

Delorme, L. D.

2001   Ostracoda. In *Ecology and Classification of North American Freshwater Invertebrates*, edited by J. H. Thorp and A. P. Covich, pp. 811–849. Academic, San Diego.

d'Errico, F., J. Zilhão, M. Julien, and D. Baffier, and J. Pelegrin

1998   Neanderthal Acculturation in Western Europe? A Critical Review of the Evidence and its Interpretation. *Current Anthropology* 39 (Supplement):S1–S44.

Donham, M., R. L. Rosencrance, and K. McDonough

2019   A First Look at the Western Stemmed Tradition Lithic Reduction and Procurement Strategies at Connley Cave 4, Oregon. Poster presented at the 84th Annual Meeting of the Society for American Archaeology, Albuquerque, NM.

Dugas, D. P.

1998   Late Quaternary Variations in the Level of Paleo-Lake Malheur, Eastern Oregon. *Quaternary Research* 50(3):276–282.

Dugstad, S. A.

2010   Early Child Caught Knapping: A Novice Early Mesolithic Flintknapper in South-Western Norway. *AmS-Skrifter* 23:65–74.

Duke, D., D. C. Young, and S. K. Rice

2018   *Cultural Resources Inventory of the High-Speed Mover Test Area, a 4,548-acre Portion of the West Delta of the Old River Bed, Utah Test and Training Range, Tooele County, Utah*. Far Western Anthropological Research Group, Henderson, NV. Submitted to Hill Air Force Base, Ogden, Utah.

Eerkens, J. W., J. S. Rosenthal, H. J. Spero, R. Shiraki, and G. S. Herbert

2005   Provenance Analysis of *Olivella biplicata* Shell Beads from the California and Oregon Coast by Stable Isotope Fingerprinting. *Journal of Archaeological Science* 32:1501–1514.

Egger, A. E., R. J. Weldon, R. M. Langridge, D. E. Ibarra, B. Marion, and J. M. Hall

2016   The Influence of Pluvial Lake Cycles on Earthquake Recurrence in the Northwestern Basin and Range Extensional Province. Paper presented at Annual Meeting of the Geological Society of America, Denver.

Eisele, J. A., E. M. Hattori, and D. C. Young

1993   Lithic Artifacts. In *Archaeological Investigations in Warner Valley, Oregon, 1989–1992: An Interim Report*, edited by D. D. Fowler, pp. 35–58. Technical Report No. 93-1. Department of Anthropology, University of Nevada, Reno.

Eiselt, B. S.

1997a   *Defining Ethnicity in Warner Valley: An Analysis of House and Home*. Master's thesis, Department of Anthropology, University of Nevada, Reno.

1997b   *Defining Ethnicity in Warner Valley: An Analysis of House and Home*. Technical Report No. 97-2. Department of Anthropology, University of Nevada, Reno.

1998   *Household Activity and Marsh Utilization in the Archaeological Record of Warner Valley: The Peninsula Site*. Technical Report No. 98-2. Department of Anthropology, University of Nevada, Reno.

Elston, R. G.

1982   Good Times, Hard Times: Prehistoric Culture Change in the Western Great Basin. In *Man and Environment in the Great Basin*, edited by D. B. Madsen and J. F. O'Connell, pp. 186–206. Society for American Archaeology Papers No. 2. Washington, D.C.

1992   Modeling the Economics and Organization of Lithic Procurement. In *Archaeological Investigations at Tosawihi, a Great Basin Quarry*, edited by R. G. Elston and C. Raven, pp. 31–47. Intermountain Research Inc.,

Silver City, Nevada. Submitted to the Bureau of Land Management, Elko Resource Area, Elko.

2005   Flaked and Battered Stone Artifacts. In *Camels Back Cave*, edited by D. N. Schmitt and D. B. Madsen, pp. 92–119. University of Utah Anthropological Papers No. 125. University of Utah Press, Salt Lake City.

Elston, R. G., and D. W. Zeanah

2002   Thinking Outside the Box: A New Perspective on Diet Breadth and Sexual Division of Labor in the Prearchaic Great Basin. *World Archaeology* 34(1): 103–130.

Elston, R. G., D. W. Zeanah, and B. F. Codding

2014   Living Outside the Box: An Updated Perspective on Diet Breadth and Sexual Division of Labor in the Prearchaic Great Basin. *Quaternary International* 352(26):200–211.

Enzel, Y., D. R. Cayan, R. Y. Anderson, and S. G. Wells

1989   Atmospheric Circulation during Holocene Lake Stands in the Mojave Desert—Evidence of Regional Climate Change. *Nature* 341:44–47.

Estes, M. B.

2009   *Paleoindian Occupations in the Great Basin: A Comparative Study of Lithic Technological Organization, Mobility, and Landscape Use from Jakes Valley, Nevada.* Master's thesis, Department of Anthropology, University of Nevada, Reno.

Fagan, J. L.

1974   *Altithermal Occupation of Spring Sites in the Northern Great Basin.* University of Oregon Anthropological Papers No. 6. University of Oregon Museum of Natural and Cultural History, Eugene.

1988   Clovis and Western Pluvial Lakes Tradition Lithic Technologies at the Dietz Site in South-Central Oregon. In *Early Human Occupation in Far Western North America: The Clovis-Archaic Interface*, edited by J. A. Willig, C. M. Aikens, and J. L. Fagan, pp. 389–416. Nevada State Museum Anthropological Papers No. 21. Carson City.

Felling, D. C.

2015   *Paleoindian Settlement Strategies across Time and Space in the Northwestern Great Basin: Lithic Technological Organization at Last Supper Cave, Nevada.* Master's thesis, Department of Anthropology, University of Nevada, Reno.

Fiedel, S. J.

2014   Did Pre-Clovis People Inhabit the Paisley Caves (and Why Does it Matter)? *Human Biology* 86(1):69–74.

Fiedel, S. J., B. A. Potter, J. E. Morrow, M. K. Faught, C. V. Haynes Jr., and J. C. Chatters

2020   Pioneers from Northern Japan in Idaho 16,000 Years Ago? A Critical Evaluation of the Evidence from Cooper's Ferry. *PaleoAmerica.* DOI:10.1080/20555563.2020.1778416.

Finley, J. B.

2016   Late Holocene Geoarchaeology in the Bighorn Basin, Wyoming. In *Stones, Bones, and Profile: Papers in Honor of George C. Frison and C. Vance Haynes*, edited by M. Kornfeld and B. Huckell, pp. 259–288. University Press of Colorado, Boulder.

Forester, R. M., A. J. Smith, D. F. Palmer, and B. B. Curry

2015   NANODe: North American Non-marine Ostracode Database Project. http://www.personal.kent.edu/~alisonjs/nanode/.

Foster, D.

1996   Endangered Sucker Fish: The Klamath Tribes Struggle to Save a Native Fishery. *Southern Oregon Heritage* 2(1):30–35.

Fowler, C. S.

1983   Some Lexical Clues to Uto-Aztecan Prehistory. *International Journal of American Linguistics* 49(3):224–257.

1989   *Willard Z. Park's Ethnographic Notes on the Northern Paiute of Western Nevada, 1933–1944.* University of Utah Anthropological Papers No. 114. University of Utah Press, Salt Lake City.

1990a   Ethnographic Perspectives on Marsh-Based Cultures in Western Nevada. In *Wetland Adaptations in the Great Basin*, edited by J. C. Janetski and D. D. Fowler, pp. 17–32. Brigham Young University Museum of Peoples and Cultures Occasional Papers No. 1. Provo, UT.

1990b   *Tule Technology: Northern Paiute Uses of Marsh Resources in Western Nevada.* Smithsonian Institution Press, Washington, D.C.

1992   *In the Shadow of Fox Peak: An Ethnography of the Cattail-Water Northern Paiute People of Stillwater Marsh.* U. S. Fish and Wildlife Service Cultural Resource Series No. 5. Portland, OR.

1994   Material Culture and the Proposed Numic Expansion. In *Across the West: Human Population Movement and the Expansion of the Numa*, edited by D. B. Madsen and D. Rhode, pp. 103–113. University of Utah Press, Salt Lake City.

Fowler, C. S., and J. E. Bath

1981   Pyramid Lake Northern Paiute Fishing: The Ethnographic Record. *Journal of California and Great Basin Anthropology* 3(2):176–186.

Fowler, C. S., and E. M. Hattori

2011   Exploring Prehistoric Trade in Western Great Basin Textiles. In *Perspectives on Prehistoric Trade and Exchange in California and the Great Basin*, edited by R. E. Hughes, pp. 201–220. University of Utah Press, Salt Lake City.

2012   Prehistoric Textile Trade and Exchange in the Western Great Basin: Outland Coiling and Catlow Twining. In *Meeting at the Margins: Prehistoric Cultural Interactions in the Intermountain West*, edited by D. Rhode, pp. 92–102. University of Utah Press, Salt Lake City.

Fowler, C. S., and S. Liljeblad

1986   Northern Paiute. In *Great Basin*, edited by W. L. d'Azevedo, pp. 435–465. Handbook of North American Indians, Vol. 11, W. C. Sturtevant, general editor. Smithsonian Institution Press, Washington, D.C.

Fowler, C. S., and D. Rhode
2007   Great Basin Plants. In *Environment, Origins, and Population*, edited by D. Ubelaker, pp. 331–350. Handbook of North American Indians, Vol. 3, W. C. Sturtevant, general editor. Smithsonian Institution Press, Washington, D.C.

Fowler, D. D. (editor)
1993   *Archaeological Investigations in Warner Valley, Oregon, 1989–1992: An Interim Report.* Technical Report No. 93-1. Department of Anthropology, University of Nevada, Reno.

Fowler, D. D., E. M. Hattori, and C. C. Creger
1989   *Summary Report of Archaeological Investigations in Warner Valley, Lake County, Oregon, 1987–1988.* Research Report No. 89-1. Department of Anthropology, University of Nevada, Reno.

Friedel, D. E.
1994   Paleolake Shorelines and Lake Level Chronology of the Fort Rock Basin, Oregon. In *Archaeological Researches in the Northern Great Basin: Fort Rock Archaeology Since Cressman*, edited by C. M. Aikens and D. L. Jenkins, pp. 21–40. University of Oregon Anthropological Papers 50. University of Oregon Museum of Natural and Cultural History, Eugene.

Friedman, J.
1978   *Wood Identification by Microscopic Examination: A Guide for the Archaeologist on the Northwest Coast of North America.* British Columbia Provincial Museum Heritage Record No. 5. Victoria.

Frison, G. C., and B. A. Bradley
1980   *Folsom Tools and Technology at the Hanson Site.* Academic, New York.

Fullagar, R. L. K.
1991   The Role of Silica in Polish Formation. *Journal of Archaeological Science* 18(1):1–24.

Galanidou, N.
2000   Patterns in Caves: Foragers, Horticulturists, and the Use of Space. *Journal of Anthropological Archaeology* 19:243–275.

Geribàs, N., M. Mosquera, and J. P. Vergès
2010   What Novice Knappers Have to Learn to Become Expert Stone Toolmakers. *Journal of Archaeological Science* 37(11):2857–2870.

Giddings, J. L.
1956   The Burin Spall Artifact. *Arctic* 9(4):229–237.

Gilmore, H. W.
1953   Hunting Habits of the Early Nevada Paiutes. *American Anthropologist* 55(1):148–153.

Gleason, S. M.
2001   *In Search of the Intangible: Geophyte Use and Management along the Upper Klamath River Canyon.* PhD dissertation, Department of Anthropology, University of California, Riverside.

Goebel, T., and J. A. Keene
2014   Are Great Basin Stemmed Points as Old as Clovis in the Intermountain West? A Review of the Geochronological Evidence. In *Archaeology in the Great Basin and Southwest: Papers in Honor of Don D. Fowler*, edited by N. J. Parezo and J. C. Janetski, pp. 35–60. University of Utah Press, Salt Lake City.

Goebel, T., B. Hockett, K. D. Adams, D. Rhode, and K. Graf
2011   Climate, Environment, and Humans in North America's Great Basin during the Younger Dryas, 12,900–11,600 Calendar Years Ago. *Quaternary International* 242(2):479–501.

Goss, J. A.
1968   Cultural-Historical Inference. In *Utaztekan Prehistory*, edited by Earl H. Swanson Jr., pp. 1–42. Occasional Papers of the Idaho State University Museum No. 22. Pocatello.
1977   Linguistic Tools for the Great Basin Prehistorian. In *Models and Great Basin Prehistory: A Symposium*, edited by D. D. Fowler, pp. 48–70. Desert Research Publications in the Social Sciences No. 12. Reno.

Graf, K. E.
2001   *Paleoindian Technological Provisioning in the Western Great Basin.* Master's thesis, Department of Anthropology and Ethnic Studies, University of Nevada, Las Vegas.

Grayson, D. K.
1979   Mt. Mazama, Climatic Change, and Fort Rock Archaeofaunas. In *Volcanic Activity and Human Ecology*, edited by P. D. Sheets and D. K. Grayson, pp. 427–458. Academic, New York.
1988   *Danger Cave, Last Supper Cave, and Hanging Rock Shelter: The Faunas.* Anthropological Papers of the American Museum of Natural History Vol. 66, Pt. 1. New York.
2005   A Brief History of Great Basin Pikas. *Journal of Biogeography* 32(12):2101–2111.
2006   Holocene Bison in the Great Basin, Western USA. *The Holocene* 16(6):913–925.
2011   *The Great Basin: A Natural Prehistory.* University of California Press, Berkeley.
2016   *Giant Sloths and Sabertooth Cats: Extinct Mammals and the Archaeology of the Great Basin.* University of Utah Press, Salt Lake City.

Green, T. J., B. Cochran, T. W. Fenton, J. C. Woods, G. L. Titmus, L. Tieszen, M. A. Davis, and S. J. Miller
1998   The Buhl Burial: A Paleoindian Woman from Southern Idaho. *American Antiquity* 63(3):437–456.

Greenspan, R. L.
1994   Archaeological Fish Remains in the Fort Rock Basin. In *Archaeological Researches in the Northern Great Basin: Fort Rock Archaeology since Cressman*, edited by C. M. Aikens and D. L. Jenkins, pp. 485–504. University of Oregon Anthropological Papers No. 50. University of Oregon Museum of Natural and Cultural History, Eugene.

Greiser, S. T., and P. D. Sheets
1979   Raw Material as a Functional Variable in Use-Wear Studies. In *Lithic Use-Wear Analysis*, edited by B. Hayden, pp. 289–296. Academic, New York.

Grover, N.C., G.I. Parker, W.A. Lamb, G.C. Baldwin, and F.F. Henshaw

1917   *Surface Water Supply of the United States: 1913, Part 12. North Pacific Drainage Basins.* U.S. Geological Survey, Washington, D.C.

Hadden, C.S., and A. Cherkinsky

2015   ¹⁴C Variation in Pre-Bomb Nearshore Habitats of the Florida Panhandle, USA. *Radiocarbon* 57(3): 469–479.

Hansen, H.P.

1947   Vegetation of the Northern Great Basin. *American Journal of Botany* 34(3):164–171.

Harrington, M.R.

1933   *Gypsum Cave.* Southwest Museum Papers No. 8. Los Angeles.

Hartigan, J.A., and M.A. Wong

1979   Algorithm AS 136: A K-means Clustering Algorithm. *Applied Statistics* 28:100–108.

Hartman, A.J.

2019   *Identifying Cultural Migration in Western North America through Morphometric Analysis of Early Holocene Projectile Points.* Master's thesis, Department of Anthropology, University of Nevada, Reno.

Hattori, E.M.

1982   *The Archaeology of Falcon Hill, Winnemucca Lake, Washoe County, Nevada.* Nevada State Museum Anthropological Papers No. 18. Carson City.

Heizer, R.F., and A.E. Treganza

1944   Mines and Quarries of the Indians of California. *Report of the California State Mineralogist* 40(3): 292–359.

Helzer, M.M.

2001   *Paleoethnobotany and Household Archaeology at the Bergen Site: A Middle Holocene Occupation in the Fort Rock Basin, Oregon.* PhD dissertation. Department of Anthropology, University of Oregon, Eugene.

Herrington, H.B.

1962   *A Revision of the Sphaeriidae of North America (Mollusca: Pelecypoda).* Miscellaneous Publications of the Museum of Zoology No. 118. University of Michigan, Ann Arbor.

Herzog, N.M., and A.T. Lawlor

2016   Reevaluating Diet and Technology in the Archaic Great Basin Using Starch Grain Assemblages from Hogup Cave, Utah. *American Antiquity* 81(4):661–681.

Hilbish, J.F.

2019   Archaic Spindle Whorls of Cowboy Cave and Walters Cave in Utah. *Kiva* 85(3):257–276.

Hildebrand, J.

2012   Children in Archaeological Lithic Analysis. *Nebraska Anthropologist* 27:25–42.

Hildebrandt, W.R., and J.H. King

2002   Projectile Point Variability along the Northern California-Great Basin Interface: Results from the Tuscarora-Alturas Projects. In *Boundary Lands: Archaeological Investigations along the California-Great Basin Interface*, edited by K.R. McGuire, pp. 5–28.

Nevada State Museum Anthropological Papers No. 24. Carson City.

Hildebrandt, W.R., and K.R. McGuire

2002   The Ascendance of Hunting during the California Middle Archaic: An Evolutionary Perspective. *American Antiquity* 67(2):231–256.

Hildebrandt, W.R., K. McGuire, J. King, A. Ruby, and D.C. Young (editors)

2016   *Prehistory of Nevada's Northern Tier.* Anthropological Papers of the American Museum of Natural History Vol. 101. New York.

Hill, J.N.

2001   Proto-Uto-Aztecan: A Community of Cultivators in Central Mexico? *American Anthropologist* 103(4): 913–934.

2002   Towards a Linguistic Prehistory of the Southwest: "Azteco-Tanoan" and the Arrival of Maize Cultivation. *Journal of Anthropological Research* 58(4):457–475.

2006   *Uto-Aztecan Hunter-Gatherers: Language Change in the Takic Spread and Numic Spread Compared.* Abstract for Historical Linguistics and Hunter-Gatherer Populations in Global Perspective, 2006. Electronic document, http://www.eva.mpg.de/HunterGatherer Workshop2006/Abstracts, accessed July 30, 2020.

Hitchcock, C.L., and A. Cronquist

1973   *Flora of the Pacific Northwest.* University of Washington Press, Seattle.

Hoadley, R.B.

1990   *Identifying Wood: Accurate Results with Simple Tools.* Taunton Press, Newtown.

Hockett, B.S.

1991   Toward Distinguishing Human and Raptor Patterning on Leporid Bones. *American Antiquity* 56(4): 667–679.

1994   A Descriptive Reanalysis of the Leporid Bones from Hogup Cave, Utah. *Journal of California and Great Basin Anthropology* 16(1):106–117.

1998   Sociopolitical Meaning of Faunal Remains from Baker Village. *American Antiquity* 63(2):289–302.

2007   Nutritional Ecology of Late Pleistocene to Middle Holocene Subsistence in the Great Basin: Zooarchaeological Evidence from Bonneville Estates Rockshelter. In *Paleoindian or Paleoarchaic? Great Basin Human Ecology at the Pleistocene-Holocene Transition*, edited by K.E. Graf and D.N. Schmitt, pp. 204–230. University of Utah Press, Salt Lake City.

2015   The Zooarchaeology of Bonneville Estates Rockshelter: 13,000 Years of Great Basin Hunting Strategies. *Journal of Archaeological Science: Reports* 2:291–301.

Hockett, B.S., and D.L. Jenkins

2013   Identifying Stone Tool Cut Marks and the Pre-Clovis Occupation of the Paisley Caves. *American Antiquity* 78(4):762–778.

Hockett, B.S., M.E. Adams, P.M. Lubinski, V.L. Butler, and D.L. Jenkins

2017   Late Pleistocene Subsistence in the Great Basin: Younger Dryas-Aged Faunal Remains from the

Botanical Lens, Paisley Cave 2, Oregon. *Journal of Archaeological Science: Reports* 13:565–576.

Högberg, A.
2008 Playing with Flint: Tracing a Child's Imitation of Adult Work in a Lithic Assemblage. *Journal of Archaeological Method and Theory* 15(1):112–131.

Hosfield, R., and J. Chambers
2009 Genuine Diversity? The Broom Biface Assemblage. *Proceedings of the Prehistoric Society* 75:65–100.

House, P. K., A. R. Ramelli, and C. T. Wrucke
2001 *Geologic Map of the Battle Mountain Quadrangle, Lander County, Nevada.* Nevada Bureau of Mines and Geology Map No. 130. Reno.

Hurcombe, L. M.
1992 *Use Wear Analysis and Obsidian: Theory, Experiments and Results.* J. R. Collis, Sheffield.

Hurley, W. M.
1979 *Prehistoric Cordage: Identification of Impressions on Pottery.* Aldine, Chicago.

Ibarra, D. E., A. E. Egger, K. L. Weaver, C. R. Harris, and K. Maher
2014 Rise and Fall of Late Pleistocene Pluvial Lakes in Response to Reduced Evaporation and Precipitation: Evidence from Lake Surprise, California. *Geological Society of America Bulletin* 126(11–12):1387–1415.

Inizan, M. L., M. Reduron-Ballinger, H. Roche, and J. Tixier
1999 *Technology and Terminology of Knapped Stone.* Cercle de Recherches et d'Études Préhistoriques, Maison de l'Archéologie et de l'Ethnologie, Nanterre Cedex, France.

James, S. R.
1983 Surprise Valley Settlement and Subsistence: A Critical Review of the Faunal Evidence. *Journal of California and Great Basin Anthropology* 5(2):156–175.

Jenkins, D. L., T. J. Connolly, and C. M. Aikens
2004a Early and Middle Holocene Archaeology in the Northern Great Basin: Dynamic Natural and Cultural Ecologies. In *Early and Middle Holocene Archaeology of the Northern Great Basin,* edited by D. L. Jenkins, T. J. Connolly, and C. M. Aikens, pp. 1–20. University of Oregon Anthropological Papers No. 62. University of Oregon Museum of Natural and Cultural History, Eugene.

Jenkins, D. L., L. L. Largaespada, T. D. Largaespada, and M. A. McDonald
2004b Early and Middle Holocene Ornament Exchange Systems in the Fort Rock Basin of Oregon. In *Early and Middle Holocene Archaeology of the Northern Great Basin,* edited by D. L. Jenkins, T. J. Connolly, and C. M. Aikens, pp. 251–270. University of Oregon Anthropological Papers No. 62. University of Oregon Museum of Natural and Cultural History, Eugene.

Jenkins, D. L., L. G. Davis, T. W. Stafford Jr., P. F. Campos, B. Hockett, G. T. Jones, L. S. Cummings, et al.
2012 Clovis Age Western Stemmed Projectile Points and Human Coprolites at the Paisley Caves. *Science* 337:223–228.

Jenkins, D. L., L. G. Davis, T. W. Stafford Jr., P. F. Campos, T. J. Connolly, L. S. Cummings, et al.
2013 Geochronology, Archaeological Context, and DNA at the Paisley Caves. In *Paleoamerican Odyssey,* edited by K. E. Graf, C. V. Ketron, and M. R. Waters, pp. 485–510. Texas A&M University Press, College Station.

Jenkins, D. L., L. G. Davis, T. W. Stafford Jr., T. J. Connolly, G. T. Jones, M. Rondeau, L. S. Cummings, et al.
2016 Younger Dryas Archaeology and Human Experience at the Paisley Caves in the Northern Great Basin. In *Stones, Bones, and Profiles: Exploring Archaeological Context, Early American Hunter-Gatherers, and Bison,* edited by M. Kornfeld and B. B. Huckell, pp. 127–205. University Press of Colorado, Boulder.

Jenkins, D. L., J. A. Holcomb, and K. N. McDonough
2017 Current Research at the Connley Caves (35LK50): Late Pleistocene/Early Holocene Western Stemmed Tradition Occupations in the Fort Rock Basin, Oregon. *PaleoAmerica* 3(2):188–192.

Jennings, J. D.
1986 Prehistory: Introduction. In *Great Basin,* edited by W. L. d'Azevedo, pp. 113–119. Handbook of North American Indians, Vol. 11, W. C. Sturtevant, general editor. Smithsonian Institution Press, Washington, D.C.

Jennings T. A.
2011 Experimental Production of Bending and Radial Flake Fractures and Implications for Lithic Technologies. *Journal of Archaeological Science* 38(12): 3644–3651.

Jew, N. P., A. F. Ainis, P. E. Endzweig, J. M. Erlandson, C. Skinner, and K. J. Sullivan
2015 Chipped Stone Crescents from America's Far West: Descriptive and Geochemical Analyses from the Northern Great Basin. *North American Archaeologist* 36(2):119–140.

Johnson, J. K.
1979 Archaic Biface Manufacture: Production Failures, a Chronicle of the Misbegotten. *Lithic Technology* 8(2):25–35.

Jones, G. T., and C. Beck
2012 The Emergence of the Desert Archaic in the Great Basin. In *From the Pleistocene to the Holocene: Human Organization and Cultural Transformations in Prehistoric North America,* edited by C. B. Bousman and B. Vierra, pp. 105–124. Texas A&M University Press, College Station.

Jones, G. T., C. Beck, E. E. Jones, and R. E. Hughes
2003 Lithic Source Use and Paleoarchaic Foraging Territories in the Great Basin. *Journal of American Antiquity* 68(1):5–38.

Jones, G. T., L. M. Fontes, R. A. Horowitz, C. Beck, and D. G. Bailey
2012 Reconsidering Paleoarchaic Mobility in the Central Great Basin. *American Antiquity* 77(2):351–367.

Kallenbach, E.
2013   Chewaucan Cave Cache: A Specialized Tool Kit from Eastern Oregon. *Journal of California and Great Basin Anthropology* 33(1):72–87.

Kelly, I. T.
1932   Ethnography of the Surprise Valley Paiute. *University of California Publications in American Archaeology and Ethnology* 31(3):67–210.

Kelly R. L.
2001   *Prehistory of the Carson Desert and Stillwater Mountains.* University of Utah Anthropological Papers No. 123. University of Utah Press, Salt Lake City.

2011   Obsidian in the Carson Desert: Mobility or Trade? In *Perspectives on Prehistoric Trade and Exchange in California and the Great Basin*, edited by R. E. Hughes, pp. 189–200. University of Utah Press, Salt Lake City.

Kelly, R. L., and L. C. Todd
1988   Coming into the Country: Early Paleoindian Hunting and Mobility. *American Antiquity* 53(2): 231–244.

Kennedy, J. L.
2018   *A Paleoethnobotanical Approach to 14,000 Years of Great Basin Prehistory: Assessing Human-Environmental Interactions through the Analysis of Archaeological Plant Data at Two Oregon Rockshelters.* PhD dissertation, Department of Anthropology, University of Oregon, Eugene.

Kent, S.
1991   The Relationship between Mobility Strategies and Site Structure. In *The Interpretation of Archaeological Spatial Patterning*, edited by E. M. Kroll and T. D. Price, pp. 33–59. Plenum, New York.

1993   Models of Abandonment and Material Culture Frequencies. In *Abandonments of Settlement and Regions: Ethnoarchaeological and Archaeological Approaches*, edited by C. M. Cameron and S. A. Tomka, pp. 54–81. Cambridge University Press, Cambridge.

Khreisheh, N. N.
2013   *The Acquisition of Skill in Early Flaked Stone Technologies: An Experimental Study.* PhD dissertation, Department of Archaeology, University of Exeter.

King, J.
2016a   Chronological Controls. In *Prehistory of Nevada's Northern Tier*, edited by W. R. Hildebrandt, K. McGuire, J. King, A. Ruby, and D. C. Young, pp. 123–153. Anthropological Papers of the American Museum of Natural History Vol. 101. New York.

2016b   Obsidian Conveyance Patterns. In *Prehistory of Nevada's Northern Tier*, edited by W. R. Hildebrandt, K. McGuire, J. King, A. Ruby, and D. C. Young, pp. 303–327. Anthropological Papers of the American Museum of Natural History Vol. 101. New York.

Knell, E. J., and M. P. Muñiz (editors)
2013   *Paleoindian Lifeways of the Cody Complex.* University of Utah Press, Salt Lake City.

Kolvet, R. C.
1995   *Beyond the Valley Floor: Upland Adaptations in the Buffalo Hills, Northwestern Nevada.* Master's thesis, Department of Anthropology, University of Nevada, Reno.

Kononenko, N.
2011   Experimental and Archaeological Studies of Use-Wear and Residues on Obsidian Artefacts from Papua New Guinea. *Technical Reports of the Australian Museum, Online* 21:1–244.

Kuehn, S. C., and F. F. Foit Jr.
2006   Correlation of Widespread Holocene and Pleistocene Tephra Layers from Newberry Volcano, Oregon, USA, Using Glass Compositions and Numerical Analysis. *Quaternary International* 148(1):113–137.

Kuhn, S. L.
1995   *Mousterian Lithic Technology: An Ecological Perspective.* Princeton University Press, Princeton, NJ.

LaBelle, J. M., and C. Newton
2020   Cody Complex Foragers and Their Use of Grooved Abraders in Great Plains and Rocky Mountains of North America. *North American Archaeologist* 41(2–3):63–100.

Lamb, S. M.
1958   Linguistic Prehistory in the Great Basin. *International Journal of American Linguistics* 24(2): 95–100.

Largaespada, L. L.
2006   From Sand and Sea: Marine Shell Artifacts from Archaeological Sites in the Fort Rock Basin, Northern Great Basin. In *Beads, Points, and Pit Houses: A Northern Great Basin Miscellany*, edited by B. L. O'Neill, pp. 61–67. University of Oregon Anthropological Papers No. 66. University of Oregon Museum of Natural and Cultural History, Eugene.

Largaespada, T. D.
2006   Significant Points in Time: A Typology and Chronology of Middle and Late Holocene Projectile Points from the Northern Great Basin. In *Beads, Points, and Pit Houses: A Northern Great Basin Miscellany*, edited by B. L. O'Neill, pp. 69–92. University of Oregon Anthropological Papers No. 66. University of Oregon Museum of Natural and Cultural History, Eugene.

Layton, T. N.
1970   *High Rock Archaeology: An Interpretation of the Prehistory of the Northwestern Great Basin.* PhD dissertation, Department of Anthropology, Harvard University, Cambridge.

1985   Invaders from the South? Archaeological Discontinuities in the Northwestern Great Basin. *Journal of California and Great Basin Anthropology* 7(2): 183–201.

Licciardi, J. M.
2001   Chronology of Latest Pleistocene Lake-Level Fluctuations in the Pluvial Lake Chewaucan Basin, Oregon, USA. *Journal of Quaternary Science* 16(6):545–553.

Lindström, S.
1990   Submerged Tree Stumps as Indicators of Mid-
        Holocene Aridity in the Lake Tahoe Region. *Journal
        of California and Great Basin Anthropology* 12(2):
        146–157.

Long, A., and B. Rippeteau
1974   Testing Contemporaneity and Averaging Radio-
        carbon Dates. *American Antiquity* 39(2):205–215.

Loud, L. L., and M. R. Harrington
1929   *Lovelock Cave.* University of California Publications
        in American Archaeology and Ethnology No. 25.
        Berkeley.

Louderback, L. A., and B. M. Pavlik
2017   Starch Granule Evidence for the Earliest Potato Use in
        North America. *Proceedings of the National Academy
        of the Sciences* 114(29):7606–7610.

Louderback, L. A., D. K. Grayson, and M. Llobera
2010   Middle Holocene Climates and Human Population
        Densities in the Great Basin. *The Holocene* 21(2):
        366–373.

Lowie, R. H.
1924   *Notes on Shoshonean Ethnography.* Anthropological
        Papers of the American Museum of Natural History
        Vol. 20, Pt. 3. New York.

Lyons, W. H., S. P. Thomas, and C. E. Skinner
2001   Changing Obsidian Sources at the Lost Dune and
        McCoy Creek Sites, Blitzen Valley, Southeast Oregon.
        Journal of California and Great Basin Anthropology
        23(2):273–296.

Lyons, W. H., M. D. Glascock, and P. J. Mehringer Jr.
2003   Silica from Sources to Site: Ultraviolet Fluorescence
        and Trace Elements Identify Cherts from Lost Dune,
        Southeastern Oregon, USA. *Journal of Archaeological
        Science* 30(9):1139–1159.

Madsen, D. B.
2007   The Paleoarchaic to Archaic Transition in the Great
        Basin. In *Paleoindian or Paleoarchaic? Great Basin
        Human Ecology at the Pleistocene-Holocene Transi-
        tion*, edited by K. E. Graf and D. N. Schmitt, pp. 3–20.
        University of Utah Press, Salt Lake City.

Madsen, D. B., and R. L. Kelly
2008   The "Good Sweet Water" of Great Basin Marshes.
        In *The Great Basin: People and Place in Ancient
        Times*, edited by C. S. Fowler and D. D. Fowler,
        pp. 79–86. School for Advanced Research Press,
        Santa Fe.

Madsen, D. B., and D. Rhode (editors)
1994   *Across the West: Human Population Movement and
        the Expansion of the Numa.* University of Utah Press,
        Salt Lake City.

Malouf, C. I., and J. Findlay
1986   Euro-American Impact before 1870. In *Great Basin*,
        edited by W. L. d'Azevedo, pp. 499–516. Handbook
        of North American Indians, Vol. 11, W. C. Sturtevant,
        general editor. Smithsonian Institution Press, Wash-
        ington, D.C.

Manning, S. W.
2020   Comment on "Late Upper Paleolithic Occupation
        at Cooper's Ferry, Idaho, USA, ~16,000 Years Ago."
        Science 368:1–4.

Martin, A. C., and W. D. Barkley
1973   *Seed Identification Manual.* University of California
        Press, Berkeley.

McAvoy, J. M., and L. D. McAvoy
2003   *The Williamson Clovis Site, 44Dw1, Dinwiddie
        County, Virginia: An Analysis of Research Potential in
        Threatened Areas.* Virginia Department of Historic
        Resources Research Report No. 13. Richmond.

McDonough, K. N.
2019   Middle Holocene Menus: Dietary Reconstruction
        from Coprolites at the Connley Caves, Oregon, USA.
        Archaeological and Anthropological Sciences 11:
        5963–5982.

McGuire, K. R.
2002   Obsidian Production in Northeastern California and
        the Northwestern Great Basin: Implications for Land
        Use. In *Boundary Lands: Archaeological Investi-
        gations along the California-Great Basin Interface*,
        edited by K. R. McGuire, pp. 85–103. Nevada State
        Museum Anthropological Papers No. 24. Carson City.

McGuire, K. R., and W. R. Hildebrandt
2005   Rethinking Great Basin Foragers: Prestige Hunting
        and Costly Signaling during the Middle Archaic
        Period. *American Antiquity* 70(4):695–712.
2016   Cultural Context of the Northern Tier. In *Prehistory
        of Nevada's Northern Tier*, edited by W. R. Hilde-
        brandt, K. McGuire, J. King, A. Ruby, and D. C. Young,
        pp. 71–111. Anthropological Papers of the American
        Museum of Natural History Vol. 101. New York.

McGuire, K. R., and N. Stevens
2017   The Potential Role of Geophytes, Digging Sticks, and
        Formed Flake Tools in the Western North American
        Paleoarchaic Expansion. *Journal of California and
        Great Basin Anthropology* 37(1):3–21.

McGuire, K. R., A. Ugan, K. Carpenter, and L. Brinz
2016   Trans-Holocene Subsistence-Settlement Change in
        Northern Nevada. In *Prehistory of Nevada's North-
        ern Tier*, edited by W. R. Hildebrandt, K. McGuire,
        J. King, A. Ruby, and D. C. Young, pp. 261–277.
        Anthropological Papers of the American Museum
        of Natural History Vol. 101. New York.

McNabb, J., and C. Rivett
2007   Getting Round to the Point: Biface Tip Shape in
        the British Lower Palaeolithic. *Journal of the Lithic
        Studies Society* 28:20–32.

Mehringer, P. J., Jr.
1985   Late Quaternary Pollen Records from the Interior
        Pacific Northwest and Northern Great Basin of the
        United States. In *Pollen Records of Late-Quaternary
        North American Sediments*, edited by V. M. Bryant Jr.
        and R. G. Holloway, pp. 167–190. American Associa-
        tion of Stratigraphic Palynologists, Dallas.

Mehringer, P. J., Jr., and P. E. Wigand
1986   Holocene History of the Skull Creek Dunes, Catlow
        Valley, Southeastern Oregon. *Journal of Arid Environ-
        ments* 11(2):117–138.

Mensing, S. A., L. V. Benson, M. Kashgarian, and S. Lund
2004 A Holocene Pollen Record of Persistent Droughts from Pyramid Lake, Nevada, USA. *Quaternary Research* 62(1):29–38.

Merrill, W. L.
2012 The Historical Linguistics of Uto-Aztecan Agriculture. *Anthropological Linguistics* 54(3):203–260.

Merrill, W. L., R. J. Hard, J. B. Mabry, G. J. Fritz, K. R. Adams, J. R. Roney, and A. C. MacWilliams
2009 The Diffusion of Maize to the Southwestern United States and Its Impact. *PNAS* 106(50):21019–21026.

Meyers, S. C., T. Jaster, K. E. Mitchell, and L. K. Hardison (editors)
2015 *Flora of Oregon* Vol. 1, *Pteridophytes, Gymnosperms, and Monocots*. Brit Press, Botanical Research Institute of Texas, Fort Worth.

Middleton, E. S., G. M. Smith, W. J. Cannon, and M. F. Ricks
2014 Paleoindian Rock Art: Establishing the Antiquity of Great Basin Carved Abstract Petroglyphs in the Northern Great Basin. *Journal of Archaeological Science* 43:21–30.

Miller, D. S., V. T. Holliday, and J. Bright
2013 Clovis across the Continent. In *Paleoamerican Odyssey*, edited by K. E. Graf, C. V. Ketron, and M. R. Waters, pp. 207–220. Texas A&M University Press, College Station.

Miller, W. R.
1983 Uto-Aztecan Languages. In *Southwest*, edited by A. Ortiz, pp. 113–124. Handbook of North American Indians, Vol. 10, W. C. Sturtevant, general editor. Smithsonian Institution Press, Washington, D.C.
1986 Numic Languages. In *Great Basin*, edited by W. L. d'Azevedo, pp. 98–107. Handbook of North American Indians, Vol. 11, W. C. Sturtevant, general editor. Smithsonian Institution Press, Washington, D.C.

Milne, S. B.
2005 Palaeo-Eskimo Novice Flintknapping in the Eastern Canadian Arctic. *Journal of Field Archaeology* 30(3):329–245.

Minckley, T. A., P. J. Bartlein, and J. J. Shinker
2004 Paleoecological Response to Climate Change in the Great Basin since the Last Glacial Maximum. In *Early and Middle Holocene Archaeology of the Northern Great Basin*, edited by D. L. Jenkins, T. J. Connolly, and C. M. Aikens, pp. 21–30. University of Oregon Anthropological Papers No. 62. University of Oregon Museum of Natural and Cultural History, Eugene.

Minckley, T. A., C. Whitlock, and P. Bartlein
2007 Vegetation, Fire, and Climate History of the Northwestern Great Basin during the Last 14,000 Years. *Quaternary Science Reviews* 26(17–18):2167–2184.

Minnis, P. E.
1987 Identification of Wood from Archaeological Sites in the American Southwest: I. Keys for Gymnosperms. *Journal of Archaeological Science* 14:121–131.

Mohammed, I. N., and D. G. Tarboton
2012 An Examination of the Sensitivity of the Great Salt Lake to Changes in Inputs. *Water Resources Research* 48(11):1–17.

Montalvo, A. M., L. K. Goode, and J. L. Beyers
2010 Plant Profile for *Amsinckia menziesii* var. *intermedia*. Native Plant Recommendations for Southern California Ecoregions. Riverside-Corona Resource Conservation District and U.S. Department of Agriculture Pacific Southwest Research Station, Riverside.

Moore, E. M.
1995 *Analysis of Fauna from Sites in Warner Valley, Oregon*. Master's thesis, Department of Anthropology, University of Nevada, Reno.

Moss, M. L., and J. M. Erlandson
1995 *An Evaluation, Survey, and Dating Program for Archaeological Sites on State Lands of the Northern Oregon Coast*. University of Oregon Museum of Natural and Cultural History, Eugene. Submitted to the Oregon State Historic Preservation Office, Department of Parks and Recreation, Salem.

Mullineaux, D. R.
1996 *Pre-1980 Tephra-Fall Deposits Erupted from Mount St. Helens, Washington*. U.S. Geological Survey Professional Paper 1563. U.S. Government Printing Office, Washington, D.C.

Munroe, J. S., and B. T. C. Laabs
2013 Latest Pleistocene History of Pluvial Lake Franklin, Northeastern Nevada, USA. *Geological Society of America Bulletin* 125(3–4):322–342.

al-Nahar, M., and G. A. Clark
2009 The Lower Paleolithic in Jordan. *Jordan Journal for History and Archaeology* 3(2):173–215.

Napton, L. K.
1997 The Spirit Cave Mummy: Coprolite Investigations. *Nevada State Historical Society Quarterly* 40(1):97–104.

Negrini, R. M.
2002 Pluvial Lake Sizes in the Northwestern Great Basin throughout the Quaternary Period. In *Great Basin Aquatic Systems History*, edited by R. Hershler, D. B. Madsen, and D. R. Currey, pp. 11–52. Smithsonian Institution Contributions to the Earth Sciences No. 33. Washington, D.C.

Neubauer, F.
2018 Use-Alteration Analysis of Fire-Cracked Rocks. *American Antiquity* 83(4):681–700.

Nowell, A., C. Walker, C. E. Cordova, C. J. H. Ames, T. Pokines, D. Stueber, R. DeWitt, and A. S. A. al-Souliman
2016 Middle Pleistocene Subsistence in the Azraq Oasis, Jordan: Protein Residue and Other Proxies. *Journal of Archaeological Science* 73:36–44.

O'Connell, J. F.
1975 *The Prehistory of Surprise Valley*. Ballena Press Anthropological Papers No. 4. Ramona, CA.
1993 What Can Great Basin Archaeologists Learn from the Study of Site Structure? An Ethnoarchaeological Perspective. *Utah Archaeology* 6(1):7–26.

Oetting A. C.
1989 *Villages and Wetlands Adaptations in the North-*

ern Great Basin: Chronology and Land Use in the Lake Abert-Chewaucan Marsh Basin, Lake County, Oregon. University of Oregon Anthropological Papers No. 41. University of Oregon Museum of Natural and Cultural History, Eugene.

1990   Aboriginal Settlement in the Lake Abert-Chewaucan Marsh Basin, Lake County, Oregon. In *Wetlands Adaptations in the Great Basin*, edited by J. C. Janetski and D. B. Madsen, pp. 183–206. Brigham Young University Museum of Peoples and Cultures Occasional Papers No. 1. Provo, UT.

1994a   Early Holocene Rabbit Drives and Prehistoric Land Use Patterns on Buffalo Flat, Christmas Lake Valley, Oregon. In *Archaeological Researches in the Northern Great Basin: Fort Rock Archaeology since Cressman*, edited by C. M. Aikens and D. L. Jenkins, pp. 155–169. University of Oregon Anthropological Papers No. 50. University of Oregon Museum of Natural and Cultural History, Eugene.

1994b   Chronology and Time Markers in the Northwestern Great Basin: The Chewaucan Basin Cultural Chronology. In *Archaeological Researches in the Northern Great Basin: Fort Rock Archaeology since Cressman*, edited by C. M. Aikens and D. L. Jenkins, pp. 41–62. University of Oregon Anthropological Papers No. 50. University of Oregon Museum of Natural and Cultural History, Eugene.

O'Grady, P.

2004   Zooarchaeological Analysis of Cultural Features from Four Early to Middle Holocene Sites in the Fort Rock Basin. In *Early and Middle Holocene Archaeology of the Northern Great Basin*, edited by D. L. Jenkins, T. J. Connolly, and C. M. Aikens, pp. 187–208. University of Oregon Anthropological Papers No. 62. University of Oregon Museum of Natural and Cultural History, Eugene.

O'Grady, P. W., S. P. Thomas, C. E. Skinner, J. Thatcher, M. F. Rondeau, and J. L. Fagan

2012   The Dietz Site: Revisiting the Geochemical Sourcing and Hydration Measurement Properties for Fluted and Stemmed Artifacts from 35LK1529, Lake County, Oregon. Paper presented at the 33rd Biennial Great Basin Anthropological Conference, Stateline, NV.

Ollivier, A. P.

2016   *Evaluating Gaps in the Radiocarbon Sequences of Northwestern Great Basin Sandals.* Master's thesis, Department of Anthropology, University of Nevada, Reno.

Ollivier, A. P., G. M. Smith, and P. Barker

2017   A Collection of Fiber Sandals from Last Supper Cave and Its Implications for Cave and Rockshelter Abandonment during the Middle Holocene. *American Antiquity* 82(2):325–340.

Oviatt, C. G., D. B. Madsen, D. M. Miller, R. S. Thompson, and J. P. McGeehin

2015   Early Holocene Great Salt Lake, USA. *Quaternary Research* 84(1):57–68.

Ozbun, T. L., and J. L. Fagan

2010   Cascade Projectile Point Technology. *Journal of Northwest Anthropology* 44(1):1–22.

Padilla, L. A.

2017   *Groundstone Analysis at the Rock Creek Camp Site.* Master's thesis, Department of Anthropology, California State University, Bakersfield.

Park, W. Z., and C. S. Fowler

1989   *Willard Z. Park's Ethnographic Notes on the Northern Paiute of Western Nevada, 1933–1940.* University of Utah Anthropological Papers No. 114. University of Utah Press, Salt Lake City.

Patton, H. J.

1985   P-wave Fault-Plane Solutions and the Generation of Surface-Waves by Earthquakes in the Western United States. *Geophysical Research Letters* 12(8):518–521.

Pearsall, D. M.

2016   *Paleoethnobotany: A Handbook of Procedures.* Routledge, New York.

Peden, J. (producer)

1995   *Rabbit Boss.* Documentary Video. University of Nevada Oral History Program, Reno.

Pellegrini, E. J.

2014   *The Kammidikadi of Little Steamboat Point-1 Rockshelter: Terminal Early Holocene and Early Late Holocene Leporid Processing in Northern Warner Valley, Oregon.* Master's thesis, Department of Anthropology, University of Nevada, Reno.

Personius, S. F., and T. L. Sawyer

2002   Fault Number 827a: Warner Valley Faults, East Warner Valley Section, Quaternary Fault and Fold Database of the United States. Electronic document, https://earthquake.usgs.gov/cfusion/qfault/show _report_AB_archive.cfm?fault_id=827&section_id=a, accessed December 8, 2021.

Peterson, N. V.

1978   Soapstone Industry in Southwestern Oregon. *The Ore Bin* 40(9):149–157.

Pettigrew, R. M.

1984   Prehistoric Human Land-Use Patterns in the Alvord Basin, Southeastern Oregon. *Journal of California and Great Basin Anthropology* 6(1):61–90.

Pezzopane, S. K.

1993   *Active Faults and Earthquake Ground Motions in Oregon.* PhD dissertation, Department of Geological Sciences, University of Oregon.

Pezzopane, S. K., and R. J. Weldon

1993   Tectonic Role of Active Faulting in Central Oregon. *Tectonics* 12(5):1140–1169.

Pinson, A. O.

1999   *Foraging in Uncertain Times: The Effects of Risk on Subsistence Behavior during the Pleistocene–Holocene Transition in the Oregon Great Basin.* PhD dissertation, Department of Anthropology, University of New Mexico.

2007   Artiodactyl Use and Adaptive Discontinuity across the Paleoarchaic–Archaic Transition in the Great Basin. In *Paleoindian or Paleoarchaic? Great Basin*

Human Ecology at the Pleistocene–Holocene Transition, edited by K. E. Graf and D. N. Schmitt, pp. 187–203. University of Utah Press, Salt Lake City.

2011 The Clovis Occupation of the Dietz Site (35Lk1529), Lake County, Oregon, and Its Bearing on the Adaptive Diversity of Clovis Foragers. *American Antiquity* 76(2):285–313.

Pitzer, J. M.

1977 *A Guide to the Identification of Burins in Prehistoric Chipped Stone Assemblages.* University of Texas Center for Archaeological Research Guidebooks in Archaeology No. 1. San Antonio.

Porčić, M.

2012 Effects of Residential Mobility on the Ratio of Average House Floor Area to Average Household Size: Implications for Demographic Reconstructions in Archaeology. *Cross-Cultural Research* 46(1):72–86.

Pothier Bouchard, G., S. M. Mentzer, J. Riel-Salvatore, J. Hodgkins, C. E. Miller, F. Negrino, R. Wogelius, and M. Buckley

2019 Portable FTIR for On-Site Screening of Archaeological Bone Intended for ZooMS Collagen Fingerprint Analysis. *Journal of Archaeological Science* 26:1–12.

Potter, B. A., C. E. Holmes, and D. R. Yesner

2013 Technology and Economy Among the Earliest Prehistoric Foragers in Interior Eastern Beringia. In *Paleoamerican Odyssey*, edited by K. E. Graf, C. V. Ketron, and M. R. Waters, pp. 81–103. Texas A&M University Press, College Station.

Prasciunas, M. M.

2007 Expedient Cores and Flake Production Efficiency: An Experimental Test of Technological Assumptions. *American Antiquity* 72(2):334–348.

Pratt, J. E., T. Goebel, K. Graf, and M. Izuho

2020 A Circum-Pacific Perspective on the Origin of Stemmed Points in North America. *PaleoAmerica* 6(1):64–108.

Prouty, G. L.

2001 Plants and Fort Rock Basin Prehistory: Paleoethnobotanical Investigations at the Carlon Village Site. Appendix P. In *Carlon Village: Land, Water, Subsistence, and Sedentism in the Northern Great Basin*, edited by G. F. Wingard, pp. 595–606. University of Oregon Anthropological Papers No. 57. University of Oregon Museum of Natural and Cultural History, Eugene.

2004 Plants and Prehistory: Paleoethnobotanical Investigations in the Fort Rock Basin Lowlands. In *Early and Middle Holocene Archaeology of the Northern Great Basin*, edited by D. L. Jenkins, T. J. Connolly, and C. M. Aikens, pp. 157–166. University of Oregon Anthropological Papers No. 62. University of Oregon Museum of Natural and Cultural History, Eugene.

Ray, V. F.

1963 *Primitive Pragmatists: The Modoc Indians of Northern California.* American Ethnological Society Monograph No. 38. University of Washington Press, Seattle.

Raymond, A. W., and V. M. Parks

1990 Archaeological Sites Exposed by Recent Flooding of Stillwater Marsh Carson Desert, Churchill County, Nevada. In *Wetlands Adaptations in the Great Basin*, edited by J. C. Janetski and D. B. Madsen, pp. 33–62. Brigham Young University Museum of Peoples and Cultures Occasional Papers No. 1. Provo, UT.

Reaux, D. J., G. M. Smith, K. D. Adams, S. Jamaldin, N. D. George, K. Mohr, and R. L. Rosencrance

2018 A First Look at the Terminal Pleistocene/Early Holocene Record of Guano Valley, Oregon, USA. *Paleo-America* 4(2):162–176.

Reheis, M. C., K. D. Adams, C. G. Oviatt, and S. N. Bacon

2014 Pluvial Lakes in the Great Basin of the Western United States: A View from the Outcrop. *Quaternary Science Reviews* 97(1):33–57.

Reimer, P. J., E. Bard, A. Bayliss, J. W. Beck, P. G. Blackwell, C. Bronk Ramsey, C. E. Buck, et al.

2013 IntCal13 and Marine13 Radiocarbon Age Calibration Curves 0–50,000 Years Cal BP. *Radiocarbon* 55(4): 1869–1887.

Rhode, D.

2011 Constraints on Long-Distance Movement of Plant Foods in the Great Basin. In *Perspectives on Prehistoric Trade and Exchange in California and the Great Basin*, edited by R. E. Hughes, pp. 221–241. University of Utah Press, Salt Lake City.

2016 Paleoenvironments of the Northern Tier. In *Prehistory of Nevada's Northern Tier*, edited by W. R. Hildebrandt, K. McGuire, J. King, A. Ruby, and D. C. Young, pp. 57–70. Anthropological Papers of the American Museum of Natural History Vol. 101. New York.

Rice, D. G.

1972 *The Windust Phase in Lower Snake River Region Prehistory.* Report of Investigations No. 50. Washington State University Laboratory of Anthropology, Pullman.

Rice, H.

1965 *The Cultural Sequence at Windust Caves.* Master's thesis, Department of Anthropology, Washington State University, Pullman.

Ricks, M. F., and W. J. Cannon

1993 A Preliminary Report on the Lake County, Oregon, Rock Art Inventory: A Data Base for Rock Art Research. In *American Indian Rock Art* Vol. 12, edited by W. D. Hyder, pp. 93–106. American Rock Art Research Association, San Miguel, CA.

Riddell, F. A.

1978 *Honey Lake Paiute Ethnography.* Nevada State Museum Occasional Papers No. 3, Pt. 1. Carson City.

Ripley, B. D.

1977 Modelling Spatial Patterns (with Discussion). *Journal of the Royal Statistical Society Series B* 39(2):172–212.

1988 *Statistical Inference for Spatial Processes.* Cambridge University Press.

Rollefson, G. O., D. Schnurrenberger, L. A. Quintero, R. P. Watson, and R. Low

1997   'Ain Soda and 'Ain Qasiya: New Late Pleistocene and Early Holocene Sites in the Azraq Shishan Area, Eastern Jordan. In *The Prehistory of Jordan* Vol. 2, *Perspectives from 1997*, edited by H. G. K. Gebel, Z. Kafafi, and G. O. Rollefson, pp. 45–58. Ex Oriente Studies in Early Near Eastern Production, Subsistence, and Environment No. 4. Berlin.

Root, M. J., J. D. William, M. Kay, and L. K. Shifrin

1999   Folsom Ultrathin Biface and Radial Break Tools in the Knife River Flint Quarry Area. In *Folsom Lithic Technology*, edited by D. S. Amick, pp. 144–168. International Monographs in Prehistory No. 12. Ann Arbor, MI.

Rosencrance, R. L.

2019   *Assessing the Chronological Variation of Western Stemmed Tradition Projectile Points.* Master's thesis, Department of Anthropology, University of Nevada, Reno.

Rosencrance, R. L., G. M. Smith, D. L. Jenkins, T. J. Connolly, and T. N. Layton

2019   Reinvestigating Cougar Mountain Cave: New Perspectives on Stratigraphy, Chronology, and Younger Dryas Occupation in the Northern Great Basin. *American Antiquity* 84(3):559–573.

Ruby, A.

2016   High Rock Country Summary of Findings. In *Prehistory of Nevada's Northern Tier*, edited by W. R. Hildebrandt, K. McGuire, J. King, A. Ruby, and D. C. Young, pp. 155–180. Anthropological Papers of the American Museum of Natural History Vol. 101. New York.

Russell, I. C.

1884   *A Geological Reconnaissance in Southern Oregon: Extract from the Fourth Annual Report of the Director 1882–1883.* U.S. Geological Survey, Washington, D.C.

Saper, S., R. L. Rosencrance, K. McDonough, and D. L. Jenkins

2020   Assessing Typology of Pre-Mazama Corner-Notched Points in the Northern Great Basin. Poster presented for the 85th Annual Meeting of the Society for American Archaeology, Austin, TX.

Sanchez, G. M., J. M. Erlandson, and N. Tripcevich

2017   Quantifying the Association of Chipped Stone Crescents with Wetlands and Paleoshorelines of Western North America. *North American Archaeologist* 38(2):107–137.

Schmid, A. M. M., and R. M. Crawford

2001   *Ellerbeckia arenaria* (Bacillariophyceae): Formation of Auxospores and Initial Cells. *European Journal of Phycology* 36(4):307–320.

Schmitt, D. N., and K. D. Lupo

2005   The Camels Back Cave Mammalian Fauna. In *Camels Back Cave*, edited by D. N. Schmitt and D. B. Madsen, pp. 136–176. University of Utah Anthropological Papers No. 125. University of Utah Press, Salt Lake City.

Schmitt, Dave N., and David B. Madsen (editors)

2005   *Camels Back Cave.* University of Utah Anthropological Papers No. 125. University of Utah Press, Salt Lake City.

Schmitt, D. N., D. B. Madsen, and K. D. Lupo

2004   The Worst of Times, the Best of Times: Jackrabbit Hunting by Middle Holocene Human Foragers in the Bonneville Basin of Western North America. In *Colonisation, Migration, and Marginal Areas*, edited by M. Mondini, S. Muñoz, and S. Wickler, pp. 86–95. Oxbow Press, Oxford.

Scholze, G. J.

2011   *The Application of Starch Grain Analysis to Late Prehistoric Subsistence in Northeastern California.* Master's thesis, Department of Anthropology, California State University, Sacramento.

Schopmeyer, C. S.

1974   *Seeds of Woody Plants in the United States.* Agricultural Handbook No. 450. USDA Forest Service, U.S. Government Printing Office, Washington, D.C.

Schroth, A. B.

1996   An Ethnographic Review of Grinding, Pounding, Pulverizing, and Smoothing with Stones. *Pacific Coast Archaeological Society Quarterly* 32(4):55–75.

Shafer, H. J.

1983   The Tranchet Technique in Lowland Maya Lithic Tool Production. *Lithic Technology* 12(3):57–68.

Shafer, H. J., and T. R. Hester

1983   Ancient Maya Chert Workshops in Northern Belize, Central America. *American Antiquity* 48(3):519–543.

Sharp, J. B.

1990   *Wood Identification: A Manual for the Non-Professional.* University of Tennessee Agricultural Extension Service, Publication No. 1389. Knoxville.

Shaw, G. R.

1972   *Knots: Useful and Ornamental.* Bonanza Books, New York.

Shea, J. J., A. J. Stutz, and L. Nilsson-Stutz

2019   An Early Upper Palaeolithic Stone Tool Assemblage from Mughr El-Hamamah, Jordan: An Interim Report. *Journal of Field Archaeology* 44(7):420–439.

Shillito, L. M., H. L. Whelton, J. C. Blong, D. L. Jenkins, T. J. Connolly, and I. D. Bull

2020   Pre-Clovis Occupation of the Americas Identified by Human Fecal Biomarkers in Coprolites from Paisley Caves, Oregon. *Science Advances* 6:1–8.

Shimkin, D. B.

1986   Introduction of the Horse. In *Great Basin*, edited by W. L. d'Azevedo, pp. 517–524. Handbook of North American Indians, Vol. 11, W. C. Sturtevant, general editor. Smithsonian Institution Press, Washington, D.C.

Shipton, C., C. Clarkson, J. N. Pal, S. C. Jones, R. G. Roberts, C. Harris, M. C. Gupta, P. W. Ditchfield, and M. D. Petraglia

2013   Generativity, Hierarchical Action and Recursion in the Technology of the Acheulean to Middle Palaeolithic Transition: A Perspective from Patpara, the

Son Valley, India. *Journal of Human Evolution* 65(2): 93–108.

Silverman, B. W.

1986 *Density Estimation for Statistics and Data Analysis.* Chapman and Hall, New York.

Simek, J. F.

1987 Spatial Order and Behavioral Change in the French Paleolithic. *Antiquity* 61:25–40.

Simms, S. R.

2008 *Ancient Peoples of the Great Basin and Colorado Plateau.* Left Coast Press, Walnut Creek.

Singer, V. J.

2004 Faunal Assemblages of Four Early to Mid-Holocene Marsh-Side Sites in the Fort Rock Valley, South Central Oregon. In *Early and Middle Holocene Archaeology of the Northern Great Basin*, edited by D. L. Jenkins, T. J. Connolly, and C. M. Aikens, pp. 167–186. University of Oregon Anthropological Papers No. 62. University of Oregon Museum of Natural and Cultural History, Eugene.

Sistiaga, A., F. Berna, R. Laursen, and P. Goldberg

2014 Steroidal Biomarker Analysis of a 14,000 Years Old Putative Human Coprolite from Paisley Cave, Oregon. *Journal of Archaeological Science* 41:813–817.

Smith, G. M.

2007 Pre-Archaic Mobility and Technological Activities at the Parman Localities, Humboldt County, Nevada. In *Paleoindian or Paleoarchaic? Great Basin Human Ecology at the Pleistocene-Holocene Transition*, edited by K. E. Graf and D. N. Schmitt, pp. 139–155. University of Utah Press, Salt Lake City.

2010 Footprints Across the Black Rock: Temporal Variability in Prehistoric Foraging Territories and Toolstone Procurement Strategies in the Western Great Basin. *American Antiquity* 75(4):865–885.

2011 Shifting Stones and Changing Homes: Using Toolstone Ratios to Consider Relative Occupation Span in the Northwest Great Basin. *Journal of Archaeological Science* 38:461–469.

Smith, G. M., and P. Barker

2017 The Terminal Pleistocene/Early Holocene Record in the Northwestern Great Basin: What We Know, What We Don't Know, and How We May Be Wrong. *PaleoAmerica* 3(1):13–47.

Smith, G. M., and D. C. Harvey

2018 Reconstructing Prehistoric Landscape Use at a Regional Scale: A Critical Review of the Lithic Conveyance Zone Concept with a Focus on its Limitations. *Journal of Archaeological Science Reports* 19:828–835.

Smith, G. M., and T. A. Wriston

2018 *Diachronic Variability in Prehistoric Land Use in the Northern Warner Valley Study Area: The Results of Three Years of Investigation.* GBPRU Technical Report 18-1. Department of Anthropology, University of Nevada Reno. Submitted to Bureau of Land Management, Lakeview Resource Area, Lakeview, OR.

Smith, G. M., S. LaValley, and C. Skinner

2011 Looking to the North: Results from the XRF Analysis of Pre-Archaic Projectile Points from Hanging Rock Shelter, Northwest Nevada. *Current Research in the Pleistocene* 28:81–83.

Smith, G. M., P. A. Carey, E. S. Middleton, and J. Kielhofer

2012 Cascade Points in the Northern Great Basin: A Radiocarbon-Dated Foliate Point Assemblage from Warner Valley, Oregon. *North American Archaeologist* 33(1):13–34.

Smith, G. M., E. S. Middleton, and P. A. Carey

2013a Paleoindian Technological Provisioning Strategies in the Northwestern Great Basin. *Journal of Archaeological Science* 40:4180–4188.

Smith, G. M., P. Barker, E. M. Hattori, A. Raymond, and T. Goebel

2013b Points in Time: Direct Radiocarbon Dates on Great Basin Projectile Points. *American Antiquity* 78(3):580–594.

Smith, G. M., D. D. Pattee, J. B. Finley, J. L. Fagan, and E. Pellegrini

2014 A Flaked Stone Crescent from a Stratified Radiocarbon-Dated Site in the Northern Great Basin. *North American Archaeologist* 35(3):257–276.

Smith, G. M., D. C. Felling, A. W. Taylor, and T. N. Layton

2015a Evaluating the Stratigraphic and Chronological Integrity of the Last Supper Cave Deposits. *Journal of California and Great Basin Anthropology* 35(1): 99–112.

Smith, G. M., D. C. Felling, T. A. Wriston, and D. D. Pattee

2015b The Surface Paleoindian Record of Northern Warner Valley, Oregon, and Its Bearing on the Temporal and Cultural Separation of Clovis and Western Stemmed Points in the Northern Great Basin. *PaleoAmerica* 1(4):360–373.

Smith, G. M., A. Cherkinsky, C. Hadden, and A. P. Ollivier

2016a The Age and Origin of *Olivella* Beads from Oregon's LSP-1 Rockshelter: The Oldest Marine Shell Beads in the Northern Great Basin. *American Antiquity* 81(3):550–561.

Smith, G. M., A. Ollivier, P. Barker, A. J. Camp, D. C. Harvey, and H. Jones

2016b A Collection of Fiber Artifacts from Southcentral Oregon. *Journal of California and Great Basin Anthropology* 36(1):149–159.

Smith, G. M., D. Duke, D. L. Jenkins, T. Goebel, L. G. Davis, P. O'Grady, D. Stueber, J. E. Pratt, and H. L. Smith

2020 The Western Stemmed Tradition: Problems and Prospects in Paleoindian Archaeology in the Intermountain West. *PaleoAmerica* 6(1):23–42.

Smith, H. L., and T. Goebel

2018 Origins and Spread of Fluted-Point Technology in the Canadian Ice-Free Corridor and Eastern Beringia. *PNAS* 115(16):4116–4121.

Spaulding, S. A., D. J. Lubinski, and M. Potapova

2010 Diatoms of the United States. https://diatoms.org.

Spier, L.

1930 *Klamath Ethnography.* University of California Publications in American Archaeology and Ethnology No. 30. University of California Press, Berkeley.

Stapert, D.
2007   Neanderthal Children and Their Flints. *PalArch's Journal of Archaeology of Northwest Europe* 1(2):16–39.

Stenholm, N.A.
1994   Paleoethnobotanical Analysis of Archaeological Samples Recovered in the Fort Rock Basin. In *Archaeological Researches in the Northern Great Basin: Fort Rock Archaeology since Cressman*, edited by C.M. Aikens and D.L. Jenkins, pp. 531–560. University of Oregon Anthropological Papers No. 50. University of Oregon Museum of Natural and Cultural History, Eugene.

Stern, T.
1998   Klamath and Modoc. In *Plateau*, edited by D.E. Walker Jr., pp. 446–466. Handbook of North American Indians, Vol. 12, W.C. Sturtevant, general editor. Smithsonian Institution Press, Washington, D.C.

Sternke, F., and M. Sørensen
2007   The Identification of Children's Flintknapping Products in Mesolithic Scandinavia. In *Mesolithic Horizons: Papers Presented at the Seventh International Conference on the Mesolithic in Europe*, edited by S. McCartan, R. Schulting, G. Warren, and P.C. Woodman, pp. 720–726. Oxbow, Oxford.

Stevenson, M.G.
1991   Beyond the Formation of Hearth-Associated Artifact Assemblages. In *The Interpretation of Archaeological Site Patterning*, edited by E.M. Kroll and T.D. Price, pp. 269–300. Plenum, New York.

Steward, J.H.
1933   *Ethnography of the Owens Valley Paiute*. University of California Publications in American Archaeology and Ethnology No. 33, Pt. 3. University of California Press, Berkeley.
1938   *Basin-Plateau Aboriginal Sociopolitical Groups*. Smithsonian Institution Bureau of American Ethnology Bulletin No. 120. Washington, D.C. Reprint 1997, University of Utah Press, Salt Lake City.
1941   Culture Element Distributions: XIII Nevada Shoshone. *University of California Anthropological Records* (4(2):209–359.

Stewart, O.C.
1939   The Northern Paiute Bands. *University of California Anthropological Reports* 2:127–149.
1941   Culture Element Distributions: XIV Northern Paiute. *University of California Anthropological Records* 4(3):361–446.
1942   Culture Element Distributions: XVIII Ute-Southern Paiute. *University of California Anthropological Records* 6(4):231–360.

Stine, S.
1994   Extreme and Persistent Drought in California and Patagonia during Medieval Times. *Nature* 369:546–549.

Stout, D., and S. Semaw
2006   Knapping Skill of the Earliest Stone Toolmakers: Insights from the Study of Modern Human Novices. In *The Oldowan: Case Studies into the Earliest Stone Age*, edited by N. Toth and K. Schick, pp. 307–320. Stone Age Institute Publication Series No. 1. Bloomington, IN.

Stueber, D.O., and C.E. Skinner
2015   Glass Buttes, Oregon: 14,000 Years of Continuous Use. In *Toolstone Geography of the Pacific Northwest*, edited by T.L. Ozbun and R.L. Adams, pp. 193–207. Archaeology Press, Simon Frazier University, Burnaby, BC.

Stuiver, M., and H.A. Polach
1977   Discussion of Reporting of ^{14}C Data. *Radiocarbon* 19(3):355–363.

Surovell, T.A.
2009   *Toward a Behavioral Ecology of Folsom Lithic Technology*. University of Arizona Press, Tucson.

Sutton, M.Q.
1986   Warfare and Expansion: An Ethnohistoric Perspective on the Numic Spread. *Journal of California and Great Basin Anthropology* 8(1):65–82.
1993   The Numic Expansion in Great Basin Oral Tradition. *Journal of California and Great Basin Anthropology* 15(1):111–128.

Tadlock, L.W.
1966   Certain Crescentic Stone Objects as a Time Marker in the Western United States. *American Antiquity* 31(5):662–675.

Taylor, A.K.
2003   Results of a Great Basin Fluted-Point Survey. *Current Research in the Pleistocene* 20:77–79.

Taylor, D.W.
1981   Freshwater Mollusks of California: A Distributional Checklist. *California Fish and Game* 67(3):140–163.

Taylor, M., and G.W. Stone
1996   Beach-Ridges: A Review. *Journal of Coastal Research* 12:612–621.

Thomas, D.H.
1970   *The Archaeology of Monitor Valley 1. Epistemology.* Anthropological Papers of the American Museum of Natural History Vol. 58, Pt. 1. New York.
1981   How to Classify Projectile Points from Monitor Valley, Nevada. *Journal of California and Great Basin Anthropology* 3(1):7–43.
1983   *The Archaeology of Monitor Valley: 2. Gatecliff Shelter.* Anthropological Papers of the American Museum of Natural History Vol. 59, Pt. 1. New York.
1988   *The Archaeology of Monitor Valley: 3. Survey and Additional Excavations.* Anthropological Papers of the American Museum of Natural History Vol. 66, Pt. 2. New York.
1994   Chronology and the Numic Expansion. In *Across the West: Human Population Movement and the Expansion of the Numa*, edited by D.B. Madsen and D. Rhode, pp. 56–61. University of Utah Press, Salt Lake City.
2019   A Shoshonean Prayerstone Hypothesis: Ritual Cartographies of Great Basin Incised Stones. *American Antiquity* 84(1):1–25.

Thomas, S. P.

2014   Shoshone Complex in Southeastern Oregon. Paper presented at the 34th Biennial Great Basin Anthropological Conference, Boise, ID.

Thorp, J. A., and D. C. Rogers

2011   *Freshwater Invertebrates of North America.* Academic, New York.

Tipps, J. A.

1997   *High, Middle, and Low: An Analysis of Resource Zone Relationships in Warner Valley, Oregon.* Master's thesis, Department of Anthropology, University of Nevada, Reno.

1998   *High, Middle, and Low: An Analysis of Resource Zone Relationships in Warner Valley, Oregon.* Technical Report No. 98-1, Department of Anthropology, University of Nevada, Reno.

Train, P., J. R. Henrichs, and W. A. Archer

1941   *Medicinal Uses of Plants by Indian Tribes of Nevada.* U.S. Department of Agriculture, Washington, D.C.

Trammell, J., C. Parker, P. Borghi, S. Bush, L. Hunsaker, D. Bird, and J. O'Connell

2008   Geophytes North of High Rock: Nutrient Content, Handling Costs, Effects of Fire and Tillage, Archaeological Implications. Paper presented at the 31st Biennial Great Basin Anthropological Conference, Portland, OR.

Tremayne, A.

2010   An Analysis of Denbigh Flint Complex Burin Technology from Matcharak Lake, Alaska. *Alaska Journal of Anthropology* 8(1):73–85.

Tuohy, D. R.

1969   Breakage, Burin Facets, and the Probable Technological Linkage among Lake Mohave, Silver Lake, and Other Varieties of Projectile Points in the Desert West. In *Miscellaneous Papers on Nevada Archaeology*, edited by D. Rendall and D. R. Tuohy, pp. 133–152. Nevada State Museum Anthropological Papers No. 14. Carson City.

1974   A Comparative Study of Late Paleo-Indian Manifestations in the Western Great Basin. In *Collected Papers on Great Basin Archaeology*, edited by R. G. Elston, pp. 91–116. Nevada Archaeological Survey Research Paper No. 5. Reno.

1990   Pyramid Lake Fishing: The Archaeological Record. In *Wetland Adaptions in the Great Basin*, edited by Joel C. Janetski and David B. Madsen, pp. 121–158. Brigham Young University Occasional Papers No. 1. Provo, OR.

Tuohy, D. R., and A. J. Dansie

1997   New Information Regarding Early Holocene Manifestations in the Western Great Basin. *Nevada Historical Society Quarterly* 40(1):24–53.

United States Department of Agriculture (USDA)

2014   Wetland Indicator Status. Electronic document, https://plants.usda.gov/home/wetlandSearch, accessed December 11, 2021.

2019   Fire Effects Information System (FEIS). https://www.feis-crs.org/feis/. Accessed July 30, 2020.

Van der Voort, M. W.

2016   *Late Paleoindian Leporid Processing at the Little Steamboat Point-1 Rockshelter: An Experimental and Archaeological Use-Wear Analysis of Obsidian Flake Tools.* Master's thesis, Department of Anthropology, University of Nevada, Reno.

Van Rheede van Oudtshoorn, K., and M. W. van Rooyen

1999   *Dispersal Biology of Desert Plants.* Springer-Verlag, New York.

Van Winkle, W.

1914   *Quality of the Surface Waters of Oregon.* U.S. Geological Survey Supply Paper No. 363. Washington, D.C.

Venditti, F., C. Lemorini, M. Bordigoni, D. Zampetti, D., M. Amori, and A. Tagliacozzo

2016   The Role of Burins and Their Relationship with Art through Trace Analysis at the Upper Palaeolithic Site of Polesini Cave (Latium, Italy). *Origini: Prehistory and Protohistory of Ancient Civilizations* 34:7–29.

Walker, D. E. Jr., and R. Sprague

1998   History until 1846. In *Plateau*, edited by D. E. Walker Jr., pp. 139–148. Handbook of North American Indians, Vol. 12, W. C. Sturtevant, general editor. Smithsonian Institution Press, Washington, D.C.

Walker, G. W.

1979   *Revisions to the Cenozoic Stratigraphy of Harney Basin, Southeastern Oregon.* U.S. Government Printing Office, Washington, D.C.

Walthall, J. A.

1998   Rockshelters and Hunter-Gatherer Adaptation to the Pleistocene/Holocene Transition. *American Antiquity* 63(2):223–238.

Waters, M. R., S. L. Forman, T. A. Jennings, L. C. Nordt, S. G. Driese, J. M. Feinberg, J. L. Keene, et al.

2011   The Buttermilk Creek Complex and the Origins of Clovis at the Debra L. Friedkin Site, Texas. *Science* 331:1599–1603.

Weber, D. J., and J. Hanks

2008   Salt Tolerant Plants from the Great Basin Region of the United States. In *Ecophysiology of High Salinity Tolerant Plants*, edited by M. A. Khan and D. J. Weber, pp. 69–106. Springer, Dordrecht.

Weide, D. L.

1975   *Postglacial Geomorphology and Environments of the Warner Valley-Hart Mountain Area, Oregon.* PhD dissertation, Department of Geography, University of California, Los Angeles.

Weide, M. L.

1968   *Cultural Ecology of Lakeside Adaptation in the Western Great Basin.* PhD dissertation, Department of Anthropology, University of California, Los Angeles.

Weldon, R. J., D. K. Fletcher, E. M. Weldon, K. M. Scharer, and P. A. McCrory

2002   *An Update of Quaternary Faults of Central and Eastern Oregon.* Open-File Report 2002-301. U.S. Geological Survey, Washington, D.C.

Wheat, M. M.

1967   *Survival Art of the Primitive Paiutes.* University of Nevada Press, Reno.

Whistler, J. T., and J. H. Lewis

1916   *Warner Valley and White River Projects (Irrigation and Drainage)*. U.S. Reclamation Service in Cooperation with State of Oregon Government Printing Office, Washington, D.C.

Wilde, J. D.

1985   *Prehistoric Settlements in the Northern Great Basin: Excavations and Collections Analysis in the Steens Mountain Area, Southeastern Oregon*. PhD dissertation, Department of Anthropology, University of Oregon.

Wigand, P. E.

1987   Diamond Pond, Harney County, Oregon: Vegetation History and Water Table in the Eastern Oregon Desert. *Great Basin Naturalist* 47(3):427–458.

Wigand, P. E., and P. J. Mehringer Jr.

1985   Pollen and Seed Analyses. In *The Archaeology of Hidden Cave*, edited by D. H. Thomas, pp. 108–124. Anthropological Papers of the American Museum of Natural History Vol. 61, Pt. 1. New York.

Wigand, P. E., and D. Rhode

2002   Great Basin Vegetation and Aquatic Systems: The Last 150,000 Years. In *Great Basin Aquatic Systems History*, edited by R. Hershler, D. B. Madsen, and D. R. Currey, pp. 309–367. Smithsonian Institution Contributions to Earth Sciences No. 33. Smithsonian Institution Press, Washington, D.C.

Willig, J. A.

1988   Paleo-Archaic Adaptations and Lakeside Settlement Patterns in the Northern Alkali Basin, Oregon. In *Early Human Occupation in Far Western North America: The Clovis-Archaic Interface*, edited by J. A. Willig, C. M. Aikens, and J. L. Fagan, pp. 417–482 Nevada State Museum Anthropological Papers No. 21. Carson City.

1989   *Paleo-Archaic Broad Spectrum Adaptations at the Pleistocene-Holocene Boundary in Far Western North America*. PhD dissertation, Department of Anthropology, University of Oregon.

Willig, J. A., C. M. Aikens, and J. L. Fagan (editors)

1988   *Early Human Occupation in Far Western North America: The Clovis-Archaic Interface*. Nevada State Museum Anthropological Papers No. 21. Carson City.

Wingard, G. F.

2001   *Carlon Village: Land, Water, Subsistence, and Sedentism in the Northern Great Basin*. University of Oregon Anthropological Papers No. 57. University of Oregon Museum of Natural and Cultural History, Eugene.

Woodward, J. C., and P. Goldberg

2001   The Sedimentary Records in Mediterranean Rockshelters and Caves: Archives of Environmental Change. *Geoarchaeology* 16(4):327–354.

Woody, A.

1996   *Layer by Layer: A Multigenerational Analysis of the Massacre Lake Rock Art Site*. PhD dissertation, Department of Anthropology, University of Nevada, Reno.

Wriston, T.

2009   The Middle Holocene and Great Basin Archaeology: Past Ideas, Current Trends, and Future Research. In *Past, Present, and Future Issues in Great Basin Archaeology: Papers in Honor of Don D. Fowler*, edited by Bryan Hockett, pp. 218–241. Bureau of Land Management Cultural Resource Series No. 20. Elko, NV.

2016   The Assemblages of Great Basin Caves and Rockshelters: Representative or Not? Paper presented at the 35th Biennial Great Basin Anthropological Conference, Reno.

Wriston, T., and G. M. Smith

2017   Late Pleistocene to Holocene History of Lake Warner and Its Prehistoric Occupations, Warner Valley, Oregon (USA). *Quaternary Research* 88(3):491–513.

Yoder, D., J. Blood, and R. Mason

2005   How Warm Were They? Thermal Properties of Rabbit Skin Blankets. *Journal of California and Great Basin Anthropology* 25(1):55–68.

Young, D. Craig

1998   *Late Holocene Landscapes and Prehistoric Land Use in Warner Valley, Oregon*. PhD dissertation, Department of Anthropology, University of Nevada, Reno.

2000   *Late Holocene Landscapes and Prehistoric Land Use in Warner Valley, Oregon*. Technical Report No. 7, Department of Anthropology, University of Nevada, Reno.

2002   Secondary Obsidian Sources of the Madeline Plains: Paleolandscapes and Archaeological Implications. In *Boundary Lands: Archaeological Investigations along the California-Great Basin Interface*, edited by K. R. McGuire, pp. 75–84. Nevada State Museum Anthropological Papers No. 24. Carson City.

Zeanah, D. W.

2002   Central Place Foraging and Prehistoric Pinyon Utilization in the Great Basin. In *Beyond Foraging and Collecting: Evolutionary Change in Hunter-Gatherer Settlement Systems*, edited by B. Fitzhugh and J. Habu, pp. 231–256. Academic, New York.

2004   Sexual Division of Labor and Central Place Foraging: A Model for the Carson Desert of Western Nevada. *Journal of Anthropological Archaeology* 23(1):1–32.

Zeanah, D. W., and S. R. Simms

1999   Modeling the Gastric: Great Basin Subsistence Studies since 1982 and the Evolution of General Theory. In *Models for the Millennium: Great Basin Anthropology Today*, edited by C. Beck, pp. 118–140. University of Utah Press, Salt Lake City.

Contributors

Geoffrey M. Smith,
Department of Anthropology,
University of Nevada, Reno,
MS096, 1664 N. Virginia St., Reno, NV 89557

Pat Barker,
Nevada State Museum,
4523 Hells Bells Rd., Carson City, NV 89701

Erica J. Bradley,
Department of Anthropology,
University of Nevada, Reno,
MS096, 1664 N. Virginia St., Reno, NV 89557

Anna J. Camp,
Nevada State Museum,
600 North Carson St., Carson City, NV 89701

Judson B. Finley,
Department of Sociology, Social Work, and Anthropology,
Utah State University,
0730 Old Main Hill, Logan, UT 85322

Catherine S. Fowler,
Department of Anthropology,
University of Nevada, Reno,
MS096, 1664 N. Virginia St., Reno, NV 89557

Donald D. Fowler,
Department of Anthropology,
University of Nevada, Reno,
MS096, 1664 N. Virginia St., Reno, NV 89557

Denay Grund,
Far Western Anthropological Research Group,
3656 Research Way, Suite 32,
Carson City, NV 89706

Eugene M. Hattori,
Nevada State Museum,
600 N. Carson St., Carson City, NV 89701

Bryan S. Hockett,
Department of Anthropology,
University of Nevada, Reno
MS096, 1664 N. Virginia St., Reno, NV 89557

Christopher S. Jazwa,
Department of Anthropology,
University of Nevada, Reno,
MS096, 1664 N. Virginia St., Reno, NV 89557

Jaime L. Kennedy,
University of Oregon Natural and Cultural History Museum,
1680 E. 15th Ave., Eugene, OR 97401

Donald D. Pattee,
Applied Archaeological Research Inc.,
4001 NE Halsey St., Suite 3, Portland, OR 97232

Evan J. Pellegrini,
Nevada Department of Transportation,
1263 S. Stewart St., Carson City, NV 89712

Richard L. Rosencrance,
Department of Anthropology,
University of Nevada, Reno, MS096,
1664 N. Virginia St., Reno, NV 89557

Daniel O. Stueber,
Department of Anthropology, University of Victoria,
Cornett Building B228,
3800 Finnerty Rd., Victoria, BC, Canada, V8P 5C2

Madeline Ware Van der Voort,
Bureau of Land Management,
1340 Financial Blvd., Reno, NV 89502

Teresa A. Wriston,
Desert Research Institute,
2215 Raggio Parkway, Reno, NV 89512